GERMANY IN THE EARLY MIDDLE AGES

Longman History of Germany

Germany in the early middle ages c. 800–1056
Timothy Reuter

Germany under the Old Regime, 1600–1790
John Gagliardo

Germany in the early middle ages c. 800–1056

Timothy Reuter

Longman
London and New York

Longman Group UK Limited,
Longman House, Burnt Mill, Harlow,
Essex CM20 2JE, England
and Associated Companies throughout the world.

Published in the United States of America
by Longman Inc., New York

© Longman Group UK Limited 1991

First published 1991

British Library Cataloguing in Publication Data
Reuter, Timothy.
   Germany in the early Middle Ages c. 800–1056
   1. Germany 843–1519
   I. Title
   943.02

ISBN 0–582–08156–4 CSD
ISBN 0–582–49034–0 PPR

Library of Congress Cataloging in Publication Data
Reuter, Timothy.
   Germany in the early middle ages, c. 800–1056/Timothy Reuter.
   p. cm.
Includes bibliographical references and index.
ISBN 0–582–08156–4 (cased): $24.00. – ISBN 0–582–49034–0 (pbk.) $12.00
1. Germany – History – T 843. 2. Germany – History – 843–1273.
I. Title.
DD126.R48 1991   90–46393
943–dc20   CIP

Produced by Longman Singapore Publishers (Pte) Ltd.
Printed in Singapore

Contents

Contents

List of maps and genealogical tables

Abbreviations

Adam of Bremen	*Magistri Adam Bremensis Gesta Hammaburgensis ecclesiae pontificum* ed. B. Schmeidler (MGH SRG, Hannover 1917)
AfD	*Archiv für Diplomatik*
AHC	*Annuarium Historiae Conciliorum*
AHVNRh	*Annalen des historischen Vereins für den Niederrhein*
Annales Fuldenses	*Annales Fuldenses*, ed. F. Kurze (MGH SRG, Hannover 1891)
BDLG	*Blätter für deutsche Landesgeschichte*
CCM	*Cahiers de civilisation médiévale*
D	Diploma; the reference is by convention to the diplomata editions in the MGH series by number and ruler, thus D H II 143 is no. 143 in the edition of Henry II's diplomata
DA	*Deutsches Archiv für Erforschung des Mittelalters*
EHR	*English Historical Review*
Einhard	*Einhardi Vita Karoli*, ed. G. Waitz and O. Holder-Egger (MGH SRG, Hannover 1911)
FmaSt	*Frühmittelalterliche Studien*
HJb	*Historisches Jahrbuch*
HJLG	*Hessisches Jahrbuch für Landesgeschichte*
HZ	*Historische Zeitschrift*
JEccIH	*Journal of Ecclesiastical History*
JFLF	*Jahrbuch für fränkische Landesforschung*
JGF	*Jahrbuch für die Geschichte des Feudalismus*
JGMOD	*Jahrbuch für die Geschichte Mittel- und Ostdeutschlands*
JwLG	*Jahrbuch für westdeutsche Landesgeschichte*

Liutprand,	*Liudprandi Opera*, ed. J. Becker
Antapodosis	(MGH SRG, Hannover 1915)
MGH	Monumenta Germaniae Historica
SRG	Scriptores rerum Germanicarum
SRG NS	Scriptores rerum Germanicarum, nova series
SS	Scriptores in folio
MIÖG	*Mitteilungen des Instituts für österreichische Geschichtsforschung (EB = Ergänzungsband)*
NJLJ	*Niedersächsisches Jahrbuch für Landesgeschichte*
QFIAB	*Quellen und Forschungen aus italienischen Archiven und Bibliotheken*
Regino	*Reginonis abbatis Prumiensis Chronicon* ed. F. Kurze (MGH SRG, Hannover 1890)
RhVjbll	*Rheinische Vierteljahrsblätter*
Settimane	*Settimane di studi sull'alto medio evo*
Thietmar	*Thietmari episcopi Merseburgensis Chronicon*, ed. R. Holtzmann (MGH SRG NS 9, Berlin 1935)
TRHS	Transactions of the Royal Historical Society
VSWG	*Vierteljahrsschrift für Sozial- und Wirtschaftsgeschichte*
VuF	*Vorträge und Forschungen herausgegeben vom Konstanzer Arbeitskreis für mittelalterliche Geschichte*
Widukind	*Widukindi monaci Corbeiensis rerum gestarum Saxonicarum libri tres*, ed. H.-E. Lohmann and P. Hirsh (MGH SRG, Hannover 1935)
Wipo	*Wiponis Gesta Chuonradi in Wiponis Opera*, ed. H. Bresslau (MGH SRG, Hannover 1915)
ZBLG	*Zeitschrift für bayerische Landesgeschichte*
ZfG	*Zeitschrift für Geschichtswissenschaft*
ZGO	*Zeitschrift für die Geschichte des Oberrheins*
ZKG	*Zeitschrift für Kirchengeschichte*
ZRGGA	*Zeitschrift der Savigny-Stiftung für Rechtsgeschichte, Germanistische Abteilung*
ZRGKA	*Zeitschrift der Savigny-Stiftung für Rechtsgeschichte, Kanonistische Abteilung*
ZWLG	*Zeitschrift für württembergische Landesgeschichte*

Preface

Nemo autem a nobis sententias aut moralitates expectet.

Otto of Freising,
Chronica, prologue to Book 2

Selbstverständlich wird man immer eine eindeutige Entscheidung suchen, und das tue ich im folgenden auch. Aber man muß dabei zusehen, wieweit es überhaupt möglich ist, sie zu finden, und jenes Suchen scheint mir häufig in die Irre zu führen, indem es etwas wissen will und u. U. auch zu wissen vorgibt, was man nicht wissen kann.

Martin Lintzel
Miszellen zur Geschichte des zehnten Jahrhunderts

This book is the first part of a history of Germany in the early and high middle ages. The present volume stops on the eve of the great crisis of the late eleventh century; many early eleventh-century developments which were to become of real significance only during this crisis have been merely noted here, and will be treated more fully in a successor volume. This is intended to take the story on to the mid fourteenth century, when Golden Bull and Black Death provide a convenient place to stop. The book is an attempt by someone who has been trained and has worked in both an English-speaking and a German-speaking scholarly environment to convey and interpret the work of the latter to the former. This has not always been easy. I find that my vulgar English pragmatism has prevented me from believing too strongly in some of the more ethereal constructions of German medieval scholarship, but readers in the Anglo-Saxon world may still find some of what remains ethereal enough. Besides this, the political implications of the German middle ages are not so easily dismissed, even today. As a politically conscious being who currently lives in Germany I have my own views on the German present and the way in which the German past has led to it, but I have tried not to let these intrude into my account of the ninth, tenth and eleventh centuries. Still less have I felt tempted to interpret such obvious Good Things as Charles the Great or Otto I as prototypes for whatever policy is currently fashionable, having seen how often (and for what different policies) this has been done in the past.

A work of this kind depends very largely on the work of others; in spite of this, I have kept references, other than the identification of direct quotations from primary sources, to a fairly brief annotated reading-list. In some ways I should have liked to say, sentence for sentence and paragraph for paragraph, whom I was following and precisely where I disagreed with them, but it would have made the book more than twice its size without commensurate gain. On the whole I have referred to the most recent available literature, because this itself necessarily refers to older work on a topic. This does not mean that I hold the newest literature to be automatically the best; the insights and refinement of recent scholarship are undeniable, but anyone who works on this period has had the experience of working through the literature on a topic and arriving at a conclusion only to find that it had already been formulated more than a hundred years ago in a crisp aside by Georg Waitz in his *Verfassungsgeschichte*. With only one or two exceptions I have not made use of work which appeared after the end of 1987, though I refer to it in the notes on further reading and in the bibliography.

Names and terminology present some problems; it is difficult to achieve complete rationality and consistency in the face of one's own habits and prejudices (and those of the literature). On the whole I have anglicized personal names only where there is a virtually identical English name in common use: Frederick, William, Henry, Otto, Conrad, but Adalbert, Adelheid, Brun, Lothar. I have also preserved distinctions familiar in the literature: thus the count of Champagne killed in 1037 and the emperor who died in 973 both had the same name, but one is universally known as Otto and the other as Odo (or Eudes). Place-names are less problematic. I have followed the majority vote of the sources in referring to the German south-west as Alemannia in the eighth and ninth centuries and as Suabia in the tenth and eleventh centuries. The Hungarians are Magyars until the late tenth century, and I have used the German forms for some eastern European place-names, simply because I am familiar with them. I have borrowed a few technical terms from German (usually translated and glossed on their first appearance), and have made some use of the name Reich (to be translated as "realm", not "empire", which is *Kaiserreich*) to refer to what was to become the kingdom of Germany. I have avoided translating *Stamm* by "tribe", which seems to me to have misleading overtones, and for the same reason I have also deliberately made hardly any use of the feudal terminology of the high middle ages – homage, fealty, fief – even when this meant some circumlocution.

I owe more debts than can easily be repaid in a preface: to those friends and colleagues in the History Department in Exeter and at the MGH in Munich who have provided help, criticism, support and a collegial atmosphere in which to work; to Horst Fuhrmann, Wilfried Hartmann, Alexander Patschovsky and Janet Nelson, who read drafts of all or part of the book carefully and thoughtfully and pointed out much that was questionable or incomprehensible or just plain wrong, though they are not to be blamed for errors and infelicities which remain; to Gerd Althoff, with whom I had a number of helpful conversations while I was carrying out the final revision; to Karl Leyser, who twenty years ago introduced me to the strange world of medieval Germany, and has repeatedly offered fresh insights and new ways of looking at the subject; to Andrew MacLennan of Longmans, who first suggested that I should write the book and put up patiently but firmly with the long periods when I didn't; and finally to Georgina, Fenton and Natalie, who put up patiently but firmly with the long periods when I did.

Monumenta Germaniae Historica,
Munich, April 1990

CHAPTER ONE

Medieval Germany: sources and historiography

To write a history of Germany from the Carolingian period to the mid-eleventh century is of course to beg the question of whether there was such a thing at the time. This book will try, among other things, to suggest some answers, but will not start by offering any. The difficulty should in any case not be exaggerated, any more than one would criticise the title of Sir Frank Stenton's *Anglo-Saxon England* by saying that England only existed for – at most – only the last 150 years of the period covered. There is no theoretical difficulty in dealing with the origins and history of the east Frankish kingdom and of its successor, the Ottonian and Salian empire; whether these entities can properly be called Germany will emerge from the discussion. One should not in any case overemphasize the nation, either as a unit of historical being or as a unit of historical consciousness. The inhabitants of "Germany" in the ninth, tenth and eleventh centuries might on occasions see themselves as *Franci orientales* or Germans (i.e. not Italians or western Franks), but they might also in other contexts see themselves as Saxons (or members of some other ethnic grouping) or as Christians (i.e. not pagan Hungarians or Vikings), and there were other forms of group consciousness, some of which had far deeper roots in objective reality: free (i.e. not a slave), noble (i.e. not a nobody), clerical (i.e. not a layman). The reason why we generally write about and study the past on more or less national lines is not that the surviving remains of the past force themselves on our attention in this way, but rather that the political and social organization of scholarship has led them to be interpreted in this way. There is medieval German history because there have been and are modern German historians. An account of the sources for the history of the lands around the

Rhine, the Elbe and the Danube will help to show what kinds of history can and cannot be written. But it cannot sensibly be separated from an account of the historians who have used these sources, which will show what kind of history has been written. For it is no longer true, if it ever was, that the historian reaches an understanding of the past primarily through a reading of the sources, undisturbed by knowledge of the secondary literature. After more than a hundred and fifty years of professional, academic history-writing there can be few areas of the past where such an attitude of intellectual virginity is sensible or even possible, and certainly the early middle ages are not among them. Here there is little which has not been chewed over thoroughly by several generations of historians, and to discuss the sources alone without looking at what has been made of them is not very helpful. We may, however, begin with the sources themselves.

Germany, or east Francia, had its own historians in the ninth, tenth and eleventh centuries, men who recorded, sometimes in brief notes, sometimes in fuller and more continuous narrative, the doings of kings, nobles and bishops. Characteristic for the eighth and ninth centuries was the organization of such writings as annals, that is, recording the events of each year in a separate entry of anything from a shorthand sentence to several paragraphs in length. The history of the Frankish empire up to 830 was recorded in the so-called Royal Frankish Annals, a text which has evident connections with the Carolingian court but cannot be said to have been written at royal orders. The so-called Annals of Fulda had a similar function and status for the east Frankish kingdom up to 888. These were in reality written not in Fulda but by a Mainz cleric, who drew on earlier works, some now lost, for his account up to the end of the 860s, and then wrote contemporaneously with events from 869 to 887. From 882 to 901 a separate continuation was being written in Bavaria, perhaps in Regensburg. A Lotharingian monk, Regino of Prüm, wrote a disjointed world chronicle at the end of the ninth century, which is a valuable account of east Frankish affairs from about 880 until 908. After that there is a gap; substantial works of history were not produced again in eastern Francia until the 960s, when the wealth and fame of Otto I inspired a number of authors. Widukind, a monk of Corvey related to the Saxon royal house, wrote a history of the Saxons up to his own time; an Italian bishop, Liutprand of Cremona, composed several works which are particularly valuable for the information they give on Italian and Greek affairs; and the monk Adalbert of St Maximin, later to become the first archbishop of Magdeburg, wrote an annalistic continuation of Regino's chronicle which extended from 907 to 967. After that, historical writing became more plentiful. Annals were once again composed on a substantial scale – at Quedlinburg and Hersfeld, for example. Bishop Thietmar of Merseburg, writing in the first two decades of the eleventh century, wrote a chronicle which for the earlier period drew on Widukind's work but amplified it with other traditions and anecdotes; as he comes nearer his own time the work turns into what can only be described as the memoirs of a Saxon aristocrat, a source of value far beyond the mere information it provides about the flow of political events. Both Henry II and Conrad II had contemporary biographies, by Bishop Adalbold of Utrecht (most of whose work has been lost) and by the royal chaplain Wipo respectively, and their reigns and those of Henry III were fully covered by a number of annalists, notably Hermann the Lame, a monk of the Reichenau, as well as anonymous writers in Altaich, Mainz, Bamberg, Hersfeld and elsewhere.

From the late tenth century onwards we also have the Gesta kept for many bishoprics and monasteries: sometimes brief, sometimes full accounts of their church and the bishops or abbots in charge. Besides such forms of writing which can obviously be seen as historical there also survive a large number of saints' lives and of collections of the miracles worked by saints at their shrines. This kind of literature is much more varied. Some saints' lives were very historical in their approach, and can be described simply as the biographies of holy men; others concentrated much more on the saints' holiness and virtues, and say little or nothing beyond conventional phrases about their heroes' biography or the world in which they lived. The information all these writers provide can be supplemented and in some cases corrected from that given by minor sets of annals, but the small number of really full historical writings provides a crucial skeleton for our understanding because they alone offer not only "facts" about who did what but also attempt to put them into some kind of coherent sequence. We shall see later what other kinds of evaluation such sources lend themselves to.

A quite different kind of source is that represented by charters, using the word loosely to refer to any kind of written record of a legal transaction made by or for one of the parties to it. Rulers issued charters (normally known as diplomata) to their followers, lay and ecclesiastical, to confirm the latter's title to possession or to grant privileges or property. These have survived in fair, though not in enormous numbers: we have about 170 genuine ones for the first ruler of east Francia, Louis the German, and about 380 for the reign of the last ruler covered in this book, Henry III. These were solemn documents, often beginning with a preamble (arenga) setting out in terms of general principle the reasons for making the grant, proceeding to list the grants or titles, and ending with threats of penalty for those who should violate the conditions of the diploma. They generally finish with a dating clause, saying where and when they were issued, and with a reference to a confirmation by the royal seal. What are misleadingly known as private charters, meaning charters issued by anyone who was not a king, an emperor or a pope, followed more varied patterns. They were not in this period sealed, often not dated, and frequently had no arenga; what they did normally have was a list of witnesses to the transaction they recorded, and often their main purpose seems to have been to record the names of these witnesses so that these could testify to the transaction – the value of the private charter as testimony in itself was limited.

The context of charters and diplomata is law, but the sources available for the law in the period covered by this book are very patchy. The law of the church was extensively recorded: the older law, consisting of the canons of councils, the decrees issued by popes, and relevant and authoritative quotations from the church fathers, survived in collections, and it was added to regularly by church councils, which met in the late eighth and ninth centuries with great frequency and in the tenth and eleventh century not infrequently. The contribution of the popes to new church law was in this period insignificant. As far as secular law goes, there are codifications for the laws of all the major Germanic ethnic groupings – Bavarians, Alemans, Saxons, Franks, Thuringians, Frisians. The codifications were, in the form we have them, almost all made in the eighth century, though they often record much older law. They are, however, far from complete (in the sense that there must have been law on all sorts of matters, in particular on property-holding and inheritance, which they hardly cover); and it is not easy to show that they were put to practical use, that Saxon law in the early eleventh century still had anything much to do with *Lex Saxonum*. The earlier Carolingian rulers issued orders which were a mixture of new legislation and administrative regulation, called capitularies, but as we shall see, there was virtually no capitulary legislation in the lands east of the Rhine. Legal texts are indispensable sources, but their gaps, their silences and their tendency to anachronism and fossilization make them very difficult to interpret.

Standing somewhere between charters and narrative sources are the surviving letters of the period. These resemble narrative sources in their range and their frequent references to specific events, but charters in their greater degree of objectivity; they were not normally intended to interpret the present or recent past to subsequent generations, as historical writing proper was. Perhaps 200 isolated letters have survived from the area and period with which we are concerned here. More valuable than such documents, which, because we have no reply and sometimes not even a certain indication of who sent or received them, are often contextless, is the much smaller number of letter collections. Only Einhard's has survived from ninth-century east Francia; from the Ottonian and Salian Reich we have those associated with Rather of Verona, Froumond of Tegernsee, Gerbert of Rheims, Petrus Damiani, Abbot Bern of the Reichenau and the cathedral school at Worms, to name the most important. Letters in letter collections usually help to explain one another's content, so that the whole is greater than the sum of the parts considered as a number of separate letters. Letters often shade off into treatises or pamphlets (as with Rather and Damiani); letter form could be used for very different purposes, including dedicatory prefaces or theological tractates. By the nature of things letter writing was very much a minority, intellectual taste; there were "business" letters, but hardly any have survived. Other forms of literary activity, such as the writing of poetry (mostly in Latin, though there is a small corpus of vernacular poems from the ninth and tenth centuries), were still more minority activities.

It should not be supposed that the written word offers the only kind of source available for the reconstruction of the early medieval German past. Books and scripts can also be considered as artefacts, and in some cases as works of art as well. Most of the painting of the period survives in book illustrations; there is only a handful of surviving wall-paintings, and these are mostly incomplete, though we know that both the greater churches and the palaces of kings and bishops were decorated in this way; the church of St George on the Reichenau with its complete set of Ottonian wall-paintings gives an idea of how they might have looked. Crosses, copes and other liturgical objects, together with shrines and reliquaries, the containers used for preserving and honouring the relics of saints, formed a further opportunity for craftsmen to work in ivory and precious metals. A few churches have survived from this period, though almost all were either monastic churches or cathedrals and hence untypically large, and almost all have been heavily rebuilt in the following centuries. Comparatively few artefacts have survived outside this sacred context: virtually no secular buildings – for many royal palaces we do not even have a ground plan; and no implements apart from a few weapons and the fragments of pottery and other tools recovered by excavation. We owe most of our knowledge of what the world of the ninth, tenth and eleventh centuries looked like to manuscript paintings and drawings; and the relationship between such depictions and past reality is much more complex than that posed by photography.

The sources just listed and the kinds of information they offer have not all been treated with equal respect from the beginnings of the scientific study of history in the late eighteenth century. The emphases of nineteenth-century medieval scholarship lay on getting the facts right and making the sources available in order to do so. The opening of archives and the major state libraries in the nineteenth century made a flood of new source-material available, and much of the attention of nineteenth-century scholars was devoted to sifting and ordering this and fitting it into the context of what was already known. The edition of texts was given a powerful impulse from classical philology: Karl Lachmann and others in the first half of the nineteenth century developed techniques for working back as reliably as possible from a large number of surviving manuscripts of a text, some of which might be many copies removed from the original and all of which would inevitably contain copyists' errors, to recover the author's original text. In the process manuscripts which were mere copies of other manuscripts could be discarded for the purposes of textual reconstruction. These methods were applied – not always wholeheartedly – to the edition of the texts for above all the narrative history of the middle ages: annals, chronicles, saints' lives. A related technique was applied to the content of these texts: later writers who merely copied or abridged earlier annals or chroniclers were discarded as having no independent value when it came to weighing up evidence. There were also new developments in the treatment of charters (private records of property transactions) and of royal diplomata (documents issued by rulers which granted privileges or confirmed possessions). These documents had legal force and so were unusually subject to forgery and interpolation in the middle ages and afterwards (later forgeries often having the purpose of supporting bogus genealogies rather than legal claims). The new methods made it possible to determine whether or not such a document was genuine, and if it was not, the extent to which it had made use of genuine material. It was characteristic of nineteenth-century German scholarship that the results of this work should have been summarized in scholarly guides, by Wattenbach and Potthast for the narrative sources, by Breßlau and others for the diplomatic ones.[1] By the time of the outbreak of the First World War the narrative sources for German medieval history in the early and high middle ages had largely been edited; editions of the royal charters were well on the way to completion, and other sources such as letters, private charters, saints' lives and necrologies were also being worked through. Not only had these sources been edited, the individual scholar could make use of comprehensive guides to them and to summaries of them, such as the *Regesta Imperii* (a calendar of royal movements and actions which became the model for numerous Regesta for bishoprics and secular princes published by regional record societies) or the *Jahrbücher der deutschen Geschichte* ("Annals of German History"), which reconstructed as accurately and in as much detail as possible the *histoire événementielle* of the Reich from the eighth to the thirteenth centuries.[2]

It is one thing to edit and analyse sources; it is another to make use of them to write history. The conceptual apparatus used for the writing of the political and ecclesiastical history of the middle ages was thin. Although Ranke's maxim that "each age is equally close to God" – meaning that it should be studied from the standpoint of its own beliefs and priorities and not from ours – was in theory a widely accepted premiss, there was also a tendency – often unconscious – to posit a timeless *homo politicus*, with unchanging forms of action: the ninth, tenth and eleventh centuries were populated in such writing by "statesmen" practising far-sighted "policies", but also aware of realities and capable of *Realpolitik*, even of Macchiavellianism in order to achieve their aims. Anachronisms of this kind are of course common enough today, but they were far more common, and much less likely to be questioned, in the nineteenth century. Besides this, much historical writing of the nineteenth century was implicitly or explicitly political in its premisses and intentions. The movement

1. Breßlau 1912, 1931. Wattenbach–Levison 1952–90, Wattenbach, Holtzmann and Schmale 1967–71 and Wattenbach, W. and Schmale, F.-J. (1976) *Deutschlands Geschichtsquellen im Mittelalter. Vom Tode Heinrichs V. bis zum Ende des Interregnum*, 1 Darmstadt, are the latest editions of Wattenbach's original guide which was first published in 1858. A. Potthast, *Bibliotheca Historica Medii Aevi*, 2 vols, Berlin 1896, is also being reworked by an international team.
2. Guides to these and their contents can be found in many places, for example in Prinz 1985 and Hlawitschka 1986.

towards German unification had been, at least in its early stages, one dominated more by intellectuals than by politicians; not for nothing was the constitutional assembly in Frankfurt in 1848 known as a "professors' club", and a number of prominent historians of the nineteenth century, including such men as Waitz and Mommsen, had a secondary role as politician, though none was of the first rank. The period covered in this book was one of great interest; the tenth, eleventh and twelfth centuries were, after all, the period in which Germany had seemingly been united under powerful rulers who exercised de facto if not de jure hegemony in Europe. The *Kaiserzeit* was an inspiration for the present, as can still be seen today in Henry III's palace at Goslar, restored at the time of the founding of the new German empire. Historical wall-paintings depict significant scenes in medieval German history; the climax is provided by the Emperor Frederick Barbarossa blinking from his cave in the Kyffhäuser at the new Emperor William I and his court and assuring himself that all is well. The *Kaiserzeit* was also the period in which the "retarded national development" of Germany, the German *Sonderweg* ("special development", mostly with negative overtones), might be said to have begun, and there was considerable debate about whether the medieval emperors ought to have used so much of their resources on conquering and holding Italy rather than on a policy of expansion eastwards. Confessional differences also played a role; the Goslar wall-paintings include a number of the most famous scenes in the relations between emperors and popes, and when Bismarck said in the course of the conflict with the Catholic church that "we will not go to Canossa" (referring to the submission of Henry IV to Gregory VII in 1077) the allusion was clear to all.

Much of the development of nineteenth-century German historical writing was thus determined by the political history of the period, by the circumstances of German unification and by the nature of the polycentric polity which the new unified state only partially replaced. The decentralized nature of pre-1871 Germany meant that there were far more universities than in Great Britain or France. Many of the smaller states had their own university or universities, and history was established early as an academic discipline. There were at least twenty professors of medieval history by 1900. There was a comparable spread of archives and archivists, and of societies for the publication of historical records which had state backing; in English terms, it is as if every county record society of the nineteenth century had had royal patronage and money to go with it. It was a difference of kind as well as of degree. *Landesgeschichte* cannot be translated as "local" or even "regional" history, because a German *Land* was not simply a geographical unit but a historically evolved territory, evoking consciousness and loyalties. But in spite of this seeming decentralization, professors and other academics with permanent posts, such as the directors of archives and of major libraries, were and saw themselves as state officials, bound by a special kind of loyalty to the state which went beyond that demanded from ordinary citizens or subjects. One should neither oversimplify such connections, nor project the present back unchanged into the past; the role played by professors of history under, say, William II (especially during the First World War) was perhaps comparable to that played by professors in eastern Europe more recently, but it was certainly not identical. Nevertheless, both the institutional position of historians and the traditions of historical studies predisposed them to write the history of the state, history from the top, and in doing so to echo contemporary political fashions: it is no accident that the great era of writing about medieval politics as *Machtpolitik*, power politics, coincided with a similar exaltation of power in the dominant political rhetoric of the decades before 1918, nor that the unlovedness and disorientation of the Weimar republic should have been reflected in frustration and in a loss of the old certainties in the historical writing of the 1920s.

Even in the nineteenth century political history was not the only academically legitimate form of study of the past. Constitutional history, though it had started out in the hands of historians (Waitz' great eight-volume survey of German constitutional history, the model for Stubbs' constitutional history of England, was written by one of the most distinguished medievalists of the century), showed a strong tendency to be dominated by legal historians. Legal history was and in some places still is, though less prominently, an obligatory part of the curriculum for lawyers, and much effort was devoted to showing continuity and continuous development in "German" legal practice from the period of the barbarian invasions up to the codifications of the end of the nineteenth century. The legal texts of our period were often analysed and dissected using the legal conceptual apparatus of the nineteenth century. The nineteenth-century discovery that most European languages are descended from a common ancestor (Indo-Germanic) and that the Germanic languages themselves have a common ancestor within this line of descent played a role in the reconstruction of a common "Germanic" past; we have here, as with Lachmann's editorial method or the new techniques of critical source analysis, the idea of recovering information about "ancestors" by examining "descendants". The surviving remnants of law and legal practice in the first millennium were taken as fragments of a proto-Germanic legal system and constitution. Much of this reconstruction was then taken as having existed even in places and at times where there was little or no direct evidence for it. The methodology of legal history also heavily dominated the study of social and economic history. For example, there was much more of a tendency in Germany than in England or France to consider the records of estate management, both the *polyptiques* of the early middle ages and the *Urbare* (custumals) of the high middle ages, as records of legal obligations than as sources for the study of an economic unit. Social and economic history were also largely the preserve of *Landesgeschichte*; there were of course general surveys, but a work like Dopsch's classic study of economic development in the Carolingian era remained unusual in its generality. Attempts to link political history with social, economic and cultural developments were few, and were not well received. In particular Karl Lamprecht's *Deutsche Geschichte* was subject on its appearance in 1891-2 to a barrage of criticism. This was directed at Lamprecht's allegedly careless and unscholarly use of sources but its warmth was fuelled by dislike and distrust of his aims, which were to relate the political and constitutional developments of the period to socio-economic change ("superstructure" to "basis", perhaps, though Lamprecht was hardly a Marxist, and Marx and Engels had little effect on *academic* historical writing until after 1945). The resistance to Lamprecht showed an underlying attitude which was to outlast all changes of regime and intellectual climate; there have been few impulses from the *Annales* school (which itself owed something to Lamprecht) in German medieval studies (it took over forty years for Bloch's *Société Féodale* to be translated into German, for example), and though medievalists have in the last two generations been very much concerned with the study of consciousness, this is rather different from the study of *mentalités*.

The German collapse of 1918, the failed revolution which followed and the social disruption caused by the inflation of 1922-3 did not lead to the kind of conscious reflection on the past and on the historian's role in mediating between it and the present found after 1945, and such changes as did take place were unconscious. The period from 1920 to 1940 saw a boom in *Landesgeschichte* and a move away from the history of the Reich. Even in this economically troubled period institutes for the study of regional history were set up, for example at Bonn, Marburg and Freiburg. *Landesgeschichte* also came to acquire a theoretical framework and justification: in particular, it was argued, the previous tendency of constitutional historians to take evidence from widely different parts of the Reich and build a systematic picture from it was methodologically unsound. Instead, a much more intensive study of regional differences was required; only then would a comparative constitutional history be possible. It has still hardly been realized, though the intensive study of institutions on a regional basis has been going on now for three generations. The argument was related to a further criticism of traditional constitutional history, namely that this was based too much on liberal views of the bourgeois state as formulated in the nineteenth century, too systematized, and above all not sufficiently attentive to the elements of popular action and of leadership in the medieval past. Two highly influential studies which appeared at the end of the 1930s set out in a programmatic fashion to do this: Otto Brunner's study of the development of territorial lordship in late medieval Austria, and Walter Schlesinger's work on the tension between public office and private lordship in Thuringia in the early and high middle ages.[3] There were evidently connections between their lines of approach and the currently dominant ideology, but these were not simply ones of cause and effect, and this was typical of the relationship between National Socialism and the historians. The professoriate of 1933 was a fairly representative cross-section of the educated bourgeoisie. Most of its members were politically of the right and hence even where they were not members of the party shared many views held by the NSDAP, which was within the ideological mainstream of right-wing politics in the 1920s; on the other hand, many felt repelled by the vulgarity and crudity of Nazi ideas and Nazi rhetoric (on history as on other things), and their socialization as academics was an additional barrier to their acting as simple propagators of a new "Germanic" view of the middle ages. Though the hegemony exercised in Europe by the Ottonian and Salian emperors was glorified in public lectures and the German eastward colonization continued to be praised as bringing development and civilization to previously backward regions, these views and attitudes were hardly invented in the 1930s. Attempts to see Charles the Great (or, for that matter, Otto I, unfavourably compared with his supposedly more "Germanic" father Henry I by some NSDAP ideologues) as a betrayer and corrupter of German

---

3. O. Brunner, *Land und Herrschaft*, Vienna 1939; W. Schlesinger, *Die Entstehung der Landesherrschaft in Thüringen*, 1 (all published), Dresden 1941.

purity were publicly repudiated. Moreover, many of the developments in medieval historical studies which were to take off properly in the 1950s and 1960s can already be found in work of the late 1920s and 1930s, which saw the beginnings of a reaction against "straight" political history, conceived of as the projection of contemporary notions of power politics into the distant past. This reaction was found in quite different quarters. Percy Ernst Schramm began from the late 1920s to work on the ceremonial and public aspects of rulership: on the way rulers had themselves depicted in coins and paintings; on the liturgical texts used during the coronation of rulers; on the objects such as crowns, sceptres, swords and other still more unusual things which were used to represent and make concrete abstract notions such as kingship and the kingdom. At about the same time Ernst Kantorowicz published his biography of the Emperor Frederick II, inspired by the highly elitist circle around the poet Stefan Georg. Methodologically this was noteworthy for the way in which it took seriously the rhetoric of rulership used by Frederick's chancery and evaluated this to see how the ruler and his circle perceived themselves. This led at the time to attacks on the work for "mythologizing" history, but in retrospect Kantorowicz seems simply part of the new wave; at much the same time Schramm was doing a similar re-evaluation of Otto III. There was also a new interest in religious practice and experience, conceived of as something more than the study of religious institutions.

Perhaps the most important long-run development in German medieval historical writing since the Second World War has been the removal of the study of history from the political arena – at least in West Germany. This was not a deliberate decision. Medievalists played little part in the post-war debates on historical theory, and were on the whole far less disposed than their modernist colleagues to reflect on the traditional assumptions of their craft. Nor was there any great purge of medievalists from the universities of Germany and Austria after 1945; a few who had exposed themselves particularly prominently on behalf of the former regime lost their posts, but even for many of these this did not last long. Nor did depoliticization occur immediately. The historical writing of the 1950s on the middle ages saw a sharp drop in the use of words like "German" and "Germanic", but this was compensated for to some extent by an increased use of words like "Western" and "West". The unkind interpretation put on this by some medievalists in the GDR, namely that their colleagues in the FRG, after preaching German expansion in the 1910s, revenge in the 1920s and the Germanic virtues in the 1930s, had now simply turned their hand to expounding the new ideology of NATO and the Cold War, was untenable in this crude form, but it was not without a grain of truth. *Abendland* in the 1950s was a shorthand which when expanded included the two Cs which in different ways stood in opposition to communism: Catholicism and capitalism. The numerous conferences and public lectures devoted to the thousandth anniversary of Otto I's imperial coronation in 1962 may serve as a kind of chemical indicator for the depoliticization of historical studies, since Otto I was par excellence a potential inspiration for rollback and containment. As it turned out, the overtones of contemporary political concerns were still there, but they were fading. Another indicator was the subject and form of historical exhibitions. One in 1956 was entitled "The emergence of Western culture in the Rhine and Ruhr region"; in 1965 a great exhibition was devoted to Charles the Great in Aachen, history here being pressed into the service of the emergent European ideal. Since then there has been a number of major historical exhibitions devoted to medieval history in Germany, but none has taken for its occasion one of the dates which an older generation of historians might have seen as critical or significant. The centenaries of 1973 (death of Otto I), 1977 (Canossa) and 1987 (deposition of Charles the Fat) passed without public commemoration, while major exhibitions devoted to the Staufer (1977) and the Salians (1990) apparently had their dates chosen deliberately so as *not* to commemorate and hence emphasize any particular event.

The most characteristic feature of this new depoliticized historical writing has been an emphasis on the consciousness of groups and individuals, on how they saw themselves and others. This can be seen in much of the work done on rulers; in the work of the so-called "Freiburg school" on nobles and monks; and in the revival of interest in the work of medieval historians and hagiographers. We have already seen how the representative side of rulership was a matter of interest as early as the 1920s; this work was continued after the war, and new kinds of source were tapped to fuel it. It was soon realized, for instance, that seemingly quite formal parts of royal diplomata could be made to reveal the attitudes of the kings who issued them: the titles given them at the beginning or in the dating clauses at the end showed what they saw themselves as ruling over, while the arengas or preambles to diplomata, often dismissed as empty rhetoric, could be taken seriously as material on attitudes and hence in a sense on "policy". An arenga is as near as we get to an explicit justification by a ruler for a particular action, the grant of a privilege.

Nothing could be more revealing of the dominance of "consciousness" as a central theme of German medievalists than the developments in the study of the nobility and of a particular kind of source which has not been mentioned so far, the *libri memoriales* or confraternity-books, books kept in monasteries to contain the names of monks in other religious communities and of kings and aristocrats, for all of whom prayers were said. These do not survive in great numbers – for the Carolingian era we have only five more or less complete specimens – but they make up for their scarcity by the sheer bulk of information they offer in the form of long lists of names. The original impulse in the 1950s for the more intensive study of these sources, which had long been known about but little used, by the "Freiburg school" of Gerd Tellenbach and his pupils and their pupils, was a genealogical one; the observation that names entered in groups were often those of a widespread kindred gave rise to the hope that the otherwise sparse and conflicting information about the genealogies of the eighth to the eleventh centuries could be filled out, and family trees put on a new footing. This turned out to be at best a half-truth; further study showed that no particular group entry could be taken to be based purely on kinship without other supporting evidence. The genealogical interest receded into the background, and from the late 1960s *libri memoriales* were taken to be and studied primarily as evidence of consciousness. The self-assessment of a monastic community was revealed by the other communities with which associations of confraternity existed: tell me whom you pray for and I will tell you what kind of monasticism you favour. The self-assessment of individual aristocrats and of rulers showed itself in the company they kept in group entries: these showed not so much genealogy in a biological sense as the consciousness of family and group.

Consciousness as a key to understanding of the past is seen, finally, in the way historians and hagiographers have been studied. The list given earlier treated the writers of the eighth to the eleventh centuries as if they were in the first instance a source of "facts", of information about wars, peace treaties, rebellions, invasions and the other stuff of medieval politics. Of course they are that, and it is a function whose importance should not be underestimated. But their writings tell us other things about the world in which they wrote. Nineteenth-century scholars had examined these historians largely in order to be able to correct for their "bias", their prejudices and partisanships, and to check their originality in order to eliminate the information they merely copied from others. More recently it has been realized that their "bias", to use a crude word for the complex phenomenon of a historian's mental world and its horizons, is a worthwhile object of study in itself. We know what Otto I thought only from the very imperfect process of arguing backwards from what he is known to have done; but we know what Widukind thought because we have a written record of his thoughts in his History of the Saxons.[4] Knowing what Regino and Widukind and Thietmar thought is one step towards understanding how Arnulf of Carinthia or Otto I or Hermann Billung or the anonymous armed followings of Hugo of Lotharingia or Liudolf of Suabia thought. The terminology they use reflects their unspoken assumptions and those of their class. The study of medieval historians in this way has been a speciality of German historians since the Second World War, and virtually all the major historical writers of the ninth, tenth and eleventh centuries have been explored using this methodology in greater or lesser detail.

One of the drawbacks about an emphasis on consciousness is that we cannot always clearly distinguish between consciousnesses. Charles the Great and Otto III, after all, neither composed their own diplomata and coronation ordines nor illuminated their own manuscripts, let alone wrote their own annals. At best we are dealing, so far as the political elite of the period is concerned, with group consciousnesses. There is, however, more concrete evidence for the exercise of power by rulers and others, most clearly visible for rulers. The work done on this also owes much to another trend whose beginnings we saw in the 1920s and 1930s, the emphasis on Germany's regional diversity. The basic working assumption here is that royal power and influence were not evenly spread throughout the kingdom, nor were they even intended to be; they varied considerably in time and space, and the measure of this is where kings went, how they supported themselves, and for whom they issued diplomata. Kings' itineraries can be reconstructed from narrative sources and more accurately from the dating-clauses of diplomata, which usually mention the place where and day when a diploma was issued. We can thus see where kings went frequently, rarely or not at all; knowledge of the roads used and of standard practice enables us to fill in the otherwise large gaps, – essential since for about 90 per cent of the reigns of the rulers we are dealing with

---

4. Beumann 1950 was the first major study along these lines, as it happens devoted to Widukind.

we do not know precisely where they were on a given day. The recipients of diplomata and the distances they were prepared to travel in order to get them are also revealing: did Suabians go to Saxony to get diplomata from Otto I, or did they wait until he came to them, or at any rate to the mid Rhine?[5] A knowledge of who got grants, and of who persuaded rulers to make them, provides information on who was in and who was out of favour. Essential also for an understanding of itinerant kingship is a knowledge of where the rulers stayed (their palaces and those of their magnates, especially ecclesiastical ones), and of how they fed themselves and their entourages (the location and administration of important complexes of royal estates and rights). The entourages themselves, especially the royal clerics, are also a matter for prosopographical study: which men served the king or travelled with him, and with whom were they connected? This way of studying the rulers of the early and early high middle ages presupposes that there were few or no constants, little in the way of an abstract "state" with institutions. The state, such as it was, was revealed in the shifting patterns of behaviour of rulers. Their itineraries and entourages are a guide to their "policies" and intentions.

These emphases in recent scholarship are inevitably reflected in the pages that follow, and so also (I hope to a lesser extent) are the gaps and silences in the current concerns of German medievalists. These lie primarily in two areas. The first is a perhaps excessive unwillingness to generalize about the institutional basis of the "state" (because the baby of constitutional history has been thrown out with the bathwater of an ahistorical systematization). There are signs that this is coming to an end: there has been a revived interest recently in considering the Ottonian Reich as a state (though not, of course, as a primitive and imperfect version of a modern state). The second gap lies in a certainly excessive reaction against the implications of the work of two great German thinkers, Freud and Marx, both of whom in different ways insisted on the idea that there might be other reasons for men's actions than the ones they gave themselves. To see "consciousness" – meaning people's explicit and implicit statements about what they saw themselves as doing – as the principal if not the only proper object of historical study means to push to one side consideration of the "unconscious" springs of thought and action, whether these be taken to be the direct impact of social and economic

5. Müller-Mertens 1980 provides a state-of-the-art account of the methodology and a historiographical account of its development.

circumstances or that of the psyche. It may be that this one-sidedness, drawn from a long German tradition but perhaps reinforced by the ideological confrontation in Europe in the last forty years, will also come to an end. As yet there are fewer signs of this.

Part I Carolingian Germany

CHAPTER TWO
The Frankish kingdom

REGNUM FRANCORUM

In the eighth century the Franks under their Carolingian rulers put together a huge empire in western and central Europe. They were not working without tradition or precedent. The Romans had for a time tried to incorporate the lands beyond Rhine and Danube into their empire, though in the end they abandoned this aim. The Merovingian kings of the Franks, de facto successors to the emperors in the western half of the empire after the collapse of the Gothic kingdom in Italy in the mid sixth century, were more successful, and most of the Carolingian empire consisted of lands which had been under Frankish control in the time of the Merovingian rulers of the late sixth and early seventh centuries. The revival of the empire proceeded systematically. The opposition in the heartland of the Frankish kingdom was broken, and – in geographical, not chronological order – Frisia, Saxony, Thuringia, Bavaria, Alemannia and Raetia, Lombardy and central Italy, Provence, Septimania, Catalonia, Gascony and Aquitaine came under direct Frankish rule. Brittany and the principality of Benevento remained independent but had to pay tribute, as did the Slav peoples along the eastern frontier of the empire. The Avar empire was destroyed in a few short campaigns in the 790s, which brought the Franks immense plunder and also eliminated any possible rivals in central Europe. Only the British Isles, together with the Scandinavian and most of the Spanish peninsula, remained outside Frankish control, though not outside Frankish influence: Charles the Great was able to intervene with varying degrees of success in succession crises in Denmark and

Northumbria, and in the complicated internal politics of the newly founded Spanish emirate.

From about 800 expansion ceased, and during Charles's last years and the reign of his only surviving son and successor Louis the Pious the Frankish empire moved on to the defensive against threats from outside, while its rulers tried to turn an empire of conquest into something more permanent. Charles and Louis aimed at more than a mere "renewal" of "the Roman empire" or of "the realm of the Franks", to quote slogans they used. Whereas their Merovingian predecessors had been content with a general control over the outlying regions of their empire – they took tribute, appointed dukes and had law-codes drawn up – the Carolingians attempted with some success a fuller integration of the re-won or newly won territories into their empire. It is in this period, therefore, that the various Germanic peoples east of the Rhine were incorporated into an overriding political structure in a way which affected them socially and politically: a certain uniformity and harmonizing of institutions, of ideology (Christianization, either as conversion or as intensification, went hand in hand with the Frankish expansion of the eighth century) and to some extent also of the economy.

Neither the creation nor the continued existence of the Frankish empire was the Carolingians' unaided achievement, but it makes sense to begin with them because the Franks were ruled by a king or by kings, a tradition which was to be inherited by the successor-states in east Francia. The original Frankish dynasty, the Merovingians, was removed in a papally sanctioned coup in 751, and Pippin, who had previously been de facto leader of the Franks under the nominal rulership of the last Merovingian Childeric III, was anointed king. For 130 years after Pippin's accession in 751 there was no serious doubt that only a Carolingian could be a king. Carolingian blood in this sense was not transmitted by women. Even at the end of the ninth century, when non-Carolingians began to rule in several parts of the Frankish empire, they did not base their claim to rule on descent through females from a Carolingian, even though some of them could have done so. Only male Carolingians counted; but this does not mean that all male Carolingians became kings. Some died young, and some were not regarded as legitimate, though the criteria for this were not clearly defined until the late ninth century. Legitimacy was shown in the names kings gave their children – Charles, Carloman, Pippin, Louis, Lothar – as against the names for illegitimate male offspring – Hugo, Drogo, Bernard, Arnulf. The distinction between legitimate and illegitimate did not correspond

22

exactly to the nature of the union from which the child was born. Some Carolingians – Charles the Great's eldest son Pippin the Hunchback, and Carloman, Lothar I's son by a concubine, are examples – received "legitimate" names in spite of their origins, and may have been thought of as king-worthy. In exceptional circumstances "illegitimate" Carolingians could also succeed – Bernard to Italy in 811, Arnulf in east Francia in 887. Much was determined by the will (in both senses) of the father, and by other ruling Carolingians. Children could be disinherited, or deprived of their inheritance by their relatives. Carolingian succession arrangements sometimes defined the rights of kings' sons against those of kings' brothers, but these were still rights which had to be fought for.

Carolingians normally began ruling while their fathers were still alive; they received sub-kingdoms. Charles the Great was the last Carolingian to succeed as an adult without some experience of ruling, and the only minor to succeed between 751 and 887 was Charles of Provence, though several others began ruling fairly young. When Carolingians came to rule on their own, whether in a sub-kingdom assigned to them or in a larger portion of their father's kingdom, or in a nephew's or cousin's portion to which they had succeeded, they normally did so by receiving oaths and recognition from their "leading men"; sometimes this process was formal enough to be called an election. The Carolingians had begun their royal career with a new kind of king-making rite, that of anointing by churchmen. This rite continued in sporadic use, but it only gradually came to be regarded as an essential part of king-making; in this respect the east Frankish kingdom was to be particularly conservative.

Kings did not just rule from one central place, but also moved around their kingdoms. Charles the Great in later life and Louis the Pious stayed for long periods of time at Aachen, which had something of the functions of a capital. But they did not reside there permanently. Kings often made a pilgrimage to a monastery or other holy centre during Lent. After Easter, or perhaps after Whitsun if Easter fell early, the campaigning season began. Years without campaigns were exceptional in the eighth century, and unusual in the ninth. The king might be represented by his sons, or by trusted generals, but usually he would take the field in person. Between the end of campaigning and Christmas came the hunting season. None of this was immutable. Campaigns could be fought if necessary at any time of the year – Charles's Lombard campaign in 774 began with an Alpine crossing in deep winter – and the ceremonial side of

Carolingian kingship appeared at other times besides the first three months of the year. But the three-part year was the usual pattern, if nothing intervened.

The Carolingians were able to move around because they could provide for themselves and their entourages. They themselves owned very extensive lands: their own family holdings, what was left of the Merovingian royal fisc by 751, and the huge gains made in the eighth century through conquest and confiscation. Besides this, they could call on church lands for hospitality (*gistum*) and renders of food and drink (*fodrum, servitium*). It might seem that kings moved around in order to eat up the produce from their estates and thus ensure continued supplies of food for themselves, but this is at best a half-truth. The feeding and provisioning of really large groups of men such as armies did indeed present problems. The armed followings of the three Carolingian kings who came to the meeting at Coblenz in 860 (an entirely peaceful affair) did much damage to the surrounding region, presumably in their search for food and lodging. But the administrative arrangements of the Carolingian period were quite capable of dealing with the transfer of sufficient food and drink to maintain the rather smaller numbers who normally accompanied the king. They must have been, because it was during the winter, when provisions were scarcest and most difficult to transport, that kings stayed longest in one place. Kings, then, did not need to move around to ensure supplies. A closer look at their movements shows that neither did they move around in order to make their presence felt throughout their kingdoms. Apart from campaigns, Charles, Louis and his sons, even when on the move, usually stayed in a few well-defined areas, which turn out to be ones rich in royal palaces and lands (*Königslandschaften*). In the part of the empire which was to become the east Frankish kingdom, the *Königslandschaften* lay around the confluence of the Main and the Rhine, and around Regensburg. Here, a high proportion of royal lands was directly under the king's control, administered by royal agents on behalf of the king as landlord, whereas outside the *Königslandschaften* royal lands, even where they were extensive, were exploited politically rather than economically, being granted out to churches, and to laymen in benefice, or placed at the disposal of the count. We shall see shortly how kings ruled those areas where they did not normally go.

The court was where the king was; *palatium* could mean either a palace as a building, or the king and his court. Some valuables and archives might be deposited in palaces, but generally the king took his household goods, officials and servants around with him. Some officials – the seneschal and the butler – were responsible for organizing the king's journeys. Besides such household officials and the servants under them, the Carolingian king had other groups of men in attendance. The most important group, but the hardest to define, was that of the king's counsellors. Each Carolingian had his own group of such men, important lay office-holders and ecclesiastics, who spent a considerable part of their time with the king. As the name implies, they advised him, and their influence could be very considerable: men like Alcuin, Theodulf of Orleans and Wala under Charles the Great, or Benedict of Aniane, Matfrid of Orleans and Bernard of Septimania under Louis the Pious, came close to achieving the status of "mayor of the palace" from which the Carolingians themselves had begun their political career. But the status of counsellor was defined quite informally; the term was not used in official documents north of the Alps.

Another important group was the chapel. This had developed out of the group of clerics who under the Merovingians had been responsible for the royal collection of relics, including the cloak (*capella*) of Saint Martin, the Merovingians' patron saint. By the time of Charles and Louis the clerics of the chapel had acquired other functions. They still looked after the king's relics and his other treasures, including his books and such archives as existed, but they also met the court's extensive liturgical needs. Some chaplains, under a leader called the chancellor, were responsible for writing royal documents. The chapel had other, less well-defined but equally important roles. From the time of Pippin onwards, the Carolingian chapel was under an archchaplain. This was necessary for overall direction, but also from the point of view of canon law. Clerics were supposed to be under the supervision of their diocesan bishop, but the clerics in the chapel of an itinerant king obviously had no diocesan. To have them supervised by a senior ecclesiastic – the archchaplain was often, though not invariably, a bishop – gave their anomalous position some regularity, though church reformers continued to be unhappy about the chapel. But the archchaplain was far more than a senior bureaucrat; he was the king's right-hand man in ecclesiastical matters. Men like Angilram of Metz and Hildebold of Cologne advised the king, especially on church affairs and in particular about appointments to bishoprics, and they presided at synods summoned by the king, as Hildebold did at Mainz in 813. The archchaplain was not the only important member of the chapel. Originally its members may have been fairly lowly clerics, but from the time of Charles the Great at the latest a new kind of chaplain begins to appear: high-born, personally bound to the king by commendation and serving in the chapel in the expectation of future reward. Gerwald, *capellanus* to Charles's wife Berta, who became bishop of Évreux and then abbot of Saint-Wandrille, and served Charles as ambassador to the pope, is a good example of the type. This form of clerical service was another feature of Carolingian government that was to have a long future: the aristocratic cleric, who served at court and was then rewarded with a bishopric or other high church office, bound to the ruler even after leaving the chapel by ties of commendation and long familiarity.

The court had a limited military capacity. Besides officials such as the marshal, responsible for the king's stables and the collection of fodder for the army, and the standard-bearer, the king, like his Merovingian and Roman predecessors, also had with him a bodyguard who could form the nucleus of a larger army. In an emergency a detachment of these might be sent off as a *scara*, a fast-moving squadron. The court could also act as a court of justice. Important cases inevitably came before the king – "important" meaning here not so much cases of special legal difficulty as those involving the leading men of the kingdom and hence having a political dimension, though the beginnings of the idea of the king's court as a court of appeal were also visible. These cases might be heard before the count of the palace, and other leading men present might be asked for their judgement or opinion, but the judgement as finally delivered was the king's own.

The king governed from his court by making his will known, either in person, through representatives, or in writing. We should not assume that the Carolingians intended to govern as we should understand the word. Their aims were more limited: to preserve and extend their own wealth and power; to do justice and keep the peace within the borders; and to wage war and exact tribute abroad. But we should also not assume too readily that Carolingian government was non-existent or ineffective, or existed merely on parchment. These warnings delineate the problem of making sense of the very rich legal material available on Carolingian governmental institutions. Under Charles the Great and Louis the Pious legislation took two forms: revisions to the existing law-codes, which were made only on a small scale, and the issuing of capitularies – the name is contemporary, and denotes a legal or administrative text divided into chapters (*capitula*). The name says nothing about the content, and this could be very varied. A few capitularies relate to a single subject, but most cover a very wide range, usually mixing ecclesiastical and secular provisions. They can be called legislation only in a fairly general sense, for some *capitula* are mere administrative regulations, and others are more like exhortations than precise commands or prohibitions with specified penalties (though all were royal commands and hence in theory carried the penalty for disobedience of the king's *bannum*). What is important in the present context is the mass of material transmitted in this way – between 100 and 200 capitularies, depending on how and what one counts, have survived for the period 800–830, the high summer of capitulary legislation. This is a lot of material, but it deals with what *should* have happened. If we take it to describe what *did* happen, as an older generation of legal and constitutional historians generally did, we can construct a picture of a very elaborate state. If, on the other hand, we are sufficiently sceptical about how far what was supposed to happen did happen, we can deny the Carolingian "state" almost any degree of institutionalization we choose. For our purposes there is the further difficulty of deciding how far the institutions of the Frankish heartland were also found in the lands which were to make up the east Frankish kingdom; this cannot, for a number of reasons, be taken for granted.

The main component in Carolingian government was the count. The count and the county were institutions derived largely from late Roman provincial administration. In southern Gaul the count governed a definite territory which usually corresponded to a late Roman *civitas*: a city and its surrounding lands. In northern Gaul the office was more of a mixture between that of the *comes civitatis* and that of a Frankish judicial official known as the *grafio*, but the result was still by the Carolingian era an essentially territorial office. Whether the counts in east Francia had such sharply defined territories is less certain (see below, p. 92), but the office was certainly not wholly different in nature east of the Rhine. In any case a network of counties did not cover the whole of the Frankish empire, for royal demesne, church lands covered by immunity, and forests were to a greater or lesser extent outside the count's jurisdiction. In principle, the count was the king's representative and hence an "official". But the office was one frequently held by men who were in any case men of standing in their area. They and their contemporaries may not always have distinguished clearly between their "official" and their personal power. Apart from this it is often said that the Carolingian county changed over time, becoming in the course of the ninth century less of an office to which the king appointed, and more of a hereditary position; however, examples of counts' being succeeded by their sons or by other close relatives can be found in the eighth century, while a lot of the evidence for deposition of counts – obviously a sign that they could still be treated as officials – comes from the second half of the ninth century.

The count was a king in miniature. In so far as there was a general levy of troops from his county (see below, pp. 33–5), he gathered them and led them. He held courts three or four times a year within his county, at which he gave judgement (from Charles the Great's time this was done by permanent lawfinders called *scabini*) in the presence of the leading men of the county. He was responsible for making known the king's will and for enforcing it. This meant that he had the power to command and punish, just as the king did. As the king's command (*bannum*) had to be obeyed on penalty of a heavy fine, so did the count's, though the fine was less. The office was worth having for its power, but there were also lands which went with the county and were held from the king in benefice; a portion of the money received in fines went to the count. Counts all had the same responsibilities, but not all counts were equal. Some counts held more than one county, while some counties were shared by more than one count. In any case the size and importance of counties varied considerably. We occasionally find references to such distinctions in the sources, as when a capitulary of 792–3 distinguishes between powerful and less powerful counts (*comites fortes, comites mediocres*).[1] In border regions there was a clear hierarchy: in each march a number of counts were under the command of a prefect (or of a king's son). This was primarily a military command structure, but it is probable that the prefects also had powers equivalent to those which were exercised by royal emissaries (*missi*) in other parts of the empire.

This brings us to the *missus dominicus*. The Merovingians had employed royal envoys ad hoc for specific tasks, and the Carolingians continued to do this. They developed the institution, however, and sent out *missi* with a general brief to do justice in a particular area. Doing justice meant holding courts and supervising the counts and their subordinate officials. Counts had numerous opportunities for misusing their office. They could take bribes not to enforce summonses to serve in the army; they could use their powers of command to bring the less powerful into a position of dependence;

1. MGH Capitularia regum Francorum 1, ed. A. Boretius (Hannover 1893), 52, no. 23.

and they could give judgement in favour of themselves and their kinsmen and allies. The *missi* were supposed to control such abuses; in order to do so they were given extensive powers. In the heartland of the Frankish empire the system of inspection by *missi* was fully developed; from 802 at the latest, *missi* were sent out in pairs (normally a count and a high ecclesiastic) to cover a defined district, a *missaticum*. *Missatica* were also found in Italy, but not east of the Rhine, where *missi* were always rare and disappeared altogether after the death of Louis the Pious.

Missi were not the only means available to the Carolingian ruler for communicating with his counts. There is some evidence for orders, written or oral, being sent out by messengers, though few such mandates have survived. More important was the regular contact between the king and his counts at the general assemblies. Royal assemblies were frequent under Charles the Great, Louis the Pious and their descendants. There is some indication that two a year was the normal number, but in times of crisis many more than this could be held; occasionally, as in 820, a year passed without one, but this was exceptional. Some contemporary sources distinguish in principle between general assemblies (at which the army was present), more select meetings of the king's leading men, and meetings of the king's council, but we are not usually told how well attended any particular assembly was. It is clear that there was a general obligation on counts to attend such assemblies, though it is improbable that every count went every year. Regular contacts between each count and the king may be assumed, however, and these supplemented – indeed, were probably more important than – the contacts by mandate or *missus*.

It was at assemblies that two of the most important elements of Frankish political life came into play: law and war. We have already seen the king's court as a source of judicial decisions for important cases; such cases were frequently dealt with at assemblies, and this applied particularly to those involving accusations of treason or rebellion. Besides this, it was normally at assemblies that the content of legislation was made known and discussed. This can be seen from the form of surviving capitularies. Some survive only as lists of points to be discussed, others as brief notes, others as full texts. This suggests that the texts as we have them were often unofficial records of decisions announced orally, and in general we should assume that the contents of such *capitula* were made known at general assemblies (though we also know of cases where capitularies were sent out in written form from the court).

The other side of the assembly was war and diplomacy. In 790, for example, Charles the Great held an assembly at Worms. We are told by the Royal Frankish Annals that the ambassadors of the Avars were received and that the boundary disputes between the two peoples were discussed.[2] Diplomacy was a public matter. Contemporary annalists usually record the appearance of envoys at the assembly, as here; it helped to display the ruler's power and prestige. The Royal Frankish Annals often say that other peoples made agreements or treaties not just with the ruling king but also with his sons and with the Frankish "people". Such treaties normally followed a successful campaign, and it was usually the assembly where the current year's campaigning was determined. The annalist of Lorsch, commenting on the same assembly, said – obviously noting something unusual – that it was not a war-assembly (Mayfield) and that there was no campaign that year.[3] In most years in the eighth century the Franks did indeed campaign, and from the 780s on it became increasingly common for two or more armies to be raised in one year and sent against different opponents.

POPULUS FRANCORUM

With law and war we have reached the point where we turn from describing the structure of Carolingian government to examining the Frankish political community. To know who took part in legislating, passing judgement, deciding on war and peace, and campaigning is not easy, and very different answers have been given; these in turn have consequences for the view we take of the relations between the king and his leading men, and between the leading men and the rest of the population of the Frankish empire. The narrative sources for the history of the Frankish empire mention only a few people by name, apart from the Carolingians themselves. Almost all are bishops, abbots and lay office-holders, in other words the "leading men" whom we have already met. Did these men and the families from which they came have a monopoly or near-monopoly of the important business of Frankish politics, or were there others with a political role? How far was there a nobility of birth in the empire of

2. *Annales regni Francorum*, s.a. 790, ed. F. Kurze (MGH SRG, Hannover 1895), 86.
3. MGH SS 1, 34.

Charles the Great and Louis the Pious? On the whole, the tendency of the last hundred years of scholarship has been to move steadily towards the assumption that the "leading men" were drawn from an aristocracy and away from the idea of the Frankish empire as having been in essence a society of large numbers of more or less equal free men under a king. There are good reasons for this; but there was also considerable justification in the sources for the older view, which has too often been dismissed as simply a reflection of nineteenth century bourgeois liberalism (as it undoubtedly also was).

What was it which led an older generation of scholars to suppose that the Frankish empire was a society of small free men, out of which the aristocracies of post-Carolingian Europe only gradually crystallized? First of all, the Merovingian past. The seemingly uncontrolled and arbitrary way in which the Merovingians were able to act did not suggest that there was any strong counter-force in the form of established aristocratic privilege in the sixth and seventh centuries. Indeed, the Merovingians could be seen as the successors to Roman absolutism. Moreover, the legal evidence for the Franks (though not for the peoples further east) distinguishes only between free and unfree, as on the whole it continues to do in the Carolingian period. It is true that the text most frequently quoted in this context, a sentence from a capitulary of Charles which says "there is nothing other than free and slave",[4] actually means "either you're free or you're not", and does not imply that in Charles's view there is no nobility. But in fact Carolingians did not in written documents refer to such a thing. They legislated about the military service due either directly or by proxy from all free men and about the obligation these had to attend the county courts, and they tried to exact oaths of loyalty from all free men. Besides this, there is on the face of it not much evidence for what is normally held to be one of the most important features of an aristocracy, namely the inheritance of power and wealth. Not all the leading men can be fitted into definite genealogies, and where this is possible these tend to break off after at most three generations. Even the noble families of post-Carolingian Europe were not normally able to trace themselves back very far – which shows that the difficulty is not just the result of sources having disappeared – and some indeed claimed explicitly to be descended from parvenus.

The older model explained the transition from the supposed

---

4. MGH Capitularia regum Francorum 1, ed. A. Boretius (Hannover 1893), 145, no. 58.

community of free men to the later aristocratic polities as being the result of feudalism. As is well known, the combination of vassalage (a relationship of mutual trust and service between a lord and a follower) and benefice (a transfer of rights over property to another person without a permanent transfer of ownership and with the right to recall the property rights under certain circumstances) became a common one in the eighth century. In place of a political community in which the king still had a direct link with all free men because they were liable for military service and swore oaths to him, there emerged one in which only those who were directly bound to the king by office-holding and vassalage played a significant role. The more the ordinary free man was squeezed out of warfare and office-holding, the more he lost political standing and independence. The men who founded the new aristocracies were, on this view, those who rose to power as the vassals of the Carolingians.

If today's consensus is rather different, this is neither because scholars get bored with explanations after a time, however accurate these are, nor because the scholars of an earlier generation wilfully overlooked the obvious, but because the sources, especially but not only the narrative sources, will also sustain another reading which now seems closer to the truth. Few would today deny the existence of small free men in the Frankish empire (though there were attempts to do so a generation ago); but still fewer would deny the existence of an aristocracy. The change started with the realization that many of the leading men of the Carolingian empire did not come from nowhere but were related to one another and to office-holders of previous generations. Some at least of them were related to office-holders of the Merovingian period. This suggests that there was after all an aristocracy, and one which did not, moreover, owe its rise or its existence to the rise of the Carolingians. The realization owes much to a more flexible attitude to genealogy. The evidence often allows us to say that there was a relationship between two people, but not to say what it was.

This vagueness does not mean, as has sometimes been said, that there was a radically different sense of family in this period from the closer and better-defined one which was to prevail later. There may have been, but it is worth noting that there was no developed terminology for distant relations of the kind we should expect if men had had at all times and for all purposes a consciousness of belonging to a very large kin-group. Moreover, the church had considerable difficulty in preventing marriages between people who were by its standards (but evidently not by others') too closely related. What the vagueness does mean, however, is that we should not try to fill the genealogical gaps by guesswork but simply accept the limits to our genealogical knowledge. If we do so, then we can assign very many of the leading men of the late eighth and ninth centuries in a loose way to a comparatively small number of kindreds. Historians have christened these after the leading names (*Leitnamen*) which constantly recur in each generation: *Robert*ines, *Suppo*nids, *Wido*nids, *Rorgo*nids, *Unroch*ings, *Conrad*ines, *Eticho*nids. Many of these names can be found held by leading men of the late sixth and seventh centuries, and when we find that men with the same names held the same pieces of property in both periods, it suggests very strongly that their families had continued in positions of power over the two centuries, though we are not necessarily faced with direct descent in the male line.

A careful look at Carolingian warfare and Carolingian justice lends further support to the idea that Frankish society in the eighth and ninth centuries did not consist of undifferentiatedly equal free men. It is generally accepted that by the end of the ninth century Carolingian armies were no longer composed of levies of peasant free men. But nor had they been in the eighth. Armies consisted mainly of the followings of great men (including of course the Carolingians themselves) – as indeed they had done in the sixth and seventh centuries. In the eighth century, and probably for much of the ninth, we should envisage these vassalitic followings as having been generally unbeneficed, living in their lords' household, though they may have been given small benefices at the end of their active career as a reward, if Anglo-Saxon analogies are valid. The distribution of (mainly church) lands in benefice under Charles Martel and Pippin did not create large numbers of landed military vassals analogous to the knights of the high middle ages. Nor were there radical and expensive changes in military techniques such as to exclude peasant warriors from fighting and hence from political power. As in the Merovingian period cavalry warfare was not unknown, but it did not take the form of "mounted shock combat" practised by horsemen kept firmly in the saddle by stirrups. Horses continued to be used as much to move warriors rapidly round as in battle. Much of the Frankish success – against Aquitaine, Saxony, Lombardy and the Avars for example – can be ascribed to other things, such as their effective logistics and siege warfare, but here too there were Merovingian precedents.

What ruled out warfare for the free peasant and perhaps also for the small independent landlord was not its techniques but its cost.

It was annual campaigning which made participation in warfare difficult and expensive. The Carolingians were able to raise armies nevertheless because their wars were extremely profitable. They brought in slaves, treasure and land, and it was these attractions which raised armies, rather than the ties of obligation created by vassalage and benefice. The proceeds of warfare, however, were not evenly divided. There may once have been a time when German warbands shared out plunder among themselves by lot, but under the Carolingians the distribution of booty (and tribute) was clearly made by the king, and those rewarded were the leading men. In 795 the Lorsch annals record:

> In this year the treasure came from the land of the Avars, a huge quantity, for which the lord king gave thanks to the Almighty and distributed the treasure among the churches and the bishops and the abbots and the counts; and he enriched all his faithful men wondrously with that same treasure.[5]

"All his faithful men" means, not all free "subjects" but the groups referred to earlier in the passage, together perhaps with Charles's own unbeneficed vassals, who were numerous. The proceeds of Carolingian warfare were in any case not of a kind to be of use to the small independent fighting man. Slaves and treasure are of much more value to those with large estates to work and warrior followings to reward than they are to small freemen. The land which became available in the newly conquered territories consisted mostly of large estates confiscated from the leaders of the opposition. In so far as these were not kept in the king's fisc, they seem to have been granted out again in benefice to leading men, rather than parcelled out in small holdings.

At first sight the views just expressed seem to be contradicted by the evidence of some of Charles's and Louis's capitularies, which demand military service from free men with quite small holdings, and make arrangements for those too poor to serve in person to club together in twos, threes or fours to support one warrior. These have been taken to show the decline of general participation in warfare, but they will sustain a different interpretation. The provisions come from a time when the Frankish empire was itself threatened with Danish and Saracen invasion for the first time, and when the Franks had run out of opponents who were both easy and profitable to campaign against. Under these circumstances, when warfare had

5. MGH SS 1, 36.

become more a duty than a pleasure, Charles and Louis revived the old institution of levies of all free men for defence against potential invasion, and tried to extend it so that men were not simply obliged to defend their own locality but could be moved around as need arose. The provisions are more likely to represent an extension than a restriction of the obligation to do military service.

As far as justice and the courts were concerned, there was some political participation by quite small men at the local level, that of the county court or *mallus*; we find the notion of the *boni homines* of a neighbourhood, men of standing who could sit in judgement. But even here it is clear that there was not a group of small free men whose political standing depended on their jealously defended right to take part in courts; participation was expensive as well as extensive, and was evidently felt to be a burden as much as a right. The Carolingians tried to prevent counts from holding too many local assemblies (three a year was thought to be enough), so as not to impoverish those with the duty of attending them to give judgement; and there was no opposition to the introduction of permanent jurors (*scabini*) on the grounds that these deprived free men of their right to hear lawsuits and pass judgement. And at the level of the empire and its assemblies, the Carolingian political community consisted, as it had done under the Merovingians, of a small group of men, whom by position and life-style we can term a nobility.

However, the group was not a closed caste. By no means all leading men can be assigned to known kindreds. Some do indeed appear to have come from nowhere, without traceable ancestors or descendants. One possible explanation lies in the existence of regional elites, and some historians have wished to introduce a third, intermediate group between the leading men (often termed the *Reichsaristokratie* or *Reichsadel*, "imperial nobility") and the small free men: the "tribal" nobility (*Stammesadel*). These were landowners who were not poor and yet played no important role beyond the region in which they held land. The evidence of *libri memoriales* and witness-lists also reveals many relatives of known leading men about whose existence we otherwise know nothing, some of whom may be seen in this light, though it is also quite possible that some of the owners of the personality-less names recorded in witness-lists and *libri memoriales* led an existence as free peasant farmers even though they were related to men who most definitely did not. The conclusion seems to be that the boundaries between noble and free – or between the powerful and the ordinary free man, if one takes a strictly legalistic view of the nature of nobility – were not rigid, at any rate not in the time of Charles and Louis.

The Frankish elite, however composed, did not so much hold power from the king as exercise it with him. Royal legislation, for example, was not the unprepared announcement of new law by a supreme ruler. The legal force and penalties of the capitularies derived no doubt from their status as the king's command, but it is pretty certain that even a king like Charles the Great could not command anything he liked. He had to take into account what was acceptable, and this meant discussion and consultation. The king could indeed prevail against single leading men. Individuals could be disgraced, could even be tried and condemned to death, blinding, exile, loss of property or imprisonment in a monastery. But such events were comparatively rare, even in a troubled reign like that of Louis the Pious, and on the whole they occurred at times when kings were insecure; the moving force behind such executions was usually a rival aristocratic clique rather than the ruler himself. Normally, however, for all the rivalries between leading men, they also showed a certain group consciousness. Charles and Louis were careful to have their opponents tried and sentenced in due form (as in the case of Tassilo of Bavaria in 788 and 794), so that others besides the royal house were implicated in the actions taken against them, and so that the sanctions would be backed by public opinion. Summary executions and confiscations had to be justified: one of the few really apologetic passages in Einhard's *Life of Charles the Great* comes when he describes how three men accused of rebellion were killed on the spot, because they had drawn their swords against their capturers.[6] Killing those resisting arrest out of hand could be excused more readily than executing them. The leading men we have been considering were important in other ways also. They and their families held scattered property across the Frankish empire, just as their Merovingian and Roman equivalents had done, and they married into and helped to integrate the leading families of the conquered regions which came into the Frankish empire in the course of the eighth century. These ties of property and family were to be of great significance in the formation of east Francia, and in determining the history of the several Frankish kingdoms in the period after the single Frankish empire under a single ruler had ceased to exist.

6. Einhard c. 20, pp. 25–6.

ECCLESIA FRANCORUM

We have seen the Carolingian empire as a state with more or less well-functioning institutions; we have seen it as the interactions of an oligarchy. A further important facet was its understanding of itself as a Christian society. This had particular implications for the Germanic peoples east of the Rhine; here incorporation into the Frankish empire went hand in hand with conversion to Christianity. But Christianization was not confined to the edges of empire. From the mid eighth century there was a general renewal and consolidation of Christian institutions. This took many forms: internal missionary work; renewal of lapsed church institutions; the revival of learning needed to underpin mission and church reform; and an increased tendency to lay down norms drawn from Christian thought for secular politics, especially the actions of rulers. This traffic was not one-way. Bishoprics and the greater monasteries were locked into the world. Bishops and abbots were among the leading men just discussed; like their secular counterparts they, or rather their churches, held widely scattered lands, and thus acted as a force for cohesion and integration within the Frankish empire. Like the great laymen, they were drawn mainly from a small group of families, though not evenly: some kindreds produced few or no churchmen, while others, like the Hattonids of the middle Rhine or the episcopal family of Auxerre, specialized in doing so, finding their access to power by producing at least one bishop in each generation.

The bishop was at the heart of the Carolingian church. There were nearly 150 dioceses in the Frankish lands north of the Alps. The bishop controlled the wealth of the church within his diocese, wealth which carried heavy secular responsibilities. He was also responsible for Christian life within the diocese, and to some extent he still preached, taught, said mass, baptized and buried, assisted by his clerics, just as bishops in the early church had done. By the eighth century such duties had largely been delegated to parish priests, though few dioceses were fully and evenly divided into parishes, and the upkeep of parish priests presented problems. Until Charles the Great made tithes compulsory and general, parish churches and their priests had been supported by the revenues of the diocese and by offerings from the faithful, especially for baptism and burial. The right to have a font and a cemetery was jealously guarded, and did not in theory extend to the numerous private churches (*Eigenkirchen*), which belonged to the owner of the land on which they were erected, who also chose the priest. Tithes should have made it easier to support parish priests and enabled an extension of the parish system. In practice they blurred the distinction between parish churches and *Eigenkirchen*; the owners of private churches tried both to bring parish churches with their valuable rights of tithe into the status of *Eigenkirchen* and to secure tithe rights for their own *Eigenkirchen*. Even where this did not happen, the parish church tended to take on the character of an episcopal *Eigenkirche*; the tithe revenues went directly to the bishop, who provided a small stipend for the priest. Already by the time of Louis the Pious tithes were well on their way to becoming simply a 10 per cent income tax of a particularly burdensome kind and were resented and evaded by both great land-owners and dependent peasants – there are references in the 820s to tithe-strikes.

The diocese and its clergy were not an isolated or autonomous part of the church; one of the most important features of Carolingian church reform was the revival of episcopal group consciousness. The Gallic bishops of late antiquity and the early Merovingian period had met together in provincial councils (a province consisted of a number of dioceses, with one bishop as a metropolitan at its head) and occasionally in larger gatherings to discuss and legislate for the problems of the church. This came to an end in the second half of the seventh century; it was revived under Boniface and Chrodegang of Metz in the mid eighth century, and carried still further in the high summer of Carolingian church reform, which began with the synod of Frankfurt in 794 and reached its peak in the years between the five church councils of Mainz, Rheims, Tours, Châlons and Arles in 813 and the reform councils of 829. The aims of these councils, as reflected in their legislation, can be summed up under three main headings: intensification of Christian practice; greater uniformity; and preservation of the purity of the church. The reformers legislated in detail about marriage, penance and preaching, as well as about crime (violence, fraud, theft, and their consequences); they laid down norms for liturgical observance and monastic practice as well as for the equipment of parish churches and the training of their priests; and they forbade such things as hunting or womanizing for clerics. Taken together, the legislation amounted to an attempt to provide a fairly comprehensive Christian code, with penalties for its non-observance; few aspects of the life of the laity were left untouched. It was primarily parish priests who would have to put this legislation into effect, and Carolingian ecclesiastics tried to ensure that those who became priests were adequately trained for the purpose. Bishops were encouraged both by church councils and by rulers to set up schools for clerics, in order that these might have sufficient education to understand these instructions and pass them on to their flocks. Charles the Great's *epistola de litteris colendis*, the foundation charter of the Carolingian renaissance, set out clear practical aims: priests were to study the church fathers and the Latin classics so that they could properly understand and explain the Bible to the laity. A similar impulse lay behind much church legislation. The priest should be able to explain the Lord's prayer and the creed, and to preach to laymen in a language they could understand. This required training, and teachers with a higher level of education and understanding than would necessarily be demanded of priests. It is in this light that the so-called Carolingian renaissance should be understood: like the recent expansion of higher education in developed countries, it came about because there was felt to be a shortage of people with the right training for specific tasks. The things which now seem most impressive to us – the scholarship, the copying and preservation of manuscripts, the revived study of the classics, theology and canon law – were almost byproducts of this central aim. It was accident rather than design that so much of the literature of classical antiquity was preserved by the clerics of the Carolingian era.

The most concrete survivals of the Carolingian renaissance lie in the texts just mentioned: in the eighth and ninth centuries there was an enormous increase in the production of manuscripts of all kinds, and these were written in a new kind of script, Carolingian minuscule. The sources of the texts so enthusiastically copied are often hard to determine; for some kinds of text, especially secular law-codes and the Latin classics, the earliest surviving manuscripts are Carolingian ones, and we do not know what their exemplars were or where they came from. Some were probably already available in Frankish libraries; others came along with intellectuals looking for fame and reward from Anglo-Saxon England, Spain and Italy. One source of a rather special kind was Rome. Pippin and Charles acquired liturgical texts from the popes, as well as a standard canon law collection and a pure text of the monastic rule of St Benedict. These texts were copied, often with a note saying (not necessarily truthfully) that they had been directly copied from the authentic original, which implies both a special status and a measure of central direction in their spread. This centralizing influence can also be seen in Charles's interest in securing a purified text of the Bible, and in his commissioning of a collection of sermons, Paul the Deacon's *Homiliary*, also copied as an "authentic" text. Yet this standardization from the centre was less extensive than was once thought. The diffusion of "authentic" texts was perhaps greater than that of other comparable texts, but not massively so; only the *Rule of St Benedict* became a really standard text. Often the Roman texts were not in themselves enough; they had to be revised and supplemented to adapt them to Frankish needs (as in the case of the *Gelasian Sacramentary*) or be copied together with other similar texts. The canon law collection brought from Rome, the *Dionysio-Hadriana*, which in Carolingian manuscripts is more often found together with other canon law collections than alone, was the most important source of church law in the Carolingian era, but by no means the only one acknowledged. It was not just kings who helped to spread texts, but churchmen, both as individuals and as members of circles of friends; the Carolingian renaissance, even in its initial "court" phase, was not a royal monopoly any more than government was.

The fact that although the Carolingian rulers got authentic texts directly from the popes these did not become the only authentic texts tells us much about the role of the papacy in the Frankish church and kingdom. The Carolingians had had their assumption of kingship sanctioned by Popes Zachary and Stephen II in the years 749–54. In return they had protected the popes from their immediate enemies in Rome and abroad. They intervened in Italy in 754 or 755 and in 756 to secure a Lombard regime better disposed towards the papacy and a measure of territorial independence for the popes. After this failed they themselves took over the Lombard kingdom in 774. Their new function as protectors of the popes was one previously performed by the Byzantine emperors, and Charles the Great's coronation as emperor in 800 was in effect an acknowledgement of this. Relations between the Frankish rulers and the popes thus came to be close and personal in a way they had not been before: Hadrian I acted as godfather to Charles's son Pippin, and mediated in the dispute between Charles and Tassilo of Bavaria. The popes took on a political role in an empire which covered most of western Christendom, and in doing so became more than just the titular head of the church considered as a body of ecclesiastics. Yet the effects of this change on the Frankish church itself were not so marked. True, Boniface had been a papal legate and had habitually resorted to Rome for authoritative decisions on difficult matters. But this did not alter the Frankish tradition, which was to treat the pope with great respect but not to look to him as a judge or a legislator, or at least not as the only one available. Frankish church reform drew no more heavily on papal legislation than it did on Visigothic and Gallic church councils for inspiration. The popes were only one source of tradition, though an especially venerable one; they were not yet authority.

The interest of the Frankish church in authentic tradition and the copying of texts can be viewed more generally as part of a desire to restore the right order of things within the church and hence restore its purity. The effectiveness of the Carolingian church in spreading and deepening Christianity depended not only on the rational technique of producing a better-educated clergy, but also on enlisting the numinous power of the church, of setting up Christianity as an alternative to paganism and magic on all fronts, including providing a new Christian magic. Effective magic-working needs the right texts to be said in the right way; hence the preoccupation with authenticity and textual accuracy. It also depends on the purity of the performer; hence the preoccupation with the sexual purity and continence of priests, monks and nuns, and the beginnings of a conscious rejection by the higher clergy of the bloodier side of aristocratic life: fighting, feuding and hunting. Magic-working also requires props. Some of these were created. The de luxe manuscripts of the Carolingian renaissance and the newly built churches can, of course, be seen simply as pieces of conspicuous consumption produced to satisfy the nouveaux riches of the Frankish court and church. But they were also meant to impress as holy objects. Even the new minuscule script of the Carolingian era, whose introduction has often been seen as a rationalistic move because it was clearer and more elegant and hence more legible, should also be considered in this light. It is a calligrapher's script, at least as suitable for the production of works of art as for an extensive and self-evident use of writing in administrative and intellectual life.

Both "court" and "church" art were part of the production of magic and holiness. Charles's new palace church at Aachen was designed as a theatre for the drama of ceremonial kingship, and the ancient statues and columns raided from Italy for his palaces were objects chosen for their antiquity and numinous power. The churchmen of the Carolingian renaissance behaved in the same way; their new books and buildings both displayed their wealth and brought those who beheld them into contact with supernatural power. Churchmen, moreover, could draw on more impressive props, namely the relics of saints. The eighth and ninth centuries were the great age of relic-translations. The access to Rome and Italy given by the Frankish conquest of Lombardy in 774 allowed Frankish churchmen to draw on Rome's almost limitless reserves of saintly power. Many such relics were transferred to old-established churches like Saint-Denis, but still more went to new foundations, often far from towns and standing in areas only imperfectly converted to Christianity. Saxony, for example, saw a large number of relic translations in the ninth century. The saints to whom these relics belonged were held to have direct access to God, and their shrines were centres of power and magic.

The magic power of the church had a double function. Churchmen helped to preserve the distinction between the wealthy and powerful and the poor and dependent. They taught the duty of slaves to obey their lords and masters, and the saints whom they controlled reinforced this teaching: the miracles of saints were directed against the disobedient, but also against the wicked and oppressive. They thus sanctioned the existing social and economic order directly, while holding out some hope that its worst effects could be avenged in this world as well as in the next: a safety-valve. Equally importantly, the magic power of the church protected the special interests of churchmen. The lands and rights of the great churches were constantly threatened. What is surprising is not so much the losses as the fact that these were not greater. One reason is certainly the supernatural powers which churchmen controlled. These were applied in many different ways. Saints worked miracles to avenge the loss of an episcopal or monastic estate; or they appeared in visions to foretell dreadful punishments in the next life for evil-doers. In particular, they protected those places – monasteries and churches – where their relics were kept. At a seemingly more rational level, churchmen wrote treatises on the duties of Christian rulers and Christian laymen (meaning aristocrats). But the force of these came as much from the ancient tradition which their authors drew on – quotations from the Bible and the church fathers – as from close argument; Carolingian political theology was less of a rational instrument than it now seems to us.

The church did not exist just as bishops and priests; there were also monasteries, though the sharp distinctions of the high and late middle ages between monasteries, canonries, cathedral and parish churches are not always applicable to the eighth and ninth centuries; many of the new foundations of the eighth century, especially those east of the Rhine, existed for some time before their final organizational form was determined. In 800 there were perhaps 600 churches which could be called monasteries in the lands north of the Alps. The majority were private foundations by bishops and laymen, who owned them as proprietary monasteries (*Eigenklöster* by analogy with *Eigenkirchen*). Some had been founded or acquired by kings, and were royal *Eigenklöster*. The forms of monastic life varied greatly. Some monasteries, especially those in towns, had in effect become canonries: their inmates were less bound to the monastery, and often owned a fixed share of the monastery's income. In other words, they no longer observed the monastic vows of poverty and stability. But even those monasteries where a monastic life was led practised very diverse forms of monasticism. Besides Benedict's rule, there were numerous other rules dating from the fifth to the seventh centuries and many monasteries had a mixed observance based on more than one rule or on a mixture of rule and custom. There was also a great range in size and wealth, from immensely wealthy abbeys like Saint-Denis down to the small monastic cells in Alsace acquired by Saint-Denis in the eighth century.

Monasteries served a purpose in themselves within the framework of Christian institutions. They made it possible for Christians to practise virtues difficult to sustain – particularly for aristocrats – in the outside world: poverty, chastity, humility. Besides this, monasteries could provide the personnel for the work of the church in missionary areas; the conversion of Germany in the eighth century was done with strong back-up support from monastic foundations. But monasteries could also have quite different functions. Their comparative permanence and stability made them very suitable as centres from which to organize the more extensive colonization of regions with low levels of settlement. We also find them acting as mausolea, places where the founders and benefactors of monasteries and their kin were buried and where their memory was kept alive. This function was to become still more prominent in the tenth and eleventh centuries, but already in the Carolingian era it was clearly visible: monasteries were a new form of burial-mound for a Christianized ruling elite.

From the mid eighth century onwards an increasing number of monasteries came under royal control. Monasteries, like bishoprics, sought immunity for their landed possessions. It was common for a grant of immunity to be combined with the act of commending the monastery into the king's hands – the king then became in a sense the owner (though in what sense is debatable) and was responsible for protecting the monastery. From Louis the Pious on, immunity was granted only together with entry into the king's protection. This increase in royal control, especially over the larger and wealthier monasteries, was accompanied by an increase in royal interest. Already under Pippin and Charles church councils had shown a desire to standardize monastic practice and to specify the rule of St

Benedict as *the* monastic rule. This aim was realized in the early years of Louis the Pious, due largely to the influence of Benedict of Aniane, a monastic reformer from southern France. The assemblies at Aachen in 816 and 817 laid down that the rule of St Benedict was the only valid monastic rule, and also drew up a rule for canons, though as we shall see the extent to which these aspirations towards uniformity were actually realized in the ninth century was limited.

Royal interest also meant heavy burdens. It is no accident that the reforming assembly of 817 also saw the drawing up of a list of those monasteries which supplied the king with contingents of troops or with annual gifts or with both.[7] Church wealth had its own functions of course: the upkeep of the clergy and church buildings and the maintenance of some limited forms of public welfare – hospitals for travellers and the sick, and charity for the poor, especially in times of famine. But it was also drawn on for other purposes: hospitality for the king and his entourage (see above, p. 24) and for the other owners of *Eigenklöster*; contingents of troops; and, most extensively of all, for benefices, either at the king's order or as a direct arrangement between the benefice-holder and the church. This flow of lands away from the church probably came near to equalling the flow of lands towards it in the form of gifts and new monastic foundations. In any case, the church's wealth was not of quite the same kind as that of the king and the nobility; it can almost be described as their deposit account. Even the lands which remained in church hands were available for political purposes, as appointment to bishoprics and monasteries was an important form of patronage, exercised both by the king and on a smaller scale by bishops and laymen in the *Eigenkirchen* and *Eigenklöster*. The wealth of the Carolingian church was a sign of and a precondition for its success; but it tied churchmen to the world in ways which often conflicted with the values they were ex officio supposed to uphold. The tensions arising from this made an important contribution to the political history of the next few centuries, both in Germany and elsewhere in Europe.

7. MGH Capitularia regum Francorum 1, ed. A. Boretius (Hannover 1893), 349–52, no. 171.

CHAPTER THREE
Gentes ultra Rhenum

THE EMERGENCE OF THE EAST FRANKISH KINGDOM, 800–43

For a generation following Charles the Great's coronation as emperor by Pope Leo III on Christmas Day 800 there were attempts to consolidate the Carolingian empire from a loose agglomeration of *regna* bound together by a church, an aristocracy with widespread and scattered property-holdings, and a single ruler, into a more permanent structure. The Frankish custom of dividing up the kingdom among the surviving throneworthy sons was not an insuperable obstacle. When Charles drew up a division for his sons in 806, the Frankish empire was no longer to be divided equally: the eldest son Charles was to get not only a larger area, but also the part with the bulk of royal landed wealth. In the event, only one of Charles's legitimate sons, Louis the Pious, outlived him, and when he in turn came in 817 to provide for the division of the empire after his death, he was able to secure, against some opposition from traditionalists, a *de facto* primogeniture. Under the division, the *Ordinatio imperii*, his eldest son Lothar was to inherit most of the Frankish empire. The younger sons Louis and Pippin were to have sub-kingdoms in Bavaria and Aquitaine respectively, and his nephew Bernard a sub-kingdom in Italy, but these were to be genuine sub-kingdoms, of a kind previously held only by sons under their father, as Louis himself had held a sub-kingdom in Aquitaine under Charles. The sub-kings were not to have any real independence, particularly in the matter of making war; they were to be subordinate to Lothar, and in token of this were to bring him annual gifts like other holders of offices (*honores*) in the Frankish empire.

The Frankish empire was treated here as a single, Christian empire. Charles's imperial title had been an addition to his other titles – he did not cease to call himself king of the Franks and the Lombards. The division of 806 left the imperial title open and provided for joint protection of the papacy (one of the main implications of the imperial title) by all three brothers. Each had control of an Alpine pass into Italy. Louis the Pious, however, called himself simply emperor, and Lothar was also to have this title as a mark of his superiority. Just as the Frankish empire had one church, so it was also to have a single ruler. The *Ordinatio* was in one sense merely a planned division of the empire, which would only later come to be regarded as a programme. Yet it fell in a period of intensive reforming activity, of which it must be seen as a part. Between 816 and 825 a series of important capitularies was issued, culminating in the *Admonitio ad omnes regni ordines* of 825 and including substantial reforms of monastic life and of judicial procedure. Louis tried to act as the head of a Christian empire; in 822 he demonstrated how far rulership had become Christianized by doing public penance for his sins at Attigny and reconciling himself with political opponents.

Yet there were real problems. It was not so much that regional structures and loyalties continued to exist, and were done away with neither by Frankicization nor by absorbtion into a "Christian" empire. This could have been coped with, and indeed the *Ordinatio* might be compared to the very successful device of apanages used in the thirteenth and fourteenth centuries by the French kings, which gave regional loyalties a focus in a younger member of the royal house. Nor should we be too quick to see signs of decay in the legislation of the first three decades of the ninth century: the capitularies tell us more about what weaknesses were perceived (and about a willingness to perceive weaknesses at all) than about how serious or widespread they were or how well they were coped with. The problems lay more in the transition from an expanding empire of conquest to a more static structure. The Avar campaigns of the 790s and the final submission of Saxony were the last major Frankish successes. After that, not only had the Franks run out of opponents who were both easy and profitable to campaign against, but they had themselves begun to suffer serious losses. In the years between 798 and 806 a number of Frankish magnates (that is, members of the group which decided on war and peace) were killed in battle. At the

same time, Viking and Saracen raids on the Frankish coasts began –
the raiders were probably attracted by news of the wealth brought in
by Frankish successes. The reaction to these events was rapid. By
810 at the latest, the Franks had abandoned expansion and put their
defences on the alert; the campaigns against the Slavs in the 800s
were desultory affairs, while only defensive measures were taken
against the threats from the Danish king, Godfrey. This decision was
probably a sound one in terms of costs and rewards, but it left a
structural weakness in a polity very dependent on an inflow of loot
and tribute and on the charisma of militarily successful rulers. The
elite had to adjust. The alternative to raid and conquest was internal
redistribution. By working for influence at court, by taking over
offices held by rivals, individual leading men, both lay and
ecclesiastic, could maintain their access to wealth and hence the
followings which enabled them to keep it. It is significant that from
the beginning of Louis's reign we find clear and continuous evidence
for loose aristocratic groups which might be called parties. There had
been such things in Charles's reign as well, but the evidence for them
is much less clear, much more sporadic, and that is probably a sign
that they were less important then.

There were also inherent contradictions in the substitution of
Christianity for Frankishness as the ideological cement which held
the empire together. A good example can be seen in the question of
church lands. The process of secularization of church lands begun
under the earlier Carolingians had continued under Pippin and
Charles, though in a more orderly and regulated form than before.
In the last years of Charles's reign there had been complaints by
ecclesiastics, and in one of Charles's last capitularies he appears to be
accusing churchmen of being greedy.[1] Louis was more receptive to
such complaints, and in 819 he stated that he would not tolerate
further secularizations. This meant not only forbidding simple
usurpation of church lands, illegal in any case, but also ceasing to
issue *precaria de verbo regis*, by which laymen could at the king's order
hold church lands in benefice. By and large Louis seems to have kept
to this promise, but the result, though quite in keeping with his role
as a Christian ruler, was dissatisfaction on all sides. Many
ecclesiastics wanted restoration of the church lands seized in earlier
generations, not just a freezing of the existing state of affairs.
Laymen were equally concerned; it was only a step from saying that

1. MGH Capitularia regum Francorum 1, ed. A. Boretius (Hannover 1893), 162–3,
   no. 72.

precaria were in principle wrong and so there would be no future grants to saying that something had to be done about past grants in this form, and that was a threat to the status of lands which they and their ancestors had long held in benefice.

This was the drawback to the policies of reform, renewal and consolidation followed by Charles the Great in his last years and with still greater enthusiasm by Louis the Pious. The more Louis set himself up as the head of a Christian society, and the more he attempted to reform abuses through the issue of new capitularies and their enforcement by *missi*, the more he became personally identified with reform. He thus risked losing political credibility and loyalty on two sides, from those who felt they had something to lose if reforms were carried through, and from those who were disappointed at the apparent failure of reform (probably a smaller group, though because they were mostly high ecclesiastics and hence articulate and literate we know far more about them and their actions). In the late 820s it is clear that both forms of discontent were growing, and it was just at this time that the military effectiveness of Louis's government was seriously tested. Failures against the Danes, after attempts to reduce the danger through a combination of mission, diplomacy and discreet intervention in Danish royal family politics, and a rebellion on the Spanish frontier in 826, not successfully countered by an expedition in 827, together with the threat of Bulgarian attack in the south-east, with border raids providing a foretaste of the possible consequences, meant a serious crisis.

The crisis of 829–30 affected both policy and personnel. Louis appeared to abandon the policy of reform. At the end of 828 he and his son Lothar (who had ruled with him as co-emperor since 825) had followed Charles's example of 813 and summoned four church councils which were to consider the state of the empire and report to an assembly. The councils duly met, at Paris, Mainz, Lyons and Toulouse, and submitted a comprehensive report which included a lengthy section on the duties of a Christian king. Louis did not act on these recommendations. Rather, he announced at an assembly at Worms in August 829 that his youngest son Charles was to receive a principality of his own as his future inheritance, to include Alemannia, Raetia and parts of Burgundy. This was to be taken out of Lothar's portion of the empire, and Lothar must have objected for he was sent back to Italy and his name as co-emperor disappeared from documents. These changes were accompanied by a shift of power: Louis's second wife Judith, and her brothers Conrad and Rudolf, together with Bernard of Septimania, "second in the empire",[2] now dominated affairs. These changes and the reaction against them the following year brought the underlying instability of Frankish politics into the open. The instability arose not so much from hard and fast, ideologically determined political groupings, as from their absence. Only a small number of people exposed themselves to such an extent that they could not change with the political wind; but whenever a settlement appeared to have been reached, there were too many people with an interest in overturning it for it to become a point of equilibrium.

We do not here need to go into the details of the years 830–6, with their frequent changes and purges, culminating in Louis's deposition in 833 and his restoration to office in 834–5. The crucial point is that all four of Louis's sons became focuses for aristocratic and ecclesiastical followings. At first sight it might seem as if Lothar's position was different, for he was supported not only by a following but also by a number of ecclesiastics who justified their actions with the slogan of imperial unity and the need to preserve the divinely willed *Ordinatio*. But the difference is only superficial. In the first place, Lothar himself was unwilling to turn back the clock only as far as 817; he wanted to exclude his brothers as far as possible from any part in the succession. In the second place, the implied contrast between selfish and egoistic laymen and idealistic churchmen is somewhat misleading, for the ecclesiastics who spoke out most loudly in favour of the idea of imperial unity, like Wala, Louis's cousin and abbot of Corbie, or Agobard, archbishop of Lyons, were also those who had been most radical in their demands for restoration of secularized church lands in the 820s and most disappointed at Louis's failure to act effectively. In their own way they too were an interest-group. In fact it is doubtful how far there was a party of imperial unity in an ideological sense. Clearly there was a good reason for the major ecclesiastics and the more established nobility to favour Lothar's cause, once Louis appeared to have turned against the unified succession envisaged in 817: with their scattered land-holdings, they would have had the greatest difficulties to face should a genuine division along traditional lines come about. But this was only one set of pressures determining allegiances, and as so often in medieval politics, the overriding dispute seems to have worked like a magnet on personal feuds and expectations, propelling rivals and enemies into opposing camps.

It was in the course of the manoeuvrings of the 830s that the

---

2. Nithard, *Historiae*, I 4, ed. E. Müller (MGH SRG, Hannover 1907), 5.

future east Frankish kingdom began to take shape. Louis the German had gone to Bavaria as an active sub-king in 825, taking up the position assigned to him in 817. After the coup of 830 he began to issue charters in which he styled himself "by the grace of God king of the Bavarians". This was a claim to independent rule, not to an enlarged sphere of authority, but in 831 Louis the Pious arranged for a new division of the Frankish empire north of the Alps. In this the Germanic lands were not kept together, just as they had not been in 806 and 817. Louis the German was to get Bavaria, the Frankish lands east of the Rhine, Thuringia, Saxony, Frisia and the northernmost lands west of the Rhine, while Charles received Alemannia, Alsace, and the lands along the upper Meuse and Moselle valleys up to the west bank of the Rhine. Like the *Ordinatio*, this was an arrangement to take effect on Louis's death, but it seems that after Lothar's successful rebellion in 833 and Louis the Pious's deposition Louis the German did actually rule over most of the lands assigned to him in 831 and some of Charles's share as well. From late 833 his charters call him simply "king by the grace of God", with no restriction to Bavaria, and they date by his regnal years "in eastern *Francia*". After his father's restoration in 834–5 he kept Alsace, Alemannia, Franconia, Thuringia and Saxony as well as his heartland of Bavaria, but had to hand over the other lands west of the Rhine to his father. This kingdom was something like a kingdom of Germany, and it is in fact called a kingdom of the eastern Franks in the Fulda annals, but Louis's hold on it was insecure. When in 838 he fell into disgrace with his father it was only Bavaria which he could hold on to and which offered him a refuge.[3]

When Louis the Pious died on June 20 840, there was no general consensus about the succession. The programme of imperial reform and unification died in 829; a reform council held at Aachen in 836 repeated in essentials the proposals of 829, but found no echo. Lothar, using the *Ordinatio* as a slogan, wanted sole rule. Louis the German wanted to secure at least the portion assigned to him in 835. Louis the Pious himself had made a last division in 839 between Charles and Lothar, excluding Pippin II of Aquitaine (Pippin I had died in 838) and allowing only Bavaria to Louis the German. At first it looked as if Lothar might succeed: his advance across the Rhine showed (as in 838) that Louis the German's support in eastern Francia was weak outside Bavaria. But in the end Lothar overreached

---

3. For Louis's titles, official and unofficial, in this period, see Eggert 1973: 15–25, 245–58.

himself, forced Louis and Charles to form an alliance against him, and was defeated by this alliance at the battle of Fontenoy in June 841. The negotiations and jockeying for position between Fontenoy and the treaty of Verdun lasted over two years; at one point, in March 842, Louis and Charles even had Lothar deposed from rulership by an assembly of clerics and divided up the Frankish lands north of the Alps. The final division agreed at Verdun in August 843 was based on a survey of the royal fisc and on the assumption that Charles would start with Aquitaine, Lothar with Italy, and Louis with Bavaria. What remained was to be divided up equally, not by surface area but so that the value of royal lands and other rights in each kingdom would be more or less equal.

The result was the creation of three kingdoms which cut the Frankish empire vertically: Charles got west Francia, Lothar the middle kingdom, and Louis east Francia. This included all the lands east of the Rhine, except for Frisia and perhaps a short stretch on the right bank of the lower Rhine, which went to Lothar, and also included the three mid-Rhenish episcopal cities – Mainz, Worms and Speyer – and their territories on the west bank of the Rhine. As it turned out, this division was to have lasting effects. As we have seen, the idea of an east Frankish kingdom was already current in the 830s; but it is important to grasp that what was created at Verdun was the result of quite different premisses: the need to accept the brothers' existing power-bases and to divide the rest equally. Given these, no radically different division was possible.

"GERMANY": NAMES AND CONCEPTS

By 800 the Germanic-speaking peoples east of the Rhine had been incorporated into the Frankish empire; in 843 they formed together a separate kingdom under the Carolingian ruler Louis the German. This development was, as we have just seen, largely a matter of Carolingian family and Frankish aristocratic politics. If we now look more closely at the territories which were to make up the east Frankish kingdom, we shall find not a people but peoples. It is easy to assume that "Germany" in the early ninth century was all much of a piece, that the level of social and economic development did not vary very much, and that its inhabitants all spoke the same language. But there were also substantial differences, some of which were to persist for centuries; and even some of the similarities are deceptive.

We may begin by looking at the notions of "German" and of "Germany". Both existed at the end of the eighth century, but not in such a sense that we can see the emergence of an east Frankish kingdom in 843 as merely the political expression of an already existing entity.

The terminology available to denote the German-speaking lands and the languages spoken there collectively was not extensive. We find the terminology of antiquity, *Germania* and *Germanicus*, in the sources; from 786 onwards there is the adjective *theodiscus*, a Latinized version of an Old High German *theod-isk (from *theoda*, "folk, people", meaning "of the people"); in the ninth century there is a revival of the classical words *Teutones, Teutonicus*, presumably because of their affinity with *theodiscus*. *Theodiscus*, the ancestor of the modern German word *Deutsch* and of the modern English word "Dutch", seems at first sight to denote an overall grouping of people; but it was for long restricted north of the Alps to a community of *language*, as in the phrase *nationes Theodiscae*, "German-speaking peoples", and this did not imply any other kind of community. Just as the Romans had been well aware that linguistic similarities did not necessarily mean ethnic or sociological identity, as Tacitus's *Germania* clearly shows, so too could Carolingian intellectuals distinguish between language and other matters. A good indication of this is Einhard's statement that the various Slav peoples to the east of the Frankish empire "are very different in their polities and way of life, though they all speak similar languages".[4] Only in Italy did *theodiscus* come early on to be used to distinguish "Germans" from native inhabitants of the peninsula. *Theodisk* was in any case not a word in common vernacular use: the earliest direct evidence for the word *diutisk* comes from the time around AD 1000, and there is no reason to suppose that those who spoke a Germanic dialect around 800 thought of themselves either as being or as speaking *theodisk*. Even the term "dialect" begs a large question. It is doubtful whether a ninth-century Bavarian could have understood a ninth-century Saxon with little difficulty, or would have felt that the two spoke essentially the same language.

Germania, "Germany", was another concept available to educated Franks, those who had read (or heard of) Caesar, Pliny and Tacitus. It was, curiously, most frequently found in an ecclesiastical context. Pope Gregory II as early as 722 could write to Boniface referring to

4. Einhard c. 15, p. 18.

the *gentes Germanicae*. The archbishop of Mainz was the metropolitan of *Germania*, and we hear of councils of the bishops of *Gallia* and *Germania*, reflecting the tendency of the early medieval church to continue to use Roman administrative terminology. The term had territorial rather than "national" implications. The conclusion to be drawn from this necessarily brief account is that there was not, in 800, either a geographical or a linguistic entity of Germany or *Deutschland* only waiting, so to speak, to take political shape. The lands around the Rhine and the Danube were inhabited by a number of *gentes* (to be translated as "peoples", with overtones of "heathens"). When they do occasionally appear collectively in the narrative sources it is as "the peoples beyond the Rhine" (*gentes ultra Rhenum*) or some such phrase; what they had in common was not so much being Germanic as not being Frankish, though there were Franks east of the Rhine as well. There are suggestions in the narrative sources for the civil wars of the 830s that Louis the Pious mistrusted the Franks and placed more reliance on the dependent peoples beyond the Rhine, but this was hardly a division along "national" lines, rather a distinction between the political elite of the Frankish empire and those who occupied a more subordinate position.

If instead of looking for Germany we look simply at the histories of the lands and peoples which came to make up the east Frankish kingdom of 843, we can distinguish three main regions. The first consisted of the two southern territories created in Merovingian times, Alemannia and Bavaria, together with the Bavarian marches – corresponding roughly to the southern regions of the modern West German *Bundesländer* of Baden-Württemberg and Bayern (excluding Franken), together with Alsace and much of Austria and German-speaking Switzerland. Although the two duchies differed considerably, they nevertheless had so much in common that they can be treated together. Above this south German belt lay the Frankish zone. It corresponds to the tenth-century territories of Lotharingia and Franconia, and stretches from the Benelux lands in the west across the Rhine into Hessen and the Frankish part of Bayern. Again, the history of the western part of this region (which in any case only later came to be part of the east Frankish kingdom) was not the same as that of the east, but the two were nevertheless closely linked. Above this zone in turn lay the north German peoples: the Frisians, and in particular the Saxons. There are other dividing lines which can be drawn. The "linguistic frontier" between Germanic and Romance speakers was of little political significance; more important was that between Roman and non-Roman Germany (roughly speaking, Roman Germany lay west of the Rhine and south of the Danube). The division above also does not include the Slav lands to the east, which were sometimes treated as if they were a part of the kingdom. Nevertheless, this triple division is the most important one; it crops up repeatedly in the ninth, tenth and eleventh centuries. By 1050 there was a much stronger consciousness, at least among the political elite, of there being a single polity, but the regional differences had hardly begun to fade, and indeed even after centuries of dynastic fragmentation and then of varying degrees of centralization under Napoleon, the Hohenzollern, Weimar, Hitler and Bonn, they are clearly visible in all kinds of ways today.

BAVARIA AND ALEMANNIA

Of the two duchies in the southern zone, Bavaria was the larger and the more important. It was bounded in the west by the river Lech and in the north-east by the mountain ranges which today separate Bavaria and Austria from Czechoslovakia. To the north it extended well beyond the Danube, though the region known as the Nordgau (roughly, today's Oberpfalz, north of Regensburg) was sometimes regarded as Frankish in later periods. In the south the border with the Lombard kingdom ran to the south of the main Alpine chain. The eastern frontier was the Enns, but in the eighth century there was to be tributary overlordship over the Carinthians to the south-east. Most of Bavaria had originally been Roman; it was not until 488 that the provinces of Noricum and Raetia were evacuated. When we next hear of the region, in the mid sixth century, it is described as being inhabited by Bavarians. The explanation offered by nineteenth-century scholarship of these events was easy to understand. The territory was evacuated and then colonized by a Germanic people, the Bavarians. All that was disputed was where the Bavarians came from and with which Germanic people known to Tacitus and Pliny they should be identified. The Bavarians could be seen either as the Celtic Boii, or as the Markomanni, a Germanic people who are known to have lived in Bohemia, or perhaps as a branch of the Alemans. For a number of reasons, explanations of this kind have come to seem unsatisfactory. The peoples of the early middle ages were not fixed and unchanging entities but rather groups whose being and consciousness could appear, change over time, and

54

disappear. The Bavarians were made, not born, and were made from a number of different ethnic elements, including Alemans and a group whose original home seems to have been in Bohemia. It was this last group which gave its name to the newly formed people, but the process of formation was determined as much by politics outside Noricum as by anything which happened there. Bavaria and the Bavarians came into existence because of the attempts made by the hegemonial powers in western Europe – the Goths under Theoderic and then the Franks under Theuderic and Theudebert – to establish political stability in a region affected by the Roman evacuation. These were assisted by the break-up of the Thuringian empire in 531, and by the beginning of the long Lombard trek southward.

Bavaria began as a Frankish protectorate, but from the mid seventh century was more or less independent. The Merovingians' loss of control seems to date from the disastrous campaign against Duke Radulf of Thuringia in 642, though the *histoire événementielle* of Francia in the second half of the seventh century is largely unknown and unknowable. Even before this Bavaria was ruled by dukes from a single family, the Agilolfings. The Bavarian law-code says that the Frankish kings had conceded the duchy to the Agilolfings in perpetuity,[5] and although the law-code as we have it is a text of the eighth century, there is nothing to contradict this account. Certainly the Agilolfings were a family of great nobility and antiquity (though their ethnic origins are disputed). A branch of the family ruled the Lombard kingdom in the late seventh century, and they were also related to some of the Alemannic dukes of the eighth century. Members of the kindred are also found holding office within Francia proper. Although the Agilolfing dukes of the seventh and eighth centuries were quasi-regal figures, they were not the only nobles in Bavaria. Unlike the laws of the Franks and the Alemans, the Bavarian law actually recognized a nobility of birth: besides the Agilolfings, five other named *genealogiae* (kindreds) are assigned a higher status than that of other free men, with a double *wergeld* (the blood-price due to the relatives of a slain person),[6] though only two of these families are referred to anywhere else except here. Other sources, in particular the early property records of the bishoprics of Freising and Salzburg, reveal a wider group of *nobiles* or *optimates* with higher social standing among the free. Unlike other free men,

5. *Lex Bauiwariorum* III, 1, ed. E. Freih. v. Schwind (MGH Leges nationum Germanicarum 5/2, Hannover 1926), 313.
6. *Ibid.*, p. 312.

they could found and make donations to churches (and thus alienate their hereditary lands) without ducal permission. Below them came, as elsewhere, the free, the freed and the unfree, at least according to the law-code. Other social divisions appear both in the law-code and in other early sources. We find men who were apparently military colonists charged with defence of the frontier (*exercitales, adalschalki*), as well as men who may have been descended from the original Roman population of the region (*tributarii*), and even among the unfree there were apparently differences of status. It is not easy to say how far the social structure of the Bavarian law-code was reflected in eighth-century reality, and in any case even pre-Carolingian Bavaria already showed the tendency of this period for both the free and the unfree to merge into a single socio-economic group, the serfs.

As in the British Isles, Christianity led a shadowy existence even after Roman political structures had disappeared, especially in the major urban centres of Noricum: Salzburg, Regensburg (though this had not been a Roman *civitas*), Passau and Lorch. As in the British Isles, its revival under the new political conditions was not due to existing native groups but to missionaries from outside supported by the political elite. The Agilolfings themselves were probably Christians from early on, and we know of a number of missionaries in Bavaria in the seventh century. It is only from the end of the seventh century that we can see positive efforts by the Agilolfings themselves, especially by Duke Theodo (*c.*680–*c.*717) both to encourage missionary work and to give Bavaria a church organization with bishops of its own. Before Theodo's time, such bishops as there had been in Bavaria had been Frankish, a tradition carried on by the episcopal missionaries prominent under Theodo: Rupert, who came from Worms to Salzburg, Emmeram, who came from Poitiers to the ducal residence of Regensburg, and Corbinian, a man probably of Franco-Irish descent, who came to Freising. In 716 Theodo, who had divided up the duchy among his four sons, got papal consent for a plan to establish an ecclesiastical province of four bishoprics in Bavaria with an archbishop at its head. His death shortly afterwards meant that the plan could not be realized, but it also shows that Christianity was firmly established in Bavaria by the early eighth century.

Theodo's action also shows just how independent Bavaria had become by the early eighth century. To divide up the duchy among his sons was to claim the status of a ruler, for such divisions had previously been reserved to the Merovingians and Carolingians. The attempt to set up a separate Bavarian church province was a further sign that the Agilolfings no longer accepted more than a nominal Frankish overlordship. The period between the death of Theodo and the deposition of the last Agilolfing duke, Tassilo III, in 788, was one in which the Carolingians became less and less willing to tolerate this. On a number of occasions the Franks invaded Bavaria, in 724–5, 743 and 749. The last duke, Tassilo, began rule as a minor and Frankish protégé in 749; in 757 he appeared at a Frankish assembly in Compiègne and according to Frankish sources became the vassal of Pippin III. Yet only six years later he withdrew from a Frankish army campaigning in Aquitaine, and between then and his fall in 787–8 Bavaria was once again virtually independent. As early as 739 it had received a papally sanctioned church organization at the hands of Boniface. Odilo, Tassilo's father, defeated the Avars and established a protectorate over the Slav Carinthians, so beginning a colonizing movement beyond the Enns into the Danube basin that was to be continued in the ninth century. During Tassilo's reign the first attempts to convert the Carinthians were made, with ducal backing; the Bavarian church also held its own councils at the duke's command, in 756, 770 and 772. Tassilo made a marriage alliance with the Lombard king Desiderius, and in 771 had his son Theodo baptized by the pope. All these things show the monarchical tendencies by now inherent in the Bavarian principality, and they explain why Charles the Great and the Franks in the end intervened to depose Tassilo. In 787 Tassilo was forced to submit; in 788 he was summoned before a Frankish assembly at Ingelheim and condemned to death for treason (his desertion of Pippin twenty-five years earlier), a sentence commuted to entry into a monastery. Charles spent most of the following five years in Bavaria establishing control there. Tassilo's last recorded appearance was at the synod of Frankfurt in 794, when he formally renounced for himself and his descendents all claim to his hereditary lands in favour of Charles the Great.

Charles took over a rich and well organized province. It was politically and ecclesiastically advanced, and after 788 the Frankish rulers were well endowed there. Apart from the Agilolfings themselves, the transfer of power affected few (though we hear of some Bavarian nobles being sent into exile); but the Agilolfing lands and rights were very extensive. Together with the fiscal lands along the middle Rhine, they were to be the basis of east Frankish royal power in the ninth century. At the same time Bavaria retained much of its separate identity. For a short time in 788 it was placed under

Frankish governors, but from 814 onwards it was a sub-kingdom, held from 817 by Louis the Pious's second son. It was never divided in any of the ninth-century partitions proposed or carried out by the Carolingians, and its status as a sub-kingdom or sub-division of the kingdom during much of the ninth century in a sense preserved the quasi-regal status of the Agilolfings. The duchy of Bavaria which emerged at the beginning of the tenth century was not a conscious revival of Agilolfing independence, but its existence is much easier to understand against the background of Bavaria's Agilolfing past.

At first sight Alemannia and Bavaria would appear to have had much in common: both were south German duchies with their own ethnic consciousness, their own law and their own dukes, under Frankish overlordship in the sixth century, increasingly independent from the mid seventh century onwards, reabsorbed into a revived Frankish empire from the mid eighth century. Yet there are also notable differences, and these are instructive. Alemannic origins are seemingly better known than those of the Bavarians. We find them as early as the early third century under kings, raiding the Roman empire. At the end of the fifth century the Alemans were defeated by the Franks under Clovis, and though they were protected for a while by Theoderic the Great, they came under Frankish overlordship by the time of Theudebert I and Theuderic I in the first half of the sixth century. Up to the time of Clothar II and Dagobert I we find Alemans above all as auxiliary troops under their own *duces* in the Frankish military expeditions into Italy; by the early eighth century the Alemans, like the Bavarians, had become sufficiently independent of Frankish rule for a series of campaigns against them to be necessary, notably between 709 and 712 and again in 743 and 746–7. In the course of these last campaigns the Alemannic dukes were deposed and what must have been a substantial part of the Alemannic nobility killed at Cannstatt (near Stuttgart) in 746.

This brief summary conceals a number of tricky problems. For a start, it is by no means certain how much the Alemans who appear in the sources at the end of the fifth century had in common with those mentioned at the beginning of the third; the name, evidently, but what else? Nor is it easy to define precisely the areas of Alemannic settlement. Alsace, though probably in some sense Alemannic, was under direct Frankish rule and from the seventh century on was ruled by separate dukes drawn from the Etichonid family (a rule which survived, in a remarkable display of noble continuity, into the reign of Otto I). Apart from the dukes of Alsace, the Alemannic dukes are shadowy figures compared with the

Agilolfings. It is by no means certain that most of those mentioned in the sources of the sixth and seventh century were anything more than military leaders, or that Alemannia was ever, except perhaps immediately before the Carolingians recovered control over it, ruled by a single duke as Agilolfing Bavaria was. If anything the presumption is against this, for the area of Alemannic settlement was cut by natural barriers not colonized until the high middle ages, the Black Forest and the Suabian Alps. If we take Alemannia as it was known in the ninth and tenth centuries it was quite definitely not a unity in Merovingian and early Carolingian times. The southern part of Carolingian Alemannia, Raetia, and in particular the region around Chur, led a separate existence following the Frankish conquest of 539. What emerged there was not an ethnically based duchy as in Bavaria and perhaps in Alemannia, but a remarkable polity. Its law was not Germanic but Roman, and it was ruled by a family known from its leading-name as the Victorids. These held the office of *praeses*, meaning both bishop and count in Merovingian terms. It was not until the early ninth century that the bishop of Chur lost his comital powers. While one should not exaggerate the Romanness of Raetia – the combination of ecclesiastical and secular office was certainly not one which had precedents in late antiquity, and the seemingly Roman name of Victor need not say anything very much about how the Victorids perceived themselves or who they were – there is a noticeable contrast between the separateness of Alemannia and Raetia on the one hand and the incorporation of Roman elements in Bavaria on the other.

There are also contrasts in the way the two duchies were absorbed into the Frankish empire. Bavaria was taken over by Charles the Great fairly peacefully; only Tassilo and his immediate followers were dispossessed. By contrast, the Alemannic duke Theudebald and much of the Alemannic nobility were removed by a military campaign, not just the threat of one. The charter evidence from Alemannia in the later eighth and ninth centuries, which is plentiful, gives little indication of a native nobility; the Alemans of high birth who appear elsewhere in the Frankish empire seem to have originated in Alsace. Moreover, the Alemannic dukes may not have controlled the whole of Alemannia. Their power lay at the southern end of the Black Forest and around Lake Constance. The original core of Alemannic settlement in the upper valleys of the Danube and Neckar and the border-lands up to the Lech was apparently under the rule of a family closely connected with the Agilolfings, the Alaholfings. All this meant that the Franks did not take over a substantially intact polity, as they did in Bavaria. Too much of the Alemannic elite was destroyed in the conquest, more land became available than could be controlled or held on to, and the confusion which this led to was still being sorted out a generation later: Cannstatt did for Alemannic land-holding what Hastings did for Anglo-Saxon land-holding. Alemannia was for a long time a land of subsidiary importance.

The early Christianization of Alemannia also followed a rather different pattern from that found in Bavaria. The lack of overall political control was reflected in the haphazard growth of ecclesiastical organization. Strasbourg and Basle were the bishoprics responsible for Alsace; Augsburg, founded in the early seventh century, covered only the eastern part of Alemannia. The remainder did not come under the Roman bishoprics at Windisch, Octodunum and Chur. The bishops of Windisch and Octodunum were forced to move south, the first to Avenches and then Lausanne, the second to Sitten. Their place was taken by Constance, a new bishopric founded around the beginning of the seventh century under circumstances still obscure (probably in cooperation between the bishops of Chur and the Merovingians). This might have become the basis for an Alemannic church, as Salzburg was to do in Bavaria, but it did not. Although revisions made to the Alemannic law in the early eighth century show that Christianity was a force to be reckoned with, it was probably less well established there than in contemporary Bavaria. The two earliest and most important Alemannic monasteries, the Reichenau and St Gallen, were endowed on a scale at least equal with that of the bishoprics, and played a substantial role in the Christianization of the country, a pattern reminiscent of Saxony rather than Bavaria. When the Franks came to define the provincial organization of the lands east of the Rhine, Constance (the largest bishopric in Germany), Strasbourg and Augsburg were placed under the "missionary" archbishopric of Mainz.

CENTRAL GERMANY

Between the ethnic duchies in the south and the Saxons and Frisians in the north lay a heterogeneous zone which early came under Frankish control. In Merovingian times Austrasia, a geographical term with shifting meaning, denoted the lands which today are Lorraine in France, southern Holland, Belgium and Luxemburg, as well as in a general manner of speaking the territories east of the Rhine under Frankish control. In Carolingian times what had been known as Austrasia came to be called *Francia media*, middle Francia. Austrasia now referred to the lands east of the Rhine – the West German states of Hessen, northern Baden-Württemberg and Bayern and the Rhenish part of Nordrhein-Westfalen – but we shall use it in what follows in its Merovingian sense. Virtually all of Austrasia both in its Merovingian and in its Carolingian sense was to come into the Ottonian empire; but this was not settled by the treaty of Verdun, which cut Austrasia through the middle between the eastern and middle kingdoms. Louis the German's kingdom extended only as far as the Rhine, except for the three counties of Mainz, Worms and Speyer; north of Cologne it probably did not even reach the Rhine. In most of western Austrasia there was continuity of Christianity from the Roman period; only in the north, in what is now Belgium and the southern Netherlands, was there sufficient disturbance in the fifth and sixth centuries for renewed missionary work to be necessary in the seventh century under Amandus, Bertinus and others, which led to the establishing of bishoprics at Tournai and Liège and was in a sense the prototype for the Bonifatian and Carolingian conversion of the lands east of the Rhine in the eighth century. Most of the Roman towns, including those along the Rhine, remained important centres, though the settlements within the walls of Trier, Cologne and elsewhere covered only a fraction of the area these towns had occupied in the third and fourth centuries. This was by early medieval standards a prosperous region, one of the heartlands of Merovingian Francia. It was in Austrasia west of the Rhine that the Carolingians themselves had their allodial lands and where many of their major aristocratic supporters were at home. The Merovingians themselves had extensive lands and rights here, much of which came to the Carolingians.

From their west Austrasian power-base, Franks had been extending their rule beyond the Roman *limes* into what is now central Germany from the time of Clovis's victory over the Alemans at the turn of the fifth century and the destruction of the Thuringian empire in 531. Austrasia east of the Rhine was a very different kind of territory. Its boundaries to the north were determined by the limits of Saxon expansion in the seventh century, in effect the Sauerland hills and those south of the Teutoberger Wald. To the south it extended into the upper valley of the Neckar and the Danube, and it was bounded to the west by the Rhine and to the east by the Saale. These are at best approximate boundaries, for the region we are about to deal with was not homogeneous. In the east it included Thuringia, the provincial remnant of an empire still powerful in the early sixth century but broken by Frankish and later by Slav attacks. In the mid seventh century Thuringia had once again a powerful duke, Radulf, but by Boniface's time it was a land under Frankish control with no separate political organization of its own, being subject rather to Austrasian dukes based on Würzburg; this southern orientation contrasts with its later associations with south-eastern Saxony in Ottonian times. Remnants of its separate past continued to exist for much longer: a Thuringian law-code has survived (presumably a Carolingian codification) and the Thuringians were still paying a tribute of pigs (presumably a Merovingian or Carolingian imposition) to the king at the end of the tenth century. Even the revolt of Hardrad and other Austrasian nobles against Charles the Great in 785–6 is described in some sources as a revolt of the Thuringians against Frankish rule. To the west of Thuringia lay Hessen, originally the territory of a non-Frankish people (the Hessi), and the territories of a number of smaller peoples whose existence can only fleetingly be glimpsed in the correspondence of Boniface; south of all these lay the area of Frankish colonization proper, in the upper Main valley. In spite of – or perhaps because of – this ethnic heterogeneity, this central region was regarded by contemporaries as "Frankish", and was in essence to become the later duchy and province of Franconia (though in the high middle ages Hessen and Thuringia were once again to become separate territories).

Eastern Austrasia was colonial country, not old-established and prosperous like western Austrasia. As befitted a territory conquered by superficial Christians, much of it was superficially Christian in the seventh century; most of the evidence for this is provided by archaeology and church dedications, but we know also that there was at least one monastery of significance as far east as Erfurt in Thuringia by the early eighth century. Above all, there is the evidence of Boniface's activity as a missionary in central Germany in the early eighth century. In spite of such dramatic episodes as the felling of the sacred oak at Geismar in 724, it is evident that he was confronted here not so much by militant paganism and people wholly innocent of Christianity as by people who had been very imperfectly exposed to it and who did not accept its claim to be an exclusive religion. His choice of central Germany also reflects the political realities of the lands beyond the Rhine before Carolingian expansion. He worked here for most of his missionary career between 722 and his final departure for Frisia in 753–4, with brief interruptions for a journey to Rome and a stay in Bavaria, because it was a region under the control of the Carolingian mayor of the palace, Charles Martel. Boniface needed secular protection for his work; Charles could give it here, but not in the south German duchies, nor in Saxony, where Boniface would have liked to have worked.

Ecclesiastically, eastern Austrasia was transformed by Boniface. The Rhenish bishoprics of Mainz, Worms and Speyer were Roman in origin and firmly established by the eighth century. But it was the reforms carried through by Boniface in collaboration with Charles Martel and his sons Pippin and Carloman which gave Mainz the status it was to enjoy in our period: the chief archbishopric in the east Frankish and Ottonian kingdoms, with a special status as the metropolitan of *Germania*, a large diocese of its own stretching from west of the Rhine to Thuringia, and an enormous province. It had subordinate bishoprics in Alemannia (Constance, Strasbourg and Augsburg), Franconia, and later on in Saxony (where it shared the Saxon bishoprics with the archbishopric of Cologne). Boniface seems to have intended its main sphere of influence to lie in central Germany: he founded bishoprics in 741 or 742 in Würzburg, Erfurt and Büraburg. Würzburg flourished; the other two disappeared rapidly (the explanation is probably that bishoprics needed a minimum endowment of fiscal land in the eighth century and the Carolingians simply did not have enough to support bishoprics) and their organizational place was taken by *chorepiscopi*, bishops without fixed sees and subordinate to Mainz, in the eighth and ninth centuries. It was the disappearance of Erfurt and Büraburg which made Mainz's own diocese so large and gave it the missionary frontier which was to be so important in the tenth century. South of Würzburg a bishopric gradually established itself in the course of the later eighth century at Eichstätt, a centre associated with a follower of Boniface, Willibald, and this too came to the province of Mainz. Almost as important both for the ecclesiastical organization of the province and for the future missionary and intellectual life of the east Frankish church was Boniface's monastic foundation of Fulda: there was an intimate connection between Fulda and Mainz, reflected in the fact that several abbots of Fulda in the ninth, tenth and eleventh centuries were promoted to the archbishopric. Fulda was richly endowed, both by the Carolingians and by the local aristocracy, and enjoyed from the beginning a certain degree of freedom from episcopal control.

For all the differences between eastern and western Austrasia, the two were linked by their noble families. It was the Frankish aristocratic families of western Austrasia who pushed through Frankish eastward expansion in the sixth and seventh centuries. Recent genealogical research, perhaps questionable in much of its detailed conclusions but cumulatively impressive, has suggested particularly strong connections between the families of the mid-Rhine (in particular from the counties of Mainz, Worms and Speyer) and those of eastern Austrasia. Such kindreds as the Robertines, the Widonids and the ancestors of the Conradines – more concretely, the nobles who appear giving land to the monasteries of Lorsch, Weißenburg and Hornbach in the eighth centuries – were at home in the mid-Rhine but are found also established in eastern Austrasia. The ties between eastern and western Austrasia were to make the position of Louis the German somewhat insecure in the early years of his reign; many families, faced with having to choose between Louis and Lothar, the ruler of the middle kingdom, inclined towards Lothar. This explains why Louis the German was so anxious to have the counties of Mainz, Worms and Speyer included in his kingdom: it was not just a matter of supplies of wine, as Regino implies,[7] but of being able to control eastern Austrasia (plus the fact that Mainz was the metropolitan see for most of Louis's bishoprics). Family ties of this kind were not confined to Francia east of the Rhine. It is evident that by the second half of the eighth century neither the Saxon nor the Bavarian aristocracies were closed groups; they were linked with Frankish kindreds, and in particular with the mid-Rhenish families. Neither Tassilo nor the leaders of Saxon resistance could be sure that those whose support they needed did not look as much to the Franks as they did to their own leaders. In Alemannia there were similar links; besides which, Warin and Ruthard, the men who ruled Alemannia on behalf of Pippin and Charles in the generation after the battle of Cannstatt, also came from this area. The Austrasian aristocracy was to be the main beneficiary – apart from the Carolingians themselves – of the Carolingian "reconquest" of the German peoples in the eighth century. This is not to say that it provided "Germany" with an integrating, supra-regional and trans-ethnic ruling class, and so gave a political meaning to "Germany"; as we shall see (below, p. 76), such family links tended to decay rapidly once they crossed political boundaries.

7. Regino s.a. 842, p. 75.

SAXONY AND FRISIA

The north German plain was occupied by two peoples long under Frankish influence but not under Frankish control, Saxons and Frisians. The early history of the Saxons is obscure; it is fairly certain that they spread southwards from what is now Schleswig-Holstein from the third century AD onwards, but the nature of the expansion is unclear. It has been held that they expanded by conquest, and that the Saxon nobility represented the original conquering element; it has also been held that they expanded through alliances and confederation, with lesser peoples "joining" the Saxons and becoming part of them. We hear of them only in their relations with the Franks. In 531 a Saxon contingent probably took part on the Frankish side in the destruction of the Thuringian kingdom, and received some Thuringian territory on a tributary basis as a reward. Later relations were less peaceful, and it is clear that the Saxons made some gains at Frankish expense in the later seventh century: the Franks lost Soest, previously a military outpost, and by 695 the Boructuari, a people on the lower Lippe under Frankish protection, came under Saxon rule, as did parts of Thuringia around the same time. By the early eighth century Saxony extended from the bight of Kiel down to the southern edge of the north German plain and included the Harz. Except in the extreme north the eastern boundary was probably the Elbe; the north-western boundary with the Frisians is now scarcely definable, and may not have been clear in the eighth century either.

The Frankish counter-attack began under Charles Martel in 718; up until the early years of Charles the Great it consisted almost entirely of punitive reprisal raids and the exaction of tribute, as in 738, 748 and 753, when the tribute was changed from 500 cows to 300 horses. Anglo-Saxon missionaries, Boniface in particular, hoped for the conversion of the Old Saxons, something which was clearly unlikely if not impossible without Frankish rule, and later Frankish historiography tended to depict Charles's campaigns as aiming from the start at forcing the Saxons to submit both to the Franks and to Christianity. However, even though the first campaign of 772 was directed at a Saxon cult centre, the Irminsul, there is much in favour of Einhard's interpretation of the Saxon wars, that they originated in border disputes.[8] It was only from around 776–7 that the Frankish

8. *Einhard* c. 7, p. 2.

strategy began to change towards one of incorporation of the Saxons into the Frankish kingdom and their conversion to Christianity. By 785 this had been provisionally accomplished, not without setbacks and severe reprisals, including a mass execution of Saxons at Verden in 782. The main leader of the resistance, a Saxon noble called Widukind, surrendered in 785 and accepted baptism; his descendents were to play an important role in ninth- and tenth-century Saxony. There was still some resistance in the north from 792 until 803–4: as late as 798 two of Charles's *missi* were killed, and it was not until 803 that peace was finally made. Peace meant full incorporation – "so that the two became one people", according to Einhard[9] – but also substantial rearrangements. The least tractable part of Saxony, that beyond the Elbe, was forcibly evacuated. The Saxon inhabitants were resettled elsewhere and the territory abandoned to the Abodrites, Slav allies of the Franks. The intention seems to have been to cut Saxony off from Danish influence and support, according to a few tantalizing hints in the narrative sources.

Saxony before the Frankish conquest had an unusual social and political structure. The basic unit was the *Gau*, an area of varying size with a single ruler. There were about a hundred of these. The next division upwards was the province, of which there were three: Westfalia, Engria and Ostfalia. Finally there was an institution representing the whole people, an annual assembly at Marklohe on the Weser (about 50 km south of Bremen). This assembly was attended by all the *Gau*-rulers, plus thirty-six representatives from each *Gau*, twelve from each of the three castes of *nobiles, frilingi* and *lazzi*. The assembly could legislate and reach political decisions; military leadership was provided when needed by one of the *Gau*-rulers, chosen by lot for the duration of the campaign. The object of this constitution seems to have been to prevent the emergence of any monarchical power, and it is hardly surprising to find in the course of the Franco-Saxon wars that not only the three provinces but also individual *Gaue* could act independently in making war or peace. The three groups should be seen as castes – marriage between members of the different groups was prohibited on pain of death – and it is clear that there were very considerable social tensions in pre-Carolingian Saxony. The *nobiles* had a very high blood-price, six times that of a *frilingus* and eight times that of a *lazzus*. They were expected to pay the equivalent of 150–300 cows for their brides, and

9. *Ibid.*, p. 10.

we should visualize them as extremely wealthy in land, animals, *lazzi* and slaves. In spite of this wealth, they did not enjoy the monopoly of political power that their equivalents enjoyed elsewhere in eighth-century Europe, and there are signs that their position was seriously threatened by the other two castes by the 770s. Probably for this reason, they were more willing to accept Frankish rule than were the *frilingi* and *lazzi*, seeing in it opportunities comparable with those offered to African chiefs by the European colonization of the nineteenth and early twentieth centuries. They accepted Christianity readily, founding monasteries and entering the church themselves, while the lower castes resisted Frankish rule and clung to paganism as a symbol of their resistance: as late as 840 a movement of the *frilingi* and *lazzi* known as the *Stellinga* revolted, demanding the right to their former religion and "resisting their lawful lords".[10]

Frankish rule meant two things in the main: the replacement of *Gaue* by counties and consequent adjustments in the judicial system; and the replacement of paganism by Christianity. The former change did not imply much alteration in personnel: many Saxons were appointed as counts under the new system. But they were now counts, royal officials (see above, p. 27); and the boundaries of the new counties were not identical with those of the *Gaue*. The provincial assemblies and the assembly at Marklohe were abolished, and indeed prohibited. Their judicial functions were taken over by the *missus dominicus* and the king's palace court. Apart from new law relating to the position of the king and his subordinates and of the church, Saxon law was apparently left untouched, though it was given a written codification, probably in the first two decades of the ninth century. The extraordinary status which the *Lex Saxonum* gave to the nobility showed how wise they had been to welcome Frankish rule; apart from this it was noteworthy for its extensive use of the death penalty, where most other Germanic laws provided for monetary compensation for offences. This helps to explain the *Capitulatio de partibus Saxoniae*,[11] the capitulary issued by Charles, probably in 785, after the submission of the Saxons: the severity of the penalties there decreed for offences against king or Christianity (mostly death) probably reflected Saxon legal practice as much as it did the inherent brutality of the Franks.

The replacement of paganism by Christianity was a much more

---

10. *Annales Fuldenses* s.a. 842, p. 33.
11. MGH Capitularia regum Francorum 1, ed. A. Boretius (Hannover 1893), pp. 68–70, no. 26.

gradual process, and one representing an immense investment on the part of the Frankish church. Saxony was not wholly pagan before the Frankish conquest: as early as the seventh century there is archaeological evidence for Christian practices. But Saxon paganism appears to have gone deep, and it was reinforced by the identification of Christianity with the Franks. There was also economic resistance to the new religion. The Franks – mistakenly, in the view of ecclesiastics like Alcuin – set up the church in Saxony from the beginning with the support of compulsory endowments and tithe-payments. The Saxon economy was less well developed than that of the lands further to the west and south – at the end of the eighth century it appears scarcely to have been monetized, and it had substantial elements both of pastoral farming and of hunting, fishing and gathering – so that compulsory tithes meant an even greater sacrifice than they did elsewhere. Nevertheless, substantial progress was made. By 814 there were bishoprics in Münster, Minden, Paderborn, Osnabrück, Verden and Bremen; the two easterly bishoprics at Hildesheim and Halberstadt were founded early in Louis the Pious's reign. Besides this there was a small number of monastic foundations: Werden, Essen, Herford and, most important of all, Corvey, founded in Louis the Pious's reign by his cousin Wala. This was endowed on a scale equal to if not greater than that of the bishoprics (not least with rights of tithe, which in principle were reserved to bishoprics and parish churches), and was evidently intended to play an important part in the second stage of the conversion of Saxony. Both bishoprics and monasteries had back up support from the regions of Francia where Christianity was well established. The bishoprics were divided up between the provinces of Cologne and Mainz, while both bishoprics and monasteries received support from Rheims, Châlons and Corbie (Corvey, as the name suggests, was in origin a daughter-foundation of Corbie, from where its first abbot and monks came). This very large-scale investment of resources and priest-power shows how important the conversion of the Saxons was to the Franks. A number of things combined to make it so. The Carolingians saw themselves as responsible for spreading and defending the faith; it was no longer acceptable for a king to rule directly over heathens. He might take tribute from them, but tributary status had not proved a stable solution for Franco-Saxon relations. Given the change in Frankish policy towards incorporation, however, Christianity was a means of extending Frankish control on a more permanent basis. The Saxon nobles had only to be persuaded that it could be made to offer just as much in the way of ritual feasting and cult of the dead as paganism had done, and hence to allow them to preserve their culture and social position within a Frankish empire.

To the north-west of Saxony lay Frisia, the coastal lands between the Rhine delta and the Weser estuary. This had been conquered by the Franks in two short campaigns in 735 and 736. Yet it does not seem that this conquest made all that much difference to the Frisians. The Frisian aristocracy, in contrast to those of the other German peoples, was to only a very limited extent absorbed into the Frankish ruling elite. Christianization was slow, and some Frisians at least sided with the Saxons in the wars against the Franks in the last third of the eighth century. Frisia early had its own missionary bishopric, Utrecht – though the most easterly parts of Frisia were in the ninth century to fall under the bishoprics of Osnabrück, Verden and Bremen – and on its southern border there lay one of the most important Carolingian palaces, Nimwegen, with a large complex of royal fiscal lands for its support surrounding it. As with the Saxons and Thuringians, the Carolingians (presumably Charles the Great, though this is nowhere stated) made a written codification of Frisian customary law; as with the Saxons and Thuringians, the manuscript transmission does not suggest that it was extensively used, though there are enough different strata of law still visible in the text to suggest that it was not merely a literary exercise.

The separate status of Frisia, which was to continue into the high and late middle ages, was largely the result of its inaccessibility by land – its marshiness made it a tough nut for both Frankish and later armies. It was also the result of its accessibility by sea. Already in the seventh and early eighth centuries Frisia had occupied a pivotal position in North Sea trade both between Francia and England and between Francia and Scandinavia. It continued to do so after the Frankish conquest, and in the ninth century it became for long stretches a kind of no-man's-land between the Frankish and Danish empires, sometimes Frankish, often held by a Danish chieftain in benefice from a Frankish king, occasionally under Danish over-lordship, frequently the scene for Danish raid and Frankish counter-attack as well as for Franco-Danish trade, particularly at the important port of Durstede, which, though it ceased to be of importance after the ninth century, seems to have continued functioning under the Carolingians in spite of repeated reports of its destruction in contemporary annals. Colonies of Frisians – presumably acting as merchants – are found outside Frisia, for example at Mainz in the late ninth century.

CHAPTER FOUR
The kingdom of the eastern Franks, 843–82

SONS AND BROTHERS

The oaths Charles the Bald and Louis the German and their followers swore to each other at Strasbourg in 842 were – like the oaths which Carolingians swore to each other on numerous subsequent occasions in the ninth century – an expression not only of brotherly solidarity but also of brotherly mistrust. The peace of Verdun did not restore concord, for all its solemnity and seeming finality; it was at the time little more than an armistice. All three brothers had other things to occupy them: Lothar was pressed by Saracens in Italy and Vikings in Frisia; Charles needed to conquer Aquitaine to make good the share of his father's kingdom allotted to him under the terms of Verdun; Louis had Vikings and Slavs to deal with. But a revision of Verdun was always on the agenda; its provisions could easily be upset, and there was no reason why they should automatically outlive the three parties to the treaty. The ideology of *imperium Christianum* survived the civil war in a weakened form: the theory that there was still a single empire under the collective rule of the three brothers. There were even some attempts to put this theory into practice. In 844 at Thionville, and again in 847 and in 851 at Meerssen, all three rulers met, accompanied by their followers, and issued communiqués after a full and frank exchange of views. Even after Lothar's death in 855 there were a number of such meetings between three or more kings in the 860s. Joint action, as in the démarche by the three brothers to the Danish king, Horic, in 847, or as in the military cooperation between Charles and Lothar I against the Vikings in 852–3 and in that planned between Louis and Lothar II against the Abodrites in 862, was also not unknown.

Nevertheless, even in the period up to the death of Lothar, meetings between two of the three brothers were much more frequent, and these were often directed against, or thought to be directed against, the third brother. Up to about 850 Lothar and Louis were usually aligned against Charles; in the early 850s Lothar and Charles came closer, and it was Louis who was excluded. One might have expected that Louis and Charles would have regarded Lothar with mistrust and his kingdom with desire; it was after all, likely that Lothar, who was some eleven years older than Louis and twenty-eight years older than Charles, would die first. But this was a probability which was far from being a certainty, and there were other possible forms of conflict. Even before Lothar's death the Aquitanians had invited Louis the German in 854 to send his son Louis the Younger to rule over them. Though Louis the Younger's attempt was quickly abandoned, this was the prelude to a more serious intervention by Louis the German himself in 858, when he invaded west Francia at the invitation of some of the west Frankish episcopate and nobility, and was recognized there for a time as king before Charles the Bald was able to rally support and Louis's following deserted him in early 859.

Lothar I had divided up his kingdom among his three sons shortly before his death: Italy went to Louis II, already crowned king of Italy in 844 and (co-)emperor in 850; Provence, the central section of the Middle Kingdom, to the youngest son, Charles; and the rich fiscal lands in the northern third went to Lothar II, after whom Lorraine (Lotharingia) is named. Between 855 and 877 Carolingian politics were to be dominated largely by the attempts of Lothar I's two surviving brothers, Charles the Bald and Louis the German, to inherit their nephews' kingdoms, punctuated by their occasional attempts to intervene in each other's kingdom. There are two reasons why they hoped to inherit from their younger nephews. The latter ruled over kingdoms which compared with east and west Francia were smaller and less powerful, so that Louis and Charles had a distinct advantage in any competition. Besides this, Charles of Provence appears to have been seriously ill even at the time of his accession, while Louis II and Lothar II had no legitimate male children. Lothar II inherited his father's friendship with Charles the Bald: in 858 they campaigned jointly against the Vikings, and after Louis the German's invasion of west Francia Lothar made some effort to reconcile his uncles, which culminated in a meeting of the three kings at Coblenz in 860. But the general pattern soon shifted to one in which Louis the German sided with Lothar I's sons against an aggressive Charles the Bald. Lothar II came to power with the support of his uncle Louis, who had already held talks, presumably to this end, with some of the Lotharingian magnates in 852. Louis the German also lined up with Lothar's three sons in 861 when Charles the Bald looked like invading Provence.

Charles was evidently interested in taking over Lotharingia (and the rest of Lothar I's realm), and it was this which explained his attitude (and to a large extent that of the west Frankish church) in the *cause célèbre* of the 860s, Lothar II's attempt to repudiate his wife Theutberga (by whom he had no children) and marry his concubine Waldrada with the consent of the church. Louis the German could not openly support Lothar II, but he was not actively hostile to Lothar's plans in the way Charles the Bald and his clergy were. He was just as interested in acquiring his nephews' kingdoms as Charles was; he simply pursued a strategy rather different from Charles's open acquisitiveness, aiming rather for the designation of himself or his sons by his nephews in return for support. When Charles of Provence died in 863, his two brothers were still able to divide his inheritance between them (though Louis the German may have acquired some of Alsace at this point), but Louis II, in spite of papal backing, had no chance against his uncles in the struggle to succeed Lothar II after the latter's unexpected death from fever in 869. The only question was whether Charles the Bald would get the whole of Lotharingia, as at first seemed likely, or whether he would have to divide it with his brother Louis, as in the end by the treaty of Meerssen in 870 he had to. Louis learned his lesson from this episode; rather than leaving Italy to chance, he negotiated actively and successfully with Louis II from 872 on to secure a designation of one of his sons as Louis II's successor.

By the mid 850s Louis the German's sons were grown men: the youngest, Charles, was born in 839, while the eldest, Carloman, was old enough to have taken part in the civil war which followed Louis the Pious's death. As Charles the Great and Louis the Pious had done, Louis began to associate his sons with the government of his kingdom. Carloman became margrave of Pannonia on the south-eastern border, and hence a leading figure in Bavaria, in 856; the second, Louis (the Younger), led armies against the Abodrites in 858 and 862 and was thus linked with the northern part of the kingdom; the young Charles (the Fat) appears as count of the Breisgau (in effect a marcher territory guarding the frontier between Alemannia and southern Lotharingia and Alsace) probably from 859. From 857 all three sons subscribed their father's diplomata occasionally, and by the mid 860s all three were married to wives taken from the aristocracy of their part of the east Frankish kingdom: Carloman to a daughter of Ernest, one of the most important Bavarian magnates; Louis the Younger to Liutgard, daughter of the Saxon margrave Liudolf; Charles to Richgard, probably the daughter of an Alemannic count, Erchanger. In 865 this division of the kingdom was confirmed and made public; in contrast to earlier Carolingian sub-kings, however, Louis's sons were not called king in official documents or in most of the narrative sources, and their father took care to delimit their authority, retaining for himself control over bishoprics, counties, the royal fisc and important judicial cases. In spite of this, all three sons built up substantial followings within their own principalities. Carloman was powerful enough to try in 862 to extend the territory allotted to him, while Louis in 866 and both Louis and Charles in 872 revolted in protest against threatened reductions of their shares and could be pacified only by the grant of more lands and greater freedom to hear cases involving the leading men of their sub-kingdoms.

Louis the German died on August 28 876; Charles the Bald on October 6 877. Louis II of Italy had died on August 12 875; each of the Frankish kingdoms had thus experienced a change of ruler within a space of two years. Louis the German was nearly seventy when he died; Charles was well over fifty. Their sons and successors were no longer young men, and much of the political turbulence of the decades which followed came about through kings' dying before they could fully establish themselves within their kingdoms. It was also a result of the numerous partitions and planned partitions of kingdoms. On Louis's death his sons succeeded in the territories already assigned to them, so that there were now three kings within the territory of the old east Frankish kingdom. It seems to have been his intention also to divide up his portion of Lotharingia, and Italy (which he claimed in succession to Louis II). The partition of Italy was overtaken by events, but eastern Lotharingia was indeed briefly divided between Louis the Younger and Charles the Fat. Louis the German's death gave Charles the Bald an opportunity to invade Lotharingia and threaten the Franco-Saxon kingdom of Louis the Younger; he probably intended to take back the portion of Lotharingia he had conceded in 870, and conceivably also the three counties (Mainz, Worms and Speyer) west of the Rhine. His unexpected defeat at the battle of Andernach in October 876 prevented any radical revision of the status quo. Louis the Stammerer, Charles the Bald's successor in West Francia, died two years after his father; the west Frankish kingdom was divided between his two young sons, Louis and Carloman, who in turn died in 882 and 884 respectively. On the death of Louis the Stammerer it was Louis the Younger's turn to invade west Francia; the price of his withdrawal, agreed on in the treaties of Fouron and Ribemont in 880, was the half of Lotharingia which Charles the Bald had acquired in 870. In Italy, Louis II was succeeded first by Charles the Bald, then by Carloman, and then in 880 by Charles the Fat, who had already made an unsuccessful attempt on the kingdom in 875. Of Louis the German's sons, Carloman was incapacitated from late 878 and died in March 880. Louis the Younger, who had succeeded Carloman in Bavaria, died in January 882 before he could re-establish his father's hegemonial position, as he seems to have intended. By 884 Charles the Fat was the only surviving Carolingian who was both adult and legitimate; as such he ruled over the whole of the Carolingian empire, having acquired Italy, inherited the remainder of east Francia from his brothers, and been invited by the magnates of west Francia to assume the kingship there.

The relations between Charles, Lothar, Louis and their descendants in the period between 843 and 884 are on the surface a sordid and repetitive tale of mistrust, intrigue and treachery, but we are here not dealing just with the moral failings of individual Carolingians but with structural characteristics of the Frankish empire. The dealings of the Carolingians with one another were a macrocosmic version of the struggles over inheritance which characterized the Frankish and German aristocratic kindreds of the early and high middle ages. In particular, they show clearly that there was no established precedence of sons over brothers in the order of inheritance, especially if the sons of a deceased ruler were still minors or young. There was some feeling that sons should inherit, but the claims of brothers were evidently felt to be legitimate as well; it is otherwise impossible to explain the frequency or the self-assuredness with which Carolingians attempted to take over the kingdoms of their deceased brothers or nephews.

Kings were not motivated only by a sense of justice, an urge to claim what was rightfully theirs. There were powerful pressures encouraging any Carolingian to meddle in the internal affairs of his brothers' and nephews' kingdoms; in the ninth century inheritance rivalled external conquest and warfare as a way in which a king could increase his power and prestige and satisfy his following. Italy was particularly attractive, probably because the Franks north of the Alps regarded it as a colony, just as the German rulers and their followers were to do in the tenth, eleventh and twelfth centuries. The *Drang nach Süden* which followed Louis II's death in 875, with Charles the Bald as well as Louis the German's sons Charles and Carloman attempting to become king and emperor there, came about not because these kings were particularly anxious to assume the burden of rule in Italy – that entailed dealing with prickly popes and fighting Arab marauders and south Italian princes; but the initial pickings – the looting which was apparently acceptable when a king first took over a kingdom, the share-out of the confiscated lands and offices of those who had jumped the wrong way – made it worth while to raise a large army and cross the Alps. There was even enough with which to buy off rivals; in 875 Charles the Bald offered Carloman "a huge sum in gold and silver and precious stones"[1] to go away.

The toings and froings of Carolingian politics were not a matter for kings alone. Kingdoms might in some respects be regarded as heritable property like any other, but the act of inheriting was still a political act in which others besides the inheritors had a say. Most important in this respect were those families whose members held office and allodial land in more than one of the three kingdoms created by Verdun. Nearly fifty years ago Gerd Tellenbach, looking at the origins of Germany, drew attention to these families and provided a list of some of their most important representatives. Subsequent research, not least Tellenbach's own, has refined his original picture of the "imperial aristocracy", while confirming the importance of the group. These men and their families were not necessarily anxious for a reunion of the Frankish empire under a single ruler. What they did have in the years following Verdun were "international" contacts. For a good while after 843 Lothar I had had some support in the centre and north of the east Frankish kingdom – notably from the ancestors of the Conradines and from the abbot of Fulda and later archbishop of Mainz, Hrabanus Maurus. A king who offended a powerful kindred had to be careful that its members did not look elsewhere for help. And kings were careful, increasingly so.

It was, paradoxically, the existence of a supra-regional aristocracy coupled with an empire divided into a number of different kingdoms which led to the regionalization of this aristocracy. We can see this

1. *Annales Fuldenses* s.a. 875, p. 85.

process at work in the purges in both east and west Francia which followed Louis the German's abortive attempt to take over west Francia in 858–9. Louis and Charles each tried to protect their supporters in the other's kingdom. The treaty of Coblenz in 860 stipulated that both kings would forgive and forget, and not deprive those who had offended them in the course of the invasion of their benefices.[2] Neither side kept the agreement. In the next year there was a major purge of the east Frankish aristocracy, in which not only Ernest, Carloman's father-in-law, but also men from families which had supported Lothar in 840–3 lost their *honores*; after the purge some of these men went to Charles the Bald. As late as 865 Louis the German was enraged at the possibility that his second son, Louis the Younger, might marry into one of the west Frankish families which had let him down in 858–9. The Welfs, who up to 858–9 had held lands and office in both east and west Francia, largely disappeared from the east after that time. Such traffic was mainly westward, but not exclusively; Louis the German gave shelter and office to the deposed archbishop of Rheims, Ebo, who became bishop of Hildesheim in 845, to Charles of Aquitaine (younger brother of Pippin II), who became archbishop of Mainz in 856, and to Charles the Bald's disgraced and blinded son Carloman.

Purges of this kind, together with the simple lapse of time, meant that in the two generations following Verdun a number of regnal aristocracies replaced what may be seen as a more wide-ranging imperial aristocracy. The international connections did not vanish completely; men were still aware of them, and continued to be so even in the tenth and eleventh centuries. But these connections no longer in normal circumstances implied a community of property, inheritance or interest. The Welfs who held duchies in southern Germany in the eleventh century were quite clearly related to the west Frankish Welfs who ruled in Burgundy and later Provence between 888 and 1034. Not quite so clear, but still certain, is the relationship between the Ottonian ruling house and certain families in the north of the west Frankish kingdom which specialized in producing bishops. In neither case is there much to suggest that these relationships were still regarded as significant or even known about in the tenth and eleventh centuries. The aristocracies coagulated in the different kingdoms, and this meant an increasing identification with a territory. In the east Frankish kingdom this process coincided

2. MGH Capitularia regum Francorum 2, ed. V. Krause and A. Boretius (Hannover 1897), 152–8, no. 242.

with the subdivision of the kingdom among Louis the German's sons already mentioned. What evolved was not so much an east Frankish aristocracy as an Alemannic, a Bavarian and a Franco-Saxon aristocracy. Naturally there were ties of blood and marriage between the three groups; but they can be clearly seen as groups – often as hostile groups – from the 870s onwards. Fifty years later the reaction of the different parts of the east Frankish kingdom to the death of Conrad I still cut along these lines.

The aristocracies were capable of collective action. Carolingians still continued to act as if they could dispose freely of their kingdoms, but increasingly the consent of the leading men of a kingdom was needed for a king to succeed, and the leading men could also "invite" a Carolingian to succeed or replace another Carolingian (as in west Francia in 858, for example). Already in 855 Lothar II had succeeded in Lotharingia with the help of his uncle Louis the German; the help lay in Louis's influence over Lothar's leading men. By the late 870s this trend was firmly established. The claimants to the Italian kingdom took care to be invited and elected by the Italian magnates, while it was the west Frankish aristocracy who decided who was throneworthy following the death of Louis the Stammerer in 879. In east Francia, the kingdom of Bavaria was not divided between Louis the Younger and Charles the Fat on Carloman's death; already during Carloman's final illness Louis the Younger had come to Bavaria and been received (and hence accepted as future king) by the leading men of the kingdom.

THE EASTERN FRONTIER

Much of the attention of the east Frankish rulers and their followers was directed west and south, but they were also active eastwards. Their relations with the peoples beyond the frontier cannot be reduced to a single formula. The frontier had to be defended, which meant fortifications (for example the Ennsburg, erected against the Magyars in 900), a military command structure, and the occasional punitive or pre-emptive raid. But to seal it off was not only not possible, it was not desirable. The peoples beyond the frontier were partners in trade as well as the objects of missionary activity and political control. At the level of the high nobility there was some intermarriage across the border, and the rebellious or the disgraced might seek refuge or help there (as Louis the German himself did in

840), just as Slav exiles looked to east Francia. At times the writers of narrative sources could talk of the Slavs as if they were part of the kingdom itself, not just tributaries beyond the border: we read of "the judgement of the Franks and the Bavarians and the Slavs" in an account of the assembly of 870 which condemned the Moravian ruler Rastiz to death.[3] The external frontier had a structural significance for the east Frankish kingdom as well. It was easily the largest of any of the external frontiers of the three kingdoms established at Verdun, and the peoples beyond it were more divided and more exploitable than those along the Spanish or Breton marches or the frontiers with the south Italian principalities. Not only did this mean income in the form of tribute, it also meant the possibility of further expansion, though no longer on the scale of the eighth century. This applied particularly in Bavaria, whose borders and marches up to 907 extended into what is now eastern Austria and western Hungary. East Frankish defeats as well as east Frankish successes had their uses: the gaps they left in the east Frankish ruling class allowed more room for those who were left. Elsewhere in the Frankish kingdoms advancement came largely through rebellions and victories at court by aristocratic factions; the feuds which arose from the trials, executions and disgraces which regularly accompanied these struggles, especially in west Francia under Charles the Bald, affected the cohesion of the political community. Such things were also known in east Francia, but the steady attrition of the east Frankish nobility and the supplies of plunder, tribute and (to a limited extent) new land helped to take the pressure off.

The east Frankish kingdom shaded off at the edges. First there came marches – stretches of territory under special military organization, generally, though not always, erected at the expense of neighbouring peoples or states. Beyond that lay the peoples or states themselves. The Franks tried to keep the nearest of these in a relationship of tribute-paying clientage. Beyond that again lay peoples whom the Franks might try to control and exact tribute from, but which were rather more independent. These arrangements were general but not universal. There were parts of the frontier with no march, as for example between Bavaria and Bohemia. There were marches with no client states beyond, as in Pannonia. In any case the graduations between clientage, tribute-paying and independence were not sharp or permanent. This means that we cannot first

3. *Annales Fuldenses*, p. 72.

describe the frontier and then the relations across it; the relations defined the frontier. Instead we shall look at the frontier as it came to be established in the time of Charles the Great and Louis the Pious, and then at the developments along it in the course of the ninth century.

The incorporation of Saxony and Bavaria and the destruction of the Avar empire in the 790s had given the Frankish empire a long eastern frontier with a number of Slav peoples along it. Along the northern part of it the Franks behaved as they had a generation earlier towards the Saxons: beginning in 789 and culminating in the campaigns of 805–8 there was a series of raids aimed at establishing Frankish supremacy and exacting tribute. In the south, the collapse of the Avar state made a reorganization necessary. An eastern march was established along the south bank of the Danube between the Enns and the Wienerwald. Beyond this, in what is now western or trans-Danubian Hungary, the remnants of the Avars were allowed a continued existence as Frankish clients. Here there was also a missionary tradition. The Bavarian church, especially the bishops (from 798 archbishops) of Salzburg, had already begun the work of converting the Carinthians, and this mission was now extended northwards and eastwards. The Slavs were not just potentially dangerous heathen peoples, they were also trading partners. This emerges clearly from the capitulary of Thionville (805), which laid down strict border controls to prevent the illegal export of advanced Frankish military technology: merchants going east had to pass through one of eight designated places under the control of a royal *missus* along a line stretching from Bardowick in the north to Lorch in Austria.

In Louis the Pious's reign the eastern frontier was not the centre of attention, and we are not well informed about developments along it, especially for the 830s. Along the northern part of the frontier military command seems to have passed from the hands of ad hoc *missi* to margraves. These were counts with their own county, but also with rights of command over other counts in their district. In the south, the Avars (last heard of in 822) ceased to exist as a separate people. The Bulgars were for a time a serious threat; after a particularly damaging raid in 827 the march of Friuli was reorganized in 828 into four counties, the two northernmost of which, Carantania and lower Pannonia, were transferred from the Lombard kingdom to east Francia and so came to Louis the German. Finally the Carinthians, who had continued to exist under their own dukes, were also reorganized into counties under counts; this may have happened at the same time as the reorganization of Friuli, or perhaps earlier: there is some evidence that an independent Slovene prince, Liudewit, who made a good deal of trouble for the Franks between 819 and his murder in 823, had support from within Carinthia. But in spite of this change there was no real break in continuity. A nobility of mixed Bavarian and Slav origins ruled here both before and long after the reorganization. There are no signs of the large-scale confiscations which would have followed a serious rebellion.

As earlier, so also under Louis the German and his descendants we have far more information about the southern half of the Slav border than about the northern half. For the northern half we must rely almost entirely on occasional notices in the annals of Fulda, which reveal much the same picture as in the earlier years of the Carolingian empire. Running from north to south we find a number of main peoples mentioned: Abodrites, Linones, Daleminzi, Sorbs. Sometimes these appear under a single ruler, sometimes under a number of *duces*. Other ethnic names also occur, and it is not always clear whether we should see these as separate peoples or as subdivisions of the main ones. We hear only of rebellions and punitive expeditions. Some of these were disastrously unsuccessful, as for example the raid against the Sorbs, Daleminzi and Bohemians in 856 in which the counts Bardo and Erpf "and many others" were killed.[4] We do not even know much about the frontier, except that there was a Sorbian march. Presumably the Liudolfing *duces* of Ostfalia held margraval functions in respect of the northern Slavs; by the end of the century at the latest they were conducting what was virtually an independent campaign of conquest and colonization against the Daleminzi and Sorbs. There is little evidence for missionary work, though Würzburg is known to have possessed churches in the Slav territories between the Main and the Rednitz. This is not very surprising, as Saxony and Thuringia themselves were still missionary country in the ninth century. Our lack of knowledge may, however, be deceptive. We know far more about the southern Slavs through the survival of a large number of different kinds of source; it does not follow from this that the only interests of the east Frankish elite lay in the lands along the Bavarian frontier, and one small piece of evidence suggests that the Slav frontier was indeed seen as a whole. Some time in the mid ninth century an author known as the "Bavarian Geographer" put together

4. *Ibid.*, p. 47.

an apparently comprehensive list of the peoples living "to the north of the Danube", which includes not only the immediate eastern neighbours of the east Frankish kingdom but those beyond, going up as far as the Baltic.[5] Whether the list was compiled for missionary, military or political purposes, it suggests that the eastern Franks may have taken more interest in the northern half of the Slav frontier than is now apparent to us.

Along the southern part of the frontier there were four peoples of importance: the Bohemians, the Moravians, the Bulgarians, and an independent Slovene principality between the Franks and the Bulgars of which little is known beyond the fact of its existence. Moravians[6] and Slovenes bordered on the region known as Pannonia, the Wild East of ninth-century Bavaria. The Bulgarians were important but more distant neighbours. Direct contacts with them ceased after the border clashes of the 820s, following which they appear as a foreign power, occasionally sending embassies to the east Frankish court or making alliances with Louis the German against the Moravians. At one point it looked as if Bulgaria might also be a field for east Frankish mission. At the request of the Bulgarian khan, Louis the German sent Ermanrich, a monk from the Suabian monastery of Ellwangen and later bishop of Passau, to Bulgaria in 867, but Ermanrich soon returned, and the rivalries for the conversion of the Bulgarians were to be fought out between Roman and Byzantine missionaries. The Bohemians were also of secondary importance. Alone among the Slav peoples they were isolated from the east Frankish kingdom by natural barriers, the Erzgebirge and Böhmerwald mountains. Like their northern neighbours the Sorbs they appear as occasional rebels and tribute-payers. Fourteen of their *duces* were baptized at Louis the German's court in 845, and there is some evidence for missionary work in Bohemia directed from Regensburg, which was also the centre for trade with them. Later in the century they came under the overlordship of the Moravians, from whom they also received missionaries. Only after the death of Zwentibald of Moravia in 894 were their ties with east Francia restored and the way was opened for further missionary work from Regensburg, which led to their conversion in the first half of the tenth century.

After the disappearance of the Avars as a separate people we find a Slav, Pribina, in charge of the lands between the Raab and the Drau.

---

5. Edited Herrmann 1965: 220–1.
6. In what follows it will be assumed that Moravia in the ninth century was more or less where it is today; for an alternative view see Boba 1971, Bowlus 1987.

He had been driven out by the Moravian ruler Moimir I from his principality in Neutra and had taken refuge first with the Bulgars and then with the Franks. Pribina was converted to Christianity and encouraged the missionary work of the church of Salzburg in his territory, which lay around his settlement of Moosburg at the west end of the Plattensee. Pribina was killed by the Moravians early in the 860s, and was succeeded by his son Kocel. The status of the territory they ruled is ambiguous. There is some evidence that it was Frankish: Louis the German not only converted Pribina's *beneficia* into allodial land but also made gifts of land to Salzburg in the same region; and both Pribina and Kocel are referred to in Frankish sources as "count". On the other hand, Kocel seems to have been independent enough to contemplate setting up his own church: he allowed Methodius to work in his territory in 869–70 in spite of the claims of Salzburg, which is not behaviour one would expect of a Frankish count. The archaeological evidence, which is rich and shows trading links both with east Francia and with Moravia and a considerable amount of land colonization, does not help. The question whether the Pribina/Kocel territory should be seen as a Frankish border county under a Slav prince or as a Slav client or buffer principality beyond the marches must remain unresolved, which in itself says a good deal about the fluidity of this part of the border. The territory was at any rate sufficiently under Frankish control to pass to Arnulf of Carinthia after Kocel's death.

Undoubtedly the most important neighbouring state for the east Frankish kingdom was the Moravian empire. The Moravians are first recorded in 822; some ten years later under their ruler Moimir I they were already expanding, as we have just seen, and by 846 they were a serious enough problem for Louis the German to mount a large expedition against them, remove Moimir, and substitute his nephew Rastiz. Rastiz, who was succeeded (again after east Frankish intervention) in 870–1 by his nephew Zwentibald, proved no more amenable than Moimir had been; nor was Zwentibald, who ruled until 894. Unlike the Sorbs and Abodrites the Moravians dealt with the Franks more or less on terms of equality. It was traditional for the Franks to harbour Slav exiles and to send them back at propitious moments, and also for them to intervene in the frequent feuds within Slav royal and ducal families; but the Moravian rulers were powerful enough to do the same for the east Frankish kingdom. As early as 852 we hear of a Frankish noble who had gone into exile among the Moravians. The long feud between the Wilhelmines and the Aribonids (see below, p. 116) was marked at every point by the support given by Zwentibald and his descendants to one of the two sides. Most remarkably of all, Rastiz and Zwentibald were seen as allies by Louis the German's sons during the succession disputes of the 860s. This de facto equality was acknowledged by the east Frankish rulers, who concluded a number of peace treaties with the Moravians: at Forchheim in 874, Tulln in 885, *Omuntesperch* (an unidentified location probably to the west of Vienna) in 890 and Regensburg in 901. Zwentibald even acted as godfather to his namesake, the illegitimate son of Arnulf of Carinthia. Until his death in 894 the Moravian state grew steadily in power and wealth; its power extended for a time over the Bohemians and probably over other Slav peoples to the north and east as well, certainly sufficiently so to threaten the Bulgarians at times. Archaeology has revealed a state rather like Poland a century later, with nobles and princes ruling from within large settlements surrounded by earth and timber fortifications. The economy was developed to a level comparable with that of the east Frankish kingdom.

Such power explains the prominence of Moravia in east Frankish politics. The Moravians were capable of large-scale incursions across the Frankish border, and the military organization of the south-east frontier was changed at regular intervals to cope with the threat. From 856, when Louis the German's eldest son Carloman was appointed, to 888, when Carloman's son Arnulf became king of the eastern Franks, there was almost always a member of the east Frankish royal house holding command on the frontier. The Moravian danger also explains the missionary conflicts of the 860s between Rome, east Francia and Byzantium. In 862 Rastiz, facing a Franco-Bulgarian alliance against him, sent to Constantinople to ask for military aid and missionaries; though the Bavarian church had already been active in Moravia, Rastiz clearly wanted a church independent of east Francia. The missionaries sent were the brothers Constantine (Cyril) and Methodius. Their first period of missionary work led to increasing difficulties with the Bavarian clergy already in the land. Methodius and Constantine went to Rome in 867, and Methodius, after Constantine's death, returned to Pannonia and Moravia as a papally consecrated archbishop in 869. Here he was caught up in the Moravian succession crisis of 870-1, captured by the Franks, and tried at a synod in Regensburg in 870 on the charge of unlawfully exercising episcopal power in a diocese not his own. He was released from prison after papal protests and returned to Moravia, but increasingly he lost influence to the east Frankish clerics around Wiching, bishop of Neutra. The support he got from the papacy declined as the popes themselves came to need east Frankish support in the years following the death of Louis II of Italy in 875. After Methodius's death in 885 his followers were driven out of Moravia, as was his rival Wiching shortly afterwards; an attempt by papal legates to reorganize the Moravian church right at the end of the ninth century drew a bitter protest from the province of Salzburg.

The whole story was a foretaste of Saxon relationships with Poland and Hungary a century later. East European rulers wanted Christianity, but preferred not to be too closely bound to the German church, and so looked to Rome and Constantinople as alternative sources of supply. The intimate dependence of missionary work on political constellations is also apparent here. Methodius's loss of influence in Moravia followed on the rapprochement between Moravia and east Francia initiated by the peace of Forchheim in 874. Yet missionary work should not be seen as just the ideology of Frankish imperialism; it could be that, and often so appeared to the Slavs, both in the ninth century and later, but it had an independent dimension. It is noticeable that the complaints against Methodius came in the first instance from the Bavarian bishops, who were concerned at the infringements of their supposed rights. There is no reliable evidence that Louis the German took a close interest in the Methodius affair, as might have been expected had it had political overtones, though the bishops could hardly have held the synod at Regensburg without his consent.

EAST FRANCIA: THE GOVERNMENT OF THE KINGDOM

It is a curious fact about the east Frankish kingdom that we know far more about its relations with its neighbours – both with the Slavs to the east and with the other Carolingian kingdoms to the west and south – than we do about its internal politics. The "international relations" of the kingdom can be seen to change with time, and something like a narrative account of them could be offered. It is otherwise with the kingdom's internal politics. It is possible to offer a reconstruction, but the result is necessarily extremely speculative and a narrative is hardly possible. Only at moments of tension do we sometimes clearly see something that looks like internal politics: aristocratic factions struggling over office and the king's favour, perhaps even disagreeing on policy. But such moments – notably the aristocratic purges of 861–2 and the disputes between Louis the German and his sons between 862 and 873 – can rarely be divorced from "international relations". Often we simply do not have the background information which would enable us to interpret isolated reports. When Louis the German had a Saxon vassal of the Babenberger Henry blinded in 871, or the nobles Poppo and Egino fought pitched battles in Thuringia in 883 and 884, we do not, if we are honest, really know what lay behind such things, though we may sometimes make plausible conjectures.

Our normal view of the kingdom is a more static one, though perhaps none the less accurate for that. The account given for the autumn of 852 by the annals of Fulda is untypical in the wealth of different activities packed into a few months, but typical in the range of these activities and in its description of a year in the history of the east Frankish kingdom with no significant external complications (though perhaps for that very reason not to be treated as "normal" in all respects):

> By the will of the same most serene prince a synod was held in the city of Mainz, the metropolitan of Germany, under the presidency of Hraban, the reverend archbishop of that city, with all the bishops and abbots of eastern Francia, Bavaria and Saxony. While they were holding meetings to settle ecclesiastical matters the king with the princes and prefects of the provinces [i.e. counts and other magnates] was busy with the affairs of the kingdom and with settling disputes. After he had confirmed by his approval the canons of the synod, and had heard and dismissed the embassies of the Bulgars and Slavs, he returned to Bavaria. He arranged and settled what seemed necessary and returned without delay to Cologne along the Rhine by ship. Here he held talks with some of the leading men of Lothar's kingdom, and then set out for Saxony, mainly in order to judge their cases, which, so they say, had been neglected by bad and unfaithful judges so that they had been deprived of their rights and suffered long and serious injury through many kinds of delay. There were also other matters which concerned him especially: lands which had come to him by hereditary right from his father and grandfather, which he needed to restore to their rightful owner through lawful claim against wicked usurpers. Therefore he held a general assembly in the place which is called Minden . . . here he not only dealt justly with the cases brought to him by the people but received the possessions belonging to him according to the judgement of men of that people learned in the law. From here he went through the lands of the Angrians, the Harudi, the [Saxon] Suabians and the Hochseegau, halting where necessary and hearing the people's cases, and came to Thuringia. He held an assembly at Erfurt and decreed amongst other things that no count or deputy should take up anyone's case as an advocate within his own county or district,

though they might freely do so in the districts of others. Leaving Erfurt he celebrated Christmas in Regensburg.[7]

The first thing to note is the extent to which Louis moved about, which was more like the pattern for the Ottonian and Salian rulers than like his father and grandfather. The secular and ecclesiastical meetings at Mainz are known to have taken place in early October; between then and Christmas, Louis travelled south to Bavaria, then north again to Cologne, then into Saxony, and back down through Thuringia to Regensburg. This is a lot of travelling, especially for a time of year when the weather was beginning to make the roads difficult, and indeed Louis's itinerary was not normally quite as crowded as this. We find him most frequently in northern Bavaria, especially in Regensburg, and in the lands around the confluence of the Rhine and Main, especially in Frankfurt. He is recorded as staying in Regensburg and Frankfurt almost as often as in all other places put together, and this probably underestimates their importance, since he stayed at both on occasions for several months. The itinerary recorded above shows the prominence of these two regions well. The journeys to Cologne and Saxony, on the other hand, were unusual. Cologne in 852 was still part of Lothar I's kingdom. Louis's visit, in view of the fact that he did not meet Lothar there, was remarkable, and is presumably to be connected with the support he gave to Lothar II on the latter's accession in 855. The visit to Saxony was still more unusual; it is the last time Louis is recorded as having gone there, except for brief occasions when he crossed it with an army in 862 and 869. The gloss just given should not make us think that royal power and authority were not felt in other ways in the lands where the king did not normally go. Louis might not often go to Saxony or Alemannia, but he issued privileges for Saxon and Alemannic recipients – in 852, for example, for the monastery of Herford in Westfalia and in July 853 for Sts Felix and Regula in Zurich[8] – and this means that these recipients were prepared to seek him out and probably pay handsomely for what they got; it must have been worth the trouble. Besides, from the mid 850s, certainly from 865, Louis had assigned parts of his kingdom to his three sons, Carloman, Louis and Charles, as their future inheritance (see above, p. 72). These divisions gave Louis some problems, but they enabled Carolingian presence and authority to be spread more evenly than it might otherwise have been.

7. *Annales Fuldenses*, pp. 42–3.
8. D Louis the German 61 (for Herford, issued there), 67 (for Zurich, issued at Regensburg).

When the king travelled he drew on royal estates and the resources of the church for supplies of food and drink, and stayed normally either in royal palaces and estates or in bishoprics and monasteries (though here less so than in west Francia). The term palace is necessarily an imprecise one: we associate it with large and impressive buildings, suitable for assemblies and ceremonies. There were such things in east Francia, notably at Ingelheim, Frankfurt and Regensburg. But it is often difficult to reconcile written and archaeological evidence: Atterhof in Austria, for example, is known from the written sources only as an estate, but appears from excavation to have had a large ninth-century building which might well be considered a palace. Nor is it always easy to say (even after excavation) whether a royal estate was the site of a palace or not: some are clearly palaces, some pretty certainly only estates, but there are many possible shadings in between. Even when these ter-minological difficulties are borne in mind, it is clear that palaces and estates were not distributed evenly throughout the kingdom. Of the places mentioned in the text quoted above, Mainz and Cologne had royal palaces of lesser importance, where Louis probably stayed (though the palace in Cologne was not Louis's own). Most of the east Frankish episcopal cities did not have royal palaces, and Minden was no exception. Bishop Haduwart of Minden would presumably have provided Louis with hospitality. Regensburg had had a palace since Agilolfing times, and Louis had rebuilt it on a larger scale.

It is worth examining Regensburg and its hinterland, together with Frankfurt and its hinterland, a little more closely. Neither Regensburg nor Frankfurt was the only palace in its region. Not too far distant from Frankfurt were the episcopal cities of Mainz and Worms (both with royal palaces), the royal palaces of Ingelheim and Tribur, and important royal *villae* at Gernsheim and Bürstadt. Within a rather larger radius of Regensburg we find the Franconian palace of Forchheim and the Bavarian one of Ötting (established in the reign of Louis's son Carloman). Both favoured residences were in the middle of regions thick with actively exploited royal lands and rights, in contrast to, say, Saxony, where as the 852 annal shows the king had some difficulty in holding on to what was his. They were the centres of fiscs, units of organization of the royal estates not subject to counts and run by officials with titles like *exactor* (though these were not necessarily, or indeed usually, menial posts – in Frankfurt we find Widonids acting as *exactor*, for example). Neither Regensburg nor Frankfurt can quite be described as a "capital" of the east Frankish kingdom, but – especially taken together with the other favoured royal residences in their neighbourhood – they came close to fulfilling such a function. Regensburg was *urbs regia*, "the royal city", while Regino of Prüm calls Frankfurt "the principal seat of the eastern kingdom".[9] Noteworthy in particular is the evidence for Regensburg that monasteries, bishoprics and aristocrats held parcels of land within the city limits where they could stay during assemblies, a phenomenon otherwise known in this period only for Aachen. Institutionally this is the ancestor of the "town house" of the aristocracy in London or Paris in the early modern era. Also important were the chapels founded at Frankfurt, Regensburg and Ötting to provide not only liturgical services for the king when he was on the spot but a permanent reminder of his existence when he was not.

The assemblies mentioned in the passage quoted above, at Mainz, Minden and Erfurt, were in many ways atypical. It was in the first place unusual for so many assemblies to be held in autumn and early winter: the majority of assemblies in east Francia were held either in February/March or in May/June. Only Mainz was typical as far as the locations are concerned. Assemblies were held for preference on Frankish territory. Louis preferred the region around Frankfurt, and this remained important under his successors, though there was a shift to Alemannia under Charles III and to east Franconia and northern Bavaria under Arnulf. Untypical also was the holding of three assemblies in short succession, though those at Minden and Erfurt were probably more in the nature of provincial assemblies for Saxony and Thuringia than full-scale assemblies for the whole of the east Frankish kingdom such as the assembly at Mainz presumably was. It was more usual to hold only one or at most two in a year: a sign of political stability. It is unusual for a narrative source to emphasize the assembly as a place where justice was done, but this element was always there. The Frankish tradition of assemblies as places where embassies were received and campaigns decided on was firmly upheld in the east Frankish kingdom; we see it in the text in the passage referring to the embassies of the Bulgars and Slavs. The phrase about "hearing and dismissing" of the legations from foreign peoples is often found, to the irritation of the historian who would like to know what was discussed. Often enough, however, the purpose of such meetings lay precisely in the formal reception of the ambassadors and in the exchange of gifts. In this way kings

9. Regensburg: see the evidence cited by Schmid 1976: 436. Frankfurt: Regino s.a. 876, p. 111.

confirmed their own status and helped to confirm (or deny) the status of fellow rulers. The ceremonial and dramatic elements in the kingship of Louis the German and his sons should not be underrated. Louis frequently visited monasteries in Lent to pray, something which should be seen not just as a private expression of devotion but as a very public display of kingship. The *adventus*, the formal arrival of a king at a monastery like Fulda or St Emmeram in Regensburg, with processions and the singing of *laudes* (prayers addressed to the saints to protect the king and his army), could make a considerable impression, as witness Notker the Stammerer's description of a visit to St. Gallen by Louis the German together with two of his sons in full Frankish uniform (scarlet garters, a white shirt and a blue cloak, with sword and staff).[10]

The east Frankish kingdom appears to have had a simpler government and one less based on the written word than those found in the kingdoms of west Francia and Italy. In west Francia the issuing of capitularies was revived under Charles the Bald and reached new levels of sophistication in the edicts of Pîtres (864) and Quiersy (877). Not a single east Frankish capitulary has survived. Nor was the chancery of Louis the German prolific: hardly more diplomata survive for his reign of over thirty years than do for the twelve years of Lothar's reign, while Louis's brother Charles, in a reign of almost identical length, issued more than twice as many diplomata. However, these appearances are a little misleading. It is true, for instance, that no east Frankish capitularies survive, but we know from references in narrative sources that east Frankish kings continued to issue them, and the passage cited above is a good example of this. The decree Louis is said to have issued at Erfurt is absolutely typical of the kind of provision found in surviving capitularies, while the reference to Louis's confirmation of the canons of the Mainz synod also fits in well with earlier Frankish tradition. The capitularies of Charles and Louis the Pious continued to be copied in the east Frankish kingdom; as examples we may take the Fulda manuscript now in Hamburg which contains Ansegis's collection of capitularies together with *Lex Salica* and the capitularies of 829 or the four Mainz manuscripts now in the Palatina collection in Rome, which bring together a large number of capitulary texts including Ansegis's collection.[11] The copying of texts is not

10. *Gesta Karoli* I 34, ed. H. Haefele (MGH SRG NS 12, Berlin 1959), 47.
11. Hamburg, Stadtbibliothek, in scrinio 141a; Vatican, Bibliotheca Apostolica, cod. lat. palatini 289, 577, 582, 583.

definitive proof that the capitularies were still of practical importance, but it shows at least that they were still of interest.

The chancery of the east Frankish kings was indeed less productive
than those of other Carolingian rulers – the difference can be only
partially explained by arguing that Louis the German lacked
influence in substantial parts of his allocated kingdom even after 843,
and fully established himself only after Lothar's death in 855. But
east Francia was very definitely a society in which writing was made
practical use of, and that goes for its government as well. We even
have one or two letters or records of letters sent from frontier
generals to the king: from Carloman to Louis the German in 869,
from Aribo to Arnulf in 892. Not only are there repeated references
in the annals of Fulda to archives and to the preservation of official
documents, there are also extensive surviving archives of private
charters from a number of monasteries and bishoprics: Corvey,
Fulda, Lorsch, Weißenburg, St Gallen, Freising, Mondsee, Salzburg.
These presumably represent only a fraction of what once existed;
several of the oldest and most important churches in the east
Frankish kingdom, including Mainz, Augsburg, Worms and Speyer,
have lost all their older archives in fires. To call these records of
property transactions charters in fact begs a question. Many of them
were more like written notices of the fact that a legally valid
transaction had taken place and been properly witnessed than like
dispositive documents whose issuing was itself the legally valid
transaction. Yet they evidently served as more than mere decoration:
Cozroe, the writer of the oldest Freising collection of such notices,
says that he had gathered the records into book form in order among
other things to guard against losses "through the wiles of the jealous
or through theft".[12] In other words, it could be worthwhile if it
came to a dispute to steal or destroy your opponent's written records
– a sign that the use of writing had penetrated deeply even into the
non-Frankish parts of the east Frankish kingdom.

The government of the east Frankish kingdom may have been less
technically advanced than those of the kingdoms to the west and
south, but in the most important business of the ninth century,
warfare, it was undoubtedly superior. Louis the German was able to
revert to earlier Carolingian practice and put several armies into the
field at once, something that west Frankish and Italian rulers could
rarely manage. In the 850s and 860s there were often several

12. T. Bitterauf, *Die Traditionen des Hochstifts Freising 1 (744–926)*, Munich 1905, 1–2.

simultaneous campaigns against the Slavs, while the attempts by his sons in the 870s to secure the kingdom of Italy did not mean that the Abodrites, Sorbs, Bohemians and Moravians had an easier time of it. The military superiority of the kingdom was reflected in the absence of serious Viking raiding beyond the Saxon and Frisian coastlines between the raid on Hamburg in 845 and that on Saxony in 880; Louis the German was able to negotiate with Danish kings from a position of strength, and did so successfully in 872–3, arranging both peace and protection for Frankish and Danish merchants. Superiority showed itself also in the occasional clashes between east and west Francia. The east Frankish rulers did rather better in west Francia than Charles the Bald did on his one attempt in 876 to invade east Francia. Unfortunately, though we can observe east Frankish military strength, it is not clear where it came from; there are no hints in the sources of new developments in military technology. It was certainly not a consequence of economic superiority, though it may have owed something to the kingdom's economic and political stability.

So far we have considered the kingdom under its itinerant king, with a ruling elite which met periodically in assemblies and councils. East Francia was not, however, a single or unified polity: the incorporation of the Germanic peoples into one kingdom did not mean that ethnic divisions ceased to be of importance. They must have been apparent even at assemblies, since a number of accounts of assemblies refer to those present as organized in ethnic groupings – Franks, Saxons, Bavarians, Alemans. The narrative sources also describe armies in this way: we find in 872 an army "of the Saxons and Thuringians" sent against the Moravians; they "had no king with them and could not agree among themselves", a sign of how strong such ethnic rivalries could be.[13] The peoples also each had their own law, though the specific evidence for the practical application of Bavarian, Alemannic, Frankish or Saxon law in the ninth century would fit neatly on to a postcard. The regions where the peoples lived were referred to by terms like *ducatus* ("duchy") or *regnum* ("kingdom"), a practice found already in the late Merovingian period and revived in the ninth century. The terminology was not meant to imply that there were dukes or kings there. We do find leading aristocrats with the title *dux* – the Liudolfings in Saxony, Ernest in Bavaria – but it is clear that at least at this stage the word

13. *Annales Fuldenses*, pp. 75–6.

has its original meaning of (military) leader rather than any more permanently institutionalized power (for the tenth century see below, p. 132). And the use of the term *regnum* for Saxony, Alemannia and Bavaria preceded Louis's division of his kingdom among his three sons; it owed nothing to them, and is better translated as "principality" or "province" than as "kingdom". Louis's division was itself along ethnic lines; there was evidently no question of an even division of the east Frankish royal fisc, just as there had not been in the Frankish divisions of 806 and 817.

Below the level of the *regnum*, political and administrative subdivisions are harder to define. In several areas we find margraves, marcher counts: there was a Sorbian march, a Bohemian and a Pannonian march, and probably the Liudolfing *duces* in Saxony should be thought of as margraves. There is only fragmentary evidence for the powers of a margrave in east Francia. Probably the title implied some kind of right of military command over the other office-holders of the area; at the battle against the Vikings in 880 in which the Liudolfing *dux* Brun was killed, so were eleven other counts, two bishops and eighteen royal vassals, and there was a similar death-roll headed by the margrave Liutpold at Preßburg (Bratislava) against the Hungarians in 907. The suggestion that such men also had powers other than those of military command, that they had the function in east Francia which earlier and especially in the Frankish heartland had been assigned to *missi* of supervising other office-holders, is not an unattractive one but is difficult to document. Regular peregrinations of the country by *missi* are no longer found in east Francia after the time of Louis the Pious, yet there are occasional references to men who are evidently ad hoc *missi*, and the Raffelstetter toll-list was drawn up as late as 903–5 by a count, a bishop and an archbishop (a classical Carolingian casting for a missatical visitation) acting as *missi* for the young Louis the Child.

The evidence of normative sources like capitularies which imply uniformity of institutions throughout the Frankish kingdom north of the Alps suggests that in the whole of the Frankish empire there were counties with clearly defined boundaries, governed by a count who held his office from the king. There are difficulties in taking this for granted for east Francia, however, for although the terminology remains the same, the reality it describes is evidently different, at any rate in non-Roman Germany. Here there can be no question of the *pagus* found in Latin written sources having been the territory of a late antique *civitas*; it is evidently a translation of words like *Gau*. *Gau* is undoubtedly a territorial word, but it does not describe the territory of a count – both in Saxony and in Alemannia we sometimes find more than one count in the same *pagus*, as well as counts active in more than one *pagus*. The term *comes* is presumably also a translation, and it may not always have been used to translate the same thing. These observations have led in the last two generations to a proliferation of different kinds of "county" in the historical literature: *Streugrafschaften*, "scattered counties", which exist only at a disparate set of places where a count exercises rights; *Königsgutgrafschaften*, "royal demesne counties", which extend only over royal lands and not over the allodial lands of the nobility; *Allodial-* or *Herrschaftsgrafschaften*, the reverse of this, where nobles appear as counts and exercise comital powers over their own lands without ever having been invested by the king. More recently still there has been a justifiable reaction by both constitutional and regional historians against some of the more baroque county theories in favour of a flexible version of the traditional view: that by and large when we find a count in ninth century east Frankish sources, whether in Saxony, Lotharingia, Alemannia or Bavaria, we are dealing with someone who exercised something which we should call public authority within a reasonably definable territory. This does not exclude the possibility of ambiguities and uncertainties; it is worth remembering that even in late Anglo-Saxon England the process of shire formation was completed only in the late eleventh century, and here the "official" nature of the institution is much clearer. Nor does it exclude the possibility of areas within or between counties where the count had no authority; apart from such things as royal fiscs and church immunities, it is difficult to imagine that a man like the Franconian military leader Henry was in practice subject to the jurisdiction of the county court for the lands he owned outside his own counties. Nor, finally, does it exclude the possibility that people other than this kind of "official" were called count in the sources or that older, pre-Frankish organizational elements survived under the names of count and county (and still more so at levels of organization below that of the county, about which far less can be said than has been). It would indeed be surprising had there not been such survivals; even in the quite different conditions of the twentieth century, local government reorganization rarely proceeds from a genuine *tabula rasa*.

The very uncertainty about the nature of countships and counties in the east Frankish kingdom, however we resolve it, is itself significant; there was here probably less of a sense of the king being present in the localities through his officials than there was to the west or south in the ninth century. The question is not so much whether east Frankish kings could treat counts as removable officials; Louis the German and Arnulf at least could, as the purges of the 860s and 890s show. The power to appoint freely and to control was more important. The east Frankish kings could not easily install "foreigners". Bavarian counts were Bavarian, Alemannic counts Alemannic, and Saxon counts Saxon, with only the smallest handful of exceptions. Nor did they make serious attempts to control the activities of counts through *missi* and directives: they perhaps did more than is now visible, as the discussion of the 852 annal above suggests, but it is clear that the institutional machinery was lacking. We can see already here some of the characteristics of the Ottonian and Salian polity: a kingdom indeed, but one with very marked regional differences (and antagonisms), a kingdom whose rulers were formidable beyond its borders, but within them exercized power and influence only very patchily.

THE EAST FRANKISH ECONOMY

The driving force behind the revived Frankish empire of the eighth century had been the distribution of booty, tribute and land among the political community, and this pattern continued in the east Frankish kingdom of the ninth century. But this had also been accompanied and indeed made possible by economic expansion, both in the Frankish heartland and in the peripheral territories. From the late seventh century the population had begun to recover from the plague-induced depression of the sixth, and by Charles the Great's time the population of the Frankish empire north of the Alps may have been as high as six or seven million. This is still a very low density of population taken against the total surface area, though a rather higher one if taken against an estimate for the actual area under cultivation, for more land was under forest than plough. Such villages as have been excavated from this period were small, but as these are necessarily all sites which were later deserted, they are not a typical sample. There is evidence in the eighth and ninth centuries for both land shortage (colonization of new land) and labour shortage (slave-raiding, enticement of peasants on to new holdings). It is very doubtful whether the increase in production was the result of anything more than this increase in population – in other words, whether if we had accurate statistics we should find an increase in output per head. Some scholars have argued for significant changes in agricultural technology in the Carolingian era: the "introduction" of the supposedly more productive three-course crop rotation and of new kinds of plough. But the evidence will not really support a thesis of a Carolingian agricultural revolution. The norm for crop yields (that is, the ratio of crop harvested to seed sown) appears to have been perhaps 3:1 or 4:1, which is not high (the seed corn for the following year has to be set aside from the harvested grain) and would have left much of the population in a very precarious position. However, it is likely that especially in the more thinly populated lands east of the Rhine pastoral farming was at least as important as agriculture, if not more so.

To talk of the economy of the east Frankish kingdom is in a sense to discuss a phantom. It is possible to talk of the economy of Europe north of the Alps and Pyrenees in the ninth century. Within this area one may perceive regions which were in relation to this larger whole economically advanced or economically backward, but these were smaller in size than even the most fragmentary Frankish sub-kingdom. So far as we can judge, even the most prosperous regions of the east Frankish kingdom, such as the area around the former ducal capital of Bavaria, Regensburg, or the lands lying along the Rhine between the confluences with Neckar and Main which were to become the core of the later German kingdom, were of only secondary importance, though cities like Cologne, Mainz and Regensburg were large and important enough to have merchant colonies. But there was apparently no lack of wealth, both from trade and from tribute. We have seen how tribute came in from the Slavs to the east. Besides this, there was a sufficiently continuous trade with eastern Europe to make it worthwhile and necessary for rulers to control and tax it. The capitulary of Thionville of 805 shows eight control-points for merchants along the eastern frontier run by counts, and the Raffelstetter customs ordinance shows that even at a time when Magyar raiding had presumably led to a reduction of economic activity there was still considerable traffic between Bavaria and the Slav lands. There was a definite solidity about the prosperity. It was in the late eighth and ninth centuries that a Christian infrastructure was hewn out in most of the territory of the east Frankish kingdom: bishoprics and monasteries needed items like churches, libraries and liturgical robes and vessels, all of which were expensive, as well as landed endowments. Though there was little in the way of new church foundation in ninth-century east Francia after the Saxon bishoprics and monasteries were established, there was plenty of church building (sometimes, as at Corvey, more than once) and rebuilding (especially after fires, as at Würzburg in 855 or Cologne in 870). The resources of the kingdom could evidently cope without difficulty.

The role played by money does not appear to have been very prominent. Even the silver penny, stabilized and reformed under Pippin and Charles the Great, though a much smaller coin than the debased Merovingian gold coinage which went out of circulation in the seventh century, still had a substantial value. In Saxony at the end of the eighth century a penny was worth a twelfth of an ox or nearly a bushel of rye. The use of money for anything below wholesale transactions must have been limited indeed. A few coins were minted at Mainz and Regensburg for Louis the German and his successors, but they did not circulate widely; the monastery of Corvey had the right to mint coins but did not exploit it. This lack of domestic production was compensated for to a limited extent by the use of other kingdoms' coinage; a recent survey of coin finds on the territory of present-day Austria, for example, counts only ten ninth-century coins, seven of which are Byzantine copper *folles*, while two more are *denarii* from Italy and west Francia. The picture for north-western Germany is similar. The distribution of coin finds in ninth-century east Francia was much the same as it had been in the Merovingian period: quite extensive along the mid-Rhine, virtually unknown elsewhere. However, all this should not be pressed too far. The seemingly different situation in ninth-century west Francia, where we find Charles the Bald paying close attention to coinage, and substantial coin-hoards, may be misleading. Charles's interest in coinage went hand in hand with a need to be able to raise taxes to pay off Vikings; the function of west Frankish coinage was by no means exclusively economic. The absence of coin-hoards shows the absence of enemies, not of money. East Frankish rulers, at least up to the reign of Charles the Fat, did not pay tribute and hence were less pressed for cash, while references to money payments from ninth century east Francia, even from its backward regions, are quite numerous.

What is most noteworthy about the ninth century is the spread of the urban model of post-Roman northern Europe to the non-Roman regions east of the Rhine; the Saxon bishoprics in particular, as well as those at Constance, Augsburg and Würzburg, became the core of urban settlements resembling those of Worms, Speyer, Metz and Verdun. Some of the Bavarian bishoprics were actually founded in Roman urban sites, yet what grew up around them in the ninth century were in effect new towns. In all cases archaeology reveals small core settlements around the cathedral and (if present) royal palace, inhabited by the providers of services for the religious community which lived there. The bishoprics of Würzburg and Eichstätt possessed royal privileges entitling them to hold markets and exact market-tolls in their cities, and others probably did so without a privilege (which was in any case needed more to defend or establish a monopoly against rivals than as a licence in its own right). Yet these towns were not primarily market centres; they were centres of consumption, and still comparatively small – it was not until the tenth and early eleventh centuries, as we shall see, that towns like Hildesheim or Constance filled up with other ecclesiastical institutions besides the bishopric and cathedral chapter, and acquired a *suburbium*, a second urban settlement alongside the older one, whereas the older episcopal cities in Roman Austrasia could already show a number of monastic foundations in the ninth century. Still, the Frankicization of the lands east of the Rhine went far deeper than at the time of the first Frankish empire in the sixth and early seventh centuries.

Long- and middle-distance trade was not necessarily closely connected with towns. Much trading – of bulk items like grain and intermediate items like wax, wine and honey as well as of luxury items – was done by the owners of scattered estates, in particular by ecclesiastical institutions and the king. This is evident from the privileges for monasteries freeing them wholly or partially from transit tolls or allowing them to transport a certain number of shiploads free of market tolls. The privilege of Louis the German for Lorsch in 858 is typical here: it frees one ship of the monastery from payment of any Rhine tolls, and allows it to unload goods in the harbour of Worms without paying dues.[14] It is also evident from production on estates on a scale greater than that needed for the needs of the estate alone, perhaps even than that needed for all the estates of the owner. Consider the estate at Lauterbach in Bavaria which was given to St Emmeram, Regensburg in 821. Here one of the eleven holdings was held by a free smith; it had on it his unfree wife and children and no fewer than thirty-seven *mancipii* (landless slaves). Together these make up some 40 per cent of the total population of the estate; the other holdings have just one or two families and their slaves. The explanation is presumably that the

14. D Louis the German 89.

slaves were engaged on iron production under the direction of the smith. The salt production in the region around Salzburg and in the Eifel are further instances. Whether the circulation of these goods was by trade or gift-exchange is another matter, but in any event it must have been quite extensive, especially from the northern coast with England and Scandinavia, where Frisian cloth and Rhenish glassware were sold, and whence furs among other things were imported. The Scandinavian trade was important enough for Louis the German to pay attention to its regulation in his treaty with two Danish rulers of 872. However, even if we are here dealing with trade as we should understand it, it did not necessarily pass through towns and urban markets. There was indeed a kind of specialized urban trading settlement – known to modern historians and archaeologists as an *emporium* – in east and middle Francia in the ninth century; Hamburg (before it was sacked in 845) and probably Magdeburg are examples, though these were smaller than that at Durstede in Frisia. But only Mainz combined this kind of function with the other characteristics which we associate with a town: size, the existence of non-agricultural specialists, different kinds of buildings from those found in rural settlements, and so on.

Though we have a great deal of information about agricultural production and the rural population, it is very uneven and refers almost entirely to the organization of the large estates of the church and of the royal fisc. We know little about the estates of the lay nobility or of the independent peasantry. It is also not easy to synthesize the information from law-codes, charters, estate-surveys and archaeology. For large estates (*villae*) we can distinguish between three main types of exploitation. Estates could be directly farmed, using slave labour. They could also be parcelled out among peasants who paid rent in money or in kind for their tenancies (and these two methods could be mixed). A third technique was to retain land under direct production, but to work it not with slave but with serf labour, that is, the labour of dependent tenants who both paid rents and performed labour services on the directly farmed lands, the demesne. This last form of estate organization has been described by Adrian Verhulst as the "classical demesne organization", and he has argued convincingly that it was less common east of the Rhine, where there was a greater tendency for dependants to pay in renders alone, and for demesne land (which in any case seems in general to have been less extensive than in western Francia) to be worked by slaves. For a pre-statistical era any such statement must necessarily be impressionistic. Not all examples of dependents making renders rather than performing services are signs of an older or more primitive form of organization: any large land-holder, whether lay or ecclesiastical, is likely to have had parcels of land and dependants which lay too far from any "classical" estate to be fitted in easily. These could be burdened only with rents; labour services are worthless where the labour cannot be put to use.

The "classical" regime certainly existed beyond the Rhine. In a diploma of 840, for example, Louis the German presented Corvey with "a lord's *mansus* with houses and other buildings and twenty other *mansi* making renders and doing service [*aspicientibus et deservientibus*] there" in Empelde, south-west of Hannover; in a diploma of the following year, Abbot Gozbald of Altaich in Bavaria received an estate at Ingolstadt with "two churches, a lord's hall . . . twenty-two male slaves and female slaves working in the workshop [*feminas genecias*] . . . twenty-two servile *mansi* with their tenants belonging to the same hall. . .".[15] The well-known description of the estate of the bishopric of Augsburg at Staffelsee from the early ninth century reveals an estate of this kind: a central house (*domus*) with 740 day-works of land dependent on it, plus twenty-three free *mansi* (dependent holdings) owing varying mixtures of rents and services and nineteen servile ones.[16] The mixture of rents and labour services made it easier for the estate-owners to adjust to imbalances between land and labour, especially as many labour services were not fixed. It also allowed them to incorporate previously independent small-holders into their own production easily, and thus increase the labour force at their disposal. A possible index to the spread of serfdom is the term *mansus*, with its Germanic equivalent "hide" or *Hoba*; although this word did not have one single meaning, it came more and more to be used for a unit of land sufficient to support a family for which services were demanded of its tenants, and its use in this sense, which was widespread in ninth-century east Francia, was thus an indication of the spread of seigneurial forms of exploitation.

There were many ways in which "free" peasant farmers could be forced into a position of dependence. Impoverishment was one, whether brought about by the imposition of public burdens (military service, attendance at courts, fines) or by bad harvests. Another was the need for protection; in surrendering his land-holding to a lord, receiving it back as a tenancy and agreeing to do labour services for

15. D Louis the German 29, 30.
16. MGH Capitularia regum Francorum 1, ed. A. Boretius (Hannover 1893), 250–2 no. 128.

it, a peasant could secure protection against the powerful, though at a high price in "protection money". The exercise of justice played an important role in bringing free men into a position of dependency. The great land owners controlled the courts, whether in the form of county courts, patrimonial courts over the unfree inhabitants of aristocratic estates, or the intermediate form of the immunity. Immunity had originally simply meant freedom from public taxation; increasingly, however, it was coming to mean freedom from the direct jurisdiction of the count, that is from "public" justice. The immunist either set up his own courts or, in the case of serious offences, handed the offender over to the count (but himself carried out the police function of capturing the offender, thus retaining control over those on the immunity). Royal lands directly held by the king had immunity, and sometimes kept it when granted out in benefice; so, by royal grant, did the lands of many churches. Courts of all kinds were a source of income, probably quite a considerable one; the power to fine also gave a means of reducing free men to poverty. But more crucially, they in the last resort determined questions of personal status if there was dispute or resistance. We have a number of charters recording court decisions that a man, a family or a group of persons were indeed unfree, that is, that in spite of their claims to be free or merely to owe a nominal rent for their land, they were in fact obliged to perform services for an abbey or bishopric or a lay land-owner.

The continuing importance of slaves in the east Frankish economy in spite of trends towards enserfment is not difficult to understand: slaves were more readily available than in the west. The word itself, etymologically cognate with Slav, shows that the east Frankish elite had good access to supplies of slaves: from the end of the ninth century in east Franconia (though not until much later in the rest of Europe) the word *sclavus* comes to displace the classical *servus* as the word for a slave. Besides slave-raiding and -trading there were also areas along the boundary between German and Slav settlement (Thuringia, east Franconia, Bavaria north of the Danube) where Slav "families" were left with their economic and social organization intact and merely made to pay rents. Not only were slaves still plentiful; the land was less densely populated. The pressures leading to more efficient and flexible exploitation of resources of land and labour in the regions of the "classical regime" were less strongly felt.

The "east Frankish economy" may have been less "advanced" than that in the west, but that does not mean that it was less vigorous. One sign of economic vigour is the evidence for land clearance in the eighth and ninth centuries. This is particularly clear in central Germany, thanks to the existence of extensive charter-material from Fulda; here we find very large clearances of 80 or 90 square kilometres being presented to Fulda by groups of aristocrats who presumably had organized the clearance in the first place. The Danube basin and the valleys of the Austrian Danube tributary rivers were also areas of clearance; here much of the work was organized by churches, in particular by the bishoprics of Salzburg and Freising. Further north in Saxony, though land clearance is not unknown (for example in the area around Münster), it seems to have been less extensive, a sign of the continuing importance of pastoral farming in Saxony after the Frankish conquest. In Alemannia also, land colonization was not so prominent. This perhaps reflected the absence of extensive royal fiscs, of major churches – apart from the region around Lake Constance – and of important noble families: the organizational impulses behind colonization were weaker. It was not until the eleventh century that serious efforts were made to open up the Black Forest.

The estates referred to in the documents did not necessarily coincide with the settlements in which the population lived. It was common enough for more than one lord to hold land in a village, while on the other hand large estates covering many settlements might be referred to in documents only by the name of a central location. This is characteristic of much early medieval settlement, in England as well as on the continent; from the point of view of the owner the estate was run from one place, where dues were paid and around which the demesne lands were grouped. This form of organization, the "multiple estate" of English scholarship or *Villikation* of German, need not coincide with settlement – there might well be many villages, hamlets and isolated farmsteads owing dues and services which were collected and administered by the lord's agents from the central place. We know comparatively little about the internal life of these and other kinds of settlement. The homogenizing effects of serfdom on the status both of slaves and of the dependent and impoverished free were present in the east Frankish kingdom, but were less apparent than in the west; differences of status and wealth were sharper at low levels of society as well as at higher ones. Apart perhaps from Saxony, there can be no question of these differences having taken the form of caste: the barriers were permeable. We have already met the free smith of Lauterbach with an unfree wife (and hence unfree children), and east Frankish church councils as well as west Frankish ones had to deal with the problem of marriages between partners who, so they said, discovered each other's status only after marriage.

There is scattered evidence for collective resistance by the dependent population. Open rebellion was rare – the *Stellinga* uprising in Saxony in the early 840s was a notable exception which should not too readily be taken as typical – and when it did occur, was always confined to a single area or estate, and was easily and brutally dealt with. More common was flight or passive resistance, sometimes long drawn out. Carolingian kings and church councils legislated against all kinds of sworn associations (*coniurationes*), and it is clear that this was aimed primarily at the dependent population. Carolingian theologians also stressed the duty of slaves to obey their lords, and the value of Christianity as a means of securing assent to the existing hierarchical organization of society was no doubt one of the reasons why such large resources were put into missionary work, both in the newly conquered territories and in "internal" mission in the countryside. It would be wrong to think of the Carolingian elite as riding on a tiger; they knew that they could control the agricultural population, but they knew also that this required vigilance and willingness to apply brute force when necessary.

THE EAST FRANKISH CHURCH

The history of the east Frankish church resembled that of the east Frankish kingdom after Verdun: in spite of surviving remnants of a supra-regnal sense of Frankishness (east Frankish ecclesiastics occasionally appeared at west Frankish councils in the 840s and again in the 860s, for example) there rapidly developed a separate east Frankish church. Its sense of collectivity was based on the kingdom, not on the provincial organization set up by Charles the Great. So strong was the pull of the kingdom that the bishopric of Chur was transferred from the province of Milan to that of Mainz in the course of the ninth century. If elsewhere provincial organization was strong enough to resist these pressures, the Saxon suffragans of the archbishop of Cologne still attended east Frankish councils, not Lotharingian ones. Not that councils were frequent by west Frankish standards. Major church councils are recorded at Mainz (847, 848, 852, 857, 888), Worms (868), Tribur (895) and Hohenaltheim (916); in the same period the west Frankish church managed at least three times as many councils. From the list it is clear that all the councils were held on Frankish territory; in that they resembled secular assemblies, which, though they could be held in Alemannia, Bavaria or Saxony, normally took place in the Frankish zone around Rhine and Main. Councils were also like assemblies in that they were summoned by the king, though in the east Frankish kingdom there was a more scrupulous division between ecclesiastical synod and secular assembly than was usual in the west or had been usual under Charles and Louis. So far as we know the king did not attend council sessions (though Hohenaltheim may have been an exception). However, the king was not the only factor. All the councils listed above, except perhaps Hohenaltheim, were presided over by the archbishop of Mainz, the primate of Germany. His authority over the bishops and archbishops of other provinces, in spite of his title, was much less than that over his own suffragans; outside the province of Mainz he had rivalries and jealousies to contend with. In consequence all the councils listed had to some extent the character of a Mainz provincial council: the province of Salzburg was rarely anything like fully represented and in 847 not represented at all, and the attendance from the provinces of Cologne and Trier was also spasmodic, even after 870 when the cities of Cologne and Trier came to Louis the German under the treaty of Meerssen.

Above the level of the council there was little; the east Frankish church was much less close to the papacy than the west Frankish church. In the 860s and 870s there were disputes between Popes Nicholas I, Hadrian II and John VIII and the west Frankish episcopate about a number of issues, including appointments to and depositions from several bishoprics. The complex of legal texts forged in the west Frankish kingdom in the 840s and known collectively as the Pseudo-Isidorian forgeries, which among other things assigned the papacy a quite different jurisdictional role within the church from the one it had previously played, was used in several of these disputes. In the middle kingdom Nicholas I was able to prevent Lothar II having his remarriage recognized by the Lotharingian church, and to depose the archbishops of Trier and Cologne for having attempted to meet Lothar's wishes at the council of Metz in 863; it is true that Günther of Cologne issued a counter-manifesto and took very little notice of his deposition, but Theodgaud of Trier accepted his sentence, and at least some of the suffragans of the two archbishops wrote to Nicholas to excuse themselves for their participation in the council. The east Frankish church was hardly touched by such developments, though it knew about them. We know from surviving papal correspondence that Ermanrich of Passau was suspended from office and the bishops of Freising and Salzburg threatened with suspension for their part in the Methodius affair in 870, but there is little sign that they took any notice of this. Only a handful of east Frankish monasteries, like Boniface's foundation at Fulda or the important foundations at Corvey, Hersfeld or the Reichenau, had papal privileges confirming and securing their status. Rome was a holy city, and a supplier of relics; its bishop was perhaps owed special reverence, but he was not a judge or a law-giver. The Pseudo-Isidorian forgeries were not made use of in east Francia until the council of Mainz in 888, and even then it was not their doctrines of papal jurisdiction which received attention.

If there was a separate consciousness at the level of councils and legislation, this did not mean that there was a great gulf between the different regnal churches. There were exchanges of ideas and of manuscripts across regnal boundaries, and Frankishness probably survived longer as a collective ideal in ecclesiastical circles than it did elsewhere. The grass-roots application of Carolingian church reform took similar forms in east and west, and the east Frankish church drew on the experience of the west. East Frankish bishops, like their colleagues in the west and middle kingdoms, imitated the capitularies of rulers and issued diocesan statutes, instructions for their parish clergy on how these were to behave, how they were to carry out their duties, and what rules of canon law they were to enforce on the laity. Not only did east Frankish bishops issue their own; they also made use of texts originating in the west. Of forty-nine surviving manuscripts of Theodulf of Orleans' first episcopal capitulary, for example, no fewer than eight were written in east Francia in the ninth century; we have manuscripts from Fulda, St Gallen, Ellwangen, Mainz and Lorsch among others. These texts were used in the sense that they provided inspiration (and wording) for the east Frankish episcopate's own texts; and their provisions can also be shown to have had some effect, being drawn on by the council of Mainz in 852, for example. The frequent provision in episcopal capitularies that priests are to have a certain minimum stock of books with their church with which to teach their flocks and carry out their liturgical duties is echoed in Bavarian estate inventories of the ninth century, where the books, as valuable movable items belonging to the churches which were part of the estates, are often separately listed.

The institution of bishops' capitularies presupposes the existence of parishes and parish priests, though in the ninth century parishes were larger and less well defined than in the high middle ages. They may be assumed for Bavaria outside the marches, for Raetia and for western Franconia, but less so for Alemannia and certainly not for Saxony, Frisia, Thuringia or eastern Franconia. Here, as also in Pannonia, conversion was still very much in progress even in the second half of the ninth century, and monasteries still played an important role in the Christianization of the countryside, far more so than secular priests and in some ways more so than bishops. Whereas in more settled parts the church's income from tithes was clearly under the control of the bishop (in so far as it did not flow into the pockets of the owners of churches; see above, p. 38), the monasteries of Corvey, Fulda and Hersfeld received substantial endowments of tithe incomes in the ninth century. We know about these endowments mainly because of the (generally successful) efforts of post-Carolingian bishops to get their hands on them and the disputes which their attempts provoked; but the original intention was presumably to support the missionary work of the monasteries at a time when there was no network of parish churches which tithes could finance. Even dioceses did not yet all have defined boundaries setting them off from neighbouring dioceses; like their secular equivalents, counties and kingdoms, those who held office within them were much more fully present in some parts than in others. Some of the largest dioceses, notably those of Mainz and Constance, made use of auxiliary bishops, *chorepiscopi*, to make sacraments such as the consecration of churches or the confirmation of the young available to those parts which the bishop was unable to reach.

Outside their dioceses bishops were generally not active. The main missionary effort of the east Frankish church lay in converting the population of the kingdom; it did not concern itself overmuch with the peoples to the north and east, although some missionary efforts were made in the south-east. In continuation of the eighth-century traditions of the Bavarian church, the bishoprics of Freising and Salzburg were active in Pannonia, while the bishopric of Regensburg seems to have done some missionary work among the Bohemians. Further north there was much less to report: neither the bishops of Würzburg and Mainz in central Germany nor the Saxon bishoprics in the north have left any trace of mission to the Slavs in the ninth century. The efforts to convert the Danes, begun under Louis the Pious, in effect came to an end with the Viking sack of Hamburg in 845, leaving in Hamburg-Bremen a curious double (arch)bishopric, with an extensively defined sphere of influence in Scandinavia and along the southern Baltic coast. Its history and aspirations were to be of some consequence in the eleventh and twelfth centuries but were of hardly any in the ninth, though Ansgar and his pupil, successor and biographer Rimbert by their efforts kept conversion of the Danes and Swedes alive as an aspiration and a possibility up to the end of the century.

One of the most striking aspects of the ninth-century east Frankish church is the rapidity with which its bishoprics, which had mostly been founded or in effect refounded in the eighth century, became established as substantial powers. Ninth-century ecclesiastics, both abbots and bishops, nowhere wholly avoided giving a literal meaning to the phrase "the church militant", but east Frankish bishops appeared far more unashamedly than their west Frankish counterparts as military leaders: Arn of Würzburg was killed in an expedition against the Sorbs in 892, while Wala of Metz and Sunderolt of Mainz both fell in battle against the Vikings, and Sunderolt's predecessor Liutbert was one of the main organizers of the defence against Viking raiders in the 880s. The disastrous Saxon battle against the Vikings in 880 saw the death of two Saxon bishops along with secular nobles. The abbots of large monasteries like Corvey also had substantial armed followings. This is not only a foretaste of the warlike German church of the tenth and eleventh centuries. It is also a sign that many of these bishoprics and monasteries had after their foundation rapidly acquired great landed wealth, the indispensable basis for supporting warbands. The loss through fire and falsification of the early property charters for such important sees as Mainz or Hildesheim makes it not always easy to say how extensive the wealth was, or where it lay. Mainz at least did not simply own estates in the immediate vicinity of the see, and nor did great monasteries like Fulda (which had estates in Italy as well as in Frisia and northern Saxony) and St Gallen, though such things as the Aquitainian possessions held by the Rhenish churches in the sixth century, for example, seem to have been lost by the ninth.

A further sign that the church in east Francia had moved from being a missionary to being an established church can be found in appointments to bishoprics. The typical eighth-century bishop in these regions (apart from those of the older bishoprics along the Rhine) had been a missionary, often a foreigner from England or Ireland. It would be wrong to picture such men – Willibald in Eichstätt, Lull in Mainz, Boniface himself – as having been wholly divorced from the aristocratic world in which they found themselves; many came from noble families, and in any case they needed to be able to deal as equals with the nobles where they worked. But their sees were not as yet centres of power. In the ninth century we find practices familiar from western Francia. Aristocratic families secured a grip on certain bishoprics. In Constance we find three bishops called Solomon and related to one another holding office continuously except for a brief interlude in the early 870s, between the late 830s and 919, and further members of the family were bishops in Chur and Freising in the early tenth century. Even the new bishoprics in Münster and Halberstadt (as well as the monastery of Werden) were ruled in the first half of the ninth century largely by members of the family of the Frisian missionary Liudger: Liudger himself and his nephew Gerfrid in Münster, and his brother Hildigrim in Halberstadt, possibly also Altfrid of Münster and Thiadgrim of Halberstadt. Members of the east Frankish royal chapel were also prominent among the appointees to bishoprics and the major royal abbeys. Ermanrich, abbot of Ellwangen and later bishop of Passau, served as a *capellanus* in the 830s. Grimald, abbot of Weißenburg, was chancellor from 833 to 837, abbot of St Gallen from 841, and chancellor again for brief periods in the 850s and between 860 and 870. Right at the end of the century Arnulf tried (unsuccessfully) to have the Aleman Wiching, who had become his chancellor after having been expelled from his missionary bishopric in Moravia, appointed to the see of Passau. It is true that many appointments cannot be seen either as "court" or as "local family" appointments, not least because we often do not know who a bishop was or where he came from in east Francia in the ninth century. It is also true that there was no necessary antithesis between "court" and "noble" bishops; the Solomons of Constance may have come from an "episcopal kindred", but they also played a prominent role as advisers at the court of Louis the German and his descendants, and it was normally the king who appointed to bishoprics. Solomon III and Waldo of Freising were *capellani* before they became bishops. A lot of bishops were drawn from monasteries, but not necessarily from local ones. Unlike counts and margraves, who generally had local roots, the east Frankish episcopate was genuinely regnal and not provincial in its composition.

In Saxony the bishoprics established under Charles the Great and Louis the Pious almost all grew out of monasteries. Besides these, there were significant monasteries at Werden, Essen and Corvey in Westfalia, and for nuns at Herford in Westfalia and Gandersheim in Ostfalia. Outside Saxony – and here only in the first half of the century – there were few new monastic foundations within the territory of the east Frankish kingdom, and Bavaria in particular, which had seen a flood of foundations in the late Agilolfing era, witnessed if anything a decline in numbers in the ninth century. This is not necessarily a sign of decline in religious fervour, though the fact that the monastic reform movement fostered by Louis the Pious and Benedict of Aniane seemingly had no resonance east of the Rhine may be. It is evidently impossible for succeeding generations of bishops and aristocrats to go on founding monasteries at a constant rate, especially if there is also to be a continuing flow of donations to existing monasteries, as indeed there was. The Corvey property records show how those members of noble families who entered the monastery had to bring a "dowry" with them: an estate, a few *mansi*, a fishery at the least, in effect something of what they might have expected to inherit had they stayed in the world. Members of the founding families of monasteries were probably not subject to such constraints, but there was a natural tendency with the course of time for such proprietary monasteries either to fall into the hands of bishops or to become royal monasteries, especially if the founding family died out in the direct line. Thus the Bavarian nunnery of Rotthalmünster, originally a noble foundation, came in the ninth century to the bishopric of Passau, which like Freising and Regensburg acquired a number of smaller monasteries at this time. Werden in Westfalia, originally a family monastery of the Liudgerids, became a royal monastery with the right of "free" election of its abbot in 877; a number of Bavarian *Eigenklöster*, not just those belonging to Tassilo and the ducal family, became royal monasteries after 788. It may well be that such tendencies deterred prospective founders; it was not until the mid eleventh century that methods were found to defend noble foundations against the enveloping tendencies inherent in royal protection and episcopal supervision. Still more frequent than royal or episcopal take-overs was the swallowing up of less successful foundations by larger ones; such monasteries become *cellae*, dependencies. Indeed, we learn about the existence of some small monasteries only through the record of the transaction by which they passed into the hands of another monastery, as in the case of Engelbrechtsmünster, granted by the founding family with its endowment to St Emmeram in 821.

Nowhere are the dangers of optical illusion more apparent than when considering the intellectual and cultural activity of the east Frankish church. The starting-point here has to be the manuscripts – though as with legal texts we should be cautious about making the jump from what was copied to what was read and thought about. But the chances of survival have been quite different in south Germany from those further north. Most medieval Bavarian monastic and cathedral libraries have survived pretty well intact, either in situ or in the *Staatsbibliothek* in Munich. This is also true of St Gallen, the Reichenau and the cathedral libraries of Cologne and Würzburg. By comparison, what survives from Mainz, Lorsch, Hersfeld and Fulda is scattered and incomplete, and what survives from Werden, Corvey, Herford and the Saxon bishoprics is so fragmentary as to make any assessment questionable. In Lotharingia, a millennium of fire, sword and more modern methods of destruction has also left great holes in our knowledge of what once existed. This can be compensated for to some extent by contemporary library catalogues, which survive for a number of east Frankish bishoprics and monasteries (Fulda, Würzburg, Lorsch, the Reichenau, Murbach, St Gallen), but as these were normally written on the fly-leaves of manuscripts they are much more likely to survive for libraries which have themselves survived than for those where the losses are high. Making allowances for all this we can say that by the mid ninth century at the latest the larger monasteries and the bishoprics in east Francia had libraries which by contemporary west Frankish or Anglo-Saxon standards were balanced and adequate: besides the books needed for liturgical purposes, they had both classical literature (used above all for teaching Latin) and patristic theology, as well as more specialized works. Such libraries could be used both for teaching and for more advanced study.

This fits in well with what we know otherwise of intellectual life in the east Frankish kingdom: it was by no means a backwater. The major figure was Hrabanus Maurus, schoolmaster and then abbot of Fulda (822–41) who became archbishop of Mainz after his reconciliation with Louis the German in 847. He had a number of distinguished pupils: Rudolf of Fulda, himself an influential teacher and author of saints' lives; Walafrid Strabo, poet and editor of Einhard's *Life of Charlemagne*; Otfrid of Weißenburg, biblical versifier. Besides this, Hrabanus left an enormous written production: biblical commentaries on almost the whole of the Old and New Testaments consisting largely of excerpts from the commentaries by Augustine, Jerome, Cassiodorus and Bede; two penitentials and other treatises on church organization and discipline; a martyrology; a homiliary; and a reworking of the *Encyclopaedia Britannica* of the early middle ages, Isidore of Seville's *Etymologiae*. One thinks here of Bede, who played a comparable role as a scholar–teacher at a similar stage in the development of the young Anglo-Saxon church; in both cases the often derivative and didactic nature of what was produced should not close our eyes to the importance of the achievement. Hrabanus was an important figure but not a brilliant one, as in general the standard of learning among the east Frankish episcopate and abbatiate was solid and respectable rather than distinguished. The east Frankish church played little part in the more advanced intellectual and theological debates of the ninth century. In theological matters, the debate over predestination which the Saxon monk Gottschalk initiated took place in Burgundy and Lotharingia, while the west Frankish discussion about the nature and duties of kingship, triggered off by the reform councils of 829 and the deposition of Louis the Pious in 833 and continued in the writings of Hincmar of Rheims and Sedulius Scotus and others and in the development of an ecclesiastical king-making ceremony in west Francia, found no echo east of the Rhine. It was an exceptional event when the east Frankish church – at the request of Pope Nicholas I, moreover – issued a treatise against the errors of the Greek church at the council of Worms in 868.

It was undoubtedly because so much of the east Frankish kingdom was still missionary territory that we find an extensive interest in the written use of the vernacular. The parallels with the developments in Anglo-Saxon during Alfred's reign are very close, except that written Old High German did not to the same extent as Anglo-Saxon become a language for administration and government, or for historical writing. As with Anglo-Saxon, much of what has survived is hardly to be described as literature. It is for the most part either vernacular versions of texts needed for Christianization – Lord's Prayer, creeds, catechism, prayers, confessional formulae and hymns – or translations of texts needed by missionaries, in particular the Psalter and the Gospels. For the Psalter we have Frankish and Alemannic interlinear translations (in fragments); for the Gospels there are fragments from Mondsee (Bavaria) of a translation of the Gospel according to Matthew, and a complete translation from Fulda of Tatian's synoptic version of the four Gospels, as well as the old Saxon Heliand, a poetic retelling of the Gospel narrative. Besides this there is a very large number of glosses preserved in manuscripts of Latin texts, both classical and patristic, which presumably reflect the use of the vernacular in teaching: the library of the Reichenau even had "poems for teaching the German [*Theodiscam*] language".[17] Compared with this, the amount of secular literature is very small: heroic poetry in the *Hildebrandslied* (the epic past) and the *Ludwigslied*

17. P. Lehmann, *Mittelalterliche Bibliothekskataloge Deutschlands und der Schweiz* 1, Munich 1918, 260.

(the heroic present – the poem celebrates the victory of Louis III of west Francia over the Normans at Saucourt in 881, though it is far from certain that it is east Frankish in origin), but otherwise only fragments (charms, satirical verses, etc.). Administratively the language was used to formulate oaths (the most famous example is the Strasbourg Oaths of 842, but there are others) and to describe estate boundaries (though here much less frequently than in Anglo-Saxon England). Otherwise it occurs only as isolated words in charters and legal texts where the drafter was unable to find a Latin word for the concept or institution he wished to refer to and so used the vernacular term instead. There are (fragmentary) Old High German translations of *Lex Salica* and of a Carolingian capitulary, but their status as isolated fragments shows that the written vernacular was not normally used for such purposes.

Part II The kingdom refounded, 882–983

CHAPTER FIVE

Kings, dukes and invaders, 882–936

CHARLES THE FAT AND ARNULF

The "reunification" of the Carolingian empire under Charles the Fat between 880 and 884 was, to use a slightly anachronistic term, only a personal union. His chancery dated his diplomata using a separate numbering of his regnal years in *Gallia*, *Italia* and *Germania*; it regarded him, in other words, as king and emperor over three separate kingdoms. Only in east Francia did it make no distinction between the Alemannic kingdom which he inherited from his father in 876 and the remainder of the east Frankish kingdom which he inherited from his older brother (Louis the Younger) in 882. The separate numbering of regnal years was not mere punctiliousness on the part of notaries; it reflected political reality. The three kingdoms remained distinct, with their own elites. Charles treated them separately: he held assemblies for each, and only to a very limited extent did he call on the military resources of the west Frankish and Italian kingdoms. In view of the rapid succession of kings in all the kingdoms in the period between 876 and 884 it is not surprising that the political communities in the various kingdoms can be seen acting independently of their rulers. In west Francia, the aristocracy had dealt collectively with Charles the Bald and Louis the Stammerer. Surprisingly, in view of the fact that he had been invited in by a noble grouping, it also did so with Louis the Younger when he attempted to invade in 879–80. It was at the invitation of the west Frankish nobles that Charles the Fat assumed power in 884. As for Lotharingia, the fact that it continued to exist and was not absorbed into east or west Francia after 869 shows still more clearly the political power of regional aristocratic groupings. Within Charles's conglomeration of *regna* no new supra-regnal aristocracy capable of exploiting the opportunities presented by a reunified Frankish empire even began to emerge.

It was not just aristocratic collectivities which were gaining in importance. In east Francia, where ethnic divisions were in any case very marked, there were signs that kings were no longer able to control even individual aristocrats. The Salzburg annals hint at an attempt on Carloman's life by some Bavarian nobles in 878.[1] Between 883 and 885 there were disputes over the Thuringian and Pannonian margravates with fighting and loss of life, in which Charles the Fat was unable to intervene to any effect. The Pannonian affair is particularly instructive. In 871 Louis the German had passed over the children of two counts killed fighting the Moravians and appointed Aribo, who had continued to hold office under Carloman and Louis the Younger. On Charles's accession the children, William and Engelschalk, claimed what they saw as their rights; and when they did not get them, they sought help from Zwentibald of Moravia, who invaded Pannonia. Aribo seems to have been backed by Arnulf of Carinthia, who for this reason was threatened by Zwentibald. Charles's role in the whole business was not a prominent one, and seems to have been confined to a meeting with Zwentibald in 885 (which by implication showed his hostility to Arnulf, but had no practical consequences) and renewing the peace of 874. The east Bavarian aristocracy was in effect left to settle its own affairs. Here and elsewhere we find members of the high aristocracy whose power, based on extensive family lands, benefices and military leadership, was so great that the king could not remove them from office at will, even had he wished to: Arnulf of Carinthia and the Babenberg duke Henry in east Francia; Wido of Spoleto and Berengar of Friuli in Italy; Bishop Gauzlin of Paris, Hugo "the Abbot" and the Robertine Odo in west Francia. The most spectacular example is Boso, count of Vienne, who married Louis II's daughter Ermengard and in 879 set himself up as king in Provence, where he held out until his death in 887 in spite of efforts by the united Carolingians of east and west Francia to dislodge him. The failure of Charles's attempt to remove Wido of Spoleto in 883–4 was almost as remarkable. Even the episcopate was not prepared to accept the king's wishes without question. Charles evidently wanted to have the succession of his young illegitimate son Bernard

1. MGH SS 30, 742.

acknowledged; to this end he invited Pope Marinus to east Francia in 885, but Marinus died on the journey. We are told that Marinus was also "unreasonably to depose certain bishops",[2] and there is a strong inference that it was these bishops who had objected to Bernard's succession.

This last episode points to the fundamental political problem of the 880s: the kingdoms which Charles had reunited were faced with a succession crisis. Charles's accession in west Francia, in Italy and in most of east Francia was rather different from those of the Carolingian kings of previous generations to neighbouring kingdoms. Charles had been invited to assume rule rather than himself playing any very active part in affairs; everything fell into his lap, as Regino of Prüm pointed out.[3] His eminence was due to the flatness of the surrounding country, and at nearly fifty he offered no hope of continuity. He was childlessly married, probably not in the best of health, and had only Bernard as a possible heir. Carolingians of any kind were getting scarce. Hugo, Lothar II's son by Waldrada, was killed in 885 in an attempt to seize his father's kingdom. In west Francia Louis the Stammerer's third, posthumous son Charles (the Simple), who had been passed over in 879, was of doubtful legitimacy. In east Francia, Louis the Younger had died without surviving male heirs, legitimate or illegitimate; Carloman had an illegitimate son, Arnulf, who was left in his position as margrave of Carinthia under both Louis the Younger and Charles the Fat. This was not a wide range of choice for the succession, if a Carolingian was still to be regarded as essential, and there was no one with a generally acknowledged or self-evident claim. Nor was Charles's authority such that he could designate a successor and have his wish generally accepted. The dramatic climax of 887, when Charles the Fat was deposed and his successor Arnulf was not acknowledged outside east Francia and parts of Lotharingia, with the other regions of the Frankish empire choosing rather to adopt kings of their own who were not Carolingians, made an immense impression on contemporaries; but it was the logical culmination to the politics of the years after 876.

All this should be borne in mind when considering what is often said to have been the chief problem of Charles's reign, namely his fairly unsuccessful attempts to deal with Viking incursions. His first action on succeeding to the whole of his father's kingdom in April

2. *Annales Fuldenses*, p. 103.
3. Regino s.a. 887, p. 128.

882 was to mount a campaign against the Vikings on the lower Rhine. Lotharingia had suffered more from Vikings than had east Francia, and after Alfred of Wessex had made peace with the Vikings at Edington in 878 the land was subject to the depredations of the great Viking host, which left England and established itself in a camp at Asselt, near the Rhine. Louis III of west Francia defeated the Vikings at Saucourt in August 881 (the victory was the historical occasion for the Old High German praise-poem, the *Ludwigslied*) and Louis the Younger had begun a campaign against them which was broken off on his death in January 882; neither ruler had made any impression on the Viking base. Local forces were inadequate to deal with a threat of this size – Bishop Wala of Metz was killed early in 882 at the head of a small army attempting to check the progress of the raiders – and a concerted campaign was clearly necessary. In the summer of 882 an east Frankish army, possibly with some Lombard reinforcements, set out against the Vikings. The siege of the Viking camp ended in a negotiated withdrawal by the Vikings; one of their leaders, Godfrey, turned Christian and received a Carolingian wife and part of Frisia as a benefice, while the other, Siegfried, was given a huge sum as Danegeld. Much of Charles's reputation as a weakling and a failure in modern historiography stems from this episode (together with the similar campaign around Paris in 886), yet it does not seem that contemporaries – apart from the Mainz cleric who composed the so-called annals of Fulda – saw it as a sign of the king's personal failure. Setting a thief to catch a thief, was after all, a policy which had had some success before; Lothar I and Lothar II had installed the Viking leader Roric in Frisia for the same purpose in the 850s. Godfrey could be controlled – he was killed on suspicion of treachery in 885 without this leading to renewed Viking incursions – and at least in east Francia and Lotharingia the defence against Viking raids led by the east Frankish *dux* Henry and Archbishop Liutbert of Mainz seems to have been reasonably successful.

It was otherwise in west Francia. Charles accepted rule here, but did little else. The Vikings, well informed as ever about the internal politics of their raiding-grounds, took the opportunity first to exact a large tribute following the death of the young Carloman of west Francia in 884, and then in 885 to advance up the Seine, for the first time in twenty years, and besiege Paris. In the course of the siege the most important and successful of the east Frankish military leaders, Henry, who had been sent by Charles at the head of a large east Frankish army to raise the siege, was killed in an ambush, while the two most experienced west Frankish generals, Hugo "the Abbot" and Bishop Gauzlin, died of natural causes. Charles himself, who appeared with a fresh army from east Francia in the summer of 886, failed to raise the siege and had to agree to a further payment of tribute. His failure got a much worse press than the Asselt campaign of four years earlier; but those who suffered most were not in a position to do much about him. Although he ruled over the whole of the Frankish empire, he remained essentially an east Frankish king whose power base lay in Alemannia. It was the eastern Franks who would decide his fate.

The first indications that Charles was in political difficulties came in the summer of 887, when he was forced at an assembly at Kirchheim in Alemannia to dismiss his chancellor and chief adviser, Bishop Liutward of Vercelli, and reappoint Louis the Younger's former chancellor, Archbishop Liutbert of Mainz. It was his Alemannic supporters, the basis of his power, who forced through the change, a sign that he was in real trouble. Such things were rare in the Carolingian world; court intrigues were common, but it was very unusual for a politician to be driven from court and office against the will of the ruler. The closest precedents lay, ominously, in the turbulent period leading up to Louis the Pious's deposition in 833. Perhaps Charles's health was thought to be failing. He was ill in the winter of 886–7, and again after the meeting at Kirchheim, and in the event he was not to live long. He was in any case no longer a young man, and the succession was a matter of increasing concern both for Charles and for his leading men. He himself received Boso's widow Ermengard and the young Louis of Provence in the summer, and adopted Louis as his son (and presumably as his heir). Besides this, several of those who on his death were to claim the kingship in their own lands, in particular Berengar, margrave of Friuli, and Odo, margrave of Neustria, are found visiting Charles in the course of 887. They may have been securing claims to succeed him in a part of the empire. However this may be (and it is dangerous to read backwards too much in view of the very rapid end to Charles's reign), matters came to a head in the autumn. Charles held an assembly at Waiblingen in September which was attended by "numerous princes";[4] he then summoned an assembly to Frankfurt for November 11. Here the news came that Arnulf of Carinthia was leading a powerful army of Bavarians and Slavs against him. Arnulf's interest was evident: he stood to lose most if Charles's

4. D Charles III 170.

adoption of Louis of Provence was to determine the succession. Arnulf himself was soon joined by others, notably the Franks and Saxons. The last to desert Charles were the Alemans, and this sealed his fate. His last diploma was issued on November 17; the first diploma of his successor is dated November 27. Charles himself was given a few estates in Alemannia as an old age pension, but he died only a few weeks later, on January 13 888.

The precise sequence of events is none too clear, in spite of the efforts of several generations of scholars to clarify it, and it is probably better not to push the accounts given by contemporary annalists too closely. In particular, we do not know how Charles's reign was ended or Arnulf's inaugurated. Presumably Charles was informally abandoned – at any rate there is not even a hint at a formal deposition along the lines of Louis the Pious's loss of rulership in 833. Arnulf may well simply have begun ruling, in Merovingian style. The east Frankish kingdom had not seen much in the way of a symbolism of state in the ninth century. It is possible that one or two east Frankish kings (including Charles the Fat) were anointed on their accession, but if they were this made little impression on contemporaries, and it is not referred to in the contemporary accounts of Charles's deposition. Nor do there seem to have been significant insignia – special crowns, swords and other objects symbolizing the kingdom and kingship – in contrast with both the west Frankish kingdom and the Ottonian Reich of the tenth century. What is certain is that the deposition of Charles was settled by the political communities of the east Frankish kingdom, and no one elsewhere in the Frankish empire quarrelled with this; nor did anyone dispute the eastern Franks' right to choose (or accept) Arnulf as their ruler. As we shall see, this choice was not regarded as binding on the other kingdoms, but there is no evidence that the eastern Franks intended it to be. On the other hand, there is also no reason to suppose that the magnates of the east Frankish kingdom were deliberately turning their backs on the Frankish empire and going their own way. The coup of late 887 was in effect a continuation of the fraternal rivalries between Louis the Younger, Carloman and Charles the Fat and their followings in the years after Louis the German's death. Its outcome was determined above all by the fact that Charles did not at the end command enough confidence in his future to get anyone to fight for him. In particular, he could not hold his Alemannic supporters in the face of the threat from Arnulf and his Bavarian army. The deposition was not, so far as we can tell, a direct response to Charles's failure as a military leader.

After Arnulf had been acknowledged king by the magnates of Louis the German's kingdom, he set off for Regensburg, presumably to consolidate his position in his home base. "While he delayed there too long, many kinglets sprang up in Europe, that is, the kingdom of Charles his uncle", as the Regensburg annalist put it.[5] This commentary implies that Arnulf himself intended, but failed, to establish rule over the whole of the Carolingian empire. Another contemporary annalist, the Lotharingian Regino of Prüm, offered a slightly different perspective:

On [Charles's] death the kingdoms he had ruled over, deprived of a legitimate heir, separated out from the body of his empire and each, instead of waiting for its natural lord, chose a king from its own bowels. This was the cause of great wars. Not that the Franks lacked princes with the nobility, courage and wisdom to rule over kingdoms; rather, the equality of ancestry, dignity and power enhanced the discord, for none was so outstanding that the others could submit to him without losing face.[6]

Significant in Regino's appraisal is the assessment of Arnulf's position – not the legitimate successor, but nevertheless the natural lord of all the Frankish kingdoms – and his clear explanation of why the newly formed dynasties were unstable; this is the key to much of the political history of the next fifty years. Those who were chosen (or put themselves forward) were almost all well established in their own region, as we might expect: Odo in west Francia; Ramnulf in Aquitaine; Berengar in Italy; Louis, son of Boso, in Provence; Rudolf in Burgundy. The one exception was Wido of Spoleto, who tried to claim kingship first in west Francia and then in Lotharingia before returning to Italy to dispute the kingdom there with Berengar. Wido was not without supporters north of the Alps, but neither these nor his family ties there were an adequate power-base – his failure shows the regionalization of the Carolingian ruling elite.

The changes of dynasty in 887 and 888 were indeed dramatic – even the *Anglo-Saxon Chronicle* recorded them in a lengthy notice – but are not easy to interpret. It is not in all cases clear whether it was the news of Charles's deposition or that of his death which led to the choice of a new ruler; only Berengar in Italy was certainly chosen king while Charles III was still alive. The almost universal recourse to non-Carolingians was not so much a deliberate rejection of the dynasty as a simple necessity: there were not enough Carolingians to

5. *Annales Fuldenses*, s.a. 888, p. 116.
6. Regino s.a. 888, p. 129.

go round. Some at least of the new rulers were perhaps conceived of (both by their supporters and by themselves) as temporary solutions: Ramnulf did not long claim to be king in Aquitaine; Odo was willing to come to terms with Charles the Simple; even in Italy there was evidently no universal desire to shut out the Carolingians permanently, as we shall see. Arnulf, though illegitimate, could still appear as *primus inter pares* – and in spite of the half-dozen new royal titles, his position was structurally not all that different from that of his predecessor. It was even possible for the Anglo-Saxon chronicler to see him as a hegemonial emperor ruling over kings who had taken office with his approval.[7]

His reign pre-echoed much which was to become established and familiar in the Ottonian Reich. He did not try to restore the empire of many kingdoms his uncle had held bit by bit. Charles had succeeded to kingship outside east Francia by invitation, and once the magnates of the other kingdoms had shown themselves willing to follow one of their own number there was no chance for Arnulf of peaceful succession in this way. Nor did he have the military resources for a general policy of force. Instead he adopted a differentiated approach. He refused an offer of the west Frankish crown in the summer of 888, and showed no inclination to change his mind later. Instead he treated both Odo, the Robertine king chosen in 888, and from 893 Charles the Simple, the Carolingian passed over in 884 and 888, as if they were in some sense his subordinates; he even supplied Odo with a crown for his coronation. His interest in the remains of the old middle kingdom was much more positive. The Lotharingians apparently played no part in the deposition of Charles III, but Arnulf claimed rule over all of Lotharingia as if by right. His hostility to Rudolf of Burgundy is probably explained by Rudolf's initial claim to be king in the whole of Lotharingia. The issue was seemingly settled at a meeting between Arnulf and Rudolf late in 888 at which Rudolf probably abandoned his claims to Lotharingia and swore fidelity to Arnulf for the rest of his kingdom, but Arnulf was still campaigning against Rudolf as late as 894. The other side of the coin was the support Arnulf gave to his rival of 887, Louis of Provence, who was crowned at Arnulf's instigation in the autumn of 890 and in 894 "granted" some territory ruled by Rudolf – a grant which in practice could not be realized. In Italy, finally, Arnulf supported Berengar of Friuli, who became his vassal, against Wido of Spoleto. At first he was unable to do more

7. D. Whitelock, *English Historical Documents* 1, 2nd edn, London 1979, 199.

than this, but in 894 he came south of the Alps and destroyed Wido's power-base, while after Wido's death in 896 he made a second expedition, this time going as far as Rome and receiving coronation as emperor by Pope Formosus (and for this reason incurring Berengar's hostility – all a remarkable anticipation of Otto I's relations with Berengar II between 951 and 962). Intervention and control without direct rule in west Francia; rule through intermediaries in Lotharingia and Italy, and overlordship in the rest of the middle kingdom – this kind of hegemonial rulership over the former Carolingian empire was to be practised again under Otto I.

At home Arnulf's reputation was also high, especially after his defeat of the Vikings at the River Dyle in 891, a victory almost as important as that of Otto I over the Magyars at the Lechfeld in 955. Viking attacks on Arnulf's kingdom ceased after 891 apart from a few raids on Lotharingia, and fell off in west Francia as well. Arnulf's main initial difficulty was Alemannia: although Charles III had commended his illegitimate son Bernard to Arnulf in the autumn of 887 as part of his submission, Bernard was still a focus of Alemannic resistance, and in 890 he led a substantial rebellion which included Count Ulrich of the Linzgau and Bernard, abbot of St Gallen, though whether this was aimed at deposing Arnulf or merely at a restoration of Charles III's Alemannic kingdom for Bernard we cannot now say. The Alemans refused to take part in Arnulf's campaign against the Vikings in 891, but after Bernard's death in 891 or 892 they are found supporting Arnulf and supplying troops for his campaigns. Arnulf seems to have been on generally good terms with the Liudolfing duke of Saxony, Otto, though like his predecessors he scarcely visited Saxony himself – once in 892 for an expedition against the Abodrites – and Otto, like his predecessors, hardly ever left Saxony. In central Germany Arnulf's relatives by marriage, Conrad and Rudolf, potentially rivals of the Liudolfings in northern Thuringia, held the Thuringian march and the key bishopric of Würzburg respectively from 892, though Conrad was unable or unwilling to stay in office for long. Although Arnulf's itinerary was confined largely to Bavaria and Franconia, an analysis of his diplomata shows that his authority was recognized throughout east Francia: there are numerous charters for Saxon, Alemannic and Lotharingian recipients, and most of these were issued in Bavaria and Franconia. In other words, Arnulf's diplomata were sufficiently worth having for recipients to seek him out in order to get them. Within the east Frankish kingdom he ruled like his predecessors. It is true that there was a flush of synodal activity by the church at the beginning of his reign – notably in the councils at Mainz (888, with attendance by an Italian and one or two west Frankish bishops) and Tribur (895). Both these councils concerned themselves with the office of the king, very much as earlier west Frankish councils had done; but neither this nor Arnulf's alliance with high ecclesiastics to put down Bernard's revolt in Alemannia justifies the interpretation occasionally offered that Arnulf allied with the church against the great lay magnates. The episcopate was silent – startlingly so – in the crisis of late 887; at Mainz and Tribur it did no more than express its desire for an effective and respected ruler who would maintain peace. No doubt Arnulf found ecclesiastical support welcome, but his power did not depend on it, any more than that of his predecessors had done.

Nevertheless, even before Arnulf suffered the stroke in 896 from which he was not to recover right up to his death in December 899, events in Bavaria and Lotharingia during his reign had shown the limits of his authority. Arnulf's old enemy Aribo had apparently retained his command of the Pannonian march after Arnulf's accession in 888; but in 893 Arnulf was strong enough to grant at least a part of Aribo's command to the Engelschalk whom he had backed in 884–5 (see above, p. 116). But because Engelschalk "acted over-boldly towards the leading men of Bavaria in the matters entrusted to him",[8] he was seized in Arnulf's palace in Regensburg and blinded by their judgement, without being brought before the king; there then followed a purge of Engelschalk's relatives. The point is not so much the refusal of the other Bavarian nobles to accept Engelschalk; such appointments were always tricky and the circle of those who were eligible was small. It is rather the quasi-judicial way in which Engelschalk was dealt with by his enemies under Arnulf's nose, and this not in some distant border region but in the heart of the kingdom. What is also characteristic is the way in which the Moravian duke was involved. Not only had Engelschalk returned from exile in Moravia; his brother William's first reaction on hearing of Engelschalk's execution was apparently to send messengers to Zwentibald of Moravia. When at the end of the reign Aribo and his son Isanrich in their turn fell out of favour with Arnulf, Isanrich was also able to seek help from the Moravians. It is a pattern we find elsewhere in the Carolingian empire (for example in the relations between the Widonid margraves on the Breton

8. *Annales Fuldenses*, s.a. 893, p. 122.

border and the Breton dukes) and we shall meet it again in the Ottonian empire; it should make us cautious about thinking of relations between the east Frankish elite and the Slavs further east only in terms of fire, sword and *Drang nach Osten.*

Lotharingia was not a march in quite the same sense that Pannonia was, but it was subject to the same kinds of outside influence. Both Rudolf of Burgundy and Wido of Italy had tried to claim it in 888, and Rudolf at least still dabbled in Lotharingian politics even after he had come to terms with Arnulf. The west Frankish rulers also showed increasing interest in it from 893 onwards, especially after Odo's death in 898 had left Charles the Simple with no rival at home. In effect this was a rerun of the disputes which had followed the death of Lothar II, though Lotharingia was less rich in fiscal lands than it had been a generation earlier. The main difference was that whereas in 869–70 and again in 879–80 the fate of Lotharingia could still be decided over the heads of its leading men, after 888 this was no longer possible. When Arnulf wanted to grant Lotharingia as a sub-kingdom to his illegitimate son Zwentibald in 894, he could not at first get the Lotharingians' agreement. Only in the following year was Zwentibald accepted, and he never wholly established his authority there. After 898 especially, when he broke with his main supporter Reginar, an ancestor of the later dukes of Lotharingia, his position was seriously weakened, and in the last year of Arnulf's reign he was in effect abandoned by the eastern Franks as the price to be paid for their keeping Lotharingia at all. On Arnulf's death the Lotharingians accepted Louis the Child as king, and Zwentibald, who tried to keep his position by force, was killed in battle against the supporters of his half-brother in August 900. Arnulf's ability to direct events here was limited; at best he could act as a kind of mediator, as in 897 when he reconciled Zwentibald with a hostile Lotharingian noble kindred, the Matfridings, at an assembly in Worms.

Arnulf was around forty when he began to rule, which was old by Carolingian standards, and from 896 on he was scarcely an effective ruler. Up until then he had been able to preserve the east Frankish hegemony within the Frankish kingdoms which had existed at least since the battle of Andernach and the death of Charles the Bald, but it was a hegemony *ad personam*, not one on which the east Frankish elites depended or for which they were willing to fight. When Arnulf died on December 8 899 there was no doubt that he would be succeeded without challenge in east Francia by his son, even though Louis was aged only six. Equally, there was little doubt that Louis would be merely an east Frankish king, and that the era of Frankish togetherness was coming to an end.

LOUIS THE CHILD AND CONRAD I

German historians interested in pinpointing the emergence of Germany have examined all the royal accessions between 888 and 936 but have paid least attention to the succession of Louis the Child in 900, though in many ways it is the most remarkable of all. Arnulf had tried as early as 889 to settle the succession by getting the east Frankish magnates to acknowledge his two illegitimate sons Zwentibald and Ratold as his successors. They agreed reluctantly, so long as no legitimate heir should be born to Arnulf. We have only a brief annalistic note of this to go on, and it is not enough for us to decide whether the main objection was to the illegitimacy, or rather to the division of the kingdom. In any event, the birth of Arnulf's legitimate son Louis in 893 changed matters. Zwentibald was provided for by his sub-kingdom in Lotharingia, and Ratold appears briefly as sub-king in Italy in 896 after Arnulf's departure before disappearing from the historical record altogether. According to a late source, Louis was formally accepted as Arnulf's successor in east Francia with oaths of fidelity in 897. The contemporary accounts simply record his succession as if it were quite straightforward, though they note that the Lotharingians accepted him separately. This separate status for Lotharingia (inherent in the fact that the region already had a king, Zwentibald) continued through the reign: Louis maintained a separate "chancery" for Lotharingia, and himself visited it only four times, in each case only for a few weeks. But Louis's accession was anything but straightforward or self-evident. What it meant was that a child of six was acclaimed and crowned as ruler over east Francia, though to the west and south there were adult rulers, both Carolingian and non-Carolingian, available. Two generations earlier this would have been an improbable thing to have happened and it would certainly not have been politically stable. But there is hardly a hint throughout the eleven years of Louis's reign either that the east Frankish magnates considered inviting a ruler from outside or that any outside ruler showed serious interest in east Francia. Nothing could demonstrate more clearly the extent to which the lands which had been ruled over by Louis the German had come to be regarded by their political communities as a single entity, in spite of ethnic differences. There are even some indications of plans for Louis to go to Rome and be crowned emperor as soon as he was old enough, though in the event these came to nothing: the hegemonial tradition did not die completely with Arnulf.

There was – formally at least – no regency, though Archbishop Hatto of Mainz and the king's tutor Bishop Adalbero of Augsburg in practice came near to fulfilling this role; as later during the minorities of Otto III and Henry IV, there was a tacit agreement to behave as if the king were a real king. Charters – seventy-eight more or less genuine ones have survived from Louis's reign – were issued in Louis's name as if he were an adult king, and like an adult king he authenticated the charters by completing the monogram of his name at the bottom. The only slight indication in the charters that things were not normal is to be found in the very large numbers of magnates, secular and ecclesiastical, listed as "intervening", that is, as supporting and consenting to the transaction recorded in the charter. A royal charter was, after all, supposed to carry weight of its own; its authority was in theory unchallengeable and certainly not dependent on anyone else's consent to its content. But these intervention-lists also show that Louis was not merely a nominal ruler but was positively recognized throughout east Francia; at least until 909 the leading men of Saxony, Alemannia and Bavaria as well as the Conradines and the bishops of Mainz, Augsburg and Constance are found as interveners in the charters. The need for kingship and the respect paid to it can be seen above all in the way in which the Conradines dealt with their rivals and enemies in 906, the Matfridings in Lotharingia and the Babenberger in Franconia, namely by formal trials in the king's court. Only in the last year and a half of Louis's reign, after the defeat of the combined east Frankish forces by the Magyars, does his kingship seem to have lost its authority and cohesive force, and this is perhaps only a reflection of the illness which led to his death on September 24 911 at the age of eighteen. Nevertheless, it was in Louis's reign that two of the most crucial elements of the politics of the following decades became visible. The first was the emergence of Magyar raiders as a major threat from without. The second was the appearance of political leaders who seemingly have exercised authority over areas larger than counties but smaller than kingdoms, areas with something like their own political community and traditions: the so-called stem-dukes. It is to these two developments, and to the possible links betwen them, that we must now turn.

The Magyars arrived on the scene at about the same time as

Arnulf defeated the Vikings at the battle of the Dyle. There is an isolated notice of a raid by them on east Francia in 863, and another of a battle fought against them by the Bavarians near Vienna in 881, but their continuous appearance in the sources starts in the early 890s. This is evidently no coincidence; they were used as mercenaries by Arnulf against the Moravians in 892, and by the Byzantines against the Bulgars in 894. The Byzantines soon reached an agreement with the Bulgars, leaving the Magyars to their fate; they were defeated by the Bulgars and shortly afterwards driven from their current homeland by the Pechenegs. By 896 Magyar settlement of the Carpathian basin had begun. They spared the east Frankish kingdom, apart from one raid on Pannonia, during Arnulf's lifetime. Tenth-century writers thought that this was because Arnulf had come to an agreement with them, and it would appear from a contemporary letter of the archbishop of Salzburg that the Moravians thought so too.[9] It may even have been with Arnulf's agreement, or at any rate connivance, that the first major Magyar raid on the west, that on Italy in 899, took place. Arnulf had no reason to be friendly towards Berengar.

The political economy of the Magyars, even more than that of the Franks, required the raiding of and exaction of tribute from the countries around them; the proceeds kept the nomadic warrior aristocracy and their followers in the style to which they wished to remain accustomed. Like Vikings, they were highly mobile; unlike Vikings, they fought from horseback and made extensive use of archery, which made them dangerous to all except well-armed opponents. Nevertheless, they were not invincible; it was possible to defeat them once they had been forced to stand and fight. As with the Vikings, their relations with the peoples they raided were more complex than might be expected; they acted as mercenaries on more than one occasion, and traded as well as raided. Though both contemporary and later writers offered any number of atrocity stories, the reality is probably better seen in a notice found in several sets of annals for the year 903, which records how the Bavarians invited the Magyars to a banquet and then murdered their leaders; shared banquets hardly imply unbridgeable cultural differences between Bavarians and Magyars, even though the Bavarian aristocracy were not nomadic and their preferred fighting tactics were rather different.

9. Liutprand, *Antapodosis* I 13, pp. 15–16; *Magnae Moraviae fontes historici* 3, Brno 1969, 263–4.

At first the Magyars seem to have been viewed as much as anything else as a handy weapon against the Moravians. Following the death of Zwentibald of Moravia in 894 civil war broke out there, and the Bavarians exploited this for some years. It was not until the Moravian empire had been virtually destroyed by Magyar attacks and the Pannonian march devastated that the Franks realized their mistake, and even then they were confident that they could deal with the threat. Within the space of ten years it was to be made clear that they could not. Already in 899 the Magyars had inflicted a major defeat on an Italian army at the battle of the Brenta; between 907 and 910 no fewer than three east Frankish armies lost pitched battles against the Magyars. In 907 the *dux* of the Bavarians, Liutpold, was killed at Preßburg [Bratislava] together with Archbishop Theotmar of Salzburg, Bishops Zachary of Säben and Uto of Freising, and numerous counts; in 908 Burchard, the commander of the Sorbian march, was killed together with a count Egino and Bishop Rudolf of Würzburg; and in 910 an attempt by Louis the Child to collect an army from the whole of east Francia ended in disaster when the Magyars inflicted severe defeats on the Frankish and Alemannic contingents, killing their leaders, the Conradine Gebhard of Lotharingia and a prominent Aleman count, Gozbert. The losses of fighting men (always a commodity in short supply) in these battles must have been substantial, for in the next decade and a half the Magyars were able to raid east Francia more or less with impunity. Only in 913 did a combined Bavarian and Alemannic army defeat the Magyars, but this did not compensate for or prevent raids which now extended right into Suabia and Burgundy as well as into Thuringia and Saxony.

Yet the battles show that the east Frankish elite had grasped the correct strategy for discouraging the invaders – to make the price and the risk so high that they would prefer to raid elsewhere – and also that they were confident that they could carry it out: ninth-century war leaders were cautious about giving battle unless they were sure either that the odds were heavily in their favour or that they could not avoid it. The remarkable thing about the defeats of 899–910 was the fact that it was in each case the Franks who forced battle. Preßburg in particular was evidently an attempt to attack the Magyars on their own home ground. Unfortunately we do not know enough about the battles to know why the Franks so misjudged their chances. It was perhaps because there were also numerous Magyar defeats, though these seem to have been on a smaller scale. The most successful tactics were deployed by the Bavarians after Preßburg under their new *dux* Arnulf: buy off the Magyars with tribute payments most of the time – the Magyars seem to have kept their side of such bargains well – and attack them should a favourable opportunity present itself. This was to be the recipe for the Liudolfings' ultimate success.

In September 908, a year after the disaster at Preßburg, Arnulf, the son of the *dux* Liutpold who had led the Bavarian army and been killed in the battle, confirmed an exchange of lands between Bishop Drakolf of Freising and the chorbishop Conrad of Freising. The exchange was recorded in a charter, which may have been issued at the time or perhaps somewhat later. The layout of the charter resembled that of a royal diploma, so far as one can judge (the original has not survived and we know the text only from copies); in particular, the charter began with a solemn invocation of the Trinity, and a statement of Arnulf's title: "by the ordination of divine providence *dux* of the Bavarians and even of the adjacent regions". The charter was addressed to "all bishops, counts and princes of this kingdom (*regni huius*)".[10] Here we have the essence of the so-called tribal duchy, the *jüngeres Stammesherzogtum* of German scholarship ("younger" by contrast with the "older" tribal duchies such as that of the Agilolfings in Bavaria). On the one hand, Arnulf is not a king: the clerk who drew up the charter for him entitles him *dux*. On the other hand, he behaves like a king. He exercises a royal prerogative in confirming an exchange of lands between ecclesiastical institutions. He makes the confirmation known to the magnates – counts, bishops and princes – of a "kingdom". He clearly sees himself as ruling over this kingdom, and he owes his position not to any human act but to the "ordination of divine providence", a phrase modelled closely on the titles used by Carolingian kings in their diplomata. Yet if Arnulf in or after 908 claimed to rule in Bavaria by the grace of God, contemporaries could easily have traced his rule to human acts, for Arnulf's father Liutpold had been appointed margrave of the Bavarians in 895 by his relative, King Arnulf, following the disgrace of Count Engildeo.

Conditions in Bavaria are rather better documented than those elsewhere in the east Frankish kingdom, but Arnulf is by no means an isolated phenomenon. In Saxony the position of the Liudolfing Otto (d. 912) and his son Henry was comparable to that of Arnulf,

10. Reindel 1953: 77, no. 48.

and indeed Liudolfing power in Saxony was longer established, going back at least to the mid ninth century when a Liudolf was *dux* in Ostfalia and the brother-in-law of Louis the Younger. Already in the 890s and 900s the Liudolfings were anticipating their royal successors and establishing tributary status over Slav tribes, in particular the Daleminzi. In Suabia there were two noble kin-groups claiming a pre-eminent position. The Hunfriding Burchard, "count and prince of the Alemans"[11] was executed in 911 and there was at least an attempt to exile his relatives and confiscate their lands. Erchanger, the leader of the other kin-group, revolted against Conrad I in 913–4, was acclaimed *dux* after his defeat of his rivals at Wahlwies in 915, condemned for rebellion at the synod of Hohenaltheim in 916 and executed in 917. After his execution, Burchard, the son of the Burchard killed in 911, became duke. In Lotharingia the Conradine Gebhard is described in a royal diploma of 903 as "duke of the kingdom which by many is called that of Lothar";[12] after his death in battle against the Magyars in 910 we find first Zwentibald's opponent Reginar and then Reginar's son Gilbert as dukes. The situation in central Germany is more complex. Thuringia was a march, held from 880 to 892 by the Babenberger Poppo, then briefly by the Conradine Conrad and then by a Burchard (the name suggests a Suabian connection) until his death in 908. After that references to it cease, and it is only in a notice of Burchard's death that he is called *dux*. Nearer the Rhine both the Conradines and the Babenberger held powerful positions. The leading Babenberger (Poppo and Henry) appear as *dux* only elsewhere, however: Poppo in Thuringia and Henry as leader of the east Frankish forces in the 880s. The Conradines (Conrad the Elder, killed in 906, Conrad, who became king in 911, and his brother Eberhard, killed in 939) were at first only intermittently titled *dux*; only under Eberhard in the reign of Henry I did their position become clearer. During the reign of Louis the Child there was a murderous feud between the Conradines and the Babenberger, which was conducted with full-scale warfare and ended with the deaths of two leading members of the Conradine family, followed by the execution of the Babenberger Adalbert and the breaking of Babenberger power in central Germany in 906. One should note the similarities with events in Suabia (executions and proscriptions following public trials, alternating with warfare). The differences lay

11. *Annales Alemannici*, MGH SS 1, 55.
12. D Louis the Child 20 for St Gallen.

in the heterogeneity of central Germany, plus the fact that Conrad, the leading surviving Conradine and winner of the feud, himself became king in 911; these things, coupled with the losses the feud brought with it, combined to retard the development of ducal power in Franconia.

The phrase "ducal power" of course begs a question. To say that Arnulf was by no means isolated and point to the parallels in the other regions of Germany is not to prove that all early tenth-century references to dukes refer to exactly the same phenomenon. The new dukes were also not always called *dux*, either by themselves or by others; in particular, the royal chancery tended to stick to *comes* (count) as a title. In the narrative sources for the ninth century there are numerous occurrences of *duces*, but here the word almost invariably simply means military leader. It would be methodologically very questionable to suppose that this meaning had ceased to exist or to be used in the early tenth century: was Liutpold a *dux* or a duke at Preßburg? On the other hand, it would also be questionable to draw a sharp distinction between military leaders and dukes exercising more permanent and general political power, for if one thing is certain about the early middle ages in general and ninth- and tenth-century east Francia in particular it is that military leadership and political power went hand in hand.

We can perhaps get a better idea of what was involved by looking at the differences and similarities in the positions of the men named in the preceding paragraph. In all cases we can point to royal appointment, either of these men themselves or of their ancestors, to offices which formed the basis of their later power. Most of them also came from families connected by marriage to the Carolingians. Thus the Liudolfings are first found as military leaders in Ostfalia and as the brothers-in-law of Louis the Younger; both the Conradines and the Liutpoldings were related by marriage to Arnulf of Carinthia; and Reginar and Gilbert were almost certainly descended from the Gilbert, count of the Maasgau in the second quarter of the ninth century, who had kidnapped and married a daughter of Lothar I in 846. Characteristic of all these men was that they appeared at the head of a people, and that they seem to have had within the territory of their people a position which was no longer a matter of royal appointment, or not alone. This perhaps needs some qualification. Lotharingia, for example, was not an ethnic region with its own law and deep-rooted sense of ethnic identity in the same way as Saxony or Bavaria were. Suabia showed a marked division between the Alemannic north and the Roman south (Raetia);

Alemannia was in any case not so much of a historical unity as Bavaria had been, and this was perhaps reflected in the lack of consensus about who the Alemannic/Suabian *dux* should be. Nor did all the peoples have such a leader. Thuringia had no known *dux* after Burchard's death in 908, though the Thuringians did not cease to exist as an ethnic group. Frisia, by contrast, never had one, apart perhaps from the Viking leaders established there in the ninth century.

Within their territories these men enjoyed a quasi-regal position. They summoned and led armies. Certainly in Bavaria and Suabia, and probably also in Lotharingia and Saxony, they held assemblies. The evidence for their having struck coins is patchy, but the Bavarian dukes at least seem to have done so. Their control over the church varied. Arnulf appears to have appointed to the bishoprics within Bavaria, which was a stage further than any of the other dukes got. True, no Saxon bishops appeared at the synod of Hohenaltheim, and it is a plausible inference that Henry of Saxony forbade them to attend, but so far as we know he had not appointed any of them. Nor do the Suabian dukes appear to have done so; indeed, Erchanger's initial rebellion and ultimate downfall were closely linked to his attempts to gain control over the bishopric of Constance. In Lotharingia Gilbert tried to appoint to Liège in 920, but he was not successful. All the dukes, however, controlled the royal monasteries in their territories to a sufficient extent to be able to confiscate their lands and grant them out to their followers. Again, Arnulf had a particularly bad later reputation, especially for his dealings with the monasteries of Tegernsee and Benedictbeuern, but Gilbert of Lotharingia is known to have taken lands from Remiremont, Henry of Saxony from Hersfeld, and Burchard II of Suabia from St Gallen.

It is perhaps not surprising that there has been so much debate over the nature and origins of the new duchies, since in their formative phase these are far from clear. It is evident that the dukes filled a political niche, not just in the sense that they enhanced their own power and that of their families, but also in that within a very short time the idea became established that certain territories needed a duke. What that meant exactly was still to be settled; all that was certain was that the relation between king and dukes (and between kingdom and duchies) as found in the first third of the tenth century was not a stable one and was likely to change in one direction or another. One possibility was that the ducal territories would become quite distinct small kingdoms; another was that the east Frankish kingdom would come to resemble the Frankish empire after the treaty of Verdun, with a sense among its peoples of belonging together, but with a political organization in separate units; a third was that the duchies would either cease to exist or become offices to which kings appointed. In the event it was the third possibility which prevailed; but it was accompanied by traces of the first and second.

The question of origins is a more complex one. Clearly there was an "ethnic" component in the new duchies, but they were not the result of a striving for ethnic independence. Even Arnulf of Bavaria was hardly a mere representative of Bavarian separatism. On the surface there would seem to have been an obvious link between the emergence of regional leaders and the Magyar threat; it can be explained as the east Frankish version of what happened in west Francia under the impact of Viking incursions in the ninth century. There, the speed and mobility of the invaders had led, it is held, to a loss of royal authority and an enhancing of the position of the powers on the spot since quick decisions and responses were needed. Unfortunately things are not as simple as that. The Frankish kingdoms were indeed gradually divided up into military commands under margraves, but it was the kings themselves who made the divisions; they were not the result of spontaneous self-help. Moreover, any campaigning against the invaders which aimed at long-term results against them needed kings to do it; only they carried the authority which could cement together an army drawn from several regions whose component parts had no inherent loyalty to or trust in one another. The Carolingians might leave punitive raiding or tribute-collecting to generals, but for serious fighting they had to take the field themselves, and their opponents took the kings they had to face very seriously. Louis the German's reputation was thought to be enough to keep Vikings off, while Arnulf's defeat of the Great Army at the battle of the Dyle in 891 did much for the security of the kingdom (compare the effects of Alfred's victory at Edington in 878). A six-year-old king could not provide such things. At least for Bavaria and Saxony the dukes might be seen not as alternatives to royal power but as substitutes for it. The margraves who took quasi-regal power in these regions provided points of cohesion for a local political community – one whose existence went back to the east Frankish sub-kingdoms of the mid ninth century. Here the threat from Slavs and Magyars was at its clearest, and the need for a substitute for a kingship temporarily not available at its strongest. In Suabia and Franconia matters were less clear-cut, while in Lotharingia a "separatist" element is clearly visible (though here, too, principally as background to aristocratic feuding).

On Louis the Child's death there were no remaining Carolingians, legitimate or illegitimate, in east Francia. The only Carolingians of any kind available were Louis the Blind, king in Provence, and Charles the Simple, king in west Francia. By now, however, there were enough precedents from elsewhere in the Frankish empire for choosing non-Carolingians for this not to be too great a hurdle, especially as there was an obvious choice in Conrad, *dux* in Franconia. Widukind of Corvey tells us that Otto of Saxony was offered the crown and refused on the grounds of age, advising instead that Conrad should be chosen, but this should be taken as panegyric rather than history.[13] The Conradines had established themselves well. They had made all the right moves in the medieval game of rising dynasties: they were the deceased king's cousins; they had established a substantial lordship in Franconia, Thuringia and south-eastern Saxony, as well as having connections with Lotharingia; they had eliminated their closest rivals, the Babenberger; and they had the support of the primate, Hatto of Mainz. They were also indubitably Frankish, which may have made them seem more acceptable than other possible contenders; in 919 and 936 the Frankish elements of kingship were to be stressed even though the king was no longer a Frank. The election of Conrad I at Forchheim in early November by "Franks, Saxons, Alemans and Bavarians"[14] was therefore no great surprise: either someone had to be king, or else the Franks, Saxons, Alemans and Bavarians all needed kings of their own. The question was rather what was expected of the new ruler, and what he could make of his new dignity.

What Conrad did was to try by force to get all the other great magnates to accept his authority. Lotharingia is missing from the above list, and indeed the Lotharingians chose to accept Charles the Simple of west Francia as king; this was not so much an expression of Carolingian legitimism as of the rivalry between Reginarids and Conradines in Lotharingia during the preceeding two decades. Three expeditions to Lotharingia in 912–13 failed to secure Conrad's recognition there, and from 913 Conrad's relations with the leading men of the south worsened. Arnulf and Erchanger were closely related (Arnulf's mother Kunigunde was Erchanger's sister) and the two campaigned together against the Hungarians in 913. Conrad had

13. Widukind I 16, pp. 26–7.
14. *Annales Alemannici*, MGH SS 1, 55.

tried to ally himself with the two families by himself marrying Kunigunde, but hostilities deepened, perhaps as a result of Erchanger's attacks on the bishopric of Constance. Conrad was able to drive Arnulf and Erchanger out of their duchies, but Erchanger soon returned, defeated his opponents in Suabia and had himself proclaimed *dux* on the battlefield. In the same year, 915, Conrad's brother Eberhard was defeated by Henry of Saxony, which marked the beginning of Liudolfing expansion at Conradine expense in the border regions of Ostfalia and Thuringia. Conrad launched a counter-attack but rather than driving Henry into exile seems to have reached a truce with him: there are no reports of further hostilities or even of contacts for the remaining years of the reign. Conrad's position remained weak, however. At an ecclesiastical council held in 916 at Hohenaltheim, near the border between Bavaria and Franconia, which was attended by a papal legate and the bishops from the whole of east Francia except Saxony, the bishops laid down severe penalties for opposition to the king; they condemned Berthold and Erchanger and summoned Arnulf of Bavaria to answer the charges against him at a later council. Conrad was here given impressive backing – at least, so it seemed; but it brought him little. True, Berthold and Erchanger were executed in 917, but this did not increase Conrad's authority in Suabia; it simply meant that Burchard's son Burchard became duke there. Nor was Arnulf of Bavaria more easily coerced. He was briefly forced into exile but soon returned, and it was on an expedition against him that Conrad was defeated in 918 and received a wound which was to lead to his early death. Conrad could not rule over the dukes; in the last resort he needed to rule with and through them, and he was unable, and perhaps unwilling, to find the necessary symbols and forms of action to do so and preserve everyone's face. Nor had he been able to provide the kind of successful military leadership against the Magyars which could have given his rule a greater degree of acceptance; indeed, there is no record of his having taken part in dealing with any of the Magyar incursions of his reign. The Magyar defeat of 913 gave the two southern duchies some respite (Arnulf was even able to seek temporary asylum with them), but further north there were damaging raids in 916 (reaching as far as Saxony) and 918.

On his death-bed in 918 Conrad is said to have designated Henry of Saxony as his successor rather than his own brother Eberhard, saying, according to Widukind, that the Conradines possessed everything necessary for kingship except *fortuna et mores* (luck and a suitable character).[15] Widukind may here simply have been adopting the vocabulary of his literary model Sallust, or he may have had specific notions of *Königsheil* (the magical property of a successful king which ensures prosperity of all kinds for his kingdom) in mind, but we may take the judgement quite happily on twentieth-century terms. Unlike his successors Henry and Otto, Conrad had not had the kind of luck which was essential for establishing the authority and charisma of a new ruler. And he had not been flexible. Encouraged above all by ecclesiastics – in particular Hatto and Heriger of Mainz and Solomon III of Constance – who still had firmly Carolingian ideas about kingship and wanted a quick response to their demands for protection, he had attempted to re-establish kingship as it had been under Louis the German, when margraves, however powerful, were still subject to royal control and deposition, and when a great gulf was set between kings and others. Conrad's own position in central Germany was testimony to how fast things had changed between Arnulf's illness in 896 and his own accession. The clock could not be put back overnight, and not at all by the direct application of force. Henry I and Otto I were to demonstrate how to do it.

HENRY OF SAXONY AND ARNULF OF BAVARIA

Following Conrad's death in December 918 there was an interregnum which lasted until May 919. At an assembly at Fritzlar in that month the Frankish magnates chose Henry I to be king, an election which was greeted by the Franks and Saxons present at the assembly – no Bavarians or Suabians are known to have attended – with acclamation. Some time during the same year, whether before or after the events at Fritzlar we do not know, Arnulf of Bavaria was made king. Though Arnulf soon submitted formally to Henry I, and did not use a royal title, he remained king in all but name within the confines of Bavaria until his death in 937. He acquired a bad reputation in later Bavarian sources as a despoiler of monasteries, while the major narrative sources for the 920s and 930s were written considerably after the events from a position favourable to the Liudolfing–Ottonian dynasty. These things, coupled with the fact

15. Widukind I 25, pp. 37–8.

that Bavaria did not in the end go its own way and was indeed incorporated into the Ottonian kingdom, have made it easy to see Arnulf as an over-powerful magnate. Not all contemporaries viewed him like this, however – a fragmentary narrative from Regensburg writes scathingly of the unjustified attacks by Conrad and Henry upon Arnulf and praises Arnulf in terms appropriate for a king[16] – and nor should we take a view which anticipates later developments.

A further point may be made at the start both about Henry and about Arnulf: we know very little about their enemies. It is as certain as anything can be that in spite of their powerful positions in Saxony and Bavaria respectively they were not without opposition there: the contrast between their unchallenged dominance and the struggles of the Hunfridings in Suabia or the Conradines in Franconia is more apparent than real. Both came from families whose rise had occurred within living memory, and both certainly had feuds to conduct with other aristocratic families. In Saxony we have some idea of who these other families were: the counts of Merseburg, the ancestors of the Billungs and of the counts of Walbeck and Stade, as well as a large kindred which was to play a prominent role in subsequent decades and which claimed the Saxon leader Widukind as its founding ancestor – this included the historian Widukind of Corvey and Henry I's second wife Mathilda. We can see Henry's friendships with members of these kindreds in entries in *libri memoriales*, but the conflicts in and between the kindreds are hardly visible before the time of Otto I. The position for Arnulf is even less favourable – though it is worth noting that the end of Liutpolding independence in 937–8 was apparently marked by a division within the Liutpolding family itself. Some at least of the descendants of Margrave Aribo, an important kindred in tenth- and eleventh-century Bavaria, were probably unhappy about the Liutpoldings' dominant role in Bavaria. In general, though, the micro-politics of this period are scarcely visible. An account of Germany under Henry I has to confine itself very largely to the dealings of Henry and the dukes with one another and with the outside world – Slavs, Magyars, kings of Italy, Burgundy and western Francia. It is well to remember from the beginning that this is a foreshortening.

Arnulf's election is the harder of the two to interpret. We know from Liutprand of Cremona that he was chosen king, but the most precise account is given by Salzburg annals which now survive only

16. *Fragmentum de Arnulfo duce*, MGH SS 17, 570.

in excerpts copied in the twelfth century. These say: "The Bavarians again submitted themselves freely to Duke Arnulf and made him to rule in the kingdom of the Teutons."[17] There are several difficulties here – in what sense did the Bavarians need to reaffirm their loyalty to Arnulf, for example? – but the main problem is the phrase *regnare eum fecerunt in regno Teutonicorum*. The "kingdom of the Teutons" is a term which became common only in the late eleventh century; if this instance is not in any case the result of an alteration by the twelfth-century copyist (which still seems the most likely assumption after two decades of close scholarly scrutiny of the Admont manuscript and its scribes), it is quite isolated, and it is not easy to say what Arnulf and his magnates, who would not have spoken or thought in Latin, might have envisaged or how they could have formulated the notion of a German kingdom. Nor is there any indication that Arnulf at any point claimed to rule over anything other than Bavaria – except perhaps those parts of eastern Franconia which were sometimes seen as part of Bavaria: it is presumably from here that the "eastern Franks" mentioned by Liutprand came. A Bavarian kingdom would seem the most natural thing to rule over for someone who, as we have seen, regarded himself as "duke by the grace of God of the Bavarians and adjacent provinces".[18]

At Fritzlar, Henry of Saxony was chosen king in the kingdom of the eastern Franks. Bavarians and Suabians may not have been present, but there can be no doubt that Henry and his electors thought in terms of the kingdom ruled by Arnulf and Louis the Child. It is significant that Henry, though himself a Saxon, was first of all elected by the *Frankish* magnates. Equally significant is the fact that immediately following his election he set out to compel the south German dukes to recognize him. Yet Henry did not simply take up the tradition set by his predecessor. The long delay between Conrad's death and Henry's election was presumably filled by negotiations, of which we can see only the results. The first of these was that Eberhard of Franconia, Conrad I's brother and heir and Henry's old rival, submitted to Henry and became his "friend" and vassal. The second was that at the king-making ceremony Henry was offered unction by Archbishop Heriger of Mainz but refused it. It is probable that both developments should be taken together. It is admittedly difficult to interpret the refusal of unction with certainty,

17. MGH SS 30, 742; on the reading of the text see Beumann in Beumann and Schröder 1978: 317–65 with plate.
18. Above, n. 10.

since we do not know how far it had been customary in the east Frankish kingdom. It is unlikely that it should be interpreted in terms of Henry's mistrust of "clericalizing" his kingship by making it seem too dependent on episcopal anointing. What may have played a role was Liudolfing mistrust of the archbishops of Mainz. This went back at least as far as territorial rivalries in Thuringia in the time of Louis the Child and Conrad I, if not further. For a king whose power-base lay in Saxony there were additional elements. Henry I and Otto I as kings were in much the same position with Mainz as Offa of Mercia had been with Canterbury in the eighth century: their metropolitan see lay outside the territory of their own people. However, this is certainly not the whole story. Unction had become traditional elsewhere within the Frankish empire as a means of consolidating an otherwise weak claim to rule or rule in a new kingdom, and it was presumably for this reason that Conrad I was anointed in 911. Henry's need for unction was certainly no less than Conrad's; if he refused it, then he probably did so as a signal (a spontaneous gesture is hardly likely) to other magnates, and in particular to the quasi-regal dukes in Lotharingia, Franconia, Suabia and Bavaria, that he was not by his royal title claiming to be something quite different from them.

Such an interpretation fits well with Henry's relations with Conrad's brother Eberhard, and with his first actions in southern Germany. In the year of his accession he moved against Burchard of Suabia, who was himself under attack by Rudolf II of Burgundy, and secured his submission; in 921 Arnulf of Bavaria submitted and became Henry's "friend". Both dukes retained a princely status: they controlled the church within their duchy (in Arnulf's case this included episcopal appointments), they held assemblies, and they acted beyond the borders of the kingdom of the eastern Franks apparently without consulting Henry. Lotharingia took longer: the Lotharingians were at first no more inclined to accept Henry than they had been to accept Conrad, but increasingly they became unwilling to accept Charles the Simple either. In 920 Gilbert seems to have planned for a time to set himself up as an independent ruler (whether or not with the title of king is unclear). He dropped the plan, but Lotharingia was caught up in the war between Charles the Simple and Rudolf over the west Frankish kingship. As Arnulf had done, Henry intervened in west Frankish politics in support of the rival claimants. Although, unlike Arnulf, he did not act as an overlord, he intervened for the same reason: to protect the east Frankish position in Lotharingia. From 923 onwards, and especially after 925, Lotharingia slowly came under his control, and the extent of the cooperation between Henry and the Conradines was shown by the fact that Eberhard was sent to Lotharingia with an army in 925 to secure east Frankish overlordship and make peace between the various parties. As it turned out, this incorporation of Lotharingia into the east Frankish kingdom was to prove a lasting one, though no one could have foreseen this at the time, and the fact that the west Frankish rulers never again regained control over it did not make Ottonian and Salian rule there secure. From 928 Gilbert, married to Henry's daughter Gerberga, ruled in Lotharingia as duke; the relation between Gilbert and Henry, one of *amicitia*, resembled that between Henry and Eberhard or Arnulf.

Characteristic of all these submissions is that they represented relations between more or less equals and expressed this openly. The terms used repeatedly in the sources are "friend" and "friendship" – terms by no means clear-cut but not devoid of content either. The forms used were ones which enabled all sides to preserve face. Henry was acknowledged as king, so long as he did not try to act as one directly within the duchies, while the dukes kept their authority within the duchy by appearing almost on a level with the king. Such relationships of *amicitia* were not confined to dukes; Henry had "friendships" with bishops and other magnates, particularly the Saxon ones. The arrangement was a flexible one. There is no question of any of the parties having intended a permanent "federalism". Rather they chose forms which were convenient to both sides at the time. Already by the end of Henry I's reign his "friendships" with the dukes were perhaps not quite the same as they had been at the beginning, and the changes under Otto I were to be still more marked. But at the beginning of Henry's reign no other form of rule was thinkable. As an unfriendly Bavarian writer put it, Henry in coming to Bavaria was presuming to tread "where neither he nor his ancestors held a foot of land".[19] Whether or not the Carolingian fisc was still a going concern in the southern and western duchies (or in Franconia for that matter), it was not a going concern for Henry, and without it he could do little outside the regions where he himself was well endowed. Conrad's reign had shown that it was possible to expel dukes from their duchies (with luck) but also that this was no solution. What could be done can be seen in the instructive episode of the Suabian duchy in 926 after

19. MGH SS 17, 570.

Burchard II had been killed in northern Italy in the course of an expedition in support of his son-in-law, Rudolf of Burgundy. At an assembly at Worms Henry was able to install Hermann, a cousin of Eberhard of Franconia. On the one hand, Henry was here able to treat the dukedom of Suabia as an office. The decision was made neither in Suabia nor by the Suabians (though it is possible that some were consulted). Hermann was not noticeably related to Burchard, nor had he or his ancestors held "a foot of land" in Suabia. He was not a Suabian, and owed his position to royal appointment; and this was an appointment to control over what was left of the fisc in Suabia, not to Burchard's private property, which went to his own kin. On the other hand, Henry could evidently not simply abolish the ducal office and re-establish himself as ruler in Suabia in the same sense that, say, Charles III had been ruler there, though his triumphal visit to the area around Lake Constance in 929–30 certainly marked an increase in royal control and power in Suabia. There had to be a duke; and Hermann married Burchard's widow as if to consolidate his legitimacy, a pattern found more than once in the tenth century. Hermann was not Henry's creature, though he was in the event to remain loyal to Otto I during the conflicts of 937–41; his appointment made the Conradines at least as powerful in terms of land and followings as Henry himself.

Earlier historians saw the importance of Henry's reign above all in his careful military planning which culminated in the defeat of the Magyars at Riade (location uncertain; somewhere in northern Thuringia) in 933, and this interpretation goes back to Widukind, who depicts Henry's reign as ending in glory after his great victory; as with Otto I at the Lechfeld, Widukind makes Henry's troops acclaim him emperor on the battlefield, after which all Henry has to do is to order the succession and plan a pilgrimage to Rome. Yet it is precisely the fact that this is Widukind's interpretation that should make us sceptical. It is not that Widukind invented or fantasized, but rather that he pursued clear literary purposes, including that of drawing parallels between the reigns of Henry I and his son Otto with the intention of exalting the son. A victory there undoubtedly was; other writers, including Flodoard of Rheims, mention it (Flodoard, unlike Widukind, records the presence of Bavarian contingents).[20] It is equally certain that it did not stop Magyar raiding, and Widukind's account of the battle makes it clear that it

---

20. Widukind I 38, pp. 55–7; Flodoard, *Annales*, ed. P. Lauer (Paris 1905), p. 54.

was above all a psychological victory: the Magyars refused to fight. What is most difficult is to see how Henry achieved it. Widukind describes Henry's strategy precisely enough.[21] The Magyars defeated a Saxon army in the first year of the reign, and again in 924, but the capture of a Magyar princeling enabled Henry to conduct ransom negotiations with the Magyars. A truce was agreed for nine years, perhaps in 926. Henry was to pay the Magyars tribute and in return the Magyars agreed not to raid the east Frankish kingdom. Henry took advantage of the breathing space to reorganize the Saxon army. At an assembly in that year Henry ordered the building of castles, which were to be manned by what Widukind calls *agrarii milites*, farmer-soldiers, organized in groups of nine. Normally eight would work their fields while the ninth was doing guard-duty in the castle. Only in times of invasion would all nine move to defend the fortification. Once these arrangements were working, it was decided at an assembly in 932 to withhold tribute payments to the Magyars and so break the agreement of 926. This paved the way for the Magyar invasion and the campaign of 933 which ended so gloriously.

Widukind's account presents two kinds of difficulty. The first is the technical one of deciding precisely what Henry did. Attempts to identify the fortifications built on his orders have not been successful. We know of major palaces built or extended under Henry I at Merseburg, Meißen and Quedlinburg, but these had a function which was at least as much representative as military. The fortifications were certainly not manned by peasant warriors. These, the *agrarii milites*, turn out to be equally difficult to pin down. Probably Widukind was thinking of the dependants of his own monastery of Corvey, who, like others similarly placed, were bound to provide labour services for the building of castles and as auxiliaries and servants on local campaigns. The second difficulty in Widukind's account is still more serious: Riade was neither a castle siege nor a battle conducted by peasant soldiers. The Magyar raiders fled before Henry's mounted warriors, as Widukind himself tells us. It would appear that Henry was able to improve the equipment and training of his Saxon following, or to create the conditions in which they could do this themselves. The breathing-space granted by the truce of 926 was used above all to re-establish Saxon domination over the Slavs. Successful campaigns were mounted against the

21. Widukind I 32, 35, 38, pp. 43, 48–54, 55–7.

Hevelli in 928, and then against the Daleminzi and Bohemians in 929. In the same year an attack by the Redarii was driven off, and further offensive campaigns were mounted in the 930s against the Slavs of the Lausitz and the Ucker as well as against a Danish king, Knuba, in the north. Not only did Henry not have to worry for the time being about Hungarian invasions; he does not seem to have had to fear Hungarian support for his Slav opponents, whereas before 924–6 the Daleminzi, for example, seem to have allied themselves with the Hungarians (or paid them tribute) to secure military assistance against the Saxons. The high-point was the re-establishing of Saxon overlordship over Bohemia in 929; and here we can guess that Arnulf of Bavaria had been pursuing very similar tactics, though he had no Widukind to record his successes. A Bavarian campaign in Bohemia is recorded for 922, while Arnulf made his own peace with the Hungarians in 927 (probably on terms similar to those Henry had made, which had a tradition in Bavaria). The Bavarians took part in the campaign of 929 – no doubt Arnulf acted as Henry's *amicus*, but presumably as his rival as well, one who did not want to see Bohemia totally dominated by Saxony. There are grounds for thinking that the rivalries within Bohemia between Wenceslas (the saint-king of legend and Christmas carols) and his brother Boleslav which led to Wenceslas's assassination (in 935?) reflected tensions not just between newly converted Christians and pagans in Bohemia but also between Bohemian aristocratic factions backed by the Bavarian duke and by the Saxon king. But what increasing Slav domination meant for both Henry and Arnulf was an inflow of wealth with which to reward military followings, and the sense of luck and charismatic leadership so necessary for early medieval war-lords.

The battle of Riade may have enhanced Henry's reputation, but it did not create it. Already in the early 920s, in spite of his being a new man, he had been accepted by the more established kings of western Europe. Charles the Simple had met him in 921 at Bonn; both the meeting-place (on the border between the two kingdoms) and the treaty made there established equality between the two rulers. A church council at Coblenz in the following year was attended by bishops from east and west Francia and Lotharingia, the first "pan-Frankish" council since that held at Mainz in 888. Henry's friendship-pact with the rival west Frankish ruler Robert in 923 marked the beginning of the long Ottonian tradition of maintaining good relations with as many of the powerful magnates of west Francia as possible. In 926 Rudolf II of Burgundy came to an assembly at Worms and acknowledged Henry's overlordship and thus the continuation of the relationship between the two kingdoms established by Arnulf, while in 930 Henry was able to marry his oldest son Otto to Edith, the sister of Æthelstan of Wessex. The gifts exchanged in the course of these alliances also helped to establish Henry's prestige. His *amicitia* with Charles the Simple was sealed by a present of relics of St Denis, while that with Rudolf II brought in what was to be one of the most important symbols of east Frankish/German kingship, the Holy Lance. The marriage alliance with Æthelstan not only was accompanied by exchanges of costly gifts, but also established Henry's status as king. It was almost certainly at the same time as the marriage that Otto was designated king by his father. This at least is a plausible interpretation of a diploma of Henry I granting a dowry to his wife Mathilda, one apparently confirmed by admittedly very corrupt annals from Lausanne and by other evidence. Henry's progress through the whole of the kingdom in 929–30, with stays in Franconia, Bavaria, Suabia and Lotharingia, is a further sign of the consolidation of his power. Previously he had hardly moved outside Saxony except when campaigning, but these journeyings were peaceful and were marked by *convivia*, ritual feasts, shared by Henry and his leading men. It is probable that their consent to Otto's succession was given at the same time.

The church councils of this period show a similar rise in Henry's prestige. If Henry's relations with some leading churchmen at the beginning of his reign had been clouded (and this should not be interpreted as an expression of a generally "secular" or anti-ecclesiastical policy), this soon passed. After an interlude Henry set up a royal chapel of his own, and was able on a small scale to draw on the resources of some of the major churches of his kingdom to man it with Frankish and Saxon clerics. Church councils were held at Duisburg in 929 and at Erfurt in 932. For the former we have little more than an agenda (which shows that the cases of a number of leading laymen were dealt with at the synod, as at Hohenaltheim); for the latter we have the conciliar *acta* themselves. These drew in their formulations on the *acta* of the council held at Hohenaltheim in 916, a noteworthy display of continuity. The council's legislation was of less importance than the fact that it existed. More weight should be attached to the occasion for summoning the council – a letter from the doge and patriarch of Venice reporting conspiracies between Jews and Muslims against Christianity in the east and urging a policy of forced baptism or expulsion of the Jews. No response to this is known, but the letter provided a splendid opportunity for Henry to imitate Carolingian rule by summoning a synod to discuss matters of general concern for the welfare of Christendom.

What Henry had achieved was prosperity and stability, based on freedom from Magyar attack and a re-established east Frankish (in particular Saxon) dominance in eastern Europe; his relations with the kings to the west helped to demonstrate these things, but did not create them. The position he had built up did not express itself as power over the other dukes and great men. The dukes were seen more frequently at royal assemblies from about 925–6 onwards, but this reflected relationships of cooperation rather than domination, particularly in the case of Arnulf of Bavaria. Arnulf's rule also profited from stability. Henry's church councils did not imply the full restoration of Carolingian-style kingship within the east Frankish kingdom, for at almost the same time church councils were being held in Bavaria under Arnulf, at Regensburg and again at Dingolfing in 932. The *acta* of these Bavarian synods referred in their dating-clause to the rule of Arnulf, not of Henry; and the synods were attended by the bishop of Eichstätt (a Mainz suffragan), and so were something more than provincial councils of the archbishops of Salzburg. The fact that the two rulers held synods so close together in time is perhaps neither a coincidence nor an indication of rivalry – there is a parallel in Arnulf's separate truce with the Magyars which was made in 927, shortly after the one Henry had concluded. It is not inconceivable in both cases that what we are seeing is concerted action (with comparatively light overtones of rivalry, as in the Bohemian campaign of 929). Further indications of such amicable dualism can be seen at the end of Arnulf's career. At the height of Henry's power and influence in 933 Arnulf was able to campaign in Italy at the invitation of some north Italian aristocrats, including Bishop Rather of Verona, to try to secure the throne for his eldest son Eberhard. The campaign was unsuccessful, but it is not known to have inspired any protest from Henry I. Nor did Arnulf's designation of his son Eberhard as his successor in 935. This had all the forms of a royal designation, with fidelity being sworn to Eberhard at public meetings by the leading men of Bavaria. This dualism was not to survive Henry's death for long, but it did exist, as it also did, though in a much less marked for.n, between Henry and the dukes of Franconia, Suabia and Lotharingia.

It is hard to assess the last years of Henry's reign in the face of Widukind's blinding rhetorical pathos; it remains a completely undecided issue how far we should take seriously Widukind's statement that Henry intended to go to Rome, and if we do take it seriously we still have to decide whether this is to be interpreted as an intended pilgrimage or as an intended "Italian expedition" aimed at securing imperial coronation. Pilgrimages to Rome were still established behaviour in the ninth and tenth centuries for magnates – Henry's grandfather Liudolf had been on one, and the leading margrave of Otto I's reign, Gero, was also to do so, though they were no longer in fashion for kings. If we are to take Widukind's report historically then a pilgrimage is probably more likely than the intention of imperial coronation, especially as we know that Hugo, more or less undisputed ruler of Italy from 933 onwards, also enjoyed Henry's *amicitia*. But the matter can hardly be proved one way or the other. It is equally unclear whether the "meeting of three kings" (Henry, Rudolf of west Francia and Rudolf II of Burgundy) on the western border of Lotharingia in 935 was more significant than previous such meetings; much has been made of it as a display of Henry's unchallenged hegemonial position in post-Carolingian Europe, but it is not evident that it was more than a meeting between equals at which some outstanding issues were sorted out. In any event, this was almost Henry's last public appearance; he fell ill in 935, secured Frankish and Saxon consent to Otto's succession at an assembly in Erfurt, and died on July 2 936.

CHAPTER SIX

The kingdom of the Franks and Saxons: Otto I and Otto II

OTTO I: THE EARLY YEARS

At first sight Otto I's accession, especially as depicted in loving detail by Widukind of Corvey, seems a remarkable tribute to his father's success in consolidating royal power. After his election by the Franks and Saxons, Otto proceeded to Aachen, where on August 7 936 he received the commendation of the dukes, counts and leading nobles of the kingdom, dressed in Frankish ceremonial garments and seated on a throne. These "made him thus to their king after their custom".[1] After this he was crowned and anointed king by Archbishop Hildebert of Mainz, assisted by Wichfrid of Cologne. The coronation was followed by a ceremonial banquet, at which Eberhard of Franconia, Arnulf of Bavaria, Hermann of Suabia and Gilbert of Lotharingia assumed the roles of court officials and ministered to the king. Much of this contrasted sharply with the rituals – or lack of them – used at Henry's accession, and was a clear assertion of Frankish tradition and continuity. Most noteworthy in this respect was the fact that Otto received royal unction where his father had refused it, but there were other changes as well. The kingdom to which Otto succeeded was still a Frankish one, and this was emphasized by Otto's clothing. The choice of Aachen, Charles the Great's favoured residence, demonstrated not only Otto's control over Lotharingia but also the legitimacy of his rule, as good as that of Otto's rival in west Francia, the Carolingian Louis IV, who had just become king after thirteen years of rule by non-Carolingians.

1. Widukind II 1, p. 64.

The clearly defined role of the church in the king-making rituals was also much more generally Frankish than specifically east Frankish. Yet there were other elements as well. As in 919, the use of the correct royal insignia for the coronation and the designation by the previous king were matters to be stressed, whereas neither had been of much importance in Frankish king-making. The ritual banquet also had no Frankish counterpart that we know of; the nearest parallel is the famous incident in 973 when the Anglo-Saxon King Edgar was rowed by eight other kings on the River Dee. In both cases what was demonstrated was overlordship as much as lordship: Otto was here seen to be more than just first among equals. Nevertheless, although constitutional historians have generally seen the ceremony as emphazising the nature of the dukedoms as an office, the way in which the dukes were able to appear as symbolically representing their peoples probably did their own political and constitutional position within their duchies little harm.

Otto's succession has also been seen as representing the triumph of a new principle, that of the indivisibility of the kingdom. The Carolingians had divided and subdivided their kingdoms among their sons, whereas Henry I did not attempt to provide separate kingdoms for his younger sons Henry and Brun or for his son by his first marriage, Thankmar. It is certainly true that the kingdom was not divided in 936 (or later), but it is doubtful whether this should be taken as the conscious acceptance of a new principle. It is not clear what could have been divided in 936. A division of Henry's wealth among his sons did indeed take place – both Henry and Thankmar got lands and treasure, according to Widukind. But for a division of the kingdom both the royal resources and aristocratic consent were lacking. We know that there was some disagreement in 936 about whether Otto or his younger brother Henry should succeed Henry I: Flodoard reports it, and Widukind's account can be read between the lines as showing that Henry was kept in Saxony under house arrest during the coronation.[2] But all were agreed that only one of the two could do so. This might not have been the case later, but as things turned out, 936 was the last occasion in the tenth and eleventh centuries when a German king had more than one son to pass on his kingdom to. In 973, 983 and 1039 there was only one surviving son, while in 1002 and 1024 there were no direct male heirs at all, so that indivisibility triumphed in practice as much as in principle (though a

2. Flodoard, ed. Lauer, 64; Widukind II 1, p. 67.

division may have been contemplated in 1002; see below, p. 187). The contrast with the ninth century can be overstressed. The Carolingians, especially in east Francia, had in the later ninth century already moved away from a simple division of their kingdoms, and the kingdoms could no longer just be carved up to satisfy the dynasty. Otto's accession represents rather a transition towards indivisibility, for both the revolts of the late 930s and the political settlement which was worked out in the 940s were very much concerned with the division of power and resources among members of the royal family; what happened in the end was a division of everything except the royal title, with Henry getting a position in Bavaria otherwise hardly distinguishable from kingship. This was perhaps the most appropriate solution for a kingdom which was still very much a conglomeration or federation under a hegemonial overlord, as the ceremony at Aachen clearly demonstrated.

Otto's coronation was followed almost immediately by a civil war, though such a term perhaps implies a partisan view of what happened. The great political crisis of 937–941 is commonly seen as a single episode, and there has been a tendency in recent scholarship to interpret it as opposition to a new, autocratic style of kingship practised by Otto I in contrast to the more collegiate methods of his father. There is some good evidence for this view: Otto's use of unction at the coronation ceremony; the sharp disappearance of "friendships" between the king and his leading men as recorded in the narrative sources and *libri memoriales*; his refusal in 939 (and later in 953) to accept *pacta*, settlements negotiated by intermediaries between him and his opponents. All these things suggest a new view of kingship, one which set a greater gap between the king and even the greatest of his leading men than that which had existed in Henry's time. Yet it is hardly possible to see the revolts of 937–41 as having been consciously directed against a new style of government. Otto's views, so far as we can ascertain them with certainty, probably contributed to the deterioration in the political atmosphere, but so did the fact that he was a new king: the start of a reign was *always* a difficult time. Otto was also a great deal younger than many of his magnates, particularly Eberhard of Franconia, who was of his father's generation. The weakness of his position compared with that of his father was shown in the behaviour of the peoples to the east. The Bohemians refused tribute after Henry's death, and could not be forced to pay it; there were difficulties in keeping control over the Abodrites and Elbe Slavs, who also more than once withheld tribute payments; and two Magyar attacks on Franconia and Saxony had to be driven back in 938. Such things imposed great stresses on the relations between leading men and their followings. The revolts of 937–41 can be disentangled without difficulty into a number of disputes which were only intermittently and loosely connected with one another. There were disagreements about power and inheritance between Otto I and his brothers Henry and Thankmar. This coincided with other feuds within Saxon aristocratic families, for example the Billungs, some of which were inflamed by decisions taken by Otto himself. At the same time old quarrels between Ottonians and Conradines over land and rights in the Wesergebirge and in Thuringia were revived. Outside Saxony there were the still unresolved issues of whether Lotharingia was to belong to east Francia or west Francia or perhaps to become an independent principality, and whether the coronation of Otto I had altered the status of Bavaria and perhaps also of Suabia as these had come to be defined under Henry I. All this made for an extremely dangerous mixture.

The Bavarian revolt which started everything off was dealt with surprisingly quickly. Arnulf had accepted Otto as king in 936; after the former's death on July 14 937 his son and designated successor Eberhard defied Otto in some way – Widukind says that Arnulf's sons refused to obey a royal order to accompany the king (*regis iussu contempserunt ire in comitatum*[3]) which may mean doing military service or may mean appearing before Otto and perhaps commending himself. Otto invaded Bavaria twice in 938. The first expedition was a failure, but after the second one he was able to send Eberhard into exile and install Berthold, Arnulf's brother, as duke. It was an episode which marked the beginning of the end of Bavaria's independence, though the process was not really completed until the accession of the Bavarian line of the Ottonians in 1002. There were no more separate Bavarian church councils; in theory at least the duke no longer appointed to bishoprics (though ducal influence over the Bavarian church remained considerable). As early as 938 we are told that Otto appointed the new archbishop of Salzburg, Herold – though he was probably a Liutpolding and the appointment part of Otto's arrangement with those Liutpoldings willing to come to terms. The virtual independence enjoyed by Arnulf in respect of rulers and peoples beyond the borders was also curtailed, though again this was a process rather than an event, and Otto I's brother Henry was from 948 to continue the Liutpolding tradition of interest in the kingdom of Italy. Considering how powerful Arnulf's position had seemed, Otto's intervention was remarkably painless. From then on until the end of

---

3. Widukind II 8, p. 72.

the crisis in 941 Bavaria was not involved in the fighting in the north; Berthold and his relatives did not try to take advantage of the Saxon quarrels to redefine the relationship between duchy and king as established in 938.

The Saxon revolt of 938 may have been triggered off by Otto's initial failure in Bavaria, though there was no shortage of grievances to fuel it. The revolt was led by Otto's half-brother Thankmar, Wichmann Billung and Eberhard of Franconia. Thankmar and Wichmann were dissatisfied with Otto's disposition of offices after coming to power. On the death of Count Siegfried of Merseburg, whom Widukind calls "second after the king",[4] Thankmar expected to be given his march (they were cousins through their mothers), but Otto gave it to Siegfried's brother Gero instead. Wichmann had been slighted by Otto's having conferred the military command in northern Saxony on his younger brother Hermann Billung. Eberhard seems to have felt that he was being squeezed out of power. His grievance began when a Saxon vassal of his, Bruning, refused to commend himself (on the grounds that it was not for the Saxons to become the men of lords from other peoples – a sign at the least of growing Saxon self-confidence, though Bruning may well have been encouraged in his attitude by Otto or his brother Henry). Eberhard, who had a substantial following in Saxony itself, attacked Bruning and was promptly condemned, along with his followers, by a royal court. The revolt of 938 fizzled out after Thankmar had been killed; both Wichmann and Eberhard made peace with Otto, Eberhard being sent into exile for a time. In the following year the revolt broke out again, this time under Otto's brother Henry (who the previous year had sided with Otto) together with Eberhard of Franconia and Gilbert of Lotharingia. The opposition was defeated in two battles at Birten and Andernach, but it was very close-run indeed, and at one point in his account Widukind describes Otto abandoned by all his followers "with no further hope of rule for the Saxons."[5] The conflict had spread to include Louis IV of west Francia, who allied with the opposition, and Hugo, duke in *Francia* (i.e. the Seine basin) and Louis's chief opponent, who allied himself with Otto. At Andernach both Eberhard and Gilbert were killed, and this broke the opposition and provided Otto with a breathing-space; he was able to appoint his brother Henry as duke of Lotharingia. Henry, however, was not able to establish himself in Lotharingia, and by 940 was back in Saxony. Here there were additional problems: the Slav peoples to the east had refused

4. Widukind II 1, p. 67.
5. Widukind II 24, p. 87.

tribute payments, and thus struck a serious blow at the Saxon political economy. A further conspiracy between Henry and some of the east Saxon nobility in 940–941 aimed at assassinating Otto during the Easter celebrations at Quedlinburg in 941 and establishing Henry as king; it was only after this had been uncovered that there was a final reconciliation between Otto and his brother.

A number of points need to be made about these events. First, the Saxons themselves were not disposed to call Ottonian rule in question. On the contrary, for serious opposition to Otto an Ottonian was necessary. The revolt against Otto was stopped by Thankmar's death, and could be got going again only after Henry had agreed to head it. These considerations had less force outside Saxony, though they perhaps weighed with Eberhard of Franconia. At least in Lotharingia Widukind depicted Otto's opponents as being against Saxon rule, which he himself also saw threatened, not least by the breakdown of the Franco-Saxon coalition which had done so well in the preceding twenty years; he lists the Saxons' enemies as "Slavs in the East, Franks in the South, Lotharingians in the West, Danes and Slavs again in the North".[6] The Bavarian Liutpoldings were presumably prepared to question Ottonian rule, though we know too little about their rising to be certain. The Suabians, under their Conradine duke Hermann, who on the precedent of 919 might also have been expected to offer opposition, actually supported Otto, though there are hints that they did not do so right from the start. It was they who won the crucial battle of Andernach for him, Otto himself being cut off from the action by the Rhine. Second, it was not only the Ottonians who were, as a family, divided. The Liutpoldings and the Billungs were as well, while the Conradines Eberhard and Hermann fought on opposite sides at Andernach, after Hermann's nephew had been killed in the course of Eberhard's uprising the previous year. Few families were without their internal tensions, which were inherent in the inheritance practices of the east Frankish nobility (see above, p. 74 and below, p. 223) and in the competition for high office among their leading members. Any dispute within the royal family provided an opportunity for disgruntled members of other families to try to improve their position. Third, the active role played by Henry I's widow Mathilda – who gave comfort and encouragement to Henry, and had to be included in the reconciliation of 941 – should not be overlooked, for it was characteristic not only of queens, as we shall see with Adelheid

6. Widukind II 20, pp. 84–5.

and Theophanu, and later with Conrad II's wife Gisela, but more generally of the position which could be occupied by aristocratic widows within a kindred in east Frankish, especially in Saxon society. Fourth, though Otto punished some of the lesser followers of his rebellious brother and leading men, hardly any were "executed for treason", and Ottonian historiography went out of its way to explain and justify the few exceptions. Temporary exile and confiscation of lands were the worst fate normally awaiting a rebel, if he should survive the chances of warfare. Already here, in the most serious crisis of the Reich before the second half of the eleventh century, we can see that sense of community among the political elite which prevented rivalries and feuds, however vigorously pursued, from being taken to extremes.

If the reign up to 941 had threatened to put an end to Ottonian (or at least Otto's) kingship, the following decade saw quite different developments. Eberhard's death in 939 prevented a fully fledged dukedom from emerging in Franconia. The Conradines did not lose all of their lands there, and some members of the family appear later in the century with a title of duke which appears to have been *ad personam*. But there was no longer any question of Franconia's going the same way as Bavaria and Suabia. Elsewhere the duchies were not suppressed, but they were gradually filled by members of the royal family. Lotharingia went after a brief interlude to the Franconian count Conrad in 944, who in 947 married Otto I's daughter Liutgard. In Bavaria Berthold died at the end of 947 and was succeeded by Otto's brother Henry; in Suabia Otto's son Liudolf, already designated Otto's successor in 946, became duke on Hermann's death in 949. Both Henry and Liudolf married the daughters of their predecessors. They were appointed by Otto, but they ruled in a sense also by hereditary right. Their rule (and Conrad's as well) also served to spread the presence and indeed the charisma of the ruling family more widely, and to ease the pressures and competition for resources within the family. It was more of a family settlement than an institutional extension of Ottonian rule, and so perhaps differs from the Carolingian practice of making kings' sons rule in sub-kingdoms. Conrad, Henry and Liudolf were in effect sub-kings, but they were not able to any great extent to take with them other prominent members of the Franco-Saxon aristocratic coalition on which Ottonian power was based to establish in their new territories. Even the opportunities provided by the condemnations and forfeitures of the late 930s could not be used to set up a new Franco-Saxon imperial aristocracy.

SONS AND BROTHERS, 952–68

The last major rebellion of the reign, which broke out in 953, was, like those before it, a family affair: it was headed by Otto's son Liudolf of Suabia and his son-in-law Conrad of Lotharingia. The rebellion was – at least according to Otto's opponents – directed not so much against Otto as against his brother Henry, and it does indeed seem that the rebels did not intend to kill or depose Otto. The starting-point was the sense of injury felt by both Liudolf and Conrad the Red after the Italian campaign of 951–2 (below, p. 169). Liudolf saw his position as designated successor threatened by Otto's marriage to Adelheid of Italy, while Conrad, who had sorted out Italian affairs and come to terms with King Berengar after Otto's hurried return to Saxony in early 952, was slighted by Otto's initial refusal either to receive Berengar or to accept unaltered the settlement which Conrad had made. Both claimed to be concerned at the influence which Henry of Bavaria had with Otto and Adelheid – Henry had argued against settling with Berengar, and had had his power extended by the grant of the north-east Italian marches of Verona and Aquileia.

The first sign of revolt came in 953 when Otto wished to celebrate Easter at Aachen (in Conrad's duchy) and found nothing prepared for him. Otto went instead to Mainz, where Archbishop Frederick tried to mediate between the king and his son and son-in-law. Otto at first agreed to the settlement arranged by Frederick (whose content we do not know) but then repudiated it on the grounds that it had been made under duress; Frederick was accused of favouring the opposition and in effect forced to join it. Gradually the rebellion attracted other supporters. In Bavaria the surviving Liutpoldings under Arnulf, count palatine of Bavaria and brother of the deposed Eberhard, tried to recover the position they had lost in 938, while in Saxony Wichmann the Younger, son of the Wichmann Billung who had rebelled in 938, revived the feud his father had had with Hermann Billung. Otto made things worse by offending old allies in Saxony and Thuringia, and it seemed for a time as if the rebels would have the upper hand. Otto besieged Mainz unsuccessfully, while Henry was driven out of Bavaria and his treasure-hoard in Regensburg captured by Liudolf. However, it proved to be difficult to sustain a revolt directed not against the king but against his brother – Conrad of Lotharingia drew back from giving battle to loyalist forces under Otto's youngest brother Brun, appointed archbishop of Cologne in 953. The reappearance of the Magyars in

954 led to a swift closing of ranks, especially after it appeared that both Liudolf and Conrad had allied themselves with them, if not actually summoned them into the land. At an assembly in Langenzenn near Nürnberg in June 954 Conrad and Frederick submitted; they were unable to persuade Liudolf to join them, and it was not until later in the year, after an army under Otto and Henry had besieged Regensburg and broken the Bavarian opposition, that Liudolf surrendered. Conrad and Liudolf lost their duchies but not their allodial lands; as a bishop, Frederick could not be touched, but he died in October 954 and was succeeded by Otto's illegitimate son William.

Though the origins of the last major internal crisis of Otto's reign seem simple enough, it is not at all clear what either Otto or his opponents intended. Evidently Otto felt unable to punish the leaders of the revolt severely: Conrad and Liudolf were deprived of their duchies but not of their lands, while Wichmann the Younger also suffered only honourable captivity, though his uncle Hermann was in favour of tougher punishment. Only the Liutpoldings, who had no blood ties with Otto's Franco-Saxon allies to protect them, suffered heavily: Arnulf was killed in the first siege of Regensburg, while Archbishop Herold of Salzburg was blinded on the orders of Henry of Bavaria. On the opposition side, Liudolf had been able to drive Henry out of Bavaria, but what his next step after that was to be is not obvious, while Conrad's and Frederick's intentions are even more uncertain. Frederick was perhaps primarily concerned to mediate, as befitted his episcopal office, and was driven into a rather passive opposition only by Otto's rejection of his efforts, while Otto's insult to Conrad in not accepting the Italian settlement was a question of honour and prestige which it would have been difficult and risky for Conrad to ignore – as it was it seriously threatened his position in Lotharingia. Of course, such political crises also have their own internal dynamic: both Otto and his opponents were spurred on by their backers, and were not free agents in the matter of making peace once open hostilities had broken out. The threat from Magyars and Slavs provided everyone with a way out of a deadlocked situation, taken up almost with a feeling of relief. The contrast with 938–9, when Magyar and Slav raids had stopped no one in their tracks, is worth noting; the decade and a half which had intervened had seen a consolidation of Otto's rule.

Up until recently it has been a commonplace of German historiography that the revolt of 953–4 marked a turning-point in Otto's internal policy: he is held to have abandoned attempts to rule through dukes drawn from the royal family and to have turned to the episcopate instead. Otto's brother Brun, archbishop of Cologne from 953 and "archduke" in Lotharingia from 954, was on this view both pilot project and prototype for future developments. So long as Brun lived, it is argued, his entourage provided the new royalist candidates for bishoprics, while after his death in 965 Otto and his successors, reviving Frankish tradition, used the royal chapel as a mixture of *école normale supérieure* and military college, in which future bishops were selected and trained. There is a little in this view, but it is by no means the whole story. Brun does indeed appear as *rex et sacerdos* in Ruotger's biography,[7] in other words as a high priest exercising secular power, but it is as well to remember that Brun's position in Lotharingia (and as regent during Otto's second Italian expedition) was not simply that of a bishop, but of a king's brother. His secular position in Lotharingia was a novelty, and criticized as such by his colleague and half-brother William of Mainz, but it was hardly typical for the mid tenth century. It was not until the early eleventh century that grants of secular jurisdiction to bishoprics was to become common, and then only at the level of counties, not of duchies. Brun was no prototype. His "court" was indeed a nursery for future bishops, and included such figures as the future archbishops Gero of Cologne and Egbert of Trier, but here he was essentially simply doing for his clerical following what his relatives Henry and Liudolf tried to do for their secular ones.

As for Otto's control of elections, it is in any case only from the mid 950s on that the sources become plentiful enough for us to be informed regularly about episcopal elections: the Lotharingian *gesta episcoporum* start to fill out and Thietmar of Merseburg's reminiscences swell from a trickle to a flood as he comes to the generation which was still alive when he was young. The increase in royal control over episcopal appointments after 953–4 may very well be in part an optical illusion. To the extent that it was not – and we might well expect Otto's enhanced prestige after the defeat of the rebels and of the Magyars to have been reflected in greater influence over episcopal appointments – Otto can hardly have realistically expected to control the lay nobility through the episcopate or to use bishops as a counterweight to dukes. We should bear in mind the analysis offered by Widukind, who for all his classicizing rhetoric had a firm grip of the barbarian realities of Ottonian politics, of the attitude of the Bavarian episcopate during the brief period in 953–4 when

---

7. *Vita Brunonis* c. 20, ed. I. Schmale-Ott (MGH SRG NS, Cologne 1958), 19.

Liudolf and the Liutpoldings controlled much of Bavaria: the bishops were able neither to support nor to oppose the king openly if they wished to preserve their sees.[8] It is in any case a very moot point whether this kind of rationalistic interpretation, such as the idea of a "policy" of using bishops against the lay nobility, can give us any real insight into tenth century behaviour, even if we consider it as an *ex post facto* summary of the thought behind actions rather than as a conscious guide to action. The complexity of episcopal behaviour can be seen in a figure like Ulrich of Augsburg. He and his kindred were among the few in Suabia who were loyal to Otto during the uprising of 953–4, and he led the defence of his city against the Magyars in 955 which enabled Otto and his army to close with the invaders. On the face of it this was a loyal bishop mindful of his secular responsibilities. Yet his biographer makes it clear that he was not interested primarily in these things, but rather in his pastoral responsibilities and indeed in the salvation of his own soul. Later in his episcopate he asked for an assistant to run the secular side of the diocese. Nor did his loyalty to Otto preclude local ties; his successor Henry was unable to dislodge Ulrich's kindred from their well-established positions as vassals of the bishopric, as the *Life* unwittingly makes clear.[9]

It is not even clear that we can say that Otto turned away from using dukes drawn from his own family after 953. In Lotharingia brother Brun replaced brother-in-law Conrad; in Bavaria nephew Henry succeeded brother Henry. Liudolf was sent off to Italy in 956 to deal with Berengar II, much as Arnulf of Carinthia's dispossessed sons Zwentibald and Ratold had been given Lotharingia and Italy in 895 and 896 respectively (see above, p. 126). If the 950s were a turning-point, this is rather in the sense that from then on there was always a shortage of male Ottonians (a tradition inherited by the Salian dynasty which ruled from 1024). Between 955 and 957 Otto's son-in-law Conrad (and Conrad's wife Liutgard), his only adult son Liudolf, and his only surviving brother who was not an ecclesiastic (Henry of Bavaria) all died, as did two of the three sons born to Adelheid. On the whole this made Otto's own position more secure, since there were scarcely alternatives available around whom opposition could crystallize. This security can be seen in the fact that Otto felt able to have his son Otto II elected at an assembly at

8. Widukind III 27, p. 117.
9. *Vita Udalrici Augustensis*, MGH SS 4, 377–425, especially cc. 12, 21–4, 28, pp. 401, 407–11, 416.

Worms and crowned king at Aachen in the summer of 961, and even to have him crowned co-emperor at the end of 967, though he took care not to give his son any kind of independent position even after he had come of age at the end of the 960s. Otto could even afford to spend nearly ten of the last twelve years of his reign south of the Alps. In order to do so he relied heavily on other members of his family: his mother Mathilda, his brother Brun, his illegitimate son William, archbishop of Mainz.

It is also misleading to see the uprising of 953–4 as one by dukes against the king. In Bavaria the uprising had been directed *against* the Ottonian duke; in Lotharingia Conrad the Red hardly had the nobility of the land united behind him. Only in Suabia does Liudolf – who was not just a duke but a king's son and designated successor – seem to have most of the regional nobility behind him, and even here not all of it, as Ulrich of Augsburg's kindred demonstrate. If the lesson of the 950s was that the dukes were still a danger to royal power it was lost on Otto, for the men who replaced the Ottonian ducal circle were in general directly descended from or closely related to the "native" ducal houses. The Burchard who became duke of Suabia in 954 after Liudolf had lost office was almost certainly a Hunfriding, perhaps a son, certainly a close relative of the Burchard II killed in 926. In Bavaria, Henry was succeeded by his son Henry, who was by birth both Liutpolding and Ottonian. The son was only four years old at the time, and there was a "regency" under his mother Judith, again a clear acknowledgement of the claims of heredity. The seeming exception to this general continuity was Lotharingia. Here Brun continued as overlord (*archidux* in Ruotger's phrase, by analogy with his office of *archiepiscopus*),[10] but in both upper and lower Lotharingia margraves are found, who soon came to take the title of duke (rather as in Saxony the Billungs evolved from margraves to dukes in the course of the tenth century): Frederick in upper Lotharingia, Godfrey in lower Lotharingia. These two were related by marriage to the Ottonian dynasty. To consolidate the position, Reginar III, the son of the Gilbert killed in 939, had his lands confiscated and was sent into exile. Yet the men who got Reginar's lands were Gerard and Matfrid, the current representatives of a family which had been rivals of the Reginarids for primacy in Lotharingia at least since Zwentibald's reign at the end of the 890s. In Saxony, where the Ottonians were their own

---

10. *Vita Brunonis, loc. cit.*; Widukind I 31, p. 44, speaks of Brun as "high priest and great duke".

dukes and the *dux*, when one is mentioned, was a military leader, Hermann Billung continued in office, while the division of Gero's super-march among several successors – for a time as many as six – on his death in 965 probably reflected not so much a policy of divide and conquer as Gero's immense success in enlarging his march, coupled with Otto's desire not to repeat the mistakes of 936–7 and make several enemies while pleasing only one appointee.

The uprising of 953–4 did not mark the end of all opposition to Otto I, but it was the last general uprising involving a large proportion of the leading men of the kingdom; for the next hundred years there would be only more localized and smaller-scale opposition confined to a single kindred or region. We hear little of opposition to Otto I in the last fifteen years of his reign in the regions furthest away from his rule: Lotharingia, Suabia, Bavaria. Even nearer home there was comparatively little. The most serious threat was presented by Wichmann Billung, who had not been included in the general settlement of 954. He went east beyond the marches and was able to establish a formidable position in the 960s among the Slav peoples, one strong enough to enable him to take tribute from Miesco of Poland. His opposition was directed at least as much against his uncle Hermann as against Otto I, and for a time he was reconciled and allowed to return from exile and enjoy his wife's estates, before being outmanoeuvred and driven once again into opposition by Hermann during Otto's second Italian expedition. He went back into exile, where he died on a further campaign against Miesco. Hermann Billung himself was not loyal beyond all question; he had himself received with royal honours in Magdeburg in 968 by the new archbishop, Adalbert. This has been interpreted as a symbolic public criticism of Otto's long absence in southern Italy, but it can also be seen as an early and prominent display of the almost royal status enjoyed by the Billungs in northern Saxony. Otto, who had been obviously reluctant to move against Wichmann Billung, was equally gentle in his dealings with Hermann; it was Adalbert who was forced to make heavy amends for his transgression.

THE EASTERN FRONTIER

On August 10 955 an army of Franks, Bavarians, Suabians and Bohemians under Otto I defeated a Magyar raiding army at the battle of the Lechfeld, south of Augsburg. In the rout that followed most of the remnants of the Magyar army were wiped out; the captured leaders were executed. The Saxons, apart from members of the Ottonian royal family, played little part in the victory at the Lech, for Saxony was itself threatened by a Slav offensive and the Saxons had to stay at home to meet the threat. About the same time as the Magyar defeat a Saxon army was defeated by the Slavs, and it was not until the victory of a Saxon army under Otto I over the Abodrites and their allies and tributaries at the Recknitz on October 16 that the issue was decided. Otto thus achieved his greatest victory with an army drawn from the rest of his kingdom rather than from his own home territory, a sign of his overall power and authority. The defeat of the Magyars was celebrated in Ottonian historiography and mentioned by Pope John XII as one of the reasons for crowning Otto emperor. Yet, as Marc Bloch pointed out,[11] the Magyars had long before the battle of the Lech ceased to be a serious threat to western Europe, and their raids had become increasingly infrequent. Saxony was not touched after the Magyar defeat of 938, while the Bavarians had not only defeated the Magyars in home matches in 943 and 948, but had carried warfare into Magyar territory in 950 and, according to Flodoard of Rheims, enforced tributary status on the Magyars.[12]

The Magyar raid of 954–5 looks traditional enough. It repeated a pattern already familiar from the early tenth century: no sooner is there unrest or civil war in a kingdom than well-informed Magyars appear looking for loot. Yet it can also be seen as a desperate last gamble, an attempt, by reviving a style of action already becoming less practicable with the gradual abandoning of the Magyars' previous nomadism, to unfreeze a situation already strongly favouring the Ottonians. What the battle of the Lech did was to confirm a tendency which had been there since Henry I's campaigns of 928–9 at the latest: it was to be the Saxons and not the Magyars who would exercise hegemony (including in particular tribute-taking) over the Slav peoples and principalities of central and eastern Europe; Slav auxiliaries fought on both sides at the Lechfeld. The east Frankish Carolingians had had to vie with Moravians and Bulgarians before yielding primacy to the Magyars during the first third of the tenth century. Later on Poland under Miesco I and still more under Boleslav Chrobry was to become a serious rival, while

11. M. Bloch, *Feudal Society*, London 1961, p. 11.
12. Flodoard, ed. Lauer, 128.

the great uprising of 983 was to show that Saxon control over the Slavs was not unlimited, but during the 950s and 960s at least the Saxons largely had their own way in eastern Europe. The 940s had seen substantial advances in Ottonian power over their neighbouring Slav peoples. In particular Bohemia was restored to tributary status by a campaign in 950 if not earlier, and Bohemian troops fought on the Ottonian side in both the battles of 955. Interestingly enough, Bohemia was put under the control of the duke of Bavaria, a connection which was to be of some significance in the 970s and 980s when the duke of Bohemia supported Henry the Quarrelsome against Otto II and Otto III. In Brandenburg the Ottonians had been able to install a Christian (and hence probably pro-Ottonian) prince, Tugumir, and Otto I set up bishoprics in both Brandenburg and Havelberg in 948, probably at the synod of Ingelheim.

The setting up of bishoprics was a sign that Saxon domination over the Slavs was being intensified in these decades. At an assembly held by Otto I in Saxony in 955, between the battles of the Lech and the Recknitz, a Slav embassy appeared and, according to Widukind, offered "that the allies would pay tribute as usual, but would keep the government of the region in their own hands; they would accept peace on these terms but would otherwise fight for their liberty"[13] We can here see the Slavs protesting at a new style of lordship, at overlordship turning into lordship. The various peoples were to be incorporated into the Reich and their native nobility and princes either absorbed into the nobility of the Saxon empire (as the nobilities of the German peoples had been by the Franks in the eighth century) or deposed and eliminated. This was a political necessity if the Saxons were to play the role in the Ottonians' new empire that the Franks had played in the Carolingian one. Even without rivals for hegemony, dominating the Slavs to the east of the Reich was not easy, not least because these peoples were politically highly fragmented and for that reason not as easily controlled as large peoples under a single ruler would have been. Domination was profitable, but the price was high. It meant the need to have permanent garrisons in a state of readiness, and it also meant that no king could easily draw on Saxon military strength. We have already seen how the Saxons did not play any great part on the Lechfeld; thirty years later it proved equally impossible to send Saxon troops to southern Italy to reinforce Otto II's defeated army in 982, while in

13. Widukind III 53, p. 132.

967 a substantial Saxon contingent had to remain at home while Otto I was campaigning in southern Italy, and had to make peace with the Slav Redarii against Otto I's express orders, because the Danes were threatening an invasion and there were not enough troops to fight on two fronts. The policy with a long-term future was therefore absorption and Christianization, exactly as the Franks had dealt with the Saxons themselves not quite two centuries earlier.

Christianization was on the agenda from early in the reign. Shortly after his accession Otto I had founded a new monastery at Magdeburg. This was staffed by monks drawn from the newly reformed monastery of St Maximin, Trier, and one of its principal patrons was Mauritius, an important saint very much associated with mission. It was endowed on an increasingly lavish scale – so much so that it has been supposed that Otto intended it from the start to be what in 968 it became, namely the nucleus of the foundation endowment of the new archbishopric of Magdeburg, though this is not very likely to have been his plan in 937. From the mid 940s Otto seems to have envisaged a considerable extension of the church in the regions under his control, but even a ruler of his prestige was subject to the constraints of canon law. He needed papal approval for the creation of new dioceses, and in practice he needed a reasonable degree of consent among the existing bishops of his kingdom as well. In particular the archbishops of Mainz and of Hamburg-Bremen both had claims and missionary traditions going back to the Saxon and Danish missions of the eighth and ninth centuries, and their holders were unwilling to give these up, while the bishops of Halberstadt and Würzburg were likely to lose both prestige and revenue (in the form of tithes) in the event of new bishoprics being erected. The result of this was that Otto had to carry out his intentions piecemeal, with numerous revisions of plan.

The first such changes came about in the 940s. Halberstadt's lands and rights of tithe in the Elbe marches were slowly transferred (with compensation) to Otto's new monastic foundation at Magdeburg. In 947–8 three Danish bishoprics were founded, at Aarhus, Ribe and Schleswig, and subjected to the archbishop of Hamburg-Bremen; the latter's papal privileges were renewed at around this time and his missionary responsibilities confined to Denmark and Scandinavia (up till then they had included Slavs as well). The foundation of the new bishoprics of Brandenburg and Havelberg, already mentioned, was also part of this process of reorganization: the two new bishoprics were subjected to the archbishop of Mainz and were responsible for the central part of the lands lying between the Elbe and the Oder. The northern section was entrusted to a bishopric at Oldenburg, whose foundation extended over the period from 968 to 972; unlike the other two it was made subject to Hamburg-Bremen. Otto's intentions for his own heartland are harder to make out, and it is probable that definite plans had to wait for the submission of Bohemia and the defeat of the Magyars. After the victory on the Lechfeld Otto tried to get approval from Pope Agapetus II for a proposal to transfer the bishopric of Halberstadt to Magdeburg and turn it into an archbishopric. William of Mainz protested both on his own account and on behalf of his suffragan Bernard of Halberstadt, and the project came to nothing. Seven years later Otto was able to secure a privilege from Pope John XII setting up an archbishopric at Magdeburg, but this too – though the archbishopric envisaged was still in a sense subject to Mainz – proved impossible to realize, now mainly because Bernard of Halberstadt would not give his consent. Only after the deaths of William and Bernard in early 968 could their successors Hatto and Hildiward be persuaded to agree to the new archbishopric (John XIII had already consented at the synod held in Ravenna in 967) and to the foundation of bishoprics at Merseburg, Meißen and Zeitz. Brandenburg and Havelberg were also added to the province of Magdeburg as suffragans. Other foundations are more obscure and difficult to date precisely. A bishopric was set up at Prague, perhaps in 973, perhaps in 976, which was subject to the archbishopric of Mainz; at the end of the 960s a bishopric was also established at Posen, in Miesco's territory, though its status and early history are unclear, and in particular we do not know what role Otto I played in setting it up.

On the face of it these foundations had much in common with the foundations of the Saxon bishoprics in the eighth and early ninth centuries. Yet there were also important differences. There were some disputes about which province Saxony was to fall under – hence the division of the Saxon bishoprics between the archbishops of Cologne and of Mainz – but these were not of major importance. The Saxon bishoprics were part of a concerted missionary effort, into which the Frankish church also poured other resources: manuscripts, monks, priests, relics. There is less evidence for this in the tenth century. The new foundations remained comparatively poor (except for Magdeburg) and received little support from their wealthier neighbours to the west; Otto had achieved his house archbishopric, but the Saxons had to pay for it themselves. By contrast with the Saxon bishoprics, whose dioceses do not seem to have corresponded to internal political or ethnic divisions in Saxony, some at least of the new bishoprics were clearly intended to cover a specific ethnic grouping: Prague for the Bohemians, Oldenburg for the Wagrians (the northern neighbours of the Abodrites), Havelberg for the Hevelli, Merseburg for the Sorbs, Meißen for the Misni. The intention behind the foundations was clearly among other things a missionary one, but the efforts put into converting the newly conquered Slavs varied. The missionaries could rely on a reasonable basis in the schools of the Saxon bishoprics, both old and new. There is good evidence for German clerics having taken the trouble to learn to speak Slavic languages – Boso, a monk from Regensburg and a royal *capellanus*, and Bishop Thietmar of Merseburg, for example. What was lacking was numinous power. There was no wheeling in of saints' relics on a large scale to make up for the loss of heathen shrines and deities, as there had been in ninth-century Saxony. Relics – those of Vitus and Mauritius in particular – played an important role, but they were kept in centres of concentration like Corvey and Magdeburg, or used as gifts to win over rulers (Henry or Otto I sent Vitus relics to the dukes of Bohemia, while the rulers of Poland and perhaps of Hungary got copies of the Holy Lance, associated with Mauritius, at the end of the century). They were not spread around the countryside to assist in the process of conversion. Conversion meant in the first instance political submission and the obligation to pay tithe; it cannot easily be distinguished from conquest.

Conquest and domination were a major aim not only of the Saxon rulers but of their followers, who shared in both the work and the profits – in particular of Hermann Billung and of Gero, the men appointed at the beginning of Otto's reign. Other Saxon nobles also played a part along the frontier, and some were occasionally given the title of margrave, but these two, and in particular Gero, were clearly the leaders of the Saxon thrust eastwards. After the defeat of the Magyars and the victory at the Recknitz in 955, the pressure on the Slavs increased. There were campaigns by the whole Saxon host in 957, 959 and 960, while during Otto's absence in Italy Gero was able to make the Lausitzi as well as Miesco of Poland pay tribute. In 965 Harald Bluetooth of Denmark agreed to accept Christianity. The parallel is not with the east Frankish treatment of the Slavs on their frontier but with the Frankish conquest of Saxony. The fact that Miesco of Poland moved clearly into view in the Saxon sources in the 960s shows this very well; just as the Frankish conquests east of the Rhine brought them up against the peoples beyond, the Danes and Avars, so the Saxon successes against Abodrites and other smaller peoples in the 940s and 950s expanded their horizons to include peoples further east. Where east Frankish parallels do hold good is in the position of the margraves. Otto himself was not wholly inactive in these campaigns, but he left much of the campaigning to Hermann, Gero and others, just as the Liudolfings had been largely responsible for their part of the Slav frontier in the ninth century with only occasional interruptions by royal expeditions.

Though Saxon domination still had strong tributary elements, we can see the beginnings of a more intensive style of lordship. Slav "families" begin to be donated in large numbers in royal and private charters; it is the transition from tribute-paying peoples to census-paying peasants. Burgwards were set up from the 940s in the Sorbic territories and a little later on among the Hevelli and around Brandenburg as well. These were a form of territorial organization with precedents both in the Frankish empire and among the Slavs: a fortification (*Burg*) with perhaps ten or twenty settlements dependent on it (*ward*, a district; compare the modern English word "ward" and its Anglo-Saxon equivalents). The fortification was a place of refuge in time of attack (by other Slavs, by rebels, possibly by Magyars), but it was also tax-point, church, perhaps also court: the basis for a new style of domination. The Slavs were well aware of the change, and they did not like it; but the effective reaction was not to come until 983.

HEGEMONY: FRANCE, BURGUNDY AND ITALY

From the beginning of Otto's reign the strength of the external position which had been built up by Henry I was very evident. To the west and south-west the hegemony of the east Frankish kingdom could be extended even during the initial crisis. In Burgundy, Rudolf II had died in 937; in 939 Otto made a quick expedition to the kingdom to rescue the young king Conrad from his enemies, including Hugo of Arles, king of Italy. He brought him to his court, and thus both saved his kingship and consolidated the tradition of east Frankish overlordship over Burgundy already begun under Arnulf and Henry I. Also reminiscent of Arnulf were Otto's shifting alliances with the leading men of the west Frankish kingdom. At first, and especially during the succession crisis, Otto had tended to favour Hugo the Great, while Louis IV, with eyes on Lotharingia, allied with Henry and Gilbert. In 940 Otto even received the commendation of Hugo the Great, Heribert of Vermandois and Hugo the Black of Burgundy. After the peace settlement of 941, and especially after the granting of Lotharingia to Conrad in 943–4, there was little immediate prospect for Louis of gains in Lotharingia, and Otto was able to play the role of mediator between Robertines and Carolingians. This was made all the easier by kinship ties: Hugo the Great was married to Otto's sister Hadwig, while Louis IV had as part of his attempt to regain Lotharingia married another sister of Otto's, Gilbert's widow Gerberga, immediately after Gilbert's death in 939. Already in 942 Otto had met Louis at Visé and sworn friendship with him (much as Henry I had done with Charles the Simple and with Robert).

It was partly pressure by Otto which forced Hugh the Great to release Louis IV, whom he had captured in 945, in return for the surrender of Laon. This was in July 946; a full-scale east Frankish expedition to west Francia in the autumn was not able to improve Louis's position much, though it did restore Carolingian control over the crucial archbishopric of Rheims. Otto's reputation, however, was undamaged, and it was still more enhanced by the council held at Ingelheim in 948 under the presidency of a papal legate, for here not only was the dispute over the archbishopric of Rheims settled, but also the accusations made by Louis against Hugo and his followers were discussed. Few things could have displayed Otto's hegemony more effectively than a synod, which he had summoned and which was held in his kingdom and attended in the majority by his bishops, sitting in judgement on west Frankish affairs, both secular and ecclesiastical. In all probability it was also at Ingelheim that Otto's new episcopal foundations in the Danish and Slav marches (see above, p. 163) were confirmed, a further demonstration of his power. It is no accident that the first examples of Otto's being called emperor in narrative sources and private charters come from Lotharingia in the years immediately following Ingelheim. Further synods were held at Frankfurt in January 951 (where Otto took up Carolingian tradition by issuing a capitulary) and at Augsburg in August 952.

It was, of course, one thing to make judgements and another to enforce them. In practice Otto left the sorting out of west Frankish affairs to his son-in-law Conrad of Lotharingia, who was able to mediate between Hugo and Louis and bring about a settlement in 950. This marked the beginning of a period of some fifteen years during which the duke of Lotharingia – first Conrad, then Brun – was responsible for the exercise of Ottonian hegemony in west Francia. The deaths of Louis IV in 954 and Hugo the Great in 956 made this all the easier, as the Ottonian widows Gerberga and Hadwig could act as regents for their minor sons Lothar and Hugo and relied on Brun's assistance to do this. The assistance was not confined to good advice: Brun intervened in west Francia with an army in 958, and before that he and the Carolingians had combined forces to break the power of the Reginarids in Lotharingia. The way in which Brun was able to hold assemblies in Cologne to deal with Lotharingian and west Frankish affairs was reminiscent of the Ottonians' practice towards the south German duchies: meetings with the magnates of the region were held at a place just outside (Worms for Suabia) or just inside (Regensburg for Bavaria, though Regensburg was the traditional political centre of Bavaria). Verona and Constance would later come to have a similar function on occasions for Italy, as would Basle for Burgundy. In spite of this, one cannot talk of an incorporation of west Francia into the Ottonian empire, or even a lasting entry into the Ottonian sphere of influence. The hegemonial control of the period from 940 to 965 could not in the last resort be institutionalized; it depended on marriage ties and other personal connections. These found their last expression in Lothar's marriage to Otto's stepdaughter Emma in 965, but this was followed by the deaths of Brun in 965 and Gerberga in 969, and with these the west Frankish kings began a slow process of emancipation from Ottonian control which was to be accelerated by the Capetians after 987. Already by 967 a diploma of Lothar's was expressing implicit criticism of Otto's recent actions in Rome: it praised the Emperor Constantine for having withdrawn from the city and thus freed the papacy from further troubling by royal authority.

Otto's hegemonial position, his conscious revival of Frankish traditions in his kingship, and his good relations with Pope Agapetus II all pointed to an increased interest in the lands south of the Alps. For the last years of Henry I's reign and the early years of Otto's we have only fragmentary hints at such an interest. We have already seen that Widukind's attribution to Henry I of an intention to go to Rome need not be interpreted as meaning that Henry wanted to have himself crowned emperor. Otherwise we know only that Hugo of Arles, king of Italy from 924 on, is said by Liutprand to have enjoyed Henry I's *amicitia*, a relationship comparable to that between Henry and Arnulf of Bavaria or the rulers of west Francia. The implication in one source that Otto went to Italy in 941 is probably an error,[14] but in that year Berengar of Ivrea, a margrave with claims to the Italian throne, and his wife Willa did seek protection at Otto's court. It was from there that Berengar was able to prepare his successful return to Italy in 945. Following the deaths of the kings Hugo in 948 and Lothar in 950 he became sole ruler. Italian opposition to Berengar now focused on and was led by Adelheid, sister of Conrad of Burgundy, who was Lothar's widow and as such able to confer something of a legitimate claim to rule in Italy on her new husband, should she marry again (compare the roles of dukes' widows in the duchies of Suabia and Bavaria). Adelheid, threatened and for a time imprisoned by Berengar, together with her supporters appealed to Otto for help; this was probably coupled with an offer of marriage and of the kingdom. Otto had his own reasons for responding: Berengar had, after all, been his follower, and by acting independently of him in this way had provoked reprisals. In September 951 a powerful German army moved south towards Italy. It had been immediately preceded by smaller expeditions under Henry of Bavaria, who captured Aquileia, and Liudolf of Suabia, who – not least because of Henry's intervention – achieved nothing and had to recross the Alps to join his father. Whether these events were the last flickerings of the independent "foreign policy" pursued by the south German dukes under Henry I, as they have sometimes been interpreted, or part of a concerted assault by the Ottonian family on the kingdom of Italy, cannot now be decided; probably they were both. Otto's take-over was smooth. At Pavia in September 951 he took possession of the kingdom by receiving the commendation of its magnates and by marrying Adelheid; Berengar adopted the tactic (not a new one for an Italian king confronted with a rival from north of the Alps) of taking refuge in the Alps and waiting for his opponent to go home.

Liutprand of Cremona remarked in a famous aphorism that the Italians always preferred to have two kings so that they could control the one through fear of the other.[15] In the game of tenth century Italian politics, summoning Otto was not intended to be markedly different from the other requests which had gone to rulers north of the Alps in the previous half-century, to Louis of Provence, Rudolf II of Burgundy, Hugo of Arles himself as well as to Arnulf of Bavaria and

14. Schieffer in Schieffer 1976: 684–5; but note that in that year Otto's foundation at Magdeburg received a papal privilege, which implies contact between Otto's court and Rome.
15. Liutprand, *Antapodosis* I 37, p. 27.

Berengar of Ivrea. Otto was a formidable figure north of the Alps, but his resources were far from unlimited. Tentative approaches to Pope Agapetus II about an imperial coronation were met with a firm refusal, for much the same reasons as had moved Agapetus's immediate predecessors to deny such a coronation to Otto's predecessor Hugo. Neither the popes nor the Roman aristocratic factions behind them, led by Alberic, "prince of the Romans", were interested in a potential overlord for the city. One of the effects of the politics of the first half of the tenth century was the restoration more or less of the state of affairs which had led to the Carolingian interventions of 755–6 and 774; the ruler of northern Italy threatened rather than controlled papal rule in central and southern Italy. Unlike some of his Carolingian predecessors, Otto was evidently not able in 951 to think of enforcing a coronation. Perhaps the revolt of 953 was already casting its shadow, but it is more likely that Otto's followers did not want to contemplate being away from their home base for too long. Whatever the reason, Otto set off for Saxony with his new bride in February 952, leaving his son-in-law, Conrad the Red, to complete the subjugation of the kingdom. Conrad did this by coming to terms with Berengar, and although the latter accepted Otto's overlordship at Augsburg in the summer of 952 this was in effect nullified by Otto's other preoccupations: the uprising of 953–4 and the Magyar and Slav campaigns of 955. Nominally a sub-king, Berengar, after the short-lived intervention by Liudolf in 956–7, was able to behave as if he were the unchallenged king of northern Italy, and to continue the *Drang nach Süden* already initiated by his rival and predecessor Hugo. In 959 it was no longer an Italian aristocratic party but Pope John XII who appealed to Otto to rescue the papacy from Berengar's tyranny, much as Stephan II had done in 754 and Hadrian I in 773.

This time Otto prepared his ground thoroughly before setting out from Germany in the late summer of 961. Besides making sure that the size of the army would be adequate, he had had his young son Otto crowned and acknowledged as his successor, and something like a regency was established under the two Ottonian archbishops of Mainz and Cologne. The German army arrived at Rome at the end of January 962; Otto was crowned emperor on February 2, and in return confirmed the Carolingian "donations" to the papacy in a solemn privilege, the Ottonianum, on February 13. In a noteworthy imitation of Byzantine practice, a specially luxurious copy of the privilege was drawn up on purple-coloured parchment in gold letters. Otto then turned to deal with Berengar, and soon also with the pope, John XII, who had invited him to Italy and crowned him but then repented. Berengar and his wife were captured easily; like Desiderius nearly two centuries earlier they were taken into exile north of the Alps. John XII, who had allied with Berengar's son Adalbert, presented more difficulties; he was deposed by a Roman synod in December 963, and a candidate acceptable to Otto and supported by some Romans, Leo VIII, elected in his place. Leo was driven out of Rome by an uprising inspired by John XII, and after John's death the Romans elected a new pope of their own, Benedict V, contrary to the arrangements Otto had made and had confirmed by oath after John's defection. Before Otto returned to Germany in July 964 he was able to impose his candidate. Benedict V was deposed and sent into exile at Hamburg. The reputation for holiness he enjoyed in Saxony after his death was an implicit criticism of Otto I's action, which went further than any Carolingian had dared to go.

Until comparatively recently it could be debated whether the Italian and imperial involvement of the Ottonians was a Good Thing or whether it hindered German development, but this question, whose answers were heavily influenced by the contemporary debate about the nature and purpose of a unified Germany, no longer seems very interesting. To ask what the imperial coronation meant at the time is more profitable, but it is a question which cannot have a single answer. Even contemporaries debated the subject, though the debate is known to us now more through inference and allusion than through direct statement. Widukind of Corvey and Ruotger, author of the *Life* of Otto's brother Brun, mistrusted the idea of an emperorship which was Roman in nature and conferred by the pope, not least because this would threaten the slightly uneasy compromise of consciousness which had been reached among many of the Ottonian elite, namely that the imperial people of the new empire were the Franks *and* the Saxons. It was possible to argue that Otto's rule was already imperial – either because of the hegemonial authority he had exercised for nearly two decades in Europe or because he was a king over many peoples (*imperator Romanorum, rex gentium*).[16] It was even possible to borrow from antiquity and argue that *imperator* was essentially a military title and had thus already been conferred on Otto by the acclamations of his victorious army on the Lechfeld. As in 800 the title expressed Otto's role as protector of the papacy and the city of Rome against its enemies; but in spite of

16. Widukind III 76, p. 154.

this and Otto's immediate confirmation of the privileges issued by the Carolingians it is questionable whether one should see Otto as filling an office which had existed at least in principle continuously since the time of Charles the Great, even if it had been vacant since the death of Berengar I in 924. As in 800, the imperial coronation was an event charged with a symbolism whose meaning would have to be worked out afterwards. The difference lay in the fact that 800 had occurred and could be remembered, and Charles the Great was probably more important in the minds of the participants than those rulers in between who had called themselves emperor – though as long as there were real live Carolingians around in west Francia, the Ottonians were somewhat cautious even about Charles the Great, and it was not until after 987 that Otto III and his successors could really begin to emphasize Charles as a predecessor. Otto's chancery at least was certain that Otto was not a *Roman* emperor: his title in diplomata issued after 962 was *imperator augustus*, with a very small number of exceptions which are probably not significant.

It is easier to say what the coronation did and did not do than to say what it meant. It did not, either then or later, imply more than the vaguest of supremacy over other rulers, either in eastern or in western Europe. The title of emperor reflected Otto's hegemonial position, but it did nothing for it. It gave Otto no new powers on his home ground, and by raising the question of the nature of his polity (Saxon? Frankish? Roman?) may even have created difficulties. Some German historians have stressed the importance of the title for the Christian mission to the Slavs (a similar connection has been suggested for the Carolingian imperial title); but Otto I had been able to concern himself with mission long before 962, and can scarcely be said to have increased his efforts after that date. Even the project of an archbishopric at Magdeburg was not brought much nearer. John XII issued a privilege for the new foundation a few days after Otto's coronation, but Otto's newly won title did not enable him to capitalize on it (see p. 164). His rule over Italy depended on conquest and his marriage with Adelheid, not on his being emperor, while his rule over Rome depended, as did that of his successors, very largely on his being there with an army. The title did imply a responsibility for the papacy, and this was perhaps its most important aspect; Otto and his successors acted fairly consistently to protect the papacy, though often very heavy-handedly. Otto himself almost certainly had no intention of acting instrumentally, as has sometimes been suggested, of trying to control the papacy in order to give himself additional power over his own episcopate. The popes did not have that kind of power in the tenth century, and nor did Otto's supposed reliance on the episcopate require them to do so. Otto's action in coming to Rome was in a sense altruistic; it would probably not have survived modern techniques of cost-benefit analysis. Yet these considerations were foreign to the tenth century. Quite apart from the essentially unknowable question of how far Otto's piety compelled him to act as he did, there were attitudes which we can reconstruct with more certainty. Otto, as a highly successful member of a comparatively new ruling house, owed himself imperial coronation. This imperative was felt strongly enough at the end of the eighth century by Charles the Great and the circle around him; the existence of Charles's precedent made the pressures on Otto still stronger. To ask what Otto got from the imperial title is also to ask whether he could have refused it or ignored the appeal for help from John and the Romans, and the answer to that is almost certainly no.

The most obvious and immediate consequences of the title, once Roman affairs had been sorted out, were that Otto's relations with Byzantium became much more intensive, and that he acquired with the imperial title an interest in southern Italy. This had Carolingian precedents, notably in the reigns of Charles the Great and Louis II of Italy. Moreover John XII, whose position in Rome and central Italy had in effect been taken over by Otto, had had both contacts with Byzantium and an interest in southern Italian affairs. It was the weakening of his position following his unsuccessful expedition against Capua in 959 which had given the impulse to John and the Romans to appeal to Otto I. Byzantium had before 962 been slowly coming into view on the Ottonian horizon (and vice versa). Byzantine embassies had visited Otto in 945 and 949, for the first time in east Francia since the early years of Conrad I's reign, while in the 950s the Byzantines had been interested in winning Otto's help (and that of the Abbasid caliphs in Spain) for their planned attack against the Fatimids in Egypt, as well as in an Ottonian bride for the future emperor Romanus Lecapenus. Otto's coronation thus took place in a context of rather greater familiarity than Charles's had done in 800, and the very fact of Charles's coronation meant that the Byzantines had learned to live with rivals to their emperorship. Yet we do not know what the immediate Byzantine reaction was; the coronation coincided in any case more or less with the accession of a new Byzantine emperor, Nicephorus Phocas.

Otto's activities in southern Italy from 966 on were aimed primarily at securing recognition from Byzantium (again, there is a parallel with the Franco-Byzantine war along the Adriatic coast between 802 and 812). The details of the campaigns of 966 to 972 need not concern us here. Both the Lombard and the Carolingian conquests of Italy had stopped slightly more than half-way down the peninsula, leaving a ragged edge before the firmly Byzantine south. The Arab invasion of Sicily in the second half of the ninth century meant that the south was no longer firmly Byzantine and contributed to a further fragmentation of the zone between Byzantine Calabria and the papal patrimony in central Italy: by the 960s there were principalities in Benevento, Capua and Salerno, and while Sicily was firmly Muslim, the Arabs' attempts to set up bridgeheads on the mainland had all been driven back. Byzantine concern for and control over the area varied. Otto's coronation occurred at a time when the emperor Nicephorus Phocas was taking a renewed interest in it, and it looked for a time as if it might come to open warfare between the two empires. Otto's campaigns, together with a change of ruler in Byzantium in 969, produced a temporary rapprochement between eastern and western empire. Byzantine recognition of Otto's empire was expressed in the marriage between the young Otto II and the Byzantine princess Theophanu in 972, even if Theophanu had not been born in the purple and hence did not carry quite the same status in Byzantine eyes as the princess who had been originally asked for. Otto could return north in 972 leaving reasonably stable conditions in both Lombardy and Rome, and on the southern frontier.

THE END OF EXPANSION, 968–83

By the late 960s the new empire seemed to have been re-established on Frankish lines, with a European hegemony based on prestige and authority and backed in the last instance by military power based on tribute-taking. Otto dominated Europe as Louis the German and Arnulf had done. The young Otto II had been crowned as co-emperor by John XIII in Rome at Christmas 967 – the last western emperor to be crowned in his father's lifetime, as Louis the Pious, Lothar I and Louis II had been. The foundation of the new ecclesiastical province of Magdeburg, finally set in motion by the joint synod held by emperor and pope at Ravenna in April 967, not only emancipated the Ottonians from the Rhenish archbishoprics but also placed them firmly in the Frankish tradition as missionary rulers. Otto's control over the church was seen not just here but also in the increasing importance of the royal chapel (though see above, p. 157). There was seemingly little internal opposition left: the death of Wichmann Billung had removed the most serious threat among the Saxon nobility, while the successes of the decade between 955 and 965 (together with a thinning of the ranks) meant that there was enough to go round the surviving male members of the Ottonian family to satisfy all. There was at least the possibility that a new supra-regional aristocracy might be able to emerge, one perhaps not so dominated by Saxons as its predecessor had been by Franks, but having much the same sort of function: linking scattered regions by ties of office- and property-holding. Beyond the borders, the continuation and consolidation of the Ottonians' hegemonial position seemed assured: claims had been staked in southern Italy, even if for the time being there was a rapprochement with Byzantium; the kings of west Francia and Burgundy were little more than sub-kings; the kings and dukes to the north and east, in Denmark, Poland and Bohemia, and the kinglets between Poland and Saxony were bound by tribute and other ties to the Saxon empire. All these things were reflected in the great assembly held in Quedlinburg at Easter 973, still remembered forty years later as the apotheosis of Otto I's reign by Thietmar of Merseburg, who entered in his own hand in his chronicle a list of those present: "the dukes Miesco [of Poland] and Boleslav [of Bohemia], and legates from the Greeks, the Beneventans, Magyars, Bulgars, Danes and Slavs",[17] to which should be added the Fatimid and English ambassadors who arrived in the same year.

Otto II had long been king when his father died on May 7 973; Widukind, in the closing sentences of his *Res gestae Saxonicae*, describes how the assembled notables once more commended themselves and promised fidelity and aid against all his enemies.[18] This did not come free; nearly a sixth of all the diplomata Otto II issued in his ten years as sole ruler were drawn up in the first six months of his reign. Nor did it last; there were enough enemies of the regime at home and abroad who had waited until the arrival of the new king. As in Otto I's reign, the occasion for the uprising was a feud within the Ottonian house itself. The starting-point was the death of Burchard of Suabia; Otto II appointed Otto, the son of Liudolf of Suabia, and thus affronted Henry of Bavaria, who might have expected to control Suabia through his sister Hadwig,

17. Thietmar II 31, p. 76.
18. Widukind III 76, p. 153.

Burchard's widow. An initial uprising by Henry in 974 in alliance with Boleslav II of Bohemia and Miesco of Poland was quickly ended; Henry was imprisoned and lost his duchy. Otto II reorganized the southern duchies in 976: Bavaria went to Otto of Suabia, but minus Carinthia and the Italian marches acquired in 952, which were turned into a new duchy of Carinthia and given to the Liutpolding Henry, the son of the former duke of Bavaria, Berthold. A new march was set up against the Magyars in the east and given to Liutpold, previously a count in the Nordgau, who was related both to the Liutpoldings and indirectly to the Babenberger who had been wiped out in the direct line by the feud of Louis the Child's reign.

A further uprising in 976–7 by Henry of Bavaria, the newly created Duke Henry of Carinthia, and Bishop Henry of Augsburg (himself a Liutpolding), ended with a successful siege of Passau by Otto II. The three Henries were exiled, Henry of Bavaria to distant Utrecht, and the new duchy of Carinthia was given to Otto, the son of Conrad the Red. At the same time as these events in the south-east of the Reich, the west was threatened both by the Reginarids exiled in 959 and by the west Frankish ruler, Lothar. Probably there was some collusion between Otto's western and south-eastern opponents, but Lothar had his own reasons for moving against Otto: besides the west Frankish claims on Lotharingia going back to 869–70, Lothar also had a feud to conduct with his brother Charles, whom Otto II had appointed duke in lower Lotharingia in 977. Lothar made a surprise attack on Aachen in 978 and nearly captured Otto II in person; Otto's counter-raid on Paris satisfied honour, but little more. It was not until 980 that peace was made between Otto II and Lothar at Margut; a compromise had already been reached with the Reginarids in 978.

The most significant aspect of these uprisings was the very small circle of closely interrelated magnates who led them. Apart from the two Slav dukes and Margrave Liutpold, all the protagonists we have just mentioned were descended either from Henry of Saxony or from Arnulf of Bavaria or from both. There was evidently a shortage of men who were of sufficient standing to hold the south German duchies, and the idea of appointing royal relatives to these duchies had obviously not been dropped after 953–4. We should also note the independent role played by Miesco, Boleslav and Lothar. The west Frankish kingdom in particular, after more than twenty years of tutelage following the synod at Ingelheim in 948, was slowly moving out of the Ottonian orbit, a process which would be accelerated by Otto III's minority. But Miesco, whom we have previously met on the fringe of Saxon marcher politics, had evidently come sufficiently far to be a real force in Ottonian politics, a position Poland was to retain for the next fifty years, while the renewal of opposition by the Bohemian duke was also to set a pattern for the immediate future.

However, the uprisings of the 970s show the underlying stability of the empire. We do not hear of much serious opposition to Otto II within Saxony, though one or two of the insurgents of 953–4, like Count Ekbert the One-Eyed, supported Henry against Otto. Once Otto II had finally come to terms with his southern and western enemies – after an initial period of uncertainty which lasted only a little longer than the corresponding period in his father's reign – he could think of taking up Italian politics where his father had left off, namely in the south. The initial impulse was much like that of twenty years earlier: the pope, Benedict VII, had appealed to Otto II for help in 980. But the aims of the Italian campaign were rather different. There was not much to be done in Lombardy or in Rome, and Otto II had already been crowned emperor. The thrust of the campaign lay further south; it aimed not just at extorting recognition from Byzantium, but at establishing Ottonian control over the southern part of the peninsula, against both Byzantine and Muslim Sicilian opposition. It was at this point, in 982, that Otto's chancery adopted what was, after a few hiccups, to become the normal title of *imperator Romanorum augustus*, and this is certainly more than just a coincidence in time: Otto was claiming to be a *Roman* emperor and hence rule over the whole peninsula. The initial stages of the conquest went well, until the Ottonian army came upon a strong Arab force at Cap Colonne in July 982. Though the battle at first went in the Germans' favour and the Arab emir was killed, Otto's army was in the end crushingly defeated, with heavy losses, including Bishop Henry of Augsburg, the Conradine count Udo, Margrave Günther of Merseburg and at least a dozen other German counts; Otto himself barely escaped. The death of the Arab emir meant that the Arab army returned to Sicily; but the battle, echoes of which reached even Wessex, was a serious setback. Otto might perhaps have recovered matters – he was able to get an assembly of German and north Italian magnates at Verona in the summer of 983 to agree to send reinforcements and to elect his son Otto king (thus enabling Otto II himself to stay in Italy) – but his death from malaria on December 7 983 put an end to any further campaigning in southern Italy. None of Otto II's immediate successors had the time or energy to do much more than show the flag here; the claims of the ninth and tenth centuries were not to be realised until the end of the twelfth century, and then by rather different means.

The eastern frontier saw a similar stagnation. We do not hear much about campaigns against the Elbe Slavs in Otto II's reign; one campaign is recorded for 979, but it is not certain whether it was directed against the Liutizi or against Miesco. The expansion of Otto I's time was slowing down, even before it was brought to an abrupt halt by the great Slav uprising of 983. Up until the battle of the Recknitz the most formidable Slav opponents of the Ottonians and the Saxon margraves had been the Abodrites. After the campaigns of the 950s they continued in existence, and unlike the Sorbs after the comparable campaigns under Henry I they were not taken into Saxon lordship; they were still semi-independent tributaries under their own rulers (the status which, according to Widukind, they had asked for and been refused before the Recknitz). The main thrust in the 960s was not against the Abodrites but further east and south. As we have seen, this brought the Saxons into contact with Poland, where Miesco I was building up an eastern European tributary empire not unlike that of the Ottonians. The immediate effect of this was to increase the pressure on the Elbe Slavs, and the foundation of new bishoprics at the end of the 960s meant that they were not only being required to pay secular tributes (often heavy ones) but also tithes. The connection is made clear by Thietmar of Merseburg at the beginning of his account of the uprising: "The peoples who by accepting Christianity were bound to pay tribute to our kings and emperors, provoked by the pride of Duke Dietrich, took up arms, united in their presumption."[19] The peoples involved, the Zirzipani, Tollensi, Kessini and Redarii, had come in the course of the tenth century to form a confederation based on a religious cult, with its centre at the temple of Rethre in the territory of the Redarii. A militant paganism based on worship of a god of war (the name given to the confederation, Liutizi, is probably derived from the Slav word *liut*, meaning wild) was a much more effective basis for resistance both to Saxon domination and to Christianization than a ruler who might be won over or coerced. The parallels with the Saxon uprisings of the 780s and with the *Stellinga* uprisin ʒ of the early 840s are obvious. The constellation of forces in 983 was unpropitious. Saxon losses at Cap Colonne in 982 had been heavy, and in early 983 the Danes began an attack which was serious enough for Bernard

19. Thietmar III 17, p. 118.

Billung to abandon his journey to the assembly at Verona and return north to defend the frontier. The uprising by the Liutizi at the end of June destroyed the bishoprics and garrisoned fortifications at Havelberg and Brandenburg; at the same time an attack by the Abodrites under their ruler Mistui destroyed the fortress and monastery at Calbe and reduced Hamburg to ashes. A hastily raised Saxon army under Archbishop Gisilher of Magdeburg and the eastern margraves met the insurgents in August and drove them back, but it was too late to restore the status quo.

The uprising of 983 marked the end of Saxon expansion for the next few generations. It is a sign of the stability of the empire that it had few immediate repercussions, apart from a change of the guard among the Saxon margraves in the next two or three years. Forty years earlier a hold-up in Slav tribute payments had contributed to the crisis of 941; but neither the political nor the military economy of the Ottonian Reich was any longer so wholly dependent on the motor of Slav tribute as it had been under Henry I and in the early years of Otto I's reign. Structurally there is undoubtedly a connection between the end of expansion marked by the catastrophe of 983 and the beginnings of the territorialization of lordship, a tendency which had been under way in west Francia for more than a century. The transition was cushioned for the Ottonian Reich by Saxon silver, by the possession of Italy, and by the accumulated Slav tribute of three generations; and of course the rising did not break Saxon military power. Nevertheless, by Otto II's death it was clear (though to us rather than to contemporaries) that the era of expansion was over. A total of more than ten years of campaigning in southern Italy by Otto I and Otto II had brought little more than a recognition of the Ottonians' imperial title by Byzantium – welcome, no doubt, but hardly an adequate return for the efforts put in. The 970s had seen the beginnings of emancipation from Ottonian hegemony not only for the west Frankish kingdom under Lothar but also for the princes of Poland and Bohemia. Most crucially of all, the great Slav uprising of 983 left the east Saxon nobility with no more than the early Sorb conquests to show for more than fifty years of fighting. It was a long time before the consequences of the uprising were accepted, or even recognized, as the criticism of the very different lines of policy pursued by Otto III and Henry II were to show (see below, pp. 259f.). Yet whatever happened at the level of consciousness, at the level of being the uprising – together with the other developments of Otto II's reign – was to have profound effects, to initiate a shift, clearly visible by the time of the first two

Salian rulers, away from a kingdom in many ways little more than a federation under a ruler who exercised hegemony abroad and the power of a *paterfamilias* over the leading men at home, towards a territorially more stable polity which had something more of the appearances and apparatus of a state.

Part III *The* ancien régime, *983–1056*

CHAPTER SEVEN

The politics of the kingdom

KING-MAKING

Between the death of Otto II in 983 and that of Henry III in 1056 Germany was ruled by four kings; each was also crowned emperor at some time during his reign. It is worth looking carefully at how they became king. French writers of the twelfth century liked to contrast France, where kings succeeded by inheritance, and Germany, where they were elected. The contrast was not in fact as sharp as that, even in the twelfth century. The Capetian title to the French crown was not a purely hereditary one, at least in the eleventh and twelfth centuries, while on the other hand there were strong elements of heredity in German succession practice. Of the kings we are considering, all in a sense belonged to the Ottonian royal family. Otto III succeeded his father Otto II in 983; Henry II, who became king in 1002 on Otto III's childless death, was the grandson of Otto I's younger brother Henry; Conrad II, who was elected on Henry's death without heirs in 1024, was Otto I's great-great-grandson, being descended from Otto's daughter Liutgard. Conrad was succeeded by his son Henry III in 1039 and he in turn by his son Henry IV in 1056. Conrad's accession is conventionally taken to mark the foundation of a new dynasty, that of the Salians, but the name is first found in the twelfth century, and although it is evident that Conrad and his successors had a strong sense of being a family in their own right, and themselves stressed other claims to distinguished ancestry which for them were more important than their relationship to the Ottonians, contemporaries do not seem to have seen the election of 1024 as a great break in continuity. The Salians stood in almost as close a relation to the Ottonians as, say, Plantagenets to Normans.

No king in the period we are considering had any difficulty in designating his son king during his own lifetime. Otto I had had Otto II crowned in May 961; Otto III was crowned at Christmas 983 in Aachen (Otto II was already dead, but the participants in the ceremony did not yet know this, and the coronation simply confirmed the election made at the assembly of Verona in May 983). Conrad II managed to have his son Henry III elected and crowned in April 1028 at the age of ten, less than four years after he himself had become king, while Henry III's son Henry IV received the allegiance of the magnates within six weeks of his birth in 1050, even before he had been baptized, and he was elected at the age of three. Moreover, there can be no question of rulers having forced their sons on reluctant magnates. In 983, as in 961, the election of the young son was intended to protect the kingdom's stability against the risk of the ruler dying or being killed in Italy, while the fact that Henry III and Agnes of Poitou for a long time had no male children was a matter of general concern: in 1047 the archbishop of Cologne ordered prayers to be said for the birth of a successor, and the annals of Altaich recorded the news of Henry IV's birth in 1050 with a "thanks be to God!".[1]

What has just been said might suggest that royal succession in tenth- and eleventh-century Germany resembled the dynastic practices common in western Europe from the high middle ages on: untroubled direct succession from father to son where there was a son, otherwise the succession of the closest male relative. But this is not quite the whole story. We can get a better idea of what was involved by looking more closely at the disputed successions of 983, 1002 and 1024. The fact that Otto III's coronation more or less coincided with the death of his father and that Otto was only three years old at the time meant that his succession was open to revision. The events of 983–6 look in some ways like a replay of the early years of Otto I's reign. Just as between 938 and 941 Henry, the younger son of Henry I, was not disposed to let Otto I succeed unchallenged, so Henry's son, Henry "the Quarrelsome" (the nickname is not contemporary), was not disposed to let Otto I's grandson succeed. Significantly, Bishop Folkmar of Utrecht, who

1. Annales Altahenses, ed. E.L.B. von Oefele (MGH SRG, Hannover 1891) 47.

had held him in custody since the rebellion of 976–7, released him on hearing the news of Otto II's death; it was evidently risky to go on holding him captive. At first Henry claimed only the right to act as Otto III's guardian, and it was acknowledged by all that he had such a right as the young king's nearest male relative. By March 984 it was evident that he intended more: he spent Palm Sunday in Magdeburg and Easter at Quedlinburg, in the tradition of the two previous kings. At Magdeburg he invited the magnates to commend themselves to him as king, and at Quedlinburg he not only received the commendation of the Slav dukes of Poland, Bohemia and the Abodrites but had himself acclaimed with the *laudes regiae*. His following was substantial and included the majority of the bishops, all the archbishops except Willigis of Mainz, and a number of lay magnates, as well as the Slav dukes and Lothar of France. In view of the disasters at the end of Otto II's reign there was obviously a lot to be said for a king who was of age. Nevertheless, Henry's support was not large enough to overawe all opposition, and by the time of the assembly at Bürstadt on the Rhine in May 984 he had to promise the loyalists that he would hand over the young King Otto III to his mother Theophanu at the end of June. In the course of 984 and 985 Henry's followers made their peace with Otto III (or those who were acting in his name) and they were followed by Henry himself, who submitted to Otto III at Frankfurt in June 985. This submission had been preceded by negotiations as a result of which Henry was restored to the duchy of Bavaria; the incumbent duke, the Liutpolding Henry the Younger, received the duchy of Carinthia he had lost in 977, while the Carinthian duke Otto was compensated by being able to retain his ducal title as well as by grants of lands around Worms and Frankfurt.

The final confirmation of Otto's kingship came at Quedlinburg the following Easter, when Otto was acknowledged as king by the assembled magnates (including the Slav dukes who had commended themselves to Henry the Quarrelsome there in 984). In what was no doubt a conscious imitation of Otto I's accession in 936, a ceremonial banquet at which the dukes of Bavaria, Suabia, Saxony and Carinthia acted as court officials demonstrated the young king's undisputed legitimacy. The family dispute over the succession resembled those of the two previous reigns, but it is symptomatic of the shift towards a more institutionalized polity, one governed as much by abstract rules pertaining to a state as by personal connections, that Otto III and his supporters, whose position was not nearly as strong as that of Otto I or Otto II had been, nevertheless came out on top. The last stage in Otto's accession came even later, at an assembly at Sohlingen in September 994, when he received his arms and came of age. Before that, in contrast to the reign of Louis the Child, there was a regency, exercised first by Otto's mother Theophanu, and then after her death in 991 by his grandmother, the empress Adelheid. This too can be taken as a sign of an increasing institutionalization of the kingdom, though the young Otto was treated in many ways as if he were fully king, even being called on to lead armies against the Slavs. A queen who had been designated *consors regni*, as Theophanu had been and Kunigunde was to be, carried a good deal of political weight and provided an element of continuity.

The best documented of the three successions is that following the death of Otto III in 1002. Otto had died in Umbria on January 24 at the age of twenty-one, having made no arrangements for the succession. His corpse was escorted north for burial in Aachen in accordance with his wishes. Duke Henry of Bavaria met the funeral cortege when it reached Bavaria and took charge of the body together with the royal insignia, thus laying claim to the succession. Archbishop Heribert of Cologne, who had tried to avoid having to hand over the Holy Lance, was held captive by Henry until he surrendered it. Henry also tried to win over as many of the princes as possible, but they were cautious. At about the same time, in March, the Saxon magnates met at Frohse. They were as reserved about the candidature of Margrave Ekkehard of Meißen as those accompanying Otto's corpse had been about Henry of Bavaria, and would agree only to take an oath that they would neither collectively nor singly accept anyone as king before a further assembly to be held at Werla. A meeting of the western and south-western magnates was held after Otto's funeral in Aachen in early April; the majority promised their support to Hermann of Suabia. Meanwhile some of the Saxon magnates had made contact with Henry, who sent messengers to his cousins Sophie and Adelheid (Otto III's sisters) and the other magnates at the meeting at Werla in April, promising "great rewards" in return for their support. The response of the meeting was "that Henry should become king with Christ's help and by hereditary right".[2] Not all felt this way. Ekkehard of Meißen evidently had enough support to be able to commandeer the banquet prepared for the royal sisters and dine in state together with Duke

2. Thietmar V 3, p. 196.

Bernard of Saxony and Bishop Arnulf of Halberstadt, and then to have himself received with royal honours by Bishop Bernward in Hildesheim; but he was killed shortly afterwards in Pöhlde by Saxon rivals.

By the summer it was evident that Henry of Bavaria would become king. He had the support of a large part of the Saxon nobility, he had been acknowledged by the Bavarian and east Franconian nobles at Worms, and he was crowned king by Archbishop Willigis at Mainz, in spite of efforts by Hermann of Suabia to prevent this, on June 7. Here he was accepted by the Franconian and upper Lotharingian nobles; the Saxons followed suit at a meeting of their own at Merseburg on July 24. Here they separately elected Henry king, showing that they did not regard the decisions of Worms and Mainz as binding on them; Henry himself was prepared to accept this. They acknowledged him by commending themselves and having Duke Bernard Billung invest him with the Holy Lance. On September 8 the rest of the Lotharingian nobility commended themselves to him at Aachen and set him on Charles the Great's throne. Finally, Hermann of Suabia submitted and acknowledged Henry as king on October 1; we do not hear of any acknowledgement by the Suabian nobility apart from this. Hermann had evidently not been able to compete with Henry at the military level; there are hints in the annals of St Gallen and in a diploma of Henry II that he tried to negotiate with Henry over a possible division of the kingdom, but this did not come to anything.[3]

The succession of Conrad II in 1024 was seemingly a more straightforward affair. Otto III's death was perhaps unexpected, but long before 1024 it had become apparent that Henry II would die childless, and the participants had had time to prepare their positions, though the shortage of narrative sources for the final years of Henry's reign makes it difficult for us to see how. The contrast with 1002 may also reflect differences between the principal narrative sources: Thietmar of Merseburg offers much revealing detail about 1002 and was not himself an unqualified admirer of the successful candidate, whereas Wipo, the biographer of Conrad II, was writing a panegyric of his hero. On the death of Henry II on July 13 1024 there were, according to Wipo, only two serious candidates: Conrad himself, whose position derived largely from the fact that he had

3. D H II 34 for Strasbourg; *Annales Sangallenses maiores*, MGH SS 1, 81.

married Gisela, the widow of Duke Ernest I of Suabia; and his younger cousin Conrad, son of Duke Conrad of Carinthia and successor to the family possessions around Worms. The critical assembly was held at Kamba (on the Rhine opposite Oppenheim) in early September 1024. According to Wipo the two candidates agreed to accept the decision of the magnates and share the spoils afterwards: better that either of them should rule than that they should both submit to the rule of a stranger. Conrad was then proposed by Archbishop Aribo of Mainz and elected by most of those present, including Conrad the Younger. Immediately after the election Henry II's widow Kunigunde handed over the royal insignia to Conrad "and thus confirmed his rule, so far as a member of her sex may do so."[4] The election was completed by coronation at Mainz and enthroning at Aachen in September 1024, at which most of the Lotharingians commended themselves. The meeting at Kamba was by no means drawn from the whole kingdom. The Saxons had already met separately beforehand at Werla and the Lotharingians were largely absent. As Henry II had done in 1002, Conrad had to follow up his election with a perambulation of the kingdom. Between his coronation and Whitsun of the following year Conrad visited, in order, Saxony, Thuringia, Franconia, Bavaria and Suabia, receiving the acknowledgement of the magnates of the region (and in Constance also that of some Italians). Noteworthy here was the reception in the Ottonian heartland of Saxony. At a meeting between Conrad and the Saxon nobility in Minden at Christmas 1024 Conrad promised to respect their laws in return for being acknowledged as king, much as Henry II had done in 1002. At Quedlinburg Conrad was ceremonially received by the surviving Ottonian abbesses, Adelheid of Quedlinburg and Sophie of Gandersheim: a legitimizing of the new ruler by the near kin of the old. The special importance of Saxony was seen not only in these two meetings but in the length of time – nearly three months – Conrad spent there in his tour of the kingdom. The reception was completed by the submission of the remaining Lotharingian dissidents in Aachen at Christmas 1025.

It is risky to generalize from these events. There was no book of rules which laid down how successions were to be settled; there were established liturgies, *ordines*, for the crowning of the king, but these gave no guidance as to how he was to be chosen. Few magnates participated in more than one election – it was exceptional that two

4. Wipo c. 2, p. 19.

powerful archbishops, Willigis of Mainz and Gisilher of Magdeburg, played a leading role both in 983–5 and in 1002, as did Bernard I of Saxony – and the arrangements for settling the succession were evidently made ad hoc on each occasion, often under the pressure of events. Though the way this was done reflected the participants' unspoken assumptions about their polity, these should not be read too readily as political theory. Moreover, our information is far from complete. We know a lot about 1002 because of Thietmar's very full account – without it we should have only a few hints that Henry of Bavaria did not become king without opposition. In spite of these uncertainties, however, we can see that there were a number of elements involved in succession. The new king had to be (or to have been) crowned and anointed, using the royal insignia (the Holy Lance and the imperial crown); control over these gave some claim to kingship in itself. Whether the coronation and unction were performed by the archbishop of Cologne at Aachen or by the archbishop of Mainz in Mainz was not definitively settled by 1056; much more important was the fact of unction itself. The king also had to be acknowledged by his magnates, though not necessarily all together or at the same time. To call such an acknowledgement election is justified by the sources, but to do so tends to blur the very real distinction between the royal accessions in the period covered in this book and those on later occasions (notably in 1077 and 1125), when the magnates were able to make a conscious choice and deliberately to pass over possible rights of inheritance. Where there were no immediate male heirs to the deceased ruler, a wider circle of magnates could put themselves forward as candidates. In 1002, though both Ekkehard of Meißen and Hermann of Suabia could perhaps have claimed distant relationship with the Ottonians, this was so distant as not to have distinguished them from many of those who elected them. This was in itself no liability. Thietmar of Merseburg records the taunt flung at Ekkehard of Meißen in 1002: "Can't you see that your cart is missing its fourth wheel?"[5] but this probably refers to Ekkehard's lack of the cardinal virtue of self-control rather than to his shortage of hereditary right. In 1024 also there were any number of conceivable claimants (including numerous foreign rulers) whose relationship to the Ottonians was at least as close as that of the two Conrads; this was evidently not a critical factor in the absence of direct heirs, and it is interesting that Wipo

5. Thietmar IV 52, p. 190.

refers to Conrad's descent on his mother's side from Burgundian and Lotharingian noble families, and not to his Ottonian blood through his father and grandmother. Presumably this was how the Salian rulers wished to see themselves. On the other hand, ideas of heredity were not lacking: Henry II at least claimed the throne by hereditary right.

Whether a ruler succeeded as the son of his predecessor or in more open election, this was not a mere administrative act but one publicly and solemnly carried out. What it meant was a reforging of the bonds between the new ruler and his leading men: he was their king at least as much as they were his magnates. Such acknowledgement could be given either at the king-making ceremony itself or later. The new kings in particular, Henry II and Conrad II, whose rule had not been established during the reign of their predecessor, toured their kingdom after being crowned, receiving the commendation of the magnates in the different regions, but so also did Henry III, though with less urgency. Otto III, as a child and a ruler whose position was threatened, was confined by his guardians to Saxony and western Franconia, where he was acknowledged by his magnates at assemblies. There do not seem to have been hard and fast rules about whose recognition was required. Wipo lists "all the bishops, dukes and other princes, the leading warriors and the king's bodyguard, as well as all free men of any consequence",[6] but though he is certainly right about the bishops, dukes and members of the king's own following, the most we can say about the others is that a king had to be acknowledged by a representative selection of the nobility of each of the peoples. We cannot always tell whether acknowledgement simply took the form of appearance at a royal assembly – a show of hands, so to speak – or whether an individual, person to person ceremony was required. In 1002 Henry II had in many cases to give or promise a *quid pro quo* in return for recognition, and this was also done even when succession was seemingly more straightforward: Otto I, Conrad II and Henry III could not simply command the recognition of their sons in 960, 1028 or 1053 respectively, and we have seen that Otto II paid a price in 973 (above, p. 175). Recognition could also be withheld, at least by groups, though few individuals could risk doing so. In 1002 Henry II's opponent Liudger did not acknowledge him, and in 1039 Duke Gozelo of Lotharingia is said to have considered not accepting Henry

6. Wipo c. 4, p. 24.

III, but the only serious withholding of commendation was in 1024 when a group of Lotharingian magnates including Duke Frederick of Lotharingia waited over a year before commending themselves to Conrad. Nevertheless, there was something precarious about the position of a new ruler even after he had toured the kingdom. Only after the uncertainty of the first few years of a reign had been overcome was the new king, the *novus rex*, fully king, though the length and seriousness of this period of uncertainty had declined markedly by the time of Conrad II and still more by that of Henry III.

OFFICE-HOLDING AND PATRONAGE

Kings were made by their magnates; once made, they in turn made their magnates, by appointing them to positions of power and wealth – duchies, marches, counties, archbishoprics and bishoprics – and by granting them lands and other rights as privileges. To say that kings appointed to offices is both true and misleading. It is true in the sense that in the filling of all these positions the ruler normally had at least the last word. It is misleading if it is taken to imply that there were no other claims to office except those based on the will of the ruler, who could make or break men at will. Quite apart from hereditary expectations in the case of secular positions, the ruler normally appointed after receiving gifts, advice and requests, often very pressing ones. Increasingly, appointments were made publicly. They were the products of a political collective in which the ruler played the most important but not the only part. What the holders of offices did and were expected to do once appointed – in other words, the extent to which they were "officials" – will be discussed in the final section of this chapter. Here we are concerned only with the distribution of power and privilege – probably the most important aspect of the ruler's relations with his magnates.

In the succession of dukes to duchies a number of different elements were at work: royal designation (the word is used instead of appointment in order to stress the considerable similarities with *royal* succession), election by the people, hereditary succession. Direct succession was taken for granted. On no occasion between 983 and 1056 did a son who was of age fail to succeed to a duchy on his father's death. Saxony was thus held by three generations of Billungs, grandfather, father and son, between 936 and 1059 (and by two more from 1059 to 1106), upper Lotharingia by four

191

generations between 958 and 1033. So strong were such expectations that a few sons were even given the title of duke during their father's term of office: Hermann II of Suabia from 996, Henry IV of Bavaria (the later king Henry II) from 994, Godfrey the Bearded of upper Lotharingia from 1040. Minors might be passed over, but there are examples of their succeeding after an interregnum: the Liutpolding Henry III (son of Berthold) in Bavaria in 983, Conrad II (son of Conrad I) in Carinthia in 1036. They could also succeed directly: both Hermann III and Ernest II of Suabia were minors on their accession, as perhaps was Gozelo II of lower Lotharingia. Under Henry I and Otto I, ducal widows, sisters and daughters had helped through marriage to legitimize the succession of new men. In the period we are considering, there was only one directly comparable example: on the death of Hermann III of Suabia in 1012, Henry II in effect acknowledged hereditary claims to the duchy by appointing the husband of Hermann's sister Gisela, the Babenberger Ernest. But we might note the way in which women could hold duchies in trust for children: Beatrix in upper Lotharingia for her son Dietrich in the 980s (she was even occasionally referred to in charters as duke, at much the same time as Otto III's mother Theophanu was being styled *imperator* in diplomata); Gisela briefly for Ernest II of Suabia after Ernest I's death in 1015. It was only the logical culmination of this idea when Henry III's wife Agnes was given the duchy of Bavaria to hold for a possible future son in 1055.

More generally, marriage played an important role in raising men into the very small circle of those eligible for ducal office. The families of the men with whom the Ottonians had shared the duchies in the first half of the tenth century – Conradines, Hunfridings, Liutpoldings, Reginarids – were all extinct in the direct male line by the end of the tenth century. Their successors owed their duke-worthiness, at least in part, to marriages with the Ottonians. The Ezzonids, a family which under Henry III produced the dukes Otto II of Suabia and Conrad of Bavaria, began their rise with the marriage (something of a mésalliance) between Ezzo, count palatine of Lotharingia, and Mathilda, Otto III's sister. The rise of the Luxemburger (Henry V and Henry VII of Bavaria, Frederick of lower Lotharingia) went back to the marriage between Henry II and Kunigunde, though the family was in any case a powerful one on its home ground in Lotharingia; Frederick I, the founder of the upper Lotharingian ducal line, was married to Beatrix, a niece of Otto I. The duke-worthiness of the Babenberger – Ernest I and II and Hermann IV of Suabia, Otto III of Bavaria – was founded on the marriage between Ernest and Gisela, plus the fact that Ernest's family already held the margravate of Austria. The family which supplied dukes in lower Lotharingia from 1012 and in upper Lotharingia from 1033 was closely related both to the Luxemburger and to the earlier ducal house of upper Lotharingia, as were Adalbert and Gerhard, dukes in upper Lotharingia from 1047 to 1070. The one man who does not fit – Adalbero, duke of Carinthia from 1012 until his deposition in 1035 – was a well-established local man; but Carinthia, which had grown from a march to a duchy in 976, retained for a long time its march-like character.

We have just seen how strong the claims of heredity were in the succession to duchies; yet virtually all these men were designated by the ruler. The only conclusion which can be drawn is that kings were not in practice free in their choice, except on rare occasions. Even when there was no son to succeed to a duchy, the circle of those who could be considered, who would be accepted by the other dukes and by the leading men of the duchy, was always very small. The origins of the dukedoms as principalities – something between an administrative division and a fully independent kingdom – were never entirely forgotten, and can be seen in titles like duke "of the Bavarians" (or of some other people) occasionally used even in the royal chancery. The acceptance of the leading men was important; there is evidence for an element of election in duke-making. Henry II fobbed off Henry of Schweinfurt, who wanted to be given the duchy of Bavaria in 1002, with the excuse that the Bavarians had the right to choose their dukes, and in 1009 Henry of Luxemburg tried to forestall being deposed as duke of Bavaria by persuading the leading men of the duchy to swear not to elect any other duke for three years. The duchies were not uniform institutions, of course, and we cannot simply generalize from the Bavarian evidence, but we might note that Ekkehard, margrave of Meißen, is said by Thietmar of Merseburg to have been "elected" duke of Thuringia, and that there is twelfth-century evidence for Saxon ducal elections (though this cannot just be projected back into the period we are considering). At first sight it might seem that dukedoms could also simply be conferred without reference to the leading men, as for example in the "shuffle" of 985 (above, p. 185). Yet the men involved here were all of ducal rank, not new men; and the details were worked out at assemblies at which some at least of the leading men of Bavaria and Carinthia were present. What was possible was for the king to be his own duke, either by acting as "regent" for a minor or by taking the duchy into his own hands. Lower Lotharingia was vacant between

1006 and 1012. Suabia was under royal tutelage between 1003 and 1012 and in a sense again between 1015 and 1024 (the guardian for Ernest II, after his mother Gisela had remarried, was Archbishop Poppo of Trier, who was a close associate of Henry II, but also Ernest's uncle). The duchy was held by Henry III between 1038 and 1045. Bavaria was held by the king between 1009 and 1017, by the heir-apparent between 1026 and 1042, and again in 1055, while Carinthia was held by Henry III between 1039 and 1047.

What has been said about the duchies applies as far as succession is concerned to the marches also. Of the Saxon marches, the northernmost was held by the Billungs and was the basis for their ducal title. The Nordmark was held in our period by men from the family of the counts of Walbeck until 1009, and then by the rivals of the last Walbeck count Werner, Bernard and William, from 1009 to 1056. The Meißen march was in the hands of members of the family of Ekkehard I between 985 and 1046: Ekkehard, his brother Gunzelin and his sons Hermann and Ekkehard II; the margraves who followed were drawn from the family of the counts of Weimar. The eastern and Lausitz marches were held up to 1032 by descendants of a margrave who had been prominent in the 940s, though the Lausitz in particular was held de facto for much of this time by the Polish rulers; later margraves were drawn from established Saxon comital families, including for a time that of the margraves of Meißen. In the south-east the Ostmark, the kernel of what was to become Austria, was held by the Babenberger from the beginning in 976, while the Carinthian march (later to become Styria) was held either by local men or by the duke of Carinthia. The march of Verona, which after 962 did not really have the function of a march, was held by the duke of Bavaria, later of Carinthia. The element of election was almost completely absent here but there was the same "magic circle". As with the duchies, the Saxon and Bavarian marches did not always stay with the same family, but the small circle of eligible families had formed itself by Otto III's time at the latest. But, by contrast with the duchies, the marches were always held by local men. The most distant appointment was that of the Babenberger Liutpold to the Ostmark in 976, but even this was only a move from the northern end of Bavaria to the eastern end, and Liutpold's family was rooted in eastern Franconia and northern Bavaria. If the claims of heredity in the marches were stronger than in the duchies, in counties they were stronger still. Here these applied not just to direct succession; quite distant relatives could succeed, and counties could be held by minors, or by brothers together. Wives, and occasionally widows, called themselves *comitissa* (countess): a countship was – at least as seen by its holders – more a rank than an office. Rulers could and did intervene in the succession to counties, but this did not happen nearly as often as one might expect, and it was not always successful: the Westfalian count Balderich got Henry II to depose his cousin and appoint him to a county, but he could not secure general acceptance there. Duchies, marches and counties could be forfeit for disloyalty, but this was fairly rare, and the deposed holder was often reinstated after an interval (see below, p. 207). Deposition affected dukes most frequently. Henry of Luxemburg was deposed from Bavaria in 1009, Ernest II from Suabia in 1027 and again in 1030, Adalbero from Carinthia in 1035, Godfrey from lower Lotharingia in 1044 and again in 1049, Conrad from Bavaria in 1053, Welf III from Carinthia in 1055.

The elements involved in succession to bishoprics were not so different as might be supposed from those determining access to secular office. Indeed, eleventh-century annalists often note in their accounts of assemblies which bishops and secular office-holders were appointed at them, and they use a common phraseology for both kinds of appointment. Both secular and ecclesiastical offices were conferred by the king by investing the recipient with a symbol of its authority – a banner for secular office, the staff and (from the time of Henry III) ring of office for bishoprics (and monasteries). But because bishoprics were by their nature not hereditary offices – at least not in the Ottonian and Salian kingdom – the accents were different. A bishop, once consecrated, could be deposed only under quite exceptional circumstances (no German bishop was between 958 and 1056), and for this if for no other reason rulers controlled the appointment of bishops and guarded this right jealously. Henry II in particular was rarely willing to accept even the passive role of merely confirming a candidate already chosen by the episcopal chapter. On the death of Gisilher of Magdeburg in 1004 the chapter wanted Walthard, but Henry overruled their election and appointed his own candidate, Tagino. Tagino himself had been a candidate as the duke of Bavaria's *capellanus* for the bishopric of Regensburg in 995, but Otto III had preferred to appoint his own *capellanus* Gebhard and to console Tagino by taking him into the royal chapel. Walthard did, however, get Magdeburg on Tagino's death in 1012, and on his own death a few months later the chapter elected Otto, who was again passed over by Henry II but made *capellanus* as a consolation prize. We can see here how the rights of chapters to elect and the claims of their candidates could be overridden but not simply ignored. "Free election" would become a slogan of church reformers only at the end of our period, but it was nevertheless felt that the chapter should at least confirm the ruler's candidate by a formal election. In theory the laity of the bishopric and the metropolitan in whose province the bishopric lay also had a say in choosing the bishop, but this had few practical consequences; it was an unusual event when Archbishop Aribo of Mainz complained to the chapter of Worms that he had not been consulted either by them or by the king in the appointment of a new bishop in 1025.

Those who were appointed as bishops were often members of the royal chapel, that is to say they had served the king at court and were personally commended to him. It is not easy to say precisely how often this happened. We have no membership-lists for the chapel, and often learn only by chance that a bishop had been a *capellanus*. Nor is it certain that all *capellani* had done lengthy service at court: some appear simply to have been taken on as members of a club, like Wazo, made bishop of Liège in 1042, who had been an active *capellanus* for only a few months in the early years of Conrad II's reign, or the historian Wipo, who spent most of Conrad's reign on sick leave. Nevertheless, it would seem that from the end of Otto I's reign at least a quarter of all episcopal appointments were made from the chapel, and under Henry II and Henry III this rose at times to at least a half. Whereas dukes were usually "foreigners", at least in the late tenth and eleventh centuries, and counts and margraves normally locals, bishops lay somewhere in between. In the eleventh century, about a third of the bishops whose origins are known were not natives of the region where their bishoprics lay: Bavaria and Suabia were net exporters of bishops, Saxony and Lotharingia net importers, Franconia roughly in balance.

Both the role of the chapel and the appointment of "foreigners" point to the importance of the ruler in the making of bishops. As with the duchies, the appointment to bishoprics had elements of both royal designation and election, here by the chapter or monastic community. The rulers always confirmed, so far as we know, but they designated much more frequently for some sees (notably those of Saxony and lower Lotharingia, and for the Rhenish archbishoprics and bishoprics) than for others. In any case, neither rulers nor chapters were free in their choice. There were no hereditary claims to succession (though particular bishoprics might remain for long periods in the hands of a kindred – the Luxemburger for Metz and Verdun, the Aribonids for Salzburg) but there was nevertheless the same idea of a "magic circle" of eligible candidates. To a large extent these came from the same families as those which held the highest secular offices. The number of bishops not members of the high nobility in this period can be numbered almost on the fingers of one hand: two in Eichstätt, one in Freising, one or two in Liège, one in Hildesheim (out of over 200 appointments in the hundred years preceding the death of Henry III). The genealogies of many of the major families, on the other hand, are stuffed with bishops. The Babenberger produced archbishops of Trier (Poppo, 1016–47) and Mainz (Liutpold, 1051–60). Conrad II (who, it will be remembered, was not born a member of a royal family) could name as bishops his uncle (William of Strasbourg), cousin (Brun of Würzburg) and half-brother (Gebhard of Regensburg); another uncle became pope as Gregory V, and a whole host of his more distant relatives held bishoprics in the first half of the eleventh century. Many of these bishops from the high aristocracy had also been *capellani*; as in the ninth century, aristocratic and court bishops were not two distinct groups

The main change during the period we are considering was a move from patrimonial to more formalized rulership. Otto I could give bishoprics to the first cleric of the church he met (Günther of Regensburg in 940) or as compensation to the son of a man he had executed (Hildiward of Halberstadt in 968), acting apparently spontaneously and without advice (except from God). By the time of Conrad II and Henry III, bishoprics – and other offices, including secular ones – were bestowed in a glare of publicity. The appointment was often announced at an assembly, and before it was made there was lobbying. Queens like Kunigunde and Gisela, other female members of the royal family like Sophie of Gandersheim and Mathilda of Quedlinburg under Otto III, as well as influential archbishops like Willigis of Mainz, Tagino of Magdeburg or Pilgrim of Cologne, played an important role here, but they were not the only ones. Bishops and the great lay magnates had *capellani*, clerical followers, of their own, and sought promotion for these just as they sought rewards for their lay followings. Up to the time of Henry II and Conrad II large proffers were made to the ruler to gain both secular and ecclesiastical office. Henry III gave up such practices for bishoprics because they had come to be regarded as simoniacal: they could be taken to imply the buying and selling of the sacramental powers of the bishopric. But lobbying continued, and so did what later church reformers were to term simony *per obsequium*, the purchase of office by devoted service: many of Henry III's bishops had previously been members of the royal chapel.

The bestowing of offices, secular and ecclesiastical, was only one of the ways in which the rulers we are considering exercised patronage. They made extensive grants of lands to their magnates both as benefices and as gifts. The difference was not trivial. Thietmar cites as a mark of the special favour in which Ekkehard of Meißen was held by Otto III the fact that the emperor converted most of Ekkehard's benefices into *proprietas*.[7] But in practice gifts also imposed obligations, and they were forfeit for infidelity or if the recipient or his direct descendants died without immediate heirs. Besides grants of land there were other kinds of privilege. In principle at least, certain activities – later in the eleventh century to be defined collectively as *regalia* – were royal monopolies: castle-building with compulsory labour, beer-brewing, minting coins, holding markets, exercising blood justice. Magnates, particularly ecclesiastics, queued up to receive privileges entitling them to do such things. But such privileges do not necessarily prove either that they had not been doing them before the grant of the privilege (i.e. that the royal monopolies were always respected) or that they really did them afterwards (i.e. that privileges always had practical consequences). Grants of mint in particular were commoner than mints themselves. What privileges (and grants not recorded in surviving diplomata) did in the first instance was to express the relations between the ruler and his magnates: they were favours, signs of esteem and approval, the oil which lubricated the political machine. Often they were the price for services to be granted. Late in 1001 an army set off from Germany to reinforce Otto III, made up of contingents from the archbishoprics of Cologne and Mainz, the bishoprics of Worms and Würzburg, and the abbey of Fulda. All these prelates had been favoured by Otto; the bishops of Worms and Würzburg in particular had received extensive privileges during his brief visit to Germany in the spring and summer of 1000, while the abbot of Fulda had been granted special privileges by the papacy in 994 at Otto's petition. It is not surprising to find them here, nor to find that the archbishop of Mainz, who was on rather less good terms with Otto at the time because of a disagreement about which diocese had jurisdiction over the Ottonian monastery of Gandersheim, did not appear in person but merely sent his obligatory contingent of troops. Privileges were rarely granted by rulers on their own initiative. Like appointments to offices, they were the

---

7. Thietmar V 7, p. 228.

product of intensive lobbying, which helped to create ties of mutual dependence and obligation among the magnates. Royal diplomata often tell us who "intervened" to have the grant made; sometimes the interveners were named as in effect consenting to the grant of rights which affected their own rights or of lands to which they also had claims, but often they were named as lobbyists. As with appointments to offices, members of the royal family (especially queens) and influential archbishops are met particularly frequently in this context.

REBELLION

On the face of it the period between 983 and 1056 was remarkably stable politically. True, each of the four rulers was faced with a period of unrest immediately after his accession – though in Henry III's case this was confined almost completely to Bohemia and Hungary. But the opposition never reached anything like the scale it had in 937–41 or in 953–4, and it was restricted in its aims, so far as these are known or knowable. Ottonian and Salian rule was seemingly almost unquestioned. Yet this underlying stability by no means implies that peace prevailed. Lesser disturbances were common, and made up a substantial part of the relations between the magnates and their ruler as well as of those among the magnates. "Disturbance" is a neutral term. There were different kinds of disturbance: feud, uprising, latent opposition, separatism, rebellion – and what lay behind them could vary from region to region.

In Saxony under Otto I opposition to the king had tended to group around other members of the royal house: Otto's brother Henry and his son Liudolf. This tradition was continued under Otto II and in the early years of Otto III's reign, when the opposition coalition was led by Otto I's nephew Henry the Quarrelsome, but after that it declined, not least because both under the last Ottonians and under the early Salians there was a shortage of royal princes around whom such opposition could coalesce. It did not disappear altogether: Thietmar reports a Saxon conspiracy at the end of Otto III's reign which sought the leadership of Henry of Bavaria;[8] and

8. Thietmar IV 49, p. 188.

Henry had problems with his own brother Brun, even after he had been made bishop of Augsburg in 1006. But there were other tendencies. Otto III's Rome-centredness was not well received in Saxony, and the last years of his reign were a watershed: from then on the ties between the Saxons and their rulers were less close than they had been under the first two Ottos. Henry II was admittedly in a sense a Saxon, but contemporaries evidently saw him, or at least his following, as Bavarian. "Bavaria triumphs"[9] wrote one author – incidentally a good demonstration of how quickly early medieval "nationalities" could change, for Henry's grandfather had gone to Bavaria from Saxony only fifty years earlier. Consequently the Saxons feared the worst: Thietmar of Merseburg wrote that "At home [the Bavarians] are always content with little, but once they go abroad they are absolutely insatiable", and Henry II made some attempts to assuage Saxon feelings, calling the land a "delightful paradise".[10]

It is from Henry II's reign that we find Saxon magnates in open opposition to the king without either joining the following of a discontented royal relative or going into exile among the Slavs: Duke Bernard II rebelled in 1020; his brother Thietmar and Count Hermann of Werl had done so two years before; Margrave Bernard of the Nordmark fought a feud with Archbishop Gero of Magdeburg (and so in effect with Henry II) in 1016–17. Much of this stemmed from conflicts with the church, not only in Margrave Bernard's case but also in that of Bernard Billung, whose ambitions clashed with those of Archbishop Unwan of Bremen. But their cumulation reflected a general dissatisfaction with Henry II in Saxony in the second half of his reign; it was one reason why his campaigns against Boleslav Chrobry (see below, p. 260) fared so badly. Under Conrad II we hear little of conflicts with the Saxons, but the Billungs continued in opposition, having an enormous estate at Lesum confiscated at the end of Conrad II's reign. Duke Bernard regarded the archbishop of Bremen appointed by Henry III in 1043, Adalbert, as "a spy set in the land to betray its weakness to foreigners and to the emperor";[11] this expression says much about the almost regal independence of the Billungs in northern Saxony. There was an attempt by Thietmar Billung, Bernard's brother, to

9. *Rhythmus de obitu Ottonis III et de electione Heinrici*, quoted by S. Hirsch, *Jahrbücher des deutschen Reiches unter Heinrich II* 1, Leipzig 1862, 214, n. 7.
10. Thietmar V 19, p. 243; VI 10, p. 286.
11. Adam of Bremen III 5, p. 147; cf. Genesis 42:9.

ambush Henry III in 1047 while he was visiting Adalbert; Thietmar's death in a judicial duel and the exiling of his son for killing the victorious champion began a feud between Billungs and Salians which was to find expression in Magnus's revolt under Henry IV and his leadership of the Saxon uprising of the 1070s. Otherwise we have only general indications of discontent, expressed in particular at assemblies in 1053 and in 1056–7 after Henry's death; but it is evident that Henry III had already sown the seeds of the estrangement between Saxons and their Salian rulers which his son experienced.

If opposition in Saxony changed its character under the later Ottonians and Salians, opposition in Lotharingia remained remarkably constant. The risk that Lotharingia might be detached from the Reich and fall back to west Francia declined after 987: the Capetians were less interested in recovering Lotharingia than their Carolingian predecessors had been. But that did not mean that the Ottonians' and Salians' hold over it became noticeably firmer. This is in a sense paradoxical, since lower Lotharingia was a *Königslandschaft* (see below, p. 208) and the Ottonians and Salians went there frequently. Yet in upper Lotharingia, and on the borders towards Flanders and west Francia, the ruler's hold was much less secure, and the duchy was seldom completely quiet. In the north, the Frisians were scarcely more part of the Reich than the tribute-paying Slav peoples to the east. Besides this, there was usually at least one aristocratic grouping of some weight in opposition to the king: the counts of Hainault and Louvain in particular, descendants of the Reginarid dukes of the early tenth century, were usually unfriendly. Between 1008 and 1015 there was open warfare between Henry II and the Lotharingian brothers of his wife Kunigunde. One of these, Dietrich, became bishop of Metz by a coup in 1005. Henry swallowed this, but drew the line when a second brother-in-law, Adalbero, attempted to seize the archbishopric of Trier in 1008; the result was open warfare with campaigning, ended by a compromise peace. There was Lotharingian oppposition to Conrad II's election, as we have seen, while the last ten years of Henry III's reign were marked by a feud between Godfrey the Bearded and the king. Godfrey's father Gozelo had been duke in both upper and lower Lotharingia, and Godfrey was co-duke from 1040 in upper Lotharingia. On Gozelo's death in 1044 Henry III refused to accept Godfrey's demand to be invested with both duchies and gave lower Lotharingia to Godfrey's brother Gozelo II. When Godfrey refused to accept this decision he was deprived of his own duchy. The result was an alternation between warfare and settlement; Henry III was supported above all by the bishops of Liège and

Utrecht, while Godfrey had backing from the west, from Baldwin V of Flanders and from Henry I of France. It was not until 1049 that Godfrey was forced by a combination of papal excommunication, outlawry and military force to submit, and the conflict was reopened by his marriage against Henry's wishes to the heiress Beatrix of Tuscany in 1054. The Lotharingian magnates, after 987 no longer able to look to the kings of France, turned instead to other princes closer at hand for support, in particular to Otto-William of Burgundy in Henry II's reign and to Odo of Champagne under Conrad II. Odo's designs on Lotharingia and on the kingdom of Burgundy were ended only by his death in battle against Duke Gozelo I in 1037. The counts of Flanders occupied a special position here. The tenth-century counts, in particular Arnulf I (918–65), had built up a virtually independent territory in the north-east of the west Frankish kingdom. From the early eleventh century on they are found encroaching on imperial territory: Baldwin IV was able to secure recognition of his gains around Walcheren and Cambrai in spite of concerted action against him by Henry II and Robert II in 1006–7 and again in 1023. Baldwin V was even able to have his son recognized as count of Hainault immediately after Henry III's death, and thus to confirm the results of a coup he had organized in 1050.

Unrest directed against the ruler was rarer in the south German duchies than it had been under Otto I and Otto II. In particular the dukedoms themselves were not so easily made the basis of revolt, as both Suabia and Bavaria were frequently under direct or indirect royal control. The Bavarian aristocracy were at their most difficult in the years immediately following Henry II's accession. The Babenberger Henry of Schweinfurt, margrave in the Nordgau, rebelled in 1004 because Henry II had not, as half-promised, given him the duchy of Bavaria in return for his support in the election; the hostility between the two men went back to the reign of Otto II, when Henry of Schweinfurt and his brother Liutpold had been loyal to Otto II during the rebellion of Henry II's father, Henry the Quarrelsome. The man who did get the duchy, the king's brother-in-law Henry, was deposed in 1009 in the course of the feud between his Lotharingian brothers and the king. From then until the last years of Henry III's reign there was little serious trouble in the south-east, except for the deposition of Duke Adalbero of Carinthia in 1035. Adalbero was successfully removed, but not before he had killed one of his opponents and not without creating an alarm on the south-eastern border that he intended to try to hold his position with support from the Croats and Hungarians. Much more serious was the revolt by Conrad of Bavaria, who was deposed in 1053, fled to Carinthia and was joined in rebellion by Welf III of Carinthia and Bishop Gebhard of Regensburg in 1054–5. The conspiracy was thought to have aimed at depriving Henry III of his life and his kingdom and setting up Conrad in his place. What lay behind all this is uncertain, though the strains imposed on the magnates of the south-east by Henry's aggressively interventionist policy in Hungary may have accounted for the breadth of the rebellion, which was put down without fighting and followed by large-scale confiscations. In Suabia, ducal power had been radically reduced by the settlement forced on Hermann II by Henry II in 1002. The only serious revolt in this period was that of Conrad II's young stepson Ernest II. Ernest was a member of the group initially in opposition to Conrad II, together with Welf II and Conrad the Younger. He submitted in 1027 after being deserted by his Suabian following, but was pardoned and reinstated in the duchy. In 1030 he was presented by Conrad II with the choice of dealing with one of his own supporters, Count Werner of Kiburg, or giving up the duchy. He refused to abandon his own follower (as magnates often did in the tenth and eleventh centuries when this was the price of settlement with the ruler), was excommunicated and outlawed, and died along with Werner in a battle against imperialist forces in September 1030.

There were a number of different elements at work here. First, there was the general uncertainty already mentioned immediately following a king's accession. The *novus rex*, although only recently crowned and publicly acknowleged by all, always had a rather shaky position, and there was a potential opposition consisting of defeated rivals (or other representatives of the family), those who had not done well out of the previous reign and saw their opportunity, and those who had expected to do well out of the new reign and been disappointed. This was in part the basis of the support for Henry the Quarrelsome in 984–5; it fuelled the rebellions of Henry of Schweinfurt in 1004 and of the Luxemburger in 1008, and it lay behind the opposition of Conrad the Younger, Frederick of Lotharingia, Welf II and Ernest II of Suabia to Conrad II after his election. Opposition out of disappointment could happen at any time; it is not always easily distinguished from feuding over inheritance or other quarrels conducted so vigorously as to disturb the public peace. There was a pitched battle at Ulm in 1019 between Duke Adalbero of Carinthia on one side and the two Conrads, the later Conrad II and his younger cousin Conrad, son of the former Duke Conrad of Carinthia. Conrad the Younger had as a minor been passed over in favour of Adalbero for the succession to Carinthia in 1012, but what probably lay behind the action were disputes over the inheritance of Hermann II of Suabia. Adalbero and Conrad were married to daughters of Hermann's, while another daughter had married Otto of Carinthia and was thus Conrad the Younger's mother. Later on in the 1020s there was a feud between Welf II and the bishops of Augsburg and Freising in which the count plundered Brun of Augsburg's treasury and sacked the city. Thietmar recounts a whole series of such incidents in Saxony in the closing pages of his chronicle. Rulers would be expected to support the bishop in such cases; Thietmar complained that no such support was forthcoming for him and his contemporaries, and obviously thought that it should have been. In fact the ruler usually did intervene, as Conrad II did for Bruno of Augsburg or Henry III for Gebhard of Regensburg in 1053 when he was attacked by Conrad of Bavaria. Often heavy fines were imposed in such cases; Hermann II of Suabia had to compensate the bishop of Strasbourg for his sack of the city during the succession dispute of 1002, while Bernard of the Nordmark paid Gero of Magdeburg 500 pounds of silver in 1017 to make amends for an attack by his men on Magdeburg. Rulers did not intervene so readily in feuds between lay nobles, though they could do so if it suited them, and they were then just as likely to take sides as to lay down the law impartially.

A further delicate area was the relations between the marcher lords and the rulers beyond the borders. We have already seen how ambiguous and potentially conflict-laden these could be when looking at the south-eastern marches in Carolingian times. The problems were the same in the late Ottonian and early Salian period. The margraves had to keep in touch with the rulers beyond the frontiers. They and other nobles often married across the frontier, and such connections could be (and were) subject to misinterpretation (or correct interpretation). A number of Saxon nobles were thought by Henry II to be too friendly with the Polish ruler Boleslav Chrobry, including Margrave Gunzelin of Meißen in 1009 and Werner of the Nordmark and Ekkehard, brother of Margrave Hermann of Meißen, in 1013. There were similar suspicions of the relations between the dukes of Carinthia and Bavaria and the rulers of Hungary in the reigns of Conrad II and Henry III. As in the Carolingian period, there was not always a clear idea of frontier, at least as this affected persons rather than territories: the dukes of Poland and Bohemia in particular could be considered at some times as being parts of the Reich (and mentioned in the same breath as dukes of, say, Saxony or Bavaria), while at other times they were quite definitely not. When they were so considered, their disputes with the German rulers would be described in terms no different from those applied to members of the German high nobility.

A last kind of opposition was rebellion in the sense it is understood in the late medieval and early modern era: the intention to kill or depose the ruler and replace him by someone else. This was rare. As we have seen, there were plans to kill Otto I in 937–41, but apparently none in 953–4, though in 974 Henry the Quarrelsome is said to have wanted to replace Otto II. South of the border it was another matter. The Italians did not after 951 give up the practice described by Liutprand, and there were a number of attempts to set up an alternative king to the Ottonians and Salians, though apart from Arduin's kingship between 1002 and 1014 none of the other candidacies was a really serious alternative. The failure to find such an alternative did not mean enthusiastic consent, however. Only Otto III expected to be loved in Italy, quite mistakenly. The attitude of the others is best seen in Thietmar's story about Otto I in 962. Otto told his young sword-bearer Ansfrid to hold the sword firmly over his head and not to be distracted by prayer during the imperial coronation ceremony, since the Romans were not to be trusted: "when we are back in camp in the evening you can pray as much as you like".[12] The uprising of Archbishop Aribert of Milan against Conrad II in the 1030s was – at least in the accounts of writers north of the Alps – a rebellion aimed at killing Conrad and replacing him by another ruler. In Germany it is only at the end of Henry III's reign that we again hear of conspiracies against the king's life: Thietmar Billung in 1047, and the rebellion in the south-east in 1055. Even here it is not certain whether this was the actual intention, or whether the charge was brought to make it easier to proceed against the rebels. Salian rule would not really be challenged until the reign of Henry IV.

The forms opposition took varied. Often we are told no more than that someone rebelled, without learning why, or even how this manifested itself. Sometimes rebellion seems to have been provoked by the ruler's mistrust, though this in turn may have been well founded: Ernest of Suabia was more or less driven into rebellion in 1030, and we have seen a similar example in the fate of Wichmann the Younger under Otto I. Hostilities were normally pursued as feud

---

12. Thietmar IV 32, pp. 169–71.

on both sides. It was Conrad's friends and supporters who dealt with Ernest, while Godfrey the Bearded began matters in 1046 by leading an expedition to burn the royal palace at Nimwegen: arson, cattle-raiding and harrying the dependent peasants of one's opponents were the stock-in-trade of normal aristocratic feuding, and they served for rebellions as well. We know more about the mechanisms for restoring concord. Opposition hardly ever went the whole length, forcing the issue to be decided by battle or the death of the rebel (here too Ernest was an exception, though Dietrich of Holland was also killed in 1049); usually those concerned were persuaded after a suitable interval to submit to the king. There were a few attempts to negotiate from a position of strength; Ernest II wanted to do this with the backing of his Suabian followers in 1027, and submitted only when they told him they would not support him, while the Lotharingian conflict of Henry III's reign began with exchanges of proposals between Henry and Godfrey. The only wholly successful exponent of this strategy in this period was Boleslav Chrobry of Poland, though Godfrey himself did not do too badly in the long run.

Normally, reconciliation had to be preceded by openly displayed submission. As early as 941 we find Otto I's brother Henry throwing himself at Otto's feet in a gesture which was to become common. Rebels often submitted clothed as penitents, barefoot and with bowed neck "as the royal honour demands".[13] This demonstrated the ruler's power and majesty, but the submission was rarely as complete as the gesture implied. Those who knew what they were about took care to find out how they would be treated afterwards. Submissions were often preceded by negotiations behind the scenes conducted by supporters and intermediaries – here the queen and the episcopate played a specially important role. It was Queen Kunigunde and Archbishop Unwan of Bremen who secured Bernard Billung's reconciliation in 1020, and Archbishop Tagino of Magdeburg and the older Bernard Billung who persuaded Henry II – rather against his inclinations – to listen to emissaries from Henry of Schweinfurt in 1004. The terms of the surrender were worked out before the apparently unconditional surrender in public. The intermediaries were guarantors of the settlement, and the ruler risked offending them if he broke the agreement (this was what had angered Conrad the Red in 952 after he had arranged Berengar's

---

13. *Annales Altahenses maiores* s.a. 1041, ed. E.L.B. von Oefele (MGH SRG, Hannover 1891), 27.

submission). In any case, the range of punishments available was limited. Virtually no one in the circles we are here concerned with was executed north of the Alps after 941, when some of Henry's followers were killed. Men occasionally died in judicial duels (a Thuringian count Gero in 979, Thietmar Billung in 1047), and an exception might be made for brigandage, but the death penalty was not usual, and even when it was passed for rebellion it was not carried out. Loss of office and of lands held by royal gift was the normal penalty. Confiscation of the rebel's own property, his allodial lands, was, as in Carolingian times, rarer, because it punished not only the offender but also his kin both present and to come. When it did occur it usually took the form of a "voluntary" gift to the king to buy his pardon; many of the major rebels of the eleventh century, such as Henry of Schweinfurt, Ernest of Suabia or Welf III of Carinthia, had to buy back the ruler's grace in this way. Offenders themselves might be imprisoned for a time, either in the custody of a bishop or in the fortress of the archbishops of Magdeburg at the Giebichenstein on the Elbe; they could also be sent into exile. It was unusual (though not unknown, as in the case of Gunzelin of Meißen) for this imprisonment to last more than a year or two, and quite common for an offender to be restored to power. Indeed, it was a sign of deep royal displeasure if the ruler granted offices out again before having made his peace with the offender.

What has been said so far suggests, and is meant to imply, that unrest or uprising was, up to a point at least, part of the normal stuff of politics, and as much governed by rules of behaviour as any other area of life. It was not a violent intrusion which threatened the stability of the whole system, and consequently the responses to it were rarely radical ones. In dealing with breaches of the peace or disloyalty, rulers had to tread a narrow path. To behave too arbitrarily and unpredictably was rapidly to lose one's support and credibility; yet to behave customarily and predictably was equally rapidly to lose any room for manoeuvre one might have. A competent ruler, as those we are considering were, provided a satisfactory mixture of predictability and unpredictability. Royal anger, the *ira regis* of the Old Testament, which is mentioned frequently in the narrative sources, had a valuable function in mediating between the two; it allowed a ruler to behave unpredictably but explicably, and his followers to give way. Only after Conrad II had collapsed foaming at the mouth in 1035 could his magnates, led by his son Henry III, be brought to agree to the deposition of Duke Adalbero of Carinthia. The king's conventional obligation to show clemency and magnanimity was equally important; these were royal virtues which allowed a king to behave less harshly than he might have done without seeming to show a dangerous softness. It is a plausible guess, though it can hardly be more than that, that the dealings of the great magnates of the Reich with their followers followed similar lines; rarely do we have a chance to see these in detail.

THE GOVERNMENT OF THE KINGDOM

We have seen the kingdom so far as what German historians call a *Personenverbandsstaat*, a polity defined by the relationships between its rulers and its magnates. The question of how far this polity was also a "state", with institutions, with government, with "policy", is one that has greatly exercised historians recently: the older certainties no longer look so attractive. It is much the same problem as we have already met in the Carolingian period. On the one hand there are hints of something like a state as conventionally conceived, with a hierarchy of office-holders, with the king sending out commands to the localities, and so forth. On the other hand there is much that cannot easily be fitted into this pattern, and the balance is on the whole less favourable to an *étatiste* view than for the Carolingian period, for the Ottonian and Salian rulers have left virtually no legislation of any kind – a fact no doubt significant in itself. An examination of the "institutions" perceptible in the late tenth and eleventh centuries may help to define the issue more clearly.

The Ottonian and Salian rulers, even more than their Carolingian predecessors, were itinerant. There were parts of the kingdom where the king did not reach, at least not in person. The main *Königslandschaften* were in the Harz mountains and eastwards up to the Elbe in Saxony, in lower Lotharingia around Aachen and Nimwegen, and in the Rhine and Main region around Frankfurt. Here the rulers had thick clusters of lands and rights, and numerous palaces. The Rhine valley between Cologne and Mainz, Westfalia, Hessen and Thuringia also saw frequent visits by rulers. Though they rarely stayed in these parts for long, they passed through them on their way from one *Königslandschaft* to the next. By contrast, they came to Bavaria or Suabia less frequently, apart from those occasions when they passed through on their way to Italy and Burgundy or, from 1030 onwards, on expeditions against Hungary. Upper

Lotharingia, Frisia and northern Saxony also seldom saw rulers. One might expect there to have been some shift in this pattern from the time of Conrad II onwards, for the Salians' own lands lay principally around Worms and Speyer, and Henry III was duke of Bavaria for sixteen years and of Suabia for six. Yet the shift was not all that marked. With kingship the Salians inherited much if not all of the Ottonian lands and rights in Saxony – at least, there is no indication that they had to share these on any scale with the other collateral relatives. Hence the major basis of their power was still in the northeast, even if it had been supplemented. There were indeed smaller changes. Conrad and his son broke with the Ottonian practice – already in decline under Henry II – of spending Palm Sunday at Quedlinburg and Easter at Magdeburg, a city whose importance declined steadily after 983. Henry III's new palace and collegiate church at Goslar was his favourite stopping-place in Saxony, and the two Salian rulers were rarely seen as far east as the Elbe.

With the exception of the Harz, the Ottonians' own contribution, the areas of concentrated royal wealth followed the Carolingian distribution, but that does not mean that the patterns were completely static. Even if the areas concerned remained much the same, the precise holdings changed. Much of the royal lands and rights in east Franconia, for example, were bestowed on Henry II's new episcopal foundation at Bamberg, yet confiscations following Ernest's rebellion at the beginning of Conrad's reign helped to restore royal landed wealth here. The addition of the Salian house lands strengthened still further the extensive fiscal complexes around the middle Rhine, but running counter to this were the extensive grants made by Conrad II and Henry III to the bishopric of Speyer, which they singled out for special favour almost as if it were their own family foundation. In Saxony, as we have seen, there were shifts of interest away from the Elbe towards the region around Goslar in particular. In general we should visualize the royal fisc as constantly in flux; extensive confiscations, under Otto I especially but also for example in Bavaria at the end of Henry III's reign, and windfall gains, due mainly to the provision that the king inherited where there were no heirs, were balanced by a continued outflow of gifts and favours, not only to churches but also to laymen. Land in the border regions in particular changed hands frequently. It would seem that the fisc was important more as a source of rewards and less as a source of supply than it had been in the Carolingian period; at least, that seems a reasonable inference from the fact that we know virtually nothing about the organization and management of the

Ottonian and Salian fisc, in sharp contrast to the position for the Carolingian era.

The king was not by any means wholly dependent on his lands to support himself in travelling. From the major churches – bishoprics and royal monasteries – of his realm he could claim hospitality (*gistum*) and renders of food and drink (*servitium*), and these might be sent over considerable distances: the monastery of the Reichenau sent *servitia* for the upkeep of the king to Ulm, well over a hundred kilometres distant. Lay magnates had no such obligation, and though they might occasionally invite the ruler and his entourage to a ritual banquet, a *convivium*, this was a potentially ruinous practice, as Count Udalrich of Ebersberg warned his sons. There was in any case the question of where to put up the ruler. In spite of the development of fortified residences (see below, p. 226), few lay magnates had enough room to cope with the ruler. It was otherwise with the great churches. Many of these had palaces of their own at which the king could be received – even a monastery like the Reichenau had by Otto III's time a palace for the reception of the ruler, though it was only irregularly visited by rulers (five certain visits between 929 and 1048, though there may have been others not recorded). All these things should have made it possible for rulers to cover the whole of the kingdom in their travelling, since bishoprics and major royal monasteries between them covered the country in a fairly evenly distributed manner. On the whole, though, rulers stayed on their own patch, using the churches within these areas directly and the others indirectly.

The restricted nature of the royal itinerary might be seen as a sign that there were regions where the ruler had little authority; but the attendance at assemblies (most of which were held in the *Königslandschaften* mentioned above) and the diplomata granted by rulers tell a rather different story, namely that Ottonians and Salians were powerful enough for the great to come to them rather than the other way round, at least once the initial period of *Umritt* and perhaps of rebellion was over. In particular, the diplomata show that the two southern duchies looked to the ruler as an authority, especially from the time of Henry II's accession onwards. It was at the major church feasts and at the great assemblies – held more frequently than in Carolingian times, perhaps three or four times a year on average – that most of the politics of the kingdom were transacted. Here the appointments to major ecclesiastical and secular offices were discussed and announced; rebels were proscribed and their submissions accepted; ambassadors were received. In this sense even Henry III's reign still looked not very different from that of Louis the German two hundred years earlier. In some ways Salian rule was more Carolingian in appearance than Otto I's rule a century before, for from the time of Otto III on there was a steady tendency for rulers to distance themselves from their magnates and followings. Otto III's practice of dining at a raised table alone, in imitation of Roman and Byzantine customs, was still new enough to cause unfavourable comment, but his successors did not entirely revert to a more familial atmosphere: Otto I's long drinking sessions with his warriors were not to be revived. The first two Salian rulers in particular moved from a court marked by *familiaritas* punctuated only by occasional ceremonies to a much more formal, progress-like perambulation of their realm.

During the times between assemblies the king's entourage was a much smaller body – a few favoured advisers, a bodyguard, royal *capellani*, the king's own family (although the queen by no means always travelled with the king) and the necessary servants to take care of the needs of all of these. Even the rudimentary kind of court available to Carolingian rulers, with court officials and a much more permanent entourage of intellectuals and *literati*, was hardly known in Ottonian times – an exception may perhaps be made for the brief period of Otto III's majority, but he spent most of these years in Italy. There is little evidence for the existence or activity of officials like the seneschal or butler, and outside the chapel it was unusual for intellectuals to stay for long periods in the king's entourage. The element which most made for continuity was the chapel itself and the clerics who served in it as *capellani*. It was important as a training-ground for the episcopate, and those who served in it did more than just liturgical service while waiting for their bishopric to come along. Like their east Frankish predecessors, the Ottonians and Salians knew nothing of *missi dominici* with fixed territories in which the activities of dukes and counts were controlled; but on a small scale they could use their *capellani* as ad hoc representatives, though it is in the nature of the surviving sources that we see only glimpses of this, as in a letter from the royal *capellanus* Immo apologizing to Abbot Reginbald of Lorsch for not having visited him sooner and explaining that he had been detained by an imperial legation[14] or in occasional references to royal *capellani* as witnesses in charters recording judicial decisions. The least visible members of the chapel

---

14. *Die ältere Wormser Briefsammlung* no. 31, ed. W. Bulst (MGH Briefe der deutschen Kaiserzeit 3, Weimar 1949), 56–7.

were its notaries, the royal scribes. These drew up most royal diplomata; occasionally the recipient or his clerics provided a text or even the fair copy of it for approval and sealing, but this was far less common than in contemporary England. The demand for such diplomata is in itself some indication of the extent of royal power. The average number of surviving diplomata per year is twenty-four for Otto III, twenty-three for Henry II, nineteen for Conrad II and twenty-two for Henry III; this should be compared with figures of two for Henry I, twelve for Otto I and twenty-seven for Otto II. These figures are far higher than those for contemporary rulers of west Francia (Lothar: two per year; Philip I: just over three per year) or England (where the continuing uncertainty about forgery makes precise statistics difficult – Edgar: perhaps nine; Edward the Confessor: perhaps six), but that mainly shows how much larger the Reich was. The areas effectively ruled by west Frankish and Anglo-Saxon kings were not much bigger than a German duchy. What is more impressive on closer inspection is the continuity of output, with little fluctuation from the time of Otto II onwards.

This should not, however, be taken as a sign that Ottonian and Salian rule was "modern" and made extensive use of the written word. Almost all the surviving diplomata of the period are full-blown charters, physically very large documents, usually with a long arenga, a rhetorical preamble to the actual grant. They were written in a distinctive decorative script and with a large royal seal affixed; they are the written counterpart of the ruler's ceremonial appearances on the great church feasts or at assemblies. Diplomata were normally granted in response to requests, not on the ruler's own initiative. They are not to be taken as records of government policy, though it is possible to observe some shifts of governmental practice in their texts. From the time of Henry II onwards, for example, no royal diploma confirmed an episcopal church's right of free election without a clause reserving the rights of the king. Yet this affected only a handful of episcopal churches even in principle, since not all possessed such a privilege explicitly or sought confirmations of it, while royal practice was hardly disturbed by the existence of such diplomata. More flexible and progressive uses of writing were largely unknown: only a handful of mandates (short written instructions to officials) survive from the reigns of the late Ottonians and early Salians, fewer than are recorded for the reign of Edward the Confessor alone. We may suspect, however, that royal government made more use of writing than is now visible: it was capable, for example, of keeping track of lands granted out several generations earlier and reclaiming them after rebellion or the death of the holder without heirs, or of drawing up lists of armed contingents to be sent by magnates to Italy. It is difficult to see how such things could have been done without any records at all, though it is just conceivable that they were.

With so little governmental infrastructure, it is not surprising that politics were concentrated on assemblies, the occasions when the political elite were gathered together and accessible. Here the main concerns, apart from patronage in its widest sense, were warfare and justice, as in Carolingian times. We shall look at justice in a moment; warfare was, even in a polity no longer aggressively expanding, perhaps the most important consideration. Otto III continued the earlier Ottonian tradition of campaigning against the Elbe Slavs, and Henry II also did this in his own way by his campaigns against Boleslav Chrobry of Poland. Neither was particularly successful: the efforts of the 990s were considerable, but did not win back the Brandenburg permanently or bring the Liutizi back into tributary status, while Henry II was in effect forced to acknowledge Liutizi independence in return for their support in his inconclusive wars against Poland. The warfare on the eastern frontier slackened in intensity, and it became much more defensive. Much military service in the early eleventh century took the form of rotating garrison–duty in the fortifications along the Elbe, shared by Saxon bishops and lay magnates alike. Conrad II and Henry III did some campaigning against the Liutizi (in 1035, 1036 and 1045) and against Poland, but they were more active further south, against Bohemia and Hungary. From Henry II's reign onwards Burgundy was also an object of attention, while Italy continued to be so; Henry II and the two early Salian rulers did not spend so much time there as their Ottonian predecessors, but they did not go there less frequently. But a great deal of late Ottonian and Salian campaigning was done within the borders of the Reich, with the aim of overawing and subduing rebels. It was such campaigns, together with the expeditions beyond the borders, which most disturbed the regular pattern of itineration of the rulers between the regions.

The campaigning rarely involved serious fighting. The armies were normally very powerful, not so much in numbers (an army of a thousand warriors would still be a very large fighting force) as in equipment – it was the mailed fighting man, the tank of the tenth century, who was crucial, and the Ottonians and Salians could normally outnumber their opponents in this respect: "the army is small, but it is of high quality and all in iron", as the Bohemian duke's advisers put it in the course of Otto III's campaign in 990.[15] Consequently, their opponents did not normally think of direct resistance. They preferred delaying tactics, and would even submit unconditionally in order to get the intruders to go away again. Full-scale battles, as against the Hungarians at Menfö in 1044 or against the Liutizi in the Elbe marches in 1056, when the Saxons were actually defeated, were exceptional. The technique used by the rulers from Otto III onwards – putting together a force too large to be faced – meant that they could not react quickly; it also meant that they could not rely on their own resources alone. They depended heavily on the military followings of the major churches, rather less on those of the great magnates. A document has survived from the reign of Otto II, the *Indiculus Loricatorum*, which lists the troops to be sent to Italy as a subsidiary force.[16] Here the ecclesiastical troops far outnumber those to be supplied by lay magnates. The *Indiculus* also reveals that the troops were still raised with the duchy as the unit of organization at the end of the tenth century and it gives figures for the contingents of some major churches which tally exactly with those in force two centuries later; evidently we have quotas fixed comparatively early. But in spite of the existence of such quotas the rulers could not simply order their men into the field; they had to win support from both their lay and ecclesiastical magnates (often with gifts; see above, p. 198). Campaigning was a collective decision, normally taken at assemblies; a really determined ruler, like Henry II against Poland, could perhaps force a decision through, but this in itself was not enough to secure whole-hearted support for the campaign. Rulers could claim support from all for their expedition to Rome to receive the imperial crown more or less as of right; at least, we hear neither of resistance to these expeditions nor of difficulties in raising a large enough force. Apart from that, the only service due automatically was the rotating turns of garrison–duty on the eastern frontier.

Kings gave rewards and punishments, as we have already seen; they also provided justice, potentially at any time but again normally at assemblies, because here too there was a need for decisions carrying consensual support. In theory kings gave justice for all, a theory which found expression in the royal coronation *ordo*. Wipo tells how Conrad paused on the way to his coronation to hear

15. Thietmar IV 12, p. 144.
16. MGH Constitutiones et acta publica 1, ed. L. Weiland (Hannover 1893), 632, no. 436.

the cases of a peasant of the church of Mainz, of a widow and of an orphan.[17] Conrad's attention to justice, if it really existed, was unusual. Small men who tried to get a hearing from the king could normally easily be circumvented, as were the free peasants of Wolen who tried to get Henry III to hear their case against a magnate Guntramn who was oppressing them at an assembly at Solothurn: "because of the great number of princes present and because of their rustic speech their grievance did not reach the king".[18] Even when such people reached the king's presence they could be fobbed off with excuses about how busy the ruler was and told to come back another time, according to Otloh of St Emmeram.[19] The royal court was, as it had been in Carolingian times, primarily a place where disputes between members of the political community could be settled if the conventional mixture of feud and negotiation had failed. It was not often that the ruler himself summoned a case before his court, though this was necessary on the rare occasions when a magnate was to be proscribed or deprived of office judicially and not simply by decree.

There was little notion of a general all-embracing public or king's peace – less than there had been in Carolingian times, or than existed in contemporary Anglo-Saxon England. Within limits, at least for the political elite, self-help in the form of feud was acceptable, though the king might impose reconciliation, as Henry II did in a number of Saxon feuds at an assembly at Magdeburg in 1017. The ruler was supposed by his presence and his *terror* to discourage evil-doers. This was what Thietmar of Merseburg meant when he said that if he and his fellow-bishops did not obey their local counts in everything "we are plundered as if there were no king or emperor".[20] But most attempts by kings to establish peace were by example and persuasion. Henry II made all Suabians swear to keep the peace at an assembly in Zurich in 1004, and perhaps instituted a general peace in Saxony in 1012. Henry III on several occasions – at Constance in 1043 and at Trier in the following year, among others – urged not only peace but forgiveness on all present, himself declaring forgiveness for his enemies and in effect an amnesty for crimes committed against him. We can see here a royalist version of the

17. Wipo c. 5, p. 26.
18. *Acta fundationis Murensia*, c. 22, ed. M. Kiem (Quellen zur Schweizer Geschichte 3, Basle 1883), 69.
19. Otloh of St Emmeram, *Liber Visionum* c. 15, ed. P.G. Schmidt (MGH Quellen zur Geistesgeschichte des Mittelalters 13, Weimar 1989), 86.
20. Thietmar VIII 23, p. 520.

contemporary truce and peace of God movements known in southern France and Burgundy. What is noteworthy is the collective aspect; the king got the magnates of a region, perhaps even of a kingdom, to swear to keep the peace. He might use his influence to get them to agree, but he could not simply legislate for or decree the keeping of the peace and lay down penalties for breaking it. The Ottonians and Salians were themselves often too closely linked to their magnates by ties of marriage, family or friendship to look wholly convincing as umpires, and perhaps this was not even expected of them: when Henry II tried to reconcile Wichmann and Balderich, Alpert of Metz notes that both had too many supporters "for the king to favour one or the other in imposing a reconciliation". Henry contented himself with binding both over to keep the peace, but this was unusually impartial.[21]

Not all the governance of the Reich can be described in terms of business transacted at assemblies; as in Carolingian times, there was regional and local government (using the word loosely) as well as the king's court. The outcome of the interactions between kings and dukes in the first half of the tenth century might seem to have left a more organized governmental hierarchy with greater delegation of authority than in the Carolingian period. At the head of it stood the king, who ruled the kingdom; below him came dukes, set over the provinces; below these (or alongside them) came the counts, in charge of a county. Sometimes we find rulers acting as if they thought this was the case; Conrad II, for example, wrote in 1028 about the slaves of the church of Verden to Duke Bernard Billung, Count Siegfried and Margrave Bernard "to whom we have committed the rule of these provinces".[22] Henry II could order a count to hold an inquest into the facts of a boundary dispute in the Odenwald in 1012; Conrad II initiated a full-scale investigation into royal lands and rights in the duchy of Bavaria in 1027, calling on all office-holders to bring sworn evidence on what belonged to whom (rather like the procedure used to make Domesday Book, though on a smaller scale and with no surviving written record of the results).[23] Normally, however, the governance of the Reich could not be adequately or fully described using a model of hierarchical officials.

21. *De diversitate temporum* II 4, ed. H. van Rij and A.S. Abulafia (Amsterdam 1980), 48.
22. D K II 130.
23. D H II 247; MGH Constitutiones et acta publica 1, ed. L. Weiland (Hannover 1893), 645, no. 439.

The duchies were something more than geographical terms used to describe the operations of a royally appointed official: they were communities of law and to a large extent of family as well. It is noteworthy that the sworn peaces under Henry II and Henry III almost all concerned single provinces: Saxony, Lotharingia, Suabia. Evidently the likelihood of feuds carried on across the boundaries of duchies was not thought to be high. These communities were seen in warfare – as in the Carolingian era, the contingents of large armies were often organized by provinces – and in royal elections, where the magnates clearly met and grouped themselves by people. Yet the sense in which the dukes ruled over these duchies was a limited one. They did not appoint counts or margraves, nor did they normally supervise their activities. Occasionally in the eleventh century we hear of their attempts to get the leading men of the duchy to swear to support them against others, including the king: Ernest II in 1027, Godfrey the Bearded in 1046 and Welf III in 1055 (in a sense also Henry of Luxemburg in Bavaria in 1009; see above, p. 193). These attempts were not noticeably successful, and in themselves they suggest strongly that no such bonds were normally created when they took office. Though contingents of troops were still organized on the basis of the duchy, the role of the dukes themselves as war-leaders was no longer of much importance; in our period the frontiers to the north and east where serious fighting might be expected were in the charge of marcher counts, and these were hardly responsible at all to the relevant duke. There are some grounds for thinking that dukes held provincial assemblies, at least in Lotharingia, Bavaria and Suabia, and for supposing that dukes perambulated their duchies in the same way that kings did their kingdoms (no doubt with a similar tendency to visit some parts much more frequently than others). There are better grounds for thinking that they had some responsibility for peace-keeping within their duchies, except perhaps in Saxony: the constitutions of Ranshofen, issued by Henry II's father around 990,[24] represent more elaborate legislation than anything the kings themselves produced, and we also find dukes being sent home from campaigns or left at home in order to keep the peace. Yet we do not know all that much about what dukes did within their duchies. What made dukedoms attractive and worth competing for was in the first instance the lands which went with them, and of course the title itself, which gave not

24. MGH Leges in folio 3, 484–5; see Weinfurter 1986, 253–8 for a valuable commentary.

only prestige but also freedom from the jurisdiction of others. These things continued to be worth having even after the basis of ducal power had been reduced, as happened in Suabia following the conflicts between Hermann and Henry II and between Ernest and Conrad II, and in Bavaria during the long periods of direct royal control in the first half of the eleventh century.

Office-holders below the level of the duchy were hardly visible as royal officials. With the establishing of more or less permanent boundaries in the east and the decline of expansion along the eastern frontier, the role of margraves as independent war-lords on the border declined somewhat, though it was never entirely lost sight of; the distinction between margraves and other counts became less sharp. Counts still had the judicial functions they had exercised in the Carolingian period, though these were increasingly fragmented by grants of immunity; the county court seems to have been more important as a place for the public carrying out of property transactions than as a court proper, though this may just reflect what has survived as written record. In Saxony at least, perhaps elsewhere also, we can no longer assume that the county was a contiguous block of territory. Much of the evidence for such scattered counties is drawn from fragmentary reconstructions based on late eleventh- and twelfth-century material, but there are also contemporary references, in Adam of Bremen for example, who talks of Archbishop Adalbert's acquisition of a county "which was scattered over the whole diocese of Bremen, especially around the Elbe".[25] It is difficult to visualize precisely how the "public" functions of the county – in particular those of jurisdiction – would have been carried out in such cases, though presumably they must have been. The value of counties (a function of the lands attached to them and of the extent of the jurisdiction associated with them) could be very high: Adam, in the chapter just quoted, talks of figures as high as a thousand pounds in silver annually. Yet with such scattered counties, and with the jointly held counties mentioned in a previous section, we are beginning to move towards the twelfth-century world where the title of count denoted little more than the de facto exercise of jurisdictional rights of a certain kind, with hardly more than a residual sense of public office.

Increasingly, the immunity was coming to be as important as the county. The possession of immunity had originally meant that the

25. Adam of Bremen, III 46, p. 189.

218

dependants of the magnate (normally an ecclesiastic) who held it did not have to answer directly for their doings to the count; in particular, any fining that was done was done by the immunist, which meant that wealth circulated within the estate organization and was not siphoned off outside it. In the tenth century, however, immunity came increasingly to mean the exercise of comital powers, in particular those of justice. To the extent that this involved inflicting corporal punishment, ecclesiastics had to delegate the powers to representatives, known as advocates. Originally in Carolingian times these had been ad hoc figures, whose main importance lay in representing their church in court cases and property transactions. The advocate in charge of an immunity was a different kind of figure; he was in effect the private count of the ecclesiastical immunist. Advocates, because of their power over ecclesiastical dependants, were a serious threat to ecclesiastical wealth. Bishops could perhaps cope with them; monasteries found it more difficult, especially if the monastery had been founded by the family from which the advocate was drawn. It does not seem, however, that either rulers or others regarded the fragmentation and dynasticization of judicial authority in general as a serious or dangerous development. It is true that there was a tendency from the mid tenth century to endow churches, especially bishoprics, with rights of immunity and comital rights, which strengthened steadily from the time of Henry II onwards. This can be seen as a deliberate attempt by rulers to preserve the "public" aspect of the counties concerned, to keep them in the hands of men over whose appointment they still had some control. But this was true only to a very limited extent. The ecclesiastics concerned could not be counts themselves, for the same reasons which forced them to appoint advocates for their own lands covered by immunity. They had to delegate the actual exercise of comital rights to sub-counts; they did not yet possess on any scale alternative kinds of official to whom they could entrust such posts (on the *ministeriales*, often mentioned in this context, see below, p. 231). Hence the counties so granted were normally conferred on those who had held them before the royal grant. The effect was simply that these now became vassals of the bishop (to whom they now owed service and payments for their benefices). This could be regarded by the lay magnate concerned as a loss of status (as well perhaps of income), but it hardly meant an automatic increase of supervision, or a systematic use of bishops as agents of local government by rulers. As far as the advocacy is concerned, though there is some evidence that the ruler confirmed advocates in their office, there is for this period no clear indication that the ruler conveyed the right of jurisdiction directly to the advocate, or that the advocacy was regarded as a public office. In general, we may say that in so far as local government was still thought of at all as being exercised on the ruler's behalf it was thought of – by magnates *and* by rulers – as the reward for loyalty and service rather than as a duty whose performance could or should be measured.

CHAPTER EIGHT
Being and consciousness

THE NOBILITY

The Ottonian Reich was even more exclusively aristocratic than the Frankish empire had been. In the ninth century we find the occasional example of a meritocratic rise from the lower classes to high ecclesiastical office, and Notker the Stammerer saw this as characteristic of Charles the Great's episcopal promotions.[1] It wasn't by any means, but Notker's thinking it so and commenting on it favourably mark him out as a ninth-century writer. There was little place for such things in tenth-century Germany, though there began to be again in the eleventh. In the tenth century, even a man not quite of the highest rank, like Willigis of Mainz, could be described as being of low birth. It may be that this social exclusiveness was a remnant of barriers once even stronger: the *Lex Saxonum* lays down the death penalty for marriages between members of the different Saxon social groups. On the other hand, the south German law codes know of no such prohibition, yet Bavaria and Suabia scarcely look more socially open than Saxony. For the reconstruction of aristocratic consciousness and life-style, a number of different kinds of source are available. Perhaps the most important is Thietmar of Merseburg's chronicle, almost every sentence of which is loaded with the attitudes and prejudices of an east Saxon high aristocrat. There are other sources, including some works of literature. The fragmentary late eleventh-century Latin poem from the monastery of Tegernsee in Bavaria, called *Ruodlieb* after its hero, tells of a young

1. Notker, *Gesta Karoli* I 3–6, ed. H. Haefele (MGH SRG NS 12, Berlin 1959), 4–9.

noble who begins by serving other lords and is forced because of feuds he conducts for them to go into exile and take up service with a foreign king. Here he has such a distinguished career that he is finally able to return, laden with riches, to take up the family patrimony, marry and settle down.[2] The poem has elements of fairy-tale and must be interpreted with caution, but it gives us glimpses of the aristocratic life-style – hunting, feasting, service at court, social conventions – which we would otherwise know about only indirectly.

We have already seen how in the course of the ninth century the Frankish aristocracy had tended to regionalize. Where in the late eighth and early ninth centuries the whole empire had been knit together not least by close ties of kinship between leading men who held lands and office in quite different parts of the empire, in the later ninth century men's roots in the areas where they held power and influence became stronger, and kindreds split into different branches. Unlike the Carolingians, the Ottonians did not put together their kingdom by conquest. There were dispossessions and confiscations, but not enough for Otto to endow his Saxon followers elsewhere in the kingdom on a large scale; the consensual reunification practised by Henry I had left too little room for that. The regional aristocracies of Bavaria, Suabia, Franconia and Lotharingia which had come into existence between 850 and 920 thus continued to exist, and they were not much affected by the occasional import of dukes from outside the duchy. Moreover, they married among themselves to a large extent, and this meant that there were few opportunities to inherit across provincial boundaries. There was also little chance of the emergence of a new imperial aristocracy based on office-holding for secular office, at any rate below the level of duke and margrave, was very largely hereditary, as it already had been to a great extent in the ninth century. The increasing control the Ottonians had over church appointments from the mid tenth century enabled them to reward their Saxon followers outside Saxony – though at least as many Saxon bishoprics went to non-Saxons as the other way round – but in the nature of things such movements did not have any long-term effects on the regional aristocracies. Only in the late eleventh century do we find examples of bishops who had been appointed as strangers

---

2. *Ruodlieb. Faksimile-Ausgabe des Codex Latinus Monacensis 19486 der Bayerischen Staatsbibliothek München und der Fragmente von Sankt Florian*, ed. W. Haug and B. Vollmann, 2 vols, Munich 1975 and 1985, is now the standard edition; there is an English translation in E. H. Zeydel, *Ruodlieb. The earliest courtly novel (after 1050)*, Chapel Hill 1959.

to the diocese taking their relatives with them and establishing them in the new region. The movement of clerics across regional boundaries to hold canonries in the cathedral churches, also traceable to some extent as the result of royal and episcopal patronage, had no long-term consequences for the same reasons. Yet in spite of regionalization there do not seem to have been radical divergences between the different aristocracies as far as consciousness or behaviour was concerned.

Characteristic of all the regional nobilities was the custom of partible inheritance, at least as far as the allodial lands (those lands which were the absolute property of the holder, not held in benefice or by royal gift) were concerned. Instead of primogeniture, whereby the eldest son inherited and if there were no sons the whole inheritance went to the closest surviving relative, a practice beginning to predominate in some regions of west Francia in the eleventh century, the allodial property and rights of German nobles were divided on death among the surviving heirs. Even where there were children these often had to share the inheritance with more distant kin. Adalbert of Bremen and his brothers, for example, inherited only a part of the foundation site of their monastery at Goseck on their father's death, even though they divided the inheritance equally among themselves; the rest went to kinsmen, *propinqui*.[3] At first sight it might seem that such practices were bound to lead to fragmentation of holdings and hence impoverishment, but a little reflection shows that this is not so. Partible inheritance produced a smaller average holding in the following generation only if the overall numbers of those able to inherit increased. From the point of view of the individual, the fact that siblings were potentially co-heirs was compensated for by the increased chances of inheriting something from more distant relations. Of course, the vagaries of birth and death meant that there were considerable fluctuations in the holdings of families considered as direct male lines – but so there were in a system of primogeniture.

There were, however, a number of factors making inheritance not as simple as the above description might seem. Most important was the fact that inheritance was always a political act, the expression of a constellation of forces. There was no probate office in the tenth- and eleventh-century Reich to assign everyone their due proportions of inheritances without further fuss. Ruodlieb's mother thought that if

---

3. *Chronicon Gosecense* I 2, MGH SS 10, 142.

her son died without children there would be "great dispute" over the family lands.[4] In practice this meant, as it usually does, that "to those that hath shall be given". This was all the more likely because the rules of inheritance were by no means clearly defined. Even so straightforward a question as: if a man died leaving sons, did these under Saxon law acquire his right to inherit from his father, or did this pass to his brothers? had to be decided in 938 by judicial duel. The result (yes they did) does not seem to have settled the matter once and for all, and Thietmar of Merseburg thought that it was a fact of life that uncles and nephews were hostile to one another.[5] The rules for inheritance by more distant relatives were even less certain, and much probably depended on who was on the spot at the time, and on the ability to bring power to bear. There are no indications, for example, that either Henry II or Conrad II had to share the inheritance of their royal predecessors to any extent with other relatives who might have had claims, even though the distinction between crown and family lands could be formulated in the tenth and eleventh centuries. Election to the kingship carried a jackpot in the inheritance stakes.

Office was not divisible, even where it was de facto heritable, and this caused much ill-feeling and worse among noble families. Rival branches of the Billungs fought over their march under Otto I, and under Henry II there were similar disputes over the march of Meißen. In Saxony at least, especially in the marches, much land was *not* allodial; it was held in benefice or by royal gift, and though such lands might be passed on by inheritance the circle of those who could inherit was a much narrower one. The proprietary monastery was a further restriction on division of lands, acting almost as a substitute for primogeniture. Such monasteries might remain under family control, but the offices they carried, abbacy and advocacy, could be held by only one family member at a time. Lands granted to such churches could not easily be taken away from them again. This could lead to serious problems, particularly as men who expected to die leaving no close kin often used their lands to set up or endow family monasteries rather than pass their inheritance to distant kinsmen. Those excluded often resented this; a good example is the Westfalian monastery of Elten, whose endowment was disputed by the founder's daughter Adela and had to be taken under royal protection. Such endowments might lead to lands passing out of family control

4. *Ruodlieb* XVI 1–3, ed. Vollmann, p. 166.
5. Thietmar VI 44, p. 340.

altogether. In Henry II's reign a number of bishops – Unwan of Bremen, Meinwerk of Paderborn, Thietmar of Merseburg – were granted their sees on the understanding that these would receive all or at least part of the new bishop's inheritance on his death. Control over monasteries might also be lost. Helmarshausen in Westfalia was founded by a Count Ekkehard under Otto III and given a royal diploma confirming the right of Ekkehard's family to the monastery and its advocacy. This did not prevent the monastery being adjudicated to the bishopric of Paderborn in 1017, and though Ekkehard's heirs protested and tried to recover their rights by feud, they were not successful.[6] Such dangers should not be exaggerated as a risk to noble fortunes – inheritance by churches was just as much a political outcome as that by laymen, and there were counter-flows from church to laity: advocacies, secularizations, straightforward acts of usurpation – but it was there.

Because women could inherit, and because ties of marriage affected more than the pair concerned, marriage was normally a carefully considered matter. When Ruodlieb decided on his mother's advice that it was time to settle down and marry, he summoned a family council to advise him (advice here implying consent as well, as so often in the politics of the early and high middle ages), and the discussion turned around the question of who would be a good match from the point of view of the kindred. Love-matches were rare; commoner was seizing one's intended wife by force. This was legislated against by Ottonian church councils (e.g. at Frankfurt in 951) and much frowned on in practice. Thietmar's cousin Werner was fatally injured in 1014 while trying to mend his fortunes by carrying off a rich widow under the king's protection, and he would certainly have faced a great deal of trouble had he survived. But the marriage arranged between two kindreds was probably the norm. As we have noted, it was unusual for marriages to transcend the boundaries of the internal *regna*, and where they did they did not go far. Saxons married Lotharingians or eastern Franks, perhaps, but rarely Bavarians or Suabians; Alsatians married Lotharingians or Suabians but rarely further afield; and so on. A consequence of this, as well perhaps of the growing stratification within the aristocracy, which reduced the number of available eligible candidates, was that the early eleventh century saw a not inconsiderable number of

---

6. Compare D O III 256 (falsified in the twelfth century, but this does not affect the argument here) and D H II 370 with *Vita Meinwerci* c. 144, 195, ed. F. Tenckhoff (MGH SRG, Hannover 1921), 76, 112.

disputes between aristocrats who wanted to get or stay married and clerics who wanted to separate them because they were too closely related. One such dispute, over the marriage between the Westfalian count Otto of Hammerstein and Irmingard, dragged on for over a decade before the marriage was finally allowed to stand. The proposed marriage between Otto of Schweinfurt and Mathilda, the daughter of Boleslav Chrobry, was broken off, presumably on the grounds of consanguinity, by a decision of the council of Tribur in 1036. Conrad II himself was, at least in the eyes of Archbishop Aribo of Mainz, too closely related to Gisela to have been able to marry her legitimately, and the marriage of Henry III to Agnes of Poitou was also the target for invective by leading ecclesiastics. Marriages between women and men of lower rank were also a consequence of the shortage of candidates; the marriage between Otto III's sister Mathilda and Ezzo was considered a mésalliance, as was that between the Adela mentioned above and her husband Balderich.

Though the highest circles of the aristocracy at least were still itinerant, there was a definite tendency towards permanent residences in the hundred years between 950 and 1050. The characteristic type of fortification in the tenth century – large-scale, intended to provide sanctuary in times of trouble not only for its owner but for the neighbouring rural populace – gave way from the late tenth century to smaller-scale residences, still fortified but intended to be lived in by their owners and their *familia* alone. Often such fortresses contained a collegiate church or a small religious foundation of monks or more usually canons; here the members of the dynasty which owned the castle would be buried. Early examples of this are the counts of Ebersberg in Bavaria (whose castle and associated foundation is unusual in going back as far as the early tenth century) or the Billungs, whose family monastery and family seat were at Lüneburg. One such castle was besieged in the course of Henry of Schweinfurt's rebellion with Henry's mother inside it; she secured fairly favourable treatment for it by threatening to take refuge inside its church and let herself be burnt alive there should it be sacked. The development can be seen in the history of the Salians themselves. They began with a family monastic foundation at Limburg; after rising to kingship with Conrad II they adopted and adapted the cathedral church at Speyer for similar purposes; the final stage, the setting up of a dynastic fortress on a large scale at the Harzburg with an associated religious foundation and mausoleum, was interrupted by the Saxon revolt of 1073. Castles, of course, had very important practical functions: they provided protection as well as a point from which the domination of a territory could be organized. Yet they had done this before; what was new was the crystallization of family sentiment around such fortifications, as expressed in name-giving habits, burial practice and way of life. It was for this reason that the capture and sacking of fortified residences played such an important role in eleventh-century politics; such an act had psychological as well as practical consequences, as we saw above with Henry of Schweinfurt's mother. Several of the bitterest aristocratic feuds of the early eleventh century, such as those between Gunzelin and Hermann of Meißen, or between the Westfalian counts Balderich and Wichmann, turned around the insult and humiliation entailed in taking and destroying a fortified residence.

Castles also meant social differentiation among the aristocracy; the Carolingian style of aristocracy, where the great might be related to men of much lesser importance, was giving way to a more sharply stratified world, in which a part of the aristocracy could by virtue of fortified residences set themselves apart from the rest. We see those who lost out in this process only occasionally, often as members of the military followings of the great, the expendable warriors who might be sacrificed in the course of feuds (as Ruodlieb's lords abandon him at the outset of his story). It is from the early eleventh century that we find men being named after their "family seats"; Arnold of Lambach, who became margrave of Carinthia on Duke Adalbero's deposition in 1035, is an early example, and such names would later come to dominate the aristocratic landscape. In our period such name-forms still competed with the sense of family showed by the use of leading-names. Thietmar says of a murdered count that he came from "the tribe of the Buccos".[7] Gradually the number of names in common use became too small for them to show clearly in themselves to which family their holder belonged, but this was a slow change, and the highest strata of the aristocracy were among the last to adopt the new differentiation. We begin to see a more strongly developed sense of lineage. A good demonstration of this can be found in the twelfth-century annalistic compilation known as the "Annalista Saxo". The author of this put together a very large-scale history of the Frankish and east Frankish kingdoms from 741 to 1139 with special emphasis on Saxon history. The annalist mostly used well-known sources, but

7. Thietmar VI 50, p. 336.

he added numerous genealogical glosses identifying the person referred to and giving him an ancestry. Most of these genealogies do not go back much beyond the late tenth century, and the inference, which is supported by other evidence, is that in twelfth-century Saxony not much was known about direct ancestry in the male line before that date. As a pendant to this, two early eleventh-century historians, Thietmar of Merseburg and Hermann of the Reichenau, give us extensive information about their relatives in their histories. Their sense of family was more lateral: they knew more about their contemporary first cousins, less about their parents' ancestors (though not nothing at all). Neither Thietmar, Hermann nor the sources of the "Annalista" showed much awareness of really distant kin. The change was thus not so much one from the extended family to the narrow one as from one which took in the close living relations on both father's and mother's side to one which placed more emphasis on descent in the male line.

In the private sphere, what we see the members of the high aristocracy doing most often is eating, or rather feasting. The tenth and eleventh centuries were the age of the *convivium*, the ritual banquet. Even at the highest level its symbolism could be used to demonstrate unity (as after an imperial coronation, or in the coronation ceremonies of 936 and 986) or to conceal treachery (as in the attacks on the Magyars in 903 and on the Abodrites in 940 at banquets). Virtually all important events were marked by feasts. When Thietmar of Merseburg entered the religious life, his parents gave a *convivium* lasting two days. When Wichmann and Balderich were temporarily reconciled in 1016 they invited each other to *convivia*, and it was regarded as a particularly heinous piece of treachery that Balderich's wife Adela should allegedly have arranged for killers to ambush and murder Wichmann on his way home afterwards. Marriages were, as they are today, accompanied by a banquet; it was while attending one at Persenbeug in Bavaria in 1046 that Henry III was very nearly killed when a gallery collapsed. Once again *Ruodlieb* mirrors the aristocratic world of the eleventh century. The entire narrative is punctuated by banquets and meals: in the interaction between the ruler with whom Ruodlieb took up service, the Great King, and his rival the Lesser King, in the early sections of the poem; during Ruodlieb's travels homewards, when he is given hospitality first by a man of uncertain status in a village and then by a chatelaine; and finally in the courtship of Ruodlieb's nephew.

A certain division of labour between aristocratic men and women is apparent. Women were expected to run the household, as

Ruodlieb's mother did both during his absence and after his return, and as we know queens to have done. Women were also responsible for providing the piety for a family. This kind of division of labour emerges clearly from Hermann of the Reichenau's notices on his own family in his *Chronicle*, for example. In the tenth century in particular heiresses often used their patrimony to establish a religious foundation; this was no doubt a form of protection for themselves, since the patrimony was likely to be less subject to predatory attacks if it was guarded by ecclesiastical sanctions, but it also had the purpose of keeping the family *memoria* alive. Women like Adela who took an active part in aristocratic politics were frowned upon; the expectation was that they would play, if any role, then a mediatory one – the model here was provided by the queens Kunigunde and Gisela, who as we have seen were active in intervening to secure privileges, appointments and above all the reconciliation of rebels. Male piety was by no means unacceptable; yet there were other virtues. In particular the vigorous pursuit of feud in support of one's rights (real or imagined) or in defence of one's honour, was sanctioned even by ecclesiastical writers. Thietmar describes a number of such episodes, and though he is clearly hostile to feuds conducted against bishops he is by no means so unambiguous when it comes to feuds among lay magnates. It would be wrong to assume that the lay magnates of the Reich were all brutishly illiterate, caring for nothing but feuding and feasting. They hardly participated in the intellectual and artistic worlds cultivated by clerics, but there was an aristocratic lay culture as well, which can be glimpsed in such disparate activities as hunting, the practice of arms as a skill in its own right and the cultivation of family traditions. Here too *Ruodlieb*, with its hints at the beginnings of courtly behaviour among the aristocracy, shows a side of the elite of the Reich rarely visible in the historical writings of the period.

RURAL ECONOMY AND URBAN LIFE

In the economy of the kingdom there was steady growth. The wealth and power of the Ottonians and Salians and their followers depended in the tenth century, especially in Saxony and Bavaria, on the influx of tribute from across the border, but the importance of surplus production at home rose steadily. Keynesian demand-led explanations seem appropriate. The itineration of rulers and

Germany in the early middle ages

magnates meant the transport of surplus production over substantial distances, as for different reasons did the widely scattered estates of the major churches, and hence the transfer of wealth and the establishing of market mechanisms. Social stability and security from invasion provided a climate favourable to economic growth, in spite of endemic feud and occasional uprising. The investment by rulers and prelates in particular in palaces and churches, which accelerated from the end of the tenth century, enabled the surplus wealth of the elite to percolate back through local economies (not least through the use of wage labour for building), with a multiplier effect. The effects were gradual rather than spectacular, and we can often see only the first phase of developments which were to be important in the following century and a half. The beginnings of the great land colonization of the high middle ages are already visible in the first half of the eleventh century. This was especially the case in the south-east, where much of the losses of the late ninth and early tenth centuries were recouped and land newly cleared, and in the former Sorb lands in the bishoprics of Meißen, Zeitz and Merseburg. It was less apparent on the more northerly parts of the Saxon east frontier, and still less so in the older core of the kingdom.

It may seem surprising that growth and change were gradual, for French rural history in this period, where the sources are different and rather more plentiful, appears in the literature to be full of movement. Scholars such as Duby and Fossier have pointed in particular to the growth of banal lordship in west Francia, whereby the exercise of powers of justice and command by lords meant an increase in the surplus extracted from the dependent agricultural population. They have also noted from the eleventh century a tendency towards commutation of labour services (payments in cash or kind instead of in work) – in other words, a loosening of traditional structures and a monetization of the rural economy. Neither of these trends is at first sight visible east of the Rhine. If anything, there seems to have been a tendency for the exercise of justice to have become more concerned with punishing by life and limb and less with the exacting of financial penalties for wrong-doing in the eleventh century. Jurisdiction is seen by German legal and constitutional historians as a means for consolidating political power (incipient territorialization based on the advocacy), not as a source of income for the holders. Yet this seeming difference is at least in part the result of differences in the traditional organization of the historian's subject-matter. There is an equivalent of the *seigneurie banale* of French scholarship: the advocacy (see above, p. 219), with its implications of jurisdiction and command over the dependent inhabitants of an ecclesiastical immunity. Like banal lordship this did not inherently affect estate organization; like banal lordship it implied rather the setting up of a network of demands and exactions parallel to that of the manor or *seigneurie* (in German terms the *Grundherrschaft*). Like banal lordship also it threatened the existence of manorial lordship; but it could be more effectively combated. The advocate was in theory an official of the church over whose lands he exercised the advocacy, and though this might at times have only nominal consequences it gave ecclesiastical landlords opportunities to fight back. Nor did the advocacy provide much opportunity to encroach on the lands and dependants of other lay lords. It was differences like these which made for a greater degree of stability and a greater conservatism in the organization of rural land-holding than is visible in the other Carolingian successor-states.

At the level of personal status there was a move away from slavery. Slaves were still of importance, but as an item of trade with southern Europe, starting at the slave-markets of Verdun and moving down to Muslim Spain. They were less significant as labour within the Reich. Here we can see, alongside the continuing existence of serfdom, the beginnings of a trend towards specialization and social differentiation. There are two emergent social groups which may be mentioned here: *ministeriales* and *censuales* (*Kopfzinser*, poll-tax payers). The *ministeriales* were to play an important role in the late eleventh and twelfth centuries, but their significance for the social and political history of the first half of the eleventh century has been somewhat overemphasized. They evolved out of a less differentiated group, the *familia* or household of the great, particularly of rulers and prelates. They are found from the beginning of the eleventh century in narrative sources, and from the 1020s onwards we have a number of texts regulating their rights and duties (for the *ministeriales* of the churches of Worms and Bamberg and those of the monasteries of Limburg and Weißenburg). They retained many of the characteristics of the *familia*: they were unfree, and could be granted to other lords. At the same time they were more than mere serfs. They were the members of the *familia* with specialized skills, and these soon came to include fighting; *ministeriales* were important in royal and episcopal bodyguards and in contingents of troops (the Weißenburg law regulates their service on Italian expeditions, for example). It is important to realize that they were not a dramatic administrative innovation. There is little evidence for *ministeriales* being used for local government or even estate administration in the first half of the eleventh century; they served in person, not at a distance. One diploma of Henry II's for the bishop of Paderborn granting a county specifies that the bishop is not to give it in benefice to any of his vassals or to a stranger but is to administer it through a *ministerialis*. This is just the kind of thing that *ministeriales* were later to do, yet the grant is unique in this respect for the early eleventh century, and the provision was almost certainly written into it in the twelfth century.[8] Under Henry IV and Henry V the group was to take on much sharper contours, and was moreover to be swelled by the "ministerialization" of members of the lesser nobility, but these developments had hardly begun by the time of the death of Henry III. The difficulties he had with some of his leading men were not due to any policy of favouring *ministeriales*; that accusation was to be reserved for his son and grandson.

The *censuales* were a still more heterogeneous group than the *ministeriales*, and it is not clear that they constitute a group at all. Their main characteristic was that they paid an annual sum (often, but by no means invariably, a quite nominal one – the amount varied from one to sixty pence per year) to the bishopric, monastery or canonry which took them on; they were often also obliged to pay a relief on inheriting from their parents, and a tax on their marriage. It is tempting to see in such people *déclassé* aristocrats, the equivalents of the *pauperes* of late Merovingian or Carolingian times, no longer able to survive without protection. Certainly some fitted into this category (though more so in the late eleventh and twelfth centuries), but the vast majority were in origin emancipated serfs. Becoming a *Kopfzinser* admitted one not only to duties but also to privileges, in particular to the protection of the immunity of the church to which one was commended, and conceivably also to its trading privileges. Quite other kinds of commendees – merchants especially – may have joined in order to enjoy these privileges, much as today (in Germany at any rate) there are numerous people who nominally take on the obligations of being an immatriculated student at a university in order to enjoy the very real tax and social security advantages which this provides. This would explain at least in part the fact that such *censuales* are often found living away from the estates of the church to which they owed a *census*, and in particular in towns; this can be observed in Lotharingia, in the Rhenish episcopal cities (Mainz, Worms, Speyer) and in Bavaria. The status of *censualis* was among other things a mechanism from which both lord and *censualis* could

8. D H II 440.

benefit when dependants moved from the land into towns. The lord continued to receive income; the dependant was not cut off from all protection.

In the Reich in the early eleventh century there were few towns which could be described as large, even by north European standards; almost all had grown up around a bishopric, a large monastery or a royal palace. Here there was a nucleus of consumption large enough to allow the growth of specialist settlement around it to meet its needs. We should not posit a sharp dividing-line between town and countryside even here. Regensburg, one of the largest and most important cities in southern Germany, with a bishopric, two substantial monasteries and two royal palaces, was still sufficiently rural in 1031 for the monastery of St Emmeram to have a separate villication for the city, with 132 farms associated with it.[9] Nor was there in all probability too much difference between those towns which had been towns in Roman times and the newer ones of the east. Almost all the major towns were the sites of bishoprics. The exceptions are few. Some were places like Zurich, Aachen or Dortmund which had royal palaces. Besides this, there were in the northern half of the Reich a small number of merchant settlements or trading-places owing their existence apparently to long-distance trade rather than to concentrated consumption: Tiel, Soest, Hamburg (though here there were substantial elements of ecclesiastical consumption as well), Haithabu. These were comparable with Durstede and Quentovic in Carolingian times, though not, except perhaps for Hamburg, on the same scale. No monastery was sufficiently wealthy to be the nucleus of a major town, though many smaller towns grew up around monasteries (Quedlinburg and Lüneburg for example). But it was precisely in episcopal towns that many of the largest and richest monasteries were found. There were no large towns with lay lords. At first sight this might seem to be the result of royal policy. Essential for the functioning of a town of any size was a market, and the right to hold markets could be granted only by the king; such grants are recorded in profusion for ecclesiastical recipients, rarely for lay magnates. Yet there is no reason to suppose that kings would not have granted more rights of market to lay magnates had they been asked; nor is it as certain as is sometimes confidently implied that all markets which existed in the tenth- and eleventh-century Reich were from the beginning

9. Cf. the *Urbar* of St Emmeram, ed. Dollinger 1949: 504–12 (= Dollinger 1982, 454–69).

explicitly sanctioned by the king – what look like foundation charters for markets may well be simply the grant of royal protection and consent for already existing institutions. The absence of lay towns (outside western Lotharingia) reflects much more the way of life of the magnates; even the growing concentration of consumption at family fortifications was not yet enough for these to become the nucleus of an urban settlement, and of course even the wealthiest magnates and their families scarcely consumed on a scale equivalent to that of a bishop and chapter, with their servants and associated urban monasteries.

Towns were still, as in Carolingian times, essentially seigneurially organized: they had lords (though other lords, in particular the king, might hold land within their walls, especially if the town was an important centre, like Regensburg or Magdeburg). As in west Francia in the tenth and eleventh centuries, there were some struggles for control in cathedral towns between the count and the bishop. On the whole the bishops won, as in the west. Sometimes they did so with royal assistance – a good example of this is Worms, where Bishop Burchard succeeded in levering out his Salian rivals more or less peacefully with royal backing. A counter-example is Cambrai, where Henry III refused to back Bishops Gerhard and Lietbert in their struggles with the count of the city for control. Control might be disputed between lords, but disputes between the controllers and the controlled were hardly known. There had been some conflicts in Carolingian and early Ottonian times between bishops and townspeople (in Mainz on several occasions in the ninth century, and in Cambrai in 959); there were none recorded in the kingdom of Germany between the Cambrai incident and the death of Henry III, though the north Italian cities experienced them and were also capable of collective opposition to passing German armies. Very occasionally bishops granted rights to an urban collective: Bishop Cadaloh of Naumburg recognized a merchants' guild in 1033, as did Otto I and Otto II at the request of the archbishops of Magdeburg for the merchants of their city. None of this was a direct anticipation of the more continuous movement towards urban emancipation found at least in the west of the Reich in the second half of the eleventh century. There was scarcely a burgher class as yet, and the once popular idea that the Salians pursued a pro-urban policy turns out to be questionable even for Henry IV and Henry V, and quite unfounded for Conrad II and Henry III.

The topography of the towns varied somewhat with their history, but followed a generally similar pattern. The episcopal towns, as well as the smaller urban settlements associated with monasteries (Quedlinburg for example) generally had a central ecclesiastical core – usually fortified or walled – which included at least the principal church as well as the royal palace, if there was one. This should not be visualized as large; it corresponded in size as well as in function and origin to the close of English cathedral towns. Alongside this lay an additional attached settlement, the *suburbium*, often little bigger than the core. This was true also, *mutatis mutandis*, of the Roman towns whose original area of settlement had still not in the early eleventh century been fully recolonized, such as Cologne, Mainz (described in the 960s as being largely under cultivation) and Trier. Elsewhere a royal palace might supply the core element. In the ecclesiastical towns at least this physical core also housed a crucial element of the population, the *familia* of the central church and its derivatives. The cathedral canons themselves would often have their own houses; the ideals of the common life for such groups of ecclesiastics, though theoretically a prescribed norm, were in fact only beginning to become fashionable in the early eleventh century, and Adam of Bremen records the difficulties the archbishops had in enforcing them on their canons.[10] We tend to think of the *suburbium* as having been inhabited by merchants engaged in long-distance trade, and though this is not the whole story most substantial towns did have such an element. Mainz, which we have already seen with a Frisian merchant colony in the ninth century, was a significant trading centre in the mid tenth, when it was visited by a Jewish geographer, Ibrahim ben Jakub, who found an important spice market there; slaves were also traded at Mainz. Elsewhere also the association between towns and merchants is evident. Otto II, for instance, gave the township of Zwenckau to the bishopric of Merseburg with its "market, Jews and merchants",[11] meaning the rights of lordship and taxation over the Jews and merchants. We should not assume free enterprise trading in all such cases; some of these merchants at least will have been, as in Carolingian times, procurators trading on behalf of their ecclesiastical masters, securing supplies of necessities and luxuries not available locally. This is probably what lay behind the archbishop's intervention for the merchants of Magdeburg: he was protecting men who were in some sense his servants or dependants rather than pursuing a far-sighted

10. Adam of Bremen II 47, schol. 34; II 63, schol. 42; II 69, schol. 53, pp. 107, 123, 130.
11. Thietmar III 1, p. 98; D O II 89.

and progressive policy of fostering his town's economic development.

The most evident sign that there was indeed a flourishing long-distance trade beyond the borders of the Reich is found in the tenth- and eleventh-century deposits of coins from numerous German mints in Scandinavian coin-hoards. Though northern Saxony suffered somewhat from Viking raids under Otto III and perhaps under Henry II (see below, p. 255), we can hardly suppose that most of these coins found their way directly to Scandinavia as plunder. Either they were traded there directly, or they went as tribute from places like England from where we know that there was both trade with Germany and tribute payments made to the Danes under Svein and Cnut. It was probably mostly a one-way trade; German wealth, based on Slav tribute and increasingly also on the very considerable output of the Harz silver mines, enabled the import of luxury items like furs and spices. No doubt the silver also went in other directions which have not been so well recorded by the survival of coin-hoards. An early eleventh-century document, the *Honorantie civitatis Papie*, a summary of the activities of the customs department of the Lombard kingdom based in Pavia, also gives prominence to German traders.[12] Yet the silver certainly did not all go on the export trade. From the late tenth century we find the grants of rights of mint, which rulers had been making since the early ninth century, finally becoming reality, in Saxony in particular (no doubt stimulated by Harz silver) but also elsewhere – a development reflected in the diversity of mints from which the Scandinavian hoards were drawn. Some of this wealth at least circulated locally; the very large investments in new church buildings as well as in luxury artefacts made by many bishops of the late Ottonian and early Salian era will have meant some imports, but also a substantial injection of purchasing power into the local economy, through payments to masons and other craftsmen, and to labourers.

THE CHURCH UNDER THE OTTONIANS AND SALIANS

Much of what was said earlier about the east Frankish church applies

12. C. 2, MGH SS 30, 1451–2.

to the church in the Ottonian and Salian kingdom as well. As in the ninth century, it was political not ecclesiastical boundaries which determined such things as the participation of bishops in synods – hence the bishop of Cambrai was an imperial bishop, even if his bishopric belonged to the province of Rheims. As in the ninth century, the role of the papacy in the life of the Ottonian and Salian church was a limited one. Rome was still primarily a centre of Christian tradition rather than Christian authority, an object of pilgrimage both for the lay nobility and for high ecclesiastics like Aribo of Mainz, who in effect resigned to end his life with a Rome pilgrimage. Jerusalem, fashionable as a destination in west Francia, does not seem to have had the same attraction in the east until the second half of the eleventh century. Rome was also known as the seat of a judge, of the leader of the Christian church, but it was not felt strongly in this role. The popes of the tenth and early eleventh centuries issued few privileges which did more than confirm existing rights, and few enough of these. The main exceptions were privileges which granted special marks of rank and status. Papal privileges provided ammunition for the quarrels between the three Rhenish archbishops of Mainz, Cologne and Trier (and to a lesser extent the archbishops of Salzburg and Magdeburg) over pecking-order: who presides over councils? who crowns kings and queens? who is archchaplain? who can call himself metropolitan or primate? They did not decide them. The pope's jurisdiction was accepted in theory, but often overridden or ignored in practice without any very explicit theoretical justification. When Aribo of Mainz objected to Benedict VIII's judgement against him in the dispute between Mainz and Hildesheim over which bishop had diocesan authority over the monastery of Gandersheim, he challenged the judgement more than the right to judge. When in 1033 Bishop Warmann of Constance with Conrad II's backing forced Abbot Bern of the Reichenau to burn in public in the diocesan synod a privilege renewed by Pope John XIX which gave the abbot the right to wear sandals and other episcopal insignia, it was primarily the abbot who was being humiliated, not the pope who was being rejected. Even the claim by the synod of Seligenstadt in 1023 in connection with the disputed marriage between Otto of Hammerstein and Irmingard that no one might appeal to Rome without permission from their diocesan bishop, though clearly a statement of principle, should be understood in an eleventh-century context and not in that of fully developed papal doctrines on appellate jurisdiction, which grew out of a reaction to rather later attempts by kings and prelates to restrict access to the pope as judge. Apart from questions of status, the one area where the popes did have something to say was the foundation of new bishoprics; the Saxon foundations of the ninth century had been set up with little reference to the pope, but this was no longer possible in the tenth century. At the origins of the provinces of Magdeburg, Gnesen and Gran lay papal privileges and decisions, though in no case were these enough in themselves to decide the course of events.

As in the ninth century, the main expression of the unity of the church lay in councils. There were comparatively few of these in Germany in the second half of the tenth century, and they left little in the way of lasting legislation; for many we have no canons at all, and those which did legislate did not produce much of lasting significance. The Ottonians preferred to hold synods south of the Alps, just as they issued legislation in Italy but not in Germany. It is a sign of the political routinization which set in from the early eleventh century that councils became more frequent north of the Alps: Dortmund in 1005, Frankfurt in 1007 (the founding synod for the new bishopric of Bamberg), Nimwegen in 1018, Seligenstadt in 1023, Frankfurt in 1027, Pöhlde in 1028, Tribur in 1036, Limburg in 1038. Such councils, summoned by the ruler and attended by most of the bishops of a kingdom, were the exception in the tenth and early eleventh centuries in Europe; the west Frankish kingdom saw hardly anything in this period above the level of the diocesan or provincial synod, while Anglo-Saxon England knew no clear separation between a royal assembly and an ecclesiastical council. Pope Leo IX's council at Mainz in 1050 could thus draw on an established tradition, whereas in France (Rheims 1049) and England (Westminster 1075) church reform had to restart a conciliar practice more or less from scratch. Even so, none of these councils, apart from that at Seligenstadt and the papal council of Mainz, produced legislation which would be quoted and developed by later councils. Synods at national and (less well recorded) at provincial level expressed and reinforced episcopal collectivity, as in Carolingian times. They were not the only forms this took. Prayer-confraternities (again, a Carolingian invention) like that established between Henry II and most of his bishops at the synod of Dortmund in 1005 also helped to strengthen the ties which linked bishops to their colleagues. More important here was the relatively homogeneous background of the episcopate. It was not just that most bishops were drawn from a fairly small number of families, and that many had done service in the royal chapel; the *cursus honorum* they had gone through beforehand was also a standard one. Comparatively few monks became bishops in this period – they represented at most a sixth of all appointments, often much less. Even the archbishopric of Mainz, which had traditional links with the monastery of Fulda, was only occasionally held by a Fulda monk (Hatto in 968, Bardo in 1031, Siegfried in 1059). A figure like the layman Ansfrid who became bishop of Utrecht in 995 was even more of an exception. The overwhelming majority of bishops had held canonries in a cathedral chapter before receiving promotion; often they had been provost there or held some other office. Certain chapters were drawn on far more than others: Hildesheim, Bamberg from 1007 on, Magdeburg, and to a lesser extent Halberstadt, Würzburg, Cologne, Mainz, Speyer and Liège. All this made for an episcopate not unlike that of eighteenth-century England: its members were linked in a variety of ways and hence shared both experience and assumptions. It was an establishment, conscious of its own worth and competence, prepared to acknowledge holiness and other unusual talents in some of its members but not to prescribe it for all of them, nor particularly receptive to new ideas.

When not engaged on royal service at home and abroad, bishops had dioceses for which they were responsible. Ottonian and Salian bishops in general took these responsibilities seriously, or at least were expected to. The "Lives" of these prelates laid considerable stress on the bishops' pastoral duties, more so than on their secular wealth and power. Their duties might take them away from their dioceses, but they were not supposed to be absentees; it was the exception, and a matter for unfavourable comment, when in the 1030s the newly elected archbishop of Hamburg-Bremen, Hermann, declared Hamburg to be a salty waste and refused to live there.[13] Though the centre of the diocese was the cathedral city itself with its cathedral and lesser churches, bishops – when at home – perambulated their dioceses much as rulers did the kingdom and for not dissimilar reasons. Itineration was needed to keep a hold on the material basis of the bishopric, under continuous threat from advocates and other lay magnates, but besides this bishops had to travel around for religious reasons (only they could perform confirmations or consecrate churches, for example). Internal mission was still very much needed. Thietmar describes the paganism of the Liutizi and warns his readers against it in a way which suggests that

---

13. Adam of Bremen II 68, p. 128.

he saw such practices as a real danger and not just the opportunity for a moral flourish, while Adam also records the struggles of the archbishops of Bremen with the "superstition" of the country dwellers around Bremen itself.[14] The presence of the bishop brought his diocesans into contact with numinous power. Increasingly, though, this was channelled into the visible form of the cathedral and its surrounding churches. Most cathedral cities had by the eleventh century a whole phalanx of churches, often newly built or rebuilt. At Cologne, which had no fewer than ten large Romanesque churches built or rebuilt in the tenth and early eleventh centuries, these were laid out in the form of a cross, whose long descending shaft was completed by the archiepiscopal foundation at Deutz across the Rhine in 1003. A similar pattern is found in the much smaller towns of Utrecht and Bamberg. The collective effect of this can hardly be visualized nowadays after later centuries of town growth and redevelopment, not to mention warfare and destruction, but at the time it must have been an overwhelming one, well meriting the term *Sakrallandschaft* ("sacred landscape") coined by German historians to describe it.

Whereas the two centuries preceding the death of Otto II had seen a large number of bishoprics founded, the period we are considering was one of stagnation as far as the territory of the Reich was concerned: the new foundations in Poland and Hungary were rather different from the missionary foundations of Otto I's time. Henry II set up a new bishopric at Bamberg in 1007 (its diocese was taken largely from those of Eichstätt and Würzburg), but this is more readily compared to the family mausolea of other aristocrats, scaled up, naturally, to reflect Henry II's immense wealth. It was endowed on a very lavish scale, sufficiently so for it to dominate east Franconia and northern Bavaria, where it was probably intended to play a political role after the revolt of the margraves of Schweinfurt. There was also a missionary element in its foundation, which was to be realized above all in the early twelfth century by Bishop Otto I. Henry II expressed in his foundation charter the hope that "the paganism of the Slavs might be destroyed",[15] but these were local Slavs; Bamberg had a defined diocesan territory and did not have the wider missionary responsibilities of the older foundations. Its importance within the eleventh century church lay more in its close

14. Thietmar VI 23–25, pp. 302–4; Adam of Bremen II 48, p. 108, referring to Unwan of Bremen's activities in the first two decades of the eleventh century.
15. D H II 143.

links with the imperial chapel and chancery, and with the prestige of its schools, which soon became a kind of training ground for those starting a high-flying career in the church. Apart from Bamberg there were no new foundations in this period. The bishopric of Zeitz was moved to Naumburg in 1028. Merseburg, which had been merged with Magdeburg in 981, was separated again in 1004 on Gisilher's death. Both the refoundation of Merseburg and the foundation of Bamberg met with fierce resistance from bishops whose interests were affected; the difficulties may help to explain why there were no attempts to break up those dioceses with very large territories (Mainz, Constance, Salzburg, Passau), even though this might have made good sense in terms of internal mission and the organization of the church. Several of the tenth-century foundations – Brandenburg, Havelberg, Mecklenburg, Oldenburg – became missionary bishoprics with no institutional substratum after the revolt of 983, while the three Danish bishoprics founded in 947–8 slowly drifted out of the orbit of Hamburg-Bremen, in spite of the efforts of the archbishops.

East Francia in the Carolingian era had not seen many monastic foundations, and the early tenth century had been a period of secularizations and Magyar destruction. There was thus room in the tenth and eleventh centuries for both the founding of new houses and the expansion and transformation of old ones. Once again, we find considerable regional differences in the way this was carried out. Saxony in this period saw a very large number of new monastic foundations, of a number of different kinds. Aristocrats on the whole founded nunneries; thus Margrave Gero, who died in 965, left much of his inheritance to his large foundation at Gernrode, while such houses as Fischbeck, Kemnade and Hilwartshausen were all founded by women who had come into substantial inheritances. The Ottonians themselves had founded the nunneries of Quedlinburg and Gandersheim before they became kings. Only a few aristocratic families – notably the Billungs with St Michael's at Lüneburg – were wealthy enough to found monasteries, which, because greater numbers were needed for the life according to the Rule, were more expensive than small houses of canons or canonesses. The bishops were the really great founders; this is hardly surprising, for whereas elsewhere in the east Frankish kingdom the bishoprics had mainly inherited older urban sites, in Saxony the bishopric came first and urbanization afterwards. The "sacred landscape" aimed at by Saxon bishops as well as by their Rhenish and south German colleagues had to be created here from scratch. Minden had four houses founded between 993 and 1043, while Hildesheim saw five foundations between 1011 and 1029. The example of Hildesheim shows how much depended on individual bishops: Bernward put all his energies into his foundation of St Michael (1011), while it was his successor Godehard who founded the remaining four episcopal houses within the space of a few years. In the south German duchies, including Franconia, it was again the bishops who were responsible for most of the new foundations, as in Würzburg, with four foundations between 995 and 1003 (again we see the interest of a single bishop, in this case Henry I of Würzburg). Lay founders were less common, and their foundations on the whole smaller; in particular it is very noticeable that the dukes of Bavaria and Suabia hardly appear as monastic founders. The explanation is probably that the south German dukes did not dispose of enough land to make foundations possible; what they held belonged to the dukedom. In Lotharingia the ducal families (here native) were more important, and there were significant lay foundations (for example the monasteries at Waulsort and Hastière, both from the mid tenth century); but here again these were far outnumbered by the foundations and refoundations by bishops, especially those of Liège and of the province of Trier. An excessive emphasis on foundation is perhaps misleading; lay magnates are found far more often making grants to existing houses than setting up new ones (hardly surprisingly, in view of the relative costs).

Before the death of Henry III the coenobitic life of the kingdom of Germany had hardly been touched by two of the most important monastic trends of the eleventh century: canons regular and eremitical monasticism. It is true that these forms of monastic organization had not yet made much headway anywhere in Europe, but in Italy, France and Burgundy they were further advanced. The new kinds of houses of canons, whose members lived a common life with no individual shares in the property of the church and no dwelling-quarters of their own, were to become of great importance in the second half of the century, but there were none in Germany in 1056, while the eremitically tinged monasticism associated with Fruttuaria and Camaldoli had also not reached Germany. That is not to say that there were no hermits. A number of monastic houses grew from the germ of a hermitage, notably Einsiedeln ("Hermitage", a not uncommon German place-name) in Suabia, and besides this we have isolated notices of some hermits who achieved a more than local reputation. It is a sign of the sharp social differentiation of the period that the two most prominent were treated very differently by their contemporaries. The Thuringian aristocrat Günther, who converted late in life to the religious life and died after nearly forty years as a wandering hermit and preacher, was generally accepted and admired, and as a holy man was even able to mediate between Germans and Bohemians on the campaign of 1041. Haimerad, his slightly older contemporary, was of unfree origin, and was consequently regarded with great suspicion by the established church (for example by Bishop Meinwerk of Paderborn, who had his prayer-book burnt and the hermit himself beaten). Only after his death in 1019 did he come to be regarded as sufficiently respectable to be credited with miracles.

Hermits were necessarily minority figures. Mainstream German monasticism was thoroughly Benedictine – so far as we know. Many of the smaller aristocratic foundations have left no traces of any kind of their internal life; we know of their existence only because their founders secured a royal diploma which stayed in the house's archives when it was reformed in the twelfth century (as very many such houses were). Even the line between monks and canons (or nuns and canonesses) was a blurred one, only gradually sharpened in the eleventh century; Adam of Bremen records how Archbishop Unwan was the first to abolish mixed observances in his diocese.[16] To talk of Benedictine monasticism is in any case to beg a number of questions. Much has been made of the different currents within Benedictine monasticism of the tenth and early eleventh centuries; in particular, a contrast has been drawn between "imperial" monastic reform and that found on the other side of the western border of the Reich, a contrast summed up in the antithesis between the Lotharingian house of Gorze and the Burgundian house of Cluny, both founded in the early tenth century. Cluniac monasticism is held to have meant the monastery's exemption from the power of the diocesan bishop (and hence direct dependence on the papacy) and a hostile attitude to the institution of the advocacy. Gorze, which may be taken as a symbolic shorthand for a number of tenth-century centres of monastic reform in Lotharingia, is held to have meant a more tolerant attitude to the powers that be. The contrast is supposed to explain why the German rulers made no use of Cluny for the monastic reforms they carried through, and why there was no Cluniac monasticism within the Reich until the advent of the Hirsau movement in the second half of the eleventh century. Cluny's

16. Adam of Bremen II 48, p. 108.

absence from the Reich in our period is established; what is less clear is how coherent the strands of "reform monasticism" were. In particular the clear definition of Cluniac monasticism was something which evolved only slowly and was hardly complete by 1050. Many of the filiations which have been traced out to show that such and such a house was reformed along Gorzian lines turn out to depend on no more than the known fact that a new abbot was taken from another monastery which is thought to have been Gorzian. The early reformers moved around from monastery to monastery, restoring the material basis of the houses committed to them for reform and their monastic practices, but without being able to do much that would outlive them. In the eleventh century there was perhaps a greater degree of continuity, and reformers like William of Dijon, Richard of Saint-Vannes and his pupil Poppo of Stavelot were able (not least because of the backing they received from rulers such as Henry II and Conrad II and from the owners of monasteries) to set up something like congregations of monasteries – but here, too, little survived the deaths of monastic reformers. Reform groupings should in this period be seen as small families of monasteries, linked by the changes made by a particular reformer but not necessarily still so linked two or three generations later.

Many monastic houses in the *regnum Teutonicorum* (and elsewhere in Europe) were not reformed at any time in this period, though we should not assume from that that they were decadent. Indeed, one of the most striking things about monastic reform within the Reich is that its opponents – those who were reformed against their will, and their sympathizers – were capable of very articulate and literate opposition: reform was criticized by Ekkehard of St Gallen, by Thietmar of Merseburg, by Lampert of Hersfeld, and by the monks of Monte Cassino in a letter answering a complaint about reform by the monks of Lorsch. Literacy and articulacy do not of course necessarily imply other virtues, but at least clichés about worldly monks following only a debased form of monasticism being forced to adopt a new spiritual rigour would seem to be out of place. In any case, it was on the whole only the largest and wealthiest foundations which were subject to the serious attentions of reformers, and in the whole of the Ottonian kingdom there were not many of these. In Saxony there were Corvey and Herford in Westfalia, and the newer foundations at Memleben and Berge (Magdeburg) in Ostfalia. In Franconia there were Fulda, Hersfeld and Lorsch, plus St Alban's, Mainz; in Bavaria, Tegernsee and Niederaltaich, to which should be added from the end of the tenth century the four monasteries created by the transformation of the Bavarian cathedral churches (which had up until then had monastic chapters like many English cathedrals) into normal chapters of canons; in Suabia, Ellwangen, Weißenburg, St Gallen, and the Reichenau. Lotharingia, the old Carolingian core-land, had far more houses of this kind of size and importance than the rest of the kingdom: Stavelot, St Maximin in Trier, St Pantaleon in Cologne, Prüm, Echternach, Remiremont, and others. For this reason alone monastic reform is bound to look Lotharingian, and indeed most of the reformers did come from Lotharingia or from Burgundy.

Reform, or more neutrally reorganization, often meant what seem to us comparatively small changes in monastic practice: differences in clothing, in the performance of the liturgy, in the names given to offices. It was often associated with secularizations, with the granting of monastic lands in benefice, particularly where (as under Henry II and Conrad II) it was backed by rulers; complaints about loss of lands are recorded from Corvey, St Maximin's, Trier and Kempten, to name only a few. It was often imposed from outside, and demonstrates more clearly than anything else could the way in which the owners of monasteries, whether these were rulers, bishops or lay magnates, regarded the foundations as theirs, to order and reorder as they saw fit. There was little sense of the autonomy of religious life as a value to be sought after; it was only later in the century that some currents in monasticism moved towards protecting the monasteries from their owners and guardians. Reform is also misleading as a term because of its wider connotations. There was no very visible link between monastic reform on the one hand and church reform on the other; there is no reason to suppose and no evidence to show that abbots and monks, whether reformed or not, took any great interest in the questions of simony or clerical marriage which were what dominated (if that is not too strong a word for what was in any case not a very strong movement) the interests of reform-minded canon lawyers and bishops in the first half of the eleventh century. Nor was there in this period any very strong feeling against advocacies; even Cluny was less hostile to lay patronage than has been maintained.

More interesting in many ways than small changes in the customs followed by a particular monastery in addition to the Benedictine rule, or reforms in the internal practice of a house, is the role of monasteries in interchange between the different parts of the Reich. The transfers of abbots and monks (and also of books and scribes) between monasteries may or may not have led to changes in the

245

internal life of the recipient monasteries. What they did mean was a recognition of the existence of a kingdom of Germany as something more than a collection of small provinces, either ecclesiastical or secular. In principle, a monk from Bavaria could be chosen as abbot of a Saxon house, or vice versa, and this not just at the level of the larger and better-endowed foundations. Burchard, a monk from the Reichenau (and probably a Suabian, to judge by the name), was made abbot of St Emmeram, Regensburg in 1033, for example; the counts palatine of Saxony brought in a Bavarian abbot for their new foundation at Goseck. A sense that the monasteries of the Reich had something in common is also to be seen in the clause common in royal diplomata that a monastery should enjoy the same liberties as those of Corvey or the Reichenau. Very possibly the apparent failure of Cluniac monasticism to make any impact within the Reich before the middle of the eleventh century reflects nothing more than a feeling that Cluny lay outside the kingdom and hence could not be turned to in this way. It was certainly not because of any lack of respect for Cluny as a monastery – both Adelheid, Otto I's second wife, and Henry II had close contacts with it and made it rich gifts.

INTELLECTUALS, ARTISTS AND PATRONS

One cannot really talk of an "Ottonian renaissance" in the sense that there was a "Carolingian renaissance". We may perhaps make an exception when referring to the production of really lavish works of art: illuminated manuscripts, ivories, goldsmithery. Here there was a noteworthy revival in the period 950–1050 compared with the preceding seventy years or so, but that is hardly surprising – a certain stability and prosperity are required for such arts to flourish. But the absence of an "Ottonian renaissance" as far as the life of the mind was concerned should not be taken as a sign of intellectual inactivity. Rather, it shows that the foundations laid in Carolingian east Francia had survived the difficult period in the late ninth and early tenth centuries pretty well intact, and served as a base which could be taken for granted. The preoccupations of Carolingian intellectuals and churchmen had amounted to a rediscovery of Latin, of the Bible and of the church fathers. Evidently little further was felt to be necessary in this direction in the Ottonian era. The number of manuscripts of classical authors from Germany dating from the period 950–1050 is not high; biblical commentaries and *florilegia* (collections of excerpts) of the works of the church fathers were even less common, either as copies or as new productions. Intellectual effort went on other things; particularly noteworthy was the interest in historical writing and in ecclesiastical law, as we shall see shortly.

By contrast with the courts of Charles the Great and Louis the Pious, as well as those of Charles the Bald and arguably Louis the German, the Ottonian and Salian court was not inherently a centre of learning. Occasionally intellectuals might find their way there: Liutprand of Cremona and Rather of Verona for a time in the 960s, Gerbert of Rheims in the 990s. These men were not just intellectuals; they were exiles looking for favour and support. Native intellectuals could be found visiting the court, but rarely in permanent attendance on the ruler. This was not because the rulers were uneducated and hence incapable of appreciating intellectuals. Otto II could enjoy a disputation between Gerbert of Rheims and Ohtrich of Magdeburg. Otto III and Henry II were well educated and had substantial libraries (most of whose contents were used to start off the library of Henry II's new foundation at Bamberg); Conrad II, like most medieval founders of dynasties, was illiterate, but his son received a reasonable grounding from his tutor, Bishop Egilbert of Freising. Yet apart from Otto III in his final years – and the circle around him at that time was predominantly non-German – they were evidently not regarded as patrons of intellectuals. Comparatively few works were dedicated to them – surprisingly few, given the preference of Ottonian and Salian intellectuals for historical writing and the need of rulers at all times for praise and legitimation. Henry III is here an exception: Wipo's *Life of Conrad II* was dedicated to him, as were Anselm of Besate's *Rhetorimachia*, and collections of poetry by two French clerics, Arnulf and Azelin. As with Otto III's circle, none of these authors came from the *regnum Teutonicum*.

The backbone of Ottonian and Salian intellectual (and artistic) culture was provided by the cathedral schools and by the entourages of bishops. The royal court was replaced functionally by episcopal courts, under Brun at Cologne in the 950s and 960s for example, or Notker at Liège in the last third of the tenth century. There were a few monastic schools besides these – there had to be, because of the custom of offering children as monks at an early age – but even monasteries like Corvey, the Reichenau and St Gallen could not and did not compete with the cathedral schools. Here too not all cathedrals were equal. In the late tenth century the most prestigious was probably that at Magdeburg; later this would be joined by others, at Liège, Hildesheim, Worms, Würzburg and Bamberg. The fact that both Magdeburg and Bamberg were new foundations and could nevertheless achieve distinction shows that there was a considerable reservoir of ability on which to draw. It was at these schools that the ecclesiastical elite of the Ottonian and Salian Reich were taught, to a very high level, the basic skills needed for dealing with the inherited culture of Latin Europe. The most important of these skills was a mastery of Latin. The significance attached to this is seen not least in a number of anecdotes about embarrassing howlers perpetrated by people of distinction: the bishop of Bamberg who announced that the earth was "formless and a cow" (*vacca* instead of *vacua*, "empty"); the bishop of Paderborn who read without hesitation a prayer from a liturgical manuscript in which the words "male and female servants" (*famulis et famulabus*) had been altered (by Henry II himself) to "male and female mules" (*mulis et mulabus*); the monk Gunzo, who was ridiculed at St Gallen for using the wrong case and wrote an indignant letter of justification to the monks of the rival monastery at the Reichenau in consequence.[17] Stories like these do not show widespread incompetence; on the contrary, they demonstrate that the level of Latinity to which Carolingian scholars had aspired for their pupils could now be taken for granted. How this was achieved can be seen in the few surviving relics of the teaching of grammar and rhetoric, notably the letter-collections from Tegernsee (late tenth and early eleventh centuries), Worms (1020s and 1030s) and Bamberg (late 1050s to the mid 1070s), which contain numerous letters and poems written and perhaps set as rhetorical exercises. Here a remarkable level of technical ability is displayed, but little interest in new developments; Boethius was thought of more as a source of difficult metres and obscure Greek words to be used as decoration than as a philosopher and logician. Similar preoccupations are found in the collection of poems, some in very elaborate metres, known from the home of the manuscript as the Cambridge songs; this kind of activity was also a continuation of Carolingian practice, though the Cambridge songs also include newer metrical poetry. Such an emphasis on rhetorical skills was more utilitarian than it might appear. The main use for the writing of Latin lay in the composition of letters, charters and diplomata, all of which gave scope for the well-turned phrase and

---

17. *Vita Meinwerci* c. 186, ed. F. Tenckhoff (MGH SRG, Hannover 1921), 107; *Brunos Buch vom Sachsenkrieg* c. 15, ed. H. E. Lohmann (MGH Deutsches Mittelalter 1, Leipzig 1937), 22; Gunzo, *Epistola ad Augienses* c. 3, ed. K. Manitius (MGH Quellen zur Geistesgeschichte des Mittelalters 2, Weimar 1958), 22–3.

mastery of the *colores rhetorici*. The Italian Anselm of Besate, writing
in the 1040s, was able to assume that his elaborate *Rhetorimachia*
would be appreciated by the members of the imperial chapel, and if
the poet and historian Wipo was typical of the standard then no
doubt he was correct.[18] When the need arose for a new propaganda
thrust in the 1070s the Salian chancery was able to rise effortlessly to
the occasion, drawing on the skills which had been hammered into
the pupils of cathedral schools. Most of the clerical elite mentioned
earlier in this chapter went through a training of this kind in their
teens before moving into the world as canons in a cathedral chapter.

The importance of historical writing for Ottonian and Salian
intellectuals might seem at first sight to reflect a court-centred
interest in rhetoric and panegyric; yet even for the 960s the notion of
"Ottonian house historiography" (meaning among others the
writings of Hrotswitha, Liutprand, Ruotger, Widukind and Adalbert
of St Maximin) is a debatable one, in the sense that these works were
not in any sense written to order (though some were perhaps
intended to please). Later on, the divorce between historical writing
and the court became still more complete. Of the major historical
writers of the late Ottonian and early Salian era, only Wipo, a royal
capellanus, could be said to have been a court figure. The anonymous
authors of the major annalistic compilations of the period – from
Hersfeld, Altaich and Quedlinburg – were presumably monks, as
was Hermann the Lame, a chronicler from the Reichenau whose
interests covered scientific chronography and music as well as
history. Thietmar of Merseburg and Adalbold of Utrecht were
bishops associated with Henry II, whom they wrote about, but
hardly courtiers, while Alpert of Metz's *De diversitate temporum*
mentions the king only in passing and has Adalbold of Utrecht
himself as its chief protagonist. Indeed, the association of historical
writing with bishops is closer than that with kings, especially when
the *Gesta episcoporum* and the important individual episcopal
biographies of the period are taken into account: Ruotger's *Life of
Brun of Cologne*; Thangmar's *Life of Bernward of Hildesheim*; the
anonymous *Life of Burchard of Worms*; and – in a rather different
category – the Lives of the martyred bishop Adalbert of Prague.
The flourishing of historical writing in the Reich in the tenth and
early eleventh centuries is not easy to account for, except in the
general sense that the dispersion of intellectual and cultural centres

18. Ed. K. Manitius (MGH Quellen zur Geistesgeschichte des Mittelalters 2, Weimar
1958), 96, verse 18.

rather than their concentration on the court was likely to produce more. The fact that the ethnic groupings which constituted the Reich, except for the Franks, lacked a past; the novelty of empire and the need to justify and set it in a historical context; the emphasis on rhetoric in the intellectual life of the Reich – all these can be invoked as a partial account. In the last resort the sheer range and variety of historical writing prevents a single explanation. What links the authors is their interest in the past (in most cases, the very recent past) and their willingness to reflect on their own place in it and that of their contemporaries. Here at least Ottonian culture surpassed its predecessors: there is little in Carolingian historical writing which can match the fluency, the rhetorical power or the moral awareness and reflectiveness of writers like Liutprand, Widukind, Thietmar and Wipo. Technically there were advances as well: the revival of study of the quadrivium at the end of the tenth century (in Liège for example, as well as by Gerbert of Rheims) led to a renewed interest in technical problems of chronography. It was the scientific study of chronological systems at the Reichenau and later at Bamberg which, building on Bede's *De ratione temporum*, paved the way for almost all the universal chronicles of the high middle ages.

In a quite different area, that of canon law, Ottonian and Salian intellectuals paved the way for the systematic study and application of canon law of the late eleventh and twelfth centuries. The starting-point for east Frankish canon law studies was the work of the Lotharingian monk and historian Regino of Prüm at the beginning of the tenth century, whose *De synodalibus causis et disciplinis ecclesiasticis* was intended as a kind of handbook for the enforcement of canon law at the local level by the bishop or his representative. Regino had no real following in his own region, but his work none the less provided the starting-point for the developments of the early eleventh century. At the time of writing it is not entirely clear who should be given the main credit for these. The choice lies between Freising, where a substantial canon law collection in twelve parts was probably compiled at the end of the tenth century, and the traditional candidate, Burchard of Worms, whose *Decretum* appeared around 1020. Whether the Freising collection was derived from that of Burchard, as was long supposed, or Burchard's from the Freising collection, as has recently been suggested, it was Burchard's *Decretum* which found popularity and a comparatively wide circulation. It is a sign of the growing integration of the Italian kingdom into the Reich that Burchard's collection, which within the *regnum Teutonicum* soon became the standard work (eleventh-century copies survive from a number of cathedral libraries), was also widely distributed south of the Alps by the time of Henry III's death. It was characteristic of these works that they provided at least a rudimentary grouping of the material by subject matter; this was an innovation compared with the historically ordered canon law collections of the Carolingian era, since it enabled churchmen to get at the law on a particular subject without having to know it all. The problem of resolving conflicting authorities was still to be tackled. Burchard dealt with it largely by minor adjustments to his texts, thus editing conflicts out of his collection. But it was only with the advent of collections ordered by subject-matter that this could even be perceived as a serious problem.

There was much less interest in this period than there had been in the ninth century in the use of the vernacular and in translating works into German. It is true that the work of the St Gallen monk Notker "the German", whose work was produced around the turn of the millennium, was impressive both in its quantity and in its quality. Notker translated enough to provide the basis for a vernacular study of the liberal arts and of theology, and his work had a reputation sufficient to arouse the interest of the empress Gisela, who visited St Gallen in 1027. Yet in spite of this it had hardly any echo, and Notker had no pupils of note. Partly this will have reflected the greater difficulty in establishing a tradition in monastic schools. The mid tenth century poetess Hrotswitha of Gandersheim, author of a large corpus of Latin works which included saints' lives, a history of Otto the Great and several verse plays, also had no successors and founded no school. But if the conditions for successful tradition were present in any monastery in the eleventh century, then they existed in St Gallen: the vernacular was apparently not interesting. The contrast with the east Frankish kingdom in the ninth century, or with Anglo-Saxon England, where the use of the vernacular was encouraged by the court itself, is very apparent; probably the lack of interest in the vernacular in Germany reflects the decentralization of cultural activity we have already noted. It may also be that there was a change in missionary strategy, and that an articulate vernacular command of the basics of Christianity was no longer considered necessary – but this would contrast sharply with the contemporary efforts made by at least some clerics on the eastern frontier to learn Slavonic languages.

If the later Ottonian and Salian rulers were not the targets for many dedications of literary works, they did receive, and indeed probably commissioned, a number of lavish manuscripts, almost all liturgical, many with illustrations. The most famous of these are the full-page paintings which depict rulers being blessed by Christ and the Holy Spirit. Some illustrations showed more secular though no less idealized aspects of their power, such as the well-known picture in the Gospel Book of Otto III showing the ruler receiving gifts brought to him by four personified female provinces: Roma, Germania, Gallia and Sclavinia. It is perhaps characteristic of these rulers that the works dedicated to them should have been visual and ceremonial rather than intellectual in content. Probably not many people were reached by such depictions of rulers in majesty, even among the elite; but at least we may assume that the late Ottonians and the early Salians liked to see themselves in this way. Such works represent, however, only a fraction of the resources devoted altogether by Ottonian and Salian prelates to works of art: buildings, ivories, gems, goldsmithery, high-class manuscripts. A generation after the famous manuscript paintings of the Gospels and sacramentaries presented to Otto III and Henry II we find prelates themselves expending resources with comparable lavishness on manuscripts not meant for the court: in the pontificals commissioned by Siegbert of Minden or Gundechar of Eichstätt, for example. The importance attached to church building and rebuilding, to the development of the cathedral town as a "sacred landscape", has already been noted; eleventh century prelates populated their macroscopic sacred landscapes with microscopic sacred images. As with monastic foundations, not all prelates were equally interested in such things. Brun of Cologne, whose buildings and works of art are listed at length by his biographer; Egbert of Trier, the patron of the so-called "Master of the Register of St Gregory"; Bernward of Hildesheim, who commissioned bronze doors and a bronze column for his cathedral as well as lavish manuscripts and works of gold- and silversmithery – these were perhaps unusual in their efforts, but their aspirations were shared by many of their colleagues. Itinerant kings, who had to spread their butter widely enough to make a number of royal palaces sufficiently impressive to receive them, could barely compete with this kind of fixed display of wealth and sacral power. Henry III began to do so with the resources he devoted to his newly founded palace/canonry complex at Goslar, but the development was to be cut short by the Saxon revolt under his son. Lay magnates were even more outclassed. The Billung dukes might compete with the archbishops of Bremen for control over Hamburg, but they could not compete in terms of conspicuous display within Hamburg itself, and most other magnates were even less well placed.

CHAPTER NINE
Hegemony and empire

THE EASTERN FRONTIER

The relations between the German rulers and their followers and the peoples who lay in a long arc from the north to the south-east of the Reich were inevitably somewhat different from those with the other Carolingian successor-states. The fact that the peoples were not or were only incipiently Christianized meant that an attitude of superiority and dominance was possible; it also meant that there was an obligation felt by rulers, if not always by their followers, to support missionary work. In the tenth century this was more institutionalized than it had been in the ninth. The Saxons had been converted by individual missionaries, even though these had institutional back up. But in the course of the eighth and ninth centuries the archbishoprics of Mainz and Bremen in particular had acquired "missionary territories", and hence implicitly an institutional commitment to mission. This model was followed for the tenth-century episcopal foundations, especially Magdeburg, Merseburg and Meißen, which were institutions with defined (though changeable) spheres of influence. Individual missionaries continued to play an important role, as the careers of Adalbert of Prague and Brun of Querfurt show, but it was the rights and obligations of institutions which would dominate. Almost all the peoples concerned were the immediate neighbours of the Saxons; relations with the one exception, the Hungarians, took a rather more relaxed course from those with Danes, Slavs, Poles and Bohemians. The Saxons were the military backbone of the new empire; raiding and tribute-taking continued to be the basis of their political economy up to the end of the tenth century, and it was the drying up of these opportunities among other things which was to lead to the estrangement between the Saxons and their kings in the eleventh century.

The most straightforward of the Germans' eastern neighbours were the Hungarians. Their embassy to Otto I in 973 marked the beginning of a more settled way of life. Their raiding had been stopped in the west by Otto's victory in 955, and it was ended in the east by a combined attack from Sviatoslav of Kiev and the Byzantine Emperor John Tsimisces in 970. For the next generation we hear little of them, apart from a brief resumption of raids on Bavaria in the early years of Otto III's minority. This probably reflects the paucity of narrative sources for the south-east of the Reich in the second half of the tenth century. What we do hear of are missionary activities by the bishoprics of Regensburg and Passau. The Hungarian king, Geza, remained pagan, yet his son Waik, who succeeded in 997, was able to marry the Liudolfing Gisela (sister of the future Henry II), and was presumably baptized before this, probably during his father's lifetime, though the chronology is difficult to establish. Otto III and Pope Silvester II acting together in 1001 gave the new ruler, who had taken the baptismal name of Stephen, a royal title and crown and the right to set up a Hungarian church with its own archbishopric (at Gran/Esztergom) and bishoprics. Probably Otto III sent Stephen a replica of the Holy Lance in token of his kingship; probably Stephen commended his kingdom to St Peter and hence the papacy. No one protested, and Henry of Bavaria in fact sponsored his brother-in-law at baptism. Bishop Pilgrim of Passau, though he had compiled an elaborate series of forgeries giving his see the powers of a metropolitan over Hungary in the 970s, does not seem to have tried to make anything of them, and probably did not carry enough political weight to try. The south-east section of the frontier was simply less politically sensitive at this time than the north-east section. Following Stephen's coronation and baptism the Hungarians virtually disappeared from the sources for the history of the German kingdom for a generation, which is probably a sign of peaceful relations. Only under Conrad II and especially Henry III do we again hear of campaigns against them, mostly not very successful ones. Border conflicts between Hungarians and Bavarians led to a major but fruitless campaign by Conrad II in 1030; in the following year the king's son, Henry of Bavaria, made peace with Stephen and ceded territory between the rivers Fischa and Leitha. Henry III himself was able to intervene to some effect in the succession dispute between Peter, Stephen's nephew, and Obo after Stephen I's death in 1038; after Peter had commended himself to Henry, and Obo's forces had raided the south-eastern marches of Bavaria, it was clear which side Henry would take. Campaigns in 1042 and 1043 were followed by a full-scale invasion in 1044 and the defeat of the Hungarians at Menfö. Henry was able to establish Peter as king and accept his commendation, but Peter was driven out in 1046 by another nephew of Stephen's, Andrew. The war with Andrew which broke out in 1051 was still unresolved on Henry's death, though there was evidently a group among the Bavarian magnates which favoured a permanent peace and an end to what must have been very demanding and perhaps unrewarding military exertions.

At the other end of the arc, relations between the Saxons and the kings of Denmark were also normalized in the course of the first half of the eleventh century. Harald Bluetooth had taken advantage of the troubles of the 970s and of the uprising of 983 to free himself from tributary status, and after this the Danes no longer paid tribute, but no one seems to have been very interested in making them do so. Even the emergence of a loose Danish empire under Svein Forkbeard and Cnut from the last decade of the tenth century onwards went almost unnoticed by contemporary Saxon writers. Northern Saxony suffered briefly from the rise of state Vikingism, especially during the minority of Otto III, when a count of Stade and other Saxon notables were killed in the course of a raid in 993. The sources for Henry II's reign are silent about German–Danish relations, but it is probable that in the end England and the rest of Scandinavia proved to be easier and more profitable targets for the Danes. Cnut took part along with Rudolf III of Burgundy in Conrad's imperial coronation in 1027, apparently without feeling any loss of face, and even after the death of Cnut, when the Danish empire began to decline, Conrad was still interested in a Danish bride for his son Henry, who married Cnut's daughter Gunnhilde in 1036. There was little sign that either Conrad II or Henry III wanted to restore the status quo ante Svein. Indeed, Henry III, and still more Henry IV, began to look to the Danish rulers for help in their conflicts with the Billungs. Generally friendly relations between German and Danish rulers did not mean that all relations between Germans and Danes were friendly. Even in Ottonian times northern Saxony had not been a region to which rulers paid much attention, and this was still more true of the early Salian period. Those nearer to the Danes – notably the Billung dukes, the counts of Stade and the archbishops of

Hamburg-Bremen – had rather different interests. Hamburg-Bremen's attitude is visible largely in the retrospective of Adam's history, written in the 1070s; from this it would appear that Svein and Cnut were trying from the beginning of the century to emancipate the Danish church from the tutelage of Hamburg-Bremen. To do so they were prepared to get missionaries and even on occasion bishops from western Europe, especially from England. The archbishops of Bremen could do little about this except occasionally capture such a missionary and hold him prisoner until he agreed to accept Bremen's primacy over the Danish church. Politically, the part of Saxony nearest to Denmark was dominated by the Billungs, who had links by marriage with Scandinavian royal families just as the eastern margraves were linked with the princely families of Poland and Bohemia. With increasing Danish pressure on the Slavs, especially the Abodrites, along the southern Baltic shore, the conflict of interests became more acute; the loose cooperation between the Salians and the Danish royal house in effect against the quasi-regal Billungs, which took shape from the mid eleventh century, was probably a more natural state of affairs than that reflected in Ordulf Billung's marriage with Uffhilde of Denmark.

The centres of Saxon interest in the peoples beyond the frontier lay immediately to the east and south-east of Saxony: Poland, Bohemia, and nearer home the Abodrites and Liutizi. Here above all were the regions where hegemony meant not just the ability to influence events in one's favour without having to use force but also a more intensive form of domination. Yet just as with Denmark and Hungary (and in the west as well), we can perceive a hardening of the edges of empire. By 1056 the ruler of Poland was definitely no longer within the empire, while the duke of Bohemia equally definitely was, though with a status unlike that of the other duchies: German rulers neither went there, nor did they have land there. The Bohemian duke probably paid tribute still; perhaps the Polish ruler did as well, but in neither case was this on a vast scale (for Bohemia a payment of 500 marks and 120 cows is recorded for 1039),[1] and it was hardly any longer significant by comparison with the overall gross domestic product of the Reich. Abodrites certainly paid tribute, as did the Liutizi again after the expeditions of 1035 and 1036, but payment was intermittent, and the aggressive expansion of Otto I's time had long given way to more or less stable conditions.

1. Cosmas of Prague, *Chronicon* II 8, ed. B. Bretholz (MGH SRG NS 2, Berlin 1923), 94.

The Saxon marches were no longer places where political fortunes were to be made, and the rulers themselves took part in the campaigning there increasingly rarely. None of these changes came about immediately. The years following the uprising of 983 saw serious attempts to restore the status quo. Expeditions are recorded against the Slavs, meaning the Liutizi and the Bohemians, in 985 and 986, the first in conjunction with Miesco of Poland, while attempts were made in 990 to subdue Boleslav of Bohemia, the ally of the Liutizi. Around 990 there were again conflicts with the Abodrites, who had reverted to tributary status in 984 after the uprising of the previous year. Between 991 and 994 there were repeated attempts to recapture Brandenburg and establish a client prince of the Hevelli there, Pribislav. To this end a large force was raised in 992 from Saxony, Bavaria, Bohemia and Poland (one of the rare occasions when the Ottonians were able to draw on forces from within the Reich outside Saxony and Sclavinia for their Slav wars), and Brandenburg was for a short time brought under renewed Saxon control. This was the limit of Saxon success; moreover, several of the campaigns of the 990s were accompanied by heavy losses, and the Liutizi succeeded in 997 in destroying the Arneburg, a major border fortress. It is not surprising that the Quedlinburg annals reported in 994 that only the Sorbs were left under Saxon control: all the other Slav peoples had defected.[2]

The campaigns against the Elbe Slavs cannot be separated from the Ottonians' relations with the major Slav princes further east and south. Both Miesco I of Poland and Boleslav I of Bohemia had risen with Otto I; they had paid tribute, provided contingents of troops and had probably benefitted at home from their association with so powerful a ruler. They were very much key figures on the small stage of Saxon politics, perhaps as important as the dukes of Suabia. When at the end of the 960s Hodo, one of the margraves who had succeeded to a part of Gero's huge march, launched an unsuccessful attack on Miesco, Otto I sent orders all the way from southern Italy that both were to keep the peace until he should return to judge between them. Miesco and Boleslav were also related by marriage; around 966 Miesco married Dobrava, the daughter of Boleslav I, a marriage which later had dynastic consequences. The immediate result was the beginnings of Christianization in Poland; Dobrava was

2. MGH SS 3, 72.

herself a Christian, and Miesco's conversion and the setting up of the bishopric at Posen followed shortly after the marriage. Miesco and Boleslav II (who succeeded his father in 972) supported Henry the Quarrelsome in 974 and 976–7, and again in 983–5. Theophanu was able to win Miesco's support, however, and the later 980s and 990s were characterized by a cross-alliance: Saxony and Poland (under Miesco and from 992 his son Boleslav Chrobry) against the Liutizi and Bohemia. The tensions between Bohemia and Poland were home-grown, not just the result of Saxon hegemony; Silesia was disputed between the two dukes, especially after Boleslav had brought the territories surrounding the original Piast heartland under his control in the 990s. But tensions between Saxony and Bohemia were important as well. Boleslav II had captured and held Meißen for a time in the 980s; and he was not usually on good terms with the bishops of Prague. Adalbert, a member of the Slavnikid family who were rivals of the Przemyslids, was twice forced to leave his bishopric; the last exile, which coincided with the liquidation of the rest of his family in 995, was to be permanent. Though the Slavnikid Adalbert was almost bound to be *persona non grata*, this was exacerbated by his links and those of his family with Saxony. Adalbert's successor Thiadric, a monk from Corvey, was also driven out by Boleslav II, and had to be restored by a Saxon force under Margrave Ekkehard of Meißen.

Boleslav Chrobry continued on good terms with Otto III in the 990s, and he also gave support to Adalbert of Prague, who after a time in Rome in Otto's entourage had set out to try to convert the Prussians on the Baltic coast. After Adalbert's martyrdom in 997 it was the Polish duke, not the Bohemian, who recovered his body from the Prussians and set up a shrine to Adalbert in Gnesen. In 1000 Otto III made a Lent pilgrimage to the shrine; this was the occasion for setting up a separate Polish church under an archbishopric at Gnesen, with suffragan bishoprics at Cracow, Breslau and Kolberg (held to begin with by German clerics). The new archbishop, Gaudentius, was the half-brother of the martyred Adalbert, and had already been referred to in a *placitum* recording a judgement by Otto III in Rome in December 999 as the "archbishop of St Adalbert" (*archiepiscopus sancti Adalberti martyris*).[3] This vagueness of title is probably a sign that the setting up of a new province was very much a matter for discussion and improvisation right up until the last

---

3. *I Placiti del "Regnum Italiae"*, no. 441, ed. C. Manaresi (Fonti per la storia d'Italia 96, Rome 1957), 441.

moment, and indeed the sources are far from clear about what exactly happened. Boleslav received a copy of the Holy Lance and the title of "brother and cooperator of the Empire, ally and friend of the Roman people".[4] In return he presented Otto with a gift of 300 warriors and accompanied the emperor back through Saxony to Aachen, acting as his sword-bearer. Very probably Otto intended that Boleslav should become a king, as Stephen I was to do in Hungary: the copy of the Lance, an important symbol of rulership in the Ottonian kingdom, seems to point to this, especially as Stephen also seems to have received one. For whatever reason, this plan was not carried out; nevertheless, the settlement at Gnesen turned Boleslav from a tributary into a lord, as Thietmar put it.[5] Thietmar's hostility was often echoed by German historians of the nineteenth and twentieth centuries, who saw Otto III as having betrayed vital German interests. Since 1945 an inverted variant of this has become more customary: Otto's actions in Poland and in Hungary are seen as having been inspired by a spirit of peaceful cooperation, a new vision for Europe in east and west, in which kings could co-exist under the overall umbrella of the Christian and Roman empire. It is difficult not to feel that this interpretation – which is hardly supported by anything Otto himself or his entourage said – is equally anachronistic: Otto was no more the spiritual ancestor of Rapacki, Spaak and Brandt than he was of Ebert and Schneidemann. The pilgrimage can obviously be linked with Otto's idea of a renewal of the Roman empire (on which see below, p. 279ff.). Yet the context of Otto's action was traditional enough: he made a pilgrimage to pray at a shrine during Lent, as his Carolingian and Ottonian predecessors often had done. He was also sufficiently traditionalist to ensure that he was back from Gnesen in time to spend Palm Sunday at Magdeburg and Easter at Quedlinburg, as Ottonians often did. His meeting with Boleslav looks very like Henry I's dealings with the south German dukes: the relations between Otto and Boleslav or between Otto and Waik-Stephen were ones of *amicitia*. It is improbable that these would have remained stable had Otto lived, any more than the earlier *amicitiae* had done, or even that they were intended to remain stable. Even Otto's role in the setting up of new provinces in Poland and Hungary should not be seen as overly visionary; there were already incipient ecclesiastical structures, including bishoprics at

---

4. *Chronicon Polonorum Galli Anonymi* I 6, MGH SS 9, 429; the source dates from the early twelfth century, and its reliability is disputed.
5. Thietmar V 10, p. 232.

Veszprém in Hungary and at Posen and Cracow in Poland, in the two territories, and it was only a matter of time before these took more definite shape. The alternative in the medium term was between participating and not participating in the setting up of new provinces, not between allowing and preventing their coming into existence at all.

The reign of Henry II was marked by hostilities with Boleslav Chrobry for almost the whole of its length, and by a military alliance between Henry and the pagan Liutizi. This was a reversal of alliances, but it is not clear that it was a direct reaction to the events of 1000, an attempt to turn the clock back. Boleslav had backed Ekkehard of Meißen, to whom he was related by marriage, for the succession in 1002; after Ekkehard was murdered he acknowledged Henry II, but claimed Ekkehard's march. Henry II was not prepared to let him have all of it, but he had to allow him the Lausitz march and to accept the appointment of Ekkehard's brother Gunzelin in Meißen. An additional cause of hostility was an attack on Boleslav in Merseburg, where he had come to commend himself; Boleslav thought (perhaps rightly) that Henry was behind this. What brought matters to a head was Boleslav's intervention in Bohemia, where Boleslav III faced a succession dispute. Boleslav Chrobry captured and blinded the Bohemian Boleslav, sending him into exile, and then had himself elected duke of Bohemia in 1003. The sticking-point for Henry was Boleslav's refusal to pay tribute or commend himself for the duchy. Henry II was able to drive him out of Bohemia the following year and install Boleslav III's brother Jaromir, who had taken refuge in Bavaria, as duke. Boleslav captured the Lausitz in 1007, a conquest confirmed by peace-meetings at Merseburg in 1013 and again at Bautzen in 1018. Henry mounted a number of campaigns against Poland with armies drawn from Saxony and Bohemia, with support from the Liutizi. All this looks like sustained and principled hostility, but the appearances are misleading. The hostilities began as feud, and were conducted as such. The terms of the reconciliation of 1013 show that quite different relations were thought of as being possible: Boleslav was to send troops on Henry's forthcoming Italian expedition (though he didn't), and in return Henry was to assist Boleslav in his expedition against Kiev (he didn't, but some Germans took part). There was a certain amount of muttering, but no evidence of any real desire even among the Saxon episcopate to challenge the ecclesiastical settlement of Gnesen. The new bishopric at Bamberg hardly did this, and nor did capturing the bishop of Posen and forcing him to acknowledge his subjection to the archbishopric of Magdeburg. Boleslav, a Christian ruler well known to many members of the Saxon aristocracy, evidently enjoyed sufficient reputation to be someone to whom Henry II's opponents looked for support and encouragement; the Polish campaigns were not popular.

Only at the very end of his own reign, after Henry II's death, did Boleslav actually have himself crowned and anointed, reflecting the quasi-regal status he already enjoyed. Boleslav's coronation, which was repeated by his son and successor Miesco II in 1025, was described by Wipo as being *in iniuriam regis Conradi*,[6] and it evidently made a considerable impact on Saxon consciousness. Open hostilities were begun by Miesco in 1028 with an attack on the Saxon marches, which was perhaps pre-emptive. A counter-campaign in 1030 forced Miesco to make peace in 1031 on terms which included surrendering Milzen and the Lausitz; this was the occasion for a Polish revolt against Miesco led by his brothers. The parallels with early Ottonian history here are striking. Boleslav Chrobry had built up a formidable military machine, and had probably freed his realm from all but token payments of tribute to the Ottonians (just as Henry I had done with the Magyars). Unlike Otto I, however, Miesco II did not have the luck to be able to establish indivisibility as a principle; Conrad II intervened more effectively in Polish affairs than the Magyars had done in the Reich in 938 or 954, and in 1034 he enforced a division of the principality among Boleslav Chrobry's descendants. The royal insignia had already been handed over to Conrad in 1032, and Miesco had renounced his claim to kingship. This was sufficient to re-establish German hegemony, even though the division was largely a temporary one. Miesco died in 1034 and his son and successor Casimir had a very unstable position in Poland, especially in his early years. Henry III had to intervene to prevent Poland from being seized by Bretislav of Bohemia – the events of 1003-4 with the signs reversed. In 1054 he could even settle a dispute between Casimir and Bretislav over Silesia at an assembly in Quedlinburg to which he had summoned both, much as Otto I might have done ninety years earlier.

Relations with Bohemia after the death of Otto III resembled those with Poland, but there was a crucial difference: the Bohemian dukes were apparently not interested in setting up a Bohemian

6. Wipo c. 9, pp. 31–2.

church with its own provincial organization under an archbishop. The bishops of Prague, though in many ways little more than the chaplains of the Przemyslid dukes, remained suffragans of the archbishops of Mainz, and did not become archbishops until the fourteenth century. So long as Boleslav Chrobry was alive Bohemian dukes tended to look to the German rulers for support, at least early in their reigns. Jaromir (1004–12) began his career by being reinstated by Henry. His brother Udalrich (1012–34) was able to supplant him partly because Henry II mistrusted Jaromir's contacts with Boleslav Chrobry. Udalrich went into opposition after 1024; Conrad II was able to ally with Ulrich's son Bretislav, who took part in the campaigns against the Liutizi of 1035 and 1036, but by 1039 he in turn was sufficiently well established to be openly hostile to Henry III. It took two campaigns with serious losses in 1040 and 1041 to force Bretislav to submit and commend himself to Henry III. At least as far as Saxon, Suabian and Bavarian authors were concerned there was no doubt that the duke of Bohemia was felt to be part of the Reich; but the Bohemian dukes felt that only for as long as they had to.

The alliance between Henry II and the Liutizi against Boleslav Chrobry was in one sense nothing new: Henry's Ottonian predecessors had made use of Slav auxiliaries not only in their campaigns in Italy and against the Magyars but nearer home. Its real significance was that it showed that Saxon expansion had come to an end. The Liutizi, pinned between Saxony and Poland, had had to choose between the two, and presumably chose what seemed the lesser of two evils. At any rate, the alliance lasted a whole generation. Only after the decline of Poland set in around 1030 do we again hear of campaigns against the Liutizi. Campaigns in 1035 and 1036 followed border disputes and restored their tributary status, which was renewed by an expedition in 1045. Only after 1050 were there gradual signs of change. An attack on the Saxon borders by the Liutizi during Henry III's absence in Italy in 1055 was followed by a humiliating defeat of the Saxon reprisal force sent on Henry's orders: Margrave William of the Nordmark and two counts were killed. But this defeat was not followed by a general uprising, as might have been expected (especially as Henry III's death followed shortly afterwards). Instead a civil war broke out in the Liutizic confederation in the following year, and this marked the beginning of the disintegration of the Liutizi. The difference between 983 and 1056 was that in 983 Danes and Abodrites also took part in the uprising (whether all three groups – Danes, Abodrites and Liutizi – were actually acting in concert is another question, but for the hard-pressed Saxons who had to deal with them one of secondary importance). By the 1050s, however, relations with the Danish kingdom had been normalized, and the reconversion of the Abodrites, after smaller-scale uprisings at the beginning of Henry II's reign and again in the late 1010s, was well under way; we have a more or less continuous episcopal series for Oldenburg in the eleventh century, in sharp contrast to those for the sees of Mecklenburg, Brandenburg and Havelberg. The pagan line of the Abodrite princely house, Ratibor and his sons, had been destroyed in the battles of Wollin and Haithabu against the Danes in 1043, and the prince Gottschalk, who had been educated in Saxony and returned to his people from exile in Denmark, was able to continue the consolidation of Abodrite princely power initiated by his predecessors. Surrounded by more powerful neighbours, he no longer had the room to establish a principality along the lines of Bohemia or Poland with a church of his own, but, with backing from Denmark and both Archbishop Adalbert of Bremen and Duke Bernard Billung, he was able to bring at least a part of the Liutizic confederation under his overlordship. When the echo of 983 finally did come in the uprising of 1066, it was directed in the first place against Gottschalk, who was killed in the uprising along with the bishop of Mecklenburg.

The normalization of the eastern frontier was mostly not the result of conscious policy, but there was a certain inevitability about it. Just as Magyar pressure in the first half of the century had helped to consolidate the power of the dukes of Saxony and Bavaria, so Poland and Bohemia, and to some extent Denmark and Hungary, were created by the Ottonians. Przemyslids in Bohemia and Piasts in Poland drew both on their alliances with the German rulers and on the need to be able to oppose them. The superiority of German military technology could not be maintained: eastern European princes were able in the eleventh century to meet German armies on more or less equal terms. We have already seen that in both the ninth and the tenth centuries the peoples beyond the frontier, even if pagan, might offer either refuge or support to opposition. When they were Christian (as for example the Moravian empire was) such ties could easily thicken, as they did with Poland for the Saxon aristocracy and (probably) Hungary for the Bavarian. By the early eleventh century the marriage ties between the Saxon leaders and the princely houses of the new Slav principalities were at least as extensive as those between the Saxons and the nobilities of Lotharingia, Suabia and Bavaria. Christianization had an inherent dynamic. The Ottonians were at first careful, as the Carolingians had been with the Moravians, not to allow the setting up of Polish, Bohemian or Danish national churches, following the principle: *cuius religio, eius regio*. Such bishoprics as were established were either free-standing, that is, not embedded in any provincial organization, or else subject to German metropolitans. But it proved impossible to maintain care and control for ever, and canon law meant that the setting up of a province could not easily be reversed. And once such rulers could be seen as Christian rulers it was more difficult to make war on them in the old way. In the late tenth century we still find signs of a Kaffir-bashing mentality in the Saxons' attitude to the Slavs. Thietmar proudly tells how Miesco I's respect for Margrave Hodo was such that "he would not have dared while wearing his fur coat to enter a house where he knew the margrave to be, or to remain seated when the margrave stood up". Adam has a comparable anecdote about how Margrave Dietrich prevented a marriage between the Abodrite Mistui and a niece of Bernard Billung with the remark that "the duke's kinswoman was not to be given to a dog".[7] Such attitudes might persist for the Elbe Slavs, but they could not easily be sustained for countries like Poland and Bohemia, though they perhaps lie behind some of Thietmar's criticisms of Otto III's church settlement in Poland. Henry II was criticized explicitly by Brun of Querfurt and implicitly by much of the Saxon lay nobility for his campaigns against Boleslav. Neither at the level of being nor at that of consciousness were conditions in eastern Europe so favourable for the exercise of tributary hegemony in the eleventh century as they had been in the tenth.

FRANCE, BURGUNDY AND ITALY

To the west and south of the Reich there was also a move away from the hegemonial ambiguities of the early Ottonian era; more clearly defined relationships came to dominate. Even in the 1020s and 1030s, when much of Europe was organized in multi-regnal empires, with

7. Thietmar V 10, p. 232; Adam II 42, schol. 27, p. 102.

Henry II and Conrad II ruling over Germany and Italy and about to absorb Burgundy, Cnut ruling over Denmark, England and at the end Norway, what these rulers now exercised was *rule* over the subordinate kingdoms, not just influence. This is not to say that there could be no influence without rule, but the trend which was to lead to the formation of a European system of independent (if not always in our terminology sovereign) states in the twelfth and thirteenth centuries had already begun. The fluid empire of the tenth century, with lordship shading into overlordship and hegemonial domination, was noticeably hardening at the edges in the eleventh century.

Nowhere is this more clearly visible than in the case of west Francia. Otto I had here acted as an overlord, as perhaps his father had already done in the 920s. It was a position which their successors could sustain only for brief periods. Already under Otto II Lothar had begun the process of emancipating west Francia. His renunciation of Lotharingia at Margut was no more binding than those his predecessors had made, as his attack on Verdun in 985 showed. His death in 986 and that of his son Louis V the following year put an end to the running tensions between Ottonians and Carolingians over Lotharingia. The remaining available Carolingian, Lothar's brother Charles, had been made duke in lower Lotharingia in 977. His succession in west Francia might have presented a serious threat to the Ottonians' hold on Lotharingia, but there was already strong opposition to him among the magnates of west Francia, in particular from Hugo Capet, duke of Francia, and from Adalbero of Rheims. This was backed, perhaps even orchestrated, by those in charge of the young Otto III. The tacit support given by the regency government to Hugo Capet's succession in 987 paid off immediately in that Verdun was abandoned by the west Franks, and in the long term it was to mean that Lotharingia was no longer seriously at risk from west Frankish rulers. Robert II flirted with the Lotharingians opposed to Conrad II's succession in 1024–5, and Henry I is said to have laid claim to Lotharingia in the course of his meeting with Henry III in 1056, which ended in an open breach between the two rulers, but otherwise the early Capetian rulers were not even asked to renounce claims to it. On the other hand, the accession of the Capetians, coupled with the extinction of the west Frankish Carolingians, deprived the German rulers of influence in west Francia. Henry II, Conrad II and Henry III no longer settled disputed episcopal elections or royal successions there as the early Ottonians had done. When in 991 Hugo Capet deposed the newly elected archbishop of Rheims, Arnulf, on charges of treason, he did it at his own synod at Verzy (near Rheims) on his own territory; a council held at Aachen the following year under a papal legate to discuss the matter was boycotted by the west Frankish episcopate. Hugo and the west Frankish church were in the end prepared to accept papal judgement and the consequent deposition of Hugo's candidate for the archbishopric, Gerbert, at the council of Rheims in 995, but they insisted that the council be held in west Francia and not in Germany or Rome. The contrast with Ingelheim nearly fifty years earlier is clear.

Nor did the late Ottonians and early Salians receive the commendation of west Frankish magnates as Otto I had done; Theobald of Champagne commended himself to Henry III in 1054, but this seems to have been an isolated episode, apart from the special case of the counts of Flanders, who were vassals for benefices held within the territory of the German kingdom. When the German rulers met the Capetians Robert II and Henry I, they met as (formal) equals. The meetings were held on the Meuse, the border between the two kingdoms, usually at Ivois (as in 1021, 1023, 1043, 1048 and 1056); both the choice of site and the protocol (so far as we know about it – several of these meetings are known only from the dating clauses of charters) show that the German rulers were not acting as overlords, though their superior power was still evident. Whether the two rulers cooperated against powerful west Frankish magnates like Baldwin of Flanders and Odo of Champagne, as on the whole they did under Robert II and in the early years of Henry I, or stood in opposition, as increasingly they did in the 1040s and 1050s, they conducted relations in forms appropriate to independent rulers. The cultural links between the ecclesiastics and intellectuals of Lotharingia and west Francia, which went back at least to the time of Notker of Liège, continued to exist, as did the extensive property-holdings of west Frankish monasteries in Lotharingia, the Rhineland and Alsace; but politically the two kingdoms went largely separate ways.

If west Francia moved out of the Ottonian–Salian sphere of influence, the kingdom of Burgundy moved the other way, from being under Ottonian overlordship to incorporation into the Salian empire. The details are not always clear, largely because there are so few; much depends on the interpretation of a few sentences in Thietmar of Merseburg and Wipo. Conrad, who ruled from 937 to 993, had remained wholly within the Ottonian orbit, taking part in the expeditions to Italy of 966 and 980 and that to west Francia in 946, as well as appearing at assemblies within the Reich (for example at Rohr in 984 following the death of Otto II). His son Rudolf III was childless; Henry II, whose mother Gerberga was Conrad's eldest daughter, was one of his nearest relatives. As early as 1006 Rudolf and Henry met, and probably Rudolf recognized Henry as his successor and gave Basle (which had been ceded to Rudolf II in 921) back to Henry as a pledge. At two meetings in 1016 and 1018 they agreed that Henry should succeed, and Rudolf appears to have surrendered his kingdom to Henry and received it back in benefice. Rather surprisingly, Rudolf outlived Henry, and Conrad II took over Henry's claim – evidently as Henry's successor and as ruler in Germany rather than as Henry's heir, though he himself was distantly related to Rudolf III. There were other claimants, however. It is possible that Ernest II of Suabia's repeated uprisings were connected with the rights to Burgundy which he had through his mother, though this can only be speculation. What is certain is that Odo of Champagne, who was Rudolf's nephew, also claimed the kingdom. On Rudolf's death in 1032 Conrad was able to have himself elected and crowned king of Burgundy at Peterlingen in 1033 and acknowledged by the magnates of the kingdom at Zurich. Odo, who had failed to take possession of the kingdom immediately after Rudolf's death, still had a following, but Conrad was able to bring greater forces to bear. He mounted an expedition against Odo in his own heartland of Champagne in 1033 and forced him to make peace. Even this was not definitive. It was only after Odo's death in 1037 in the course of an attack on Lotharingia that the succession to Burgundy was assured; Conrad's son Henry was elected and crowned co-king and successor at Solothurn in 1038, not long before Conrad's death.

The kingdom to which the Salians succeded was not merely an empty title; the low reputation of the Rudolfings is due as much as anything else to a few disparaging remarks by Thietmar coupled with the almost complete absence of internal narrative sources for the history of the kingdom. Rudolf was a wealthy and reasonably powerful ruler in his own territory in upper Burgundy, with lands stretching from Basle down past Lausanne and Geneva to Vienne; he also controlled the bishoprics of Basle, Lausanne and Geneva. But the tenth century had seen the emergence of a number of principalities in the south and west of the kingdom: Savoy, the Dauphiné, the Franche-Comté, Provence. Here the ruler had little or no influence; it was a replication on a small scale of the situation in the east Frankish kingdom under Conrad I and Henry I. Conrad II and Henry III did too little as kings of Burgundy for us to be able to see clearly what their long-term intentions (if they had any) were; they issued a few charters for Burgundian recipients and counted their regnal years there in the dating-clauses of most of their charters. Henry III's visits there in 1042, 1045 and 1052 are not well recorded, though we do know that Henry's rule was not accepted without question, and that there were conflicts between him and some of the Burgundian magnates as late as 1052. But evidently the Salians meant to rule there – that is confirmed by the number of Henry's visits if nothing else – and not to allow others to do so. Odo of Champagne would have been willing to rule under them as a vassal-king, but this, the tenth-century solution, was no longer acceptable in the eleventh; the options were to consolidate or to abandon. Geopolitical considerations like control of the western Alpine passes and hence of access to Italy were probably of secondary importance: neither the Salians nor their successors made much use of these passes. What the acquisition of Burgundy did mean was that the Salians now ruled over virtually all of the old middle kingdom: Lotharingia, Burgundy, Italy. This had survived in a shadowy way to a surprising extent through the tenth and early eleventh centuries: there were family ties, not least between the Burgundian and Italian royal houses, political links between the Italian and Lotharingian oppositions to the Ottonians and Salians, especially in the 1020s and 1030s, and cultural links (expressed for example in the mutual influence of Burgundian and north Italian monastic reform movements). Only the death of Odo of Champagne and the Salian take-over in Burgundy really put an end to the possibility of a political revival of the middle kingdom.

Although from 962 onwards the kingdom of Italy (in effect, Lombardy and Tuscany) was ruled by the Ottonians and Salians, it is appropriately considered here, since their rule there cannot be said to have been continuous. The north Italian political community never entirely accepted the idea that the Germans could simply choose their king for them; descendants and collateral relatives of the families which had ruled the kingdom in the first half of the tenth century remained plausible alternatives up to the end of the period we are considering. In particular, the successions of 983, 1002 and 1024, which as we have seen were not automatic in Germany either, left their mark in Italy. Otto III, though he had been elected as successor at a meeting of German and Italian magnates held at Verona on the Bavarian–Italian border, and crowned at Aachen not only by the archbishop of Cologne but also by the Italian archbishop of Ravenna, was not generally acknowledged as king in Italy until his first expedition south of the Alps in 996, to judge by the absence of references to him in the dating-clauses of charters. On his death a party among the north Italian magnates chose a king of their own, Arduin, who was a relative of Berengar II; it was not until two years later, after the defeat of a south German force under Otto of Carinthia, that Henry II had to find time to go south of the Alps. He was elected and acknowledged as king of Italy by a majority of those who counted, but Arduin had neither submitted nor been defeated; it was not until Henry's expedition to Italy and Rome in 1014 that his rule in Italy was fully established. Conrad II also had to enforce acceptance, and spent most of 1026 subduing opposition from Pavia and some of the margraves of the north-west before proceeding to Rome for coronation. A party among the Italians offered the crown first to Robert II of France and then to William of Aquitaine, though little came of this. Only Henry III was apparently accepted from the beginning of his reign without opposition.

The German rulers regarded the Italian kingdom as an integral part of their own. They did not count their regnal years there separately, nor did they usually have a separate coronation as kings of Italy or display their rule over it in any element of their royal title: Henry II's separate coronation in 1004 was the exception, though it is just possible that Conrad II was also crowned king of Italy in 1026. As far as the chancery was concerned there was no organizational separation; even when, as was frequently the case, there was a separate chancellor and archchancellor for the two kingdoms, it was the same notaries who drafted and drew up the diplomata. Nevertheless, the Ottonians and Salians were not present in Italy continuously enough to be able to rule it, even in the limited sense in which they ruled their kingdom north of the Alps. Otto I, it is true, spent nine of his last twelve years of rule south of the Alps; Otto II spent the last three years of his sole rule there, and his son Otto III spent nearly five of the seven and a half years of his majority in Italy. But neither Henry II (three appearances totalling less than two years out of twenty-two), Conrad II (two appearances totalling about three years out of fifteen) nor Henry III (two appearances totalling less than two years out of sixteen) was there often or for long. Moreover, for all these rulers one must subtract from the time they did spend there that devoted to Rome or southern Italy rather than to the kingdom itself – at least half the total, and even more for the three Ottos, who at first sight appear to have devoted more time to Italy. They had to go south of the Alps not just with a large following – that was normal – but with an army. They repeated

Otto I's conquest of 951 each time they went, as Otto I himself had had to do in 961–2, though the reconquest normally involved little actual fighting. Unlike the Carolingians, they did not have the manpower in their own families to provide sub-kings for the Italian kingdom and thus bind Italy more permanently to their realms north of the Alps. Nor were they able to displace the native aristocracy, unlike the Carolingians, who managed a substantial *revirement* after Hrodgaud's rebellion in 776. But there is another way of looking at Ottonian and Salian rule in Italy. It is true that the appearance of these rulers in Italy was sporadic; though there was only one gap of more than ten years, that between 983 and 996, there were several of seven to ten. Yet their appearance in the south German duchies was equally sporadic, and they were found in Lombardy far more often than in upper Lotharingia or northern Saxony, for example. Moreover, they were able to achieve a certain degree of rule from a distance (as they were for Suabia and Bavaria). Conrad II was recognized by some Italian magnates at Constance in 1025, and Henry III also received Italian commendations (at Augsburg in 1040 for example) long before he moved south in 1046. The majority of diplomata for Italian recipients were issued south of the Alps, but a steady trickle of impetrants came north. If we take as a sample period that between Henry II's return from Italy in 1014 and the visit to Bamberg by Pope Benedict VIII in 1020, that is, a stretch of six years when there were no special reasons for Italians to be present in the ruler's entourage, we find diplomata issued in Saxony, Franconia and Lotharingia for recipients in Novara, Pavia, Vercelli, Como, Parma, Borgo San Sepolchro, Pero, Venice, Leno and Monte Cassino, amounting to perhaps a tenth of all those surviving for the period.

The appointment of Germans to Italian bishoprics was hardly practised at all in the tenth century; Henry II and Conrad II did so more frequently, but mostly in the north-eastern bishoprics within reach of the duchies of Bavaria and Carinthia, especially the province of Aquileia. It was only under Henry III that it became a more common and widespread practice; here about a quarter of all bishoprics went to candidates from north of the Alps. We have already noted how Italian bishops made as much use of the canon law collection of Burchard of Worms as did German ones; a further sign of integration can be found in the list compiled by Gundechar of Eichstätt (1057–73) of the bishops who had died during his pontificate. This includes a large number of Italian bishops, whom Gundechar obviously considered as colleagues – not surprisingly, since many of these were German in origin. The movement of clerics to bishoprics was still a one-way process, however; just as the ninth-century Frankish divisions had made provision for Frankish monasteries holding land in Italy but not the other way round, so there were no Italians holding German bishoprics. The one example sometimes quoted, Rotho of Paderborn, turns out not to have been Italian after all. In the secular sphere there were some marriages between members of the Italian and German aristocracies: between Margrave Boniface of Canossa and Tuscany and Beatrix from the family of the dukes of upper Lotharingia, or between Margrave Azzo of Este and Chuniza, the daughter of Count Welf. Daughters of Margrave Manfred of Turin married into the leading aristocracy of the early Salian era: one married Otto of Schweinfurt, another Hermann IV of Suabia, who may even have held his deceased father-in-law's Italian march for a time. All these things taken together might suggest that the kingdom of Italy was in the eleventh century slowly becoming integrated into the Ottonian and Salian kingdom north of the Alps, much as Lotharingia had been in the tenth century. Certainly the resistance to German rulers can hardly be described as nationalist in inspiration. Arduin's support was confined largely to the north-west, while Archbishop Aribert of Milan, in opposition to Conrad II in the 1030s and after his submission in 1036 even for a time excommunicated and exiled, was also the leader of a heterogeneous minority.

For the German rulers, possession of the Italian kingdom was the *sine qua non* for being able to journey to Rome and receive imperial coronation. The lands and rights associated with the kingdom were certainly not immense – there had been heavy losses in the first half of the tenth century – but they were not negligible either, and one should not suppose that the long vacancies, changes of regime and absences in the tenth century had devoured them all. A striking example of survival and continuity is provided by the *Life of Bernward of Hildesheim*, which records how the bishop visited Rudolf III on his return from Italy in 1000 and was given three *curtiles* (small estates) of land in Pavia by the Burgundian ruler;[8] these rights must have gone back at least fifty years, and they show the continuing status of Pavia as a capital. To a limited extent, probably less so than in the late ninth century, the kingdom provided treasure: Otto I gave Bishop Ulrich of Augsburg several pounds of gold when the bishop visited him in Italy in 968 and it is a fair bet that he had not brought this with him from Saxony. Relics, both of antiquity and of saints, were at least as important. Otto I imported columns for Magdeburg from Italy, just as Charles the Great had done for Aachen, and his

---

8. Thangmar *Vita Bernwardi* c. 27, MGH SS 4, 771 = D Rudolf III 130.

bishops in particular brought back large numbers of relics: Otwin of Hildesheim brought the relics of Epiphanias back to his bishopric in 963; Dietrich of Metz used his connections with Otto I to make a massive trawl through central Italy for relics in 970; Gebhard of Constance got relics of the Apostle Philip from Otto III and of Pope Gregory from Pope John XV. Italy offered fewer opportunities for rewards which could be consumed on the spot. The German rulers barely made any attempt to appoint to high secular office, let alone to appoint their German followers, and we have seen that bishops of German origin were not the norm either. But considerations like these hardly explain the investment of time and resources in Italian expeditions; questions of cost-benefit analysis are as inappropriate here as they were when considering Otto I's imperial title. The German rulers and their followers went to Italy because it belonged to them; to have abandoned it as not worth the time and trouble would not have occurred to them.

It is equally worth asking what the Italian magnates got out of having German rulers. It might be said that they had no choice in the face of German military superiority, but in fact the rulers from Otto I to Henry III were normally accepted by a majority of Italian magnates and invited to Italy to receive their commendation. There was at least an element of free will present. It was obviously in a sense inconvenient to have a ruler who was hardly ever present and who made no attempts to set up any kind of regent or vicar to represent him when he was absent. Those who needed a king to settle their disputes either had to go north of the Alps (and, should they get a judgement, work out how to get this enforced) or wait until the next German expedition southwards, which might be several years away. Accounts of Ottonian and Salian rule south of the Alps tend to use phrases like "preserving the balance" or "pragmatic", meaning that the rulers did and intended little beyond maintaining the status quo. Yet a ruler who was only occasionally present and not particularly active, but powerful enough to prevent anyone else taking over, had some advantages at a time when the kingdom was becoming even more regionalized than it had been in the ninth and tenth centuries. It is unlikely that the Italian magnates actually thought in these terms; but functionally speaking the Ottonians and Salians preserved them both from troublesome disputes about kingship and central authority, and from troublesome demands resulting from the existence of a kingship with central authority. This may explain why the Ottonians and Salians could spend so much of their time several hundred miles from Italy without doing much either to rule it or to defend their position there.

A surprising proportion of the time and energy the Ottonian and Salian rulers gave to Italy went on the area south of the old Lombard kingdom: the Lombard principalities of Capua, Salerno and Benevento, the Calabrian remains of Byzantine southern Italy and the Arab emirate in Sicily. All six German rulers of Italy between 951 and 1056 intervened here. It is not always easy to see why the region should have been worth so much trouble, but some general reasons may be offered. In the first place, southern Italy was (as already under Louis II in the ninth century) the place where eastern and western empires met; at least up to the time of Henry II German campaigning in southern Italy was often aimed directly or indirectly at Byzantium. Even the catastrophic German defeat by the Arabs of Sicily in 982 took place in the course of a campaign also directed against the Greeks. In the second place, the Ottonians and Salians inherited the traditions of their Lombard and Carolingian predecessors as far as the non-Byzantine principalities were concerned: the exercise of overlordship here was a matter of prestige, but also of practical policy, as a means of preventing a Byzantium whose presence in Italy was far from extinct from gaining influence further north. Besides this, there was probably solid gain to be expected; the sources mention no figures, but in Carolingian times the principality of Benevento had been able to pay tribute on a scale out of all proportion to its size. Nevertheless, Cap Colonne marked the last expedition which was intended to do more than restore an acceptable balance among the south Italian principalities and enforce a loose recognition of German overlordship. Otto III made a brief appearance in Capua in 999; Henry II pushed back a Byzantine advance in 1021–2; Conrad II and Henry III ventured south in 1037 and 1047, and Henry III prepared for a further expedition in 1055 which he did not carry out. In the last resort the area was not one of central interest, and it could not be run by remote control. As it turned out, this lack of interest was to enable the Normans, present as mercenaries from the second decade of the eleventh century, to set up first principalities and then a kingdom in the hundred years between 1030 and 1130. But this was hardly a foreseeable development, or rather it was hardly foreseeable that the Norman principalities would be more militarily effective and active than their Lombardo-Byzantine predecessors had been. Conrad II and Henry III were willing to accept the commendation of Norman leaders, and even the defeat of a papal army by the Normans in 1053 after Henry

III had refused Leo IX's request for assistance was a sign of things to
come rather than one of those things itself.

ROME, THE PAPACY AND THE ROMAN EMPIRE

From 962 onwards the rulers of Germany were, either actually or
potentially, emperors. Only Otto II was consecrated emperor in his
father's lifetime, and even he had been king for some years before his
imperial coronation. Otto III and Henry II did not become emperor
until 996 and 1014 respectively, in each case more than a decade after
they had succeeded to the throne. Conrad II was crowned in Rome
in 1027 after a gap of only three years; his son Henry III waited seven
years before crossing the Alps and receiving imperial coronation in
1046. The gaps show clearly that the imperial title could not simply
be assumed. It could be used only after a ruler had been crowned
emperor by the pope – ideas of a "Rome-free" hegemonial imperial
title, thinkable in Otto I's time though not accepted in his chancery,
had probably already lost their force by the end of Otto II's reign.
The "official" view is seen clearly in the titles given to rulers in their
diplomata. Until their coronation as emperor, all the rulers we are
considering were simply *rex* – not even *rex Francorum* or *rex
Francorum et Saxonum* (with exceptions which can be counted on the
fingers of both hands). Otto I and Otto II appeared as plain *imperator
augustus*; then in 982 Otto II's chancery adopted the title *Romanorum
imperator augustus*. Otto III's chancery adopted this in 996, after an
initial reversion to the plain *imperator augustus* of Otto I's time, and –
leaving aside the variations at the end of Otto III's reign, to which
we shall come later – it became the standard title for emperors from
then on. Moreover, the dating of diplomata from the later years of
Otto I on clearly distinguished between regnal and imperial years.
Yet even if the chancery was able to be consistent, this was done as
much by avoiding awkward questions as anything else. For example,
it continued to be a moot point whether the *Romanorum imperator*
ruled over a *Romanum imperium*: he was an emperor of the Romans,
but not necessarily for that reason a Roman emperor. The use of the
simple title "king" elegantly side-stepped the question of what it
actually was the Ottonians and Salians ruled over, by saying in effect
that they were *the* king, and perhaps by implication the only real
king. Only from the beginning of the twelfth century did the
German kings come to entitle themselves *rex Romanorum*, "king of

the Romans", regularly, though they had occasionally used the title before that, and from Henry III on it was found in the monogram next to the seal on the diplomata of rulers who had not yet been crowned emperor. *Rex Romanorum* was essentially a response to the papal designation *rex Teutonicorum*, "king of the Germans", a title hardly ever used by the rulers themselves and intended by its inventors to cut them down to size.

What the imperial title did was to lock the German rulers into relationships with the popes, with the city of Rome and its nobility, and with the Byzantine emperors, relationships often best described by the German word *Intimfeindschaft*, "bosom enmity". Before we look at the changes in the imperial idea in the late Ottonian and early Salian period, we must look at the other points in this eternal quadrangle. If in western eyes only the pope could make an emperor, that did not, in the period we are considering, give the popes any degree of control over the emperor once crowned. After 962, when Otto I had guaranteed the pope's personal safety and the papal possessions, the imperial coronation was hardly even a matter for serious bargaining, as it had sometimes been in the ninth century and was to become again in the twelfth. The popes had certain advantages in their dealings with the German rulers; in particular, they possessed archives and could use these as tools in pursuit of a long tradition of redefining the present by redefining the past. But though this might provide some ideological insurance for the future, it did not help them much at the time. As in Carolingian times, the duty of the emperors was to protect the papacy; but what constituted protection, the emperors. decided. It often did not mean protection for individual popes: five out of the twenty-five who held office between 962 and 1056 were deposed or made to depose themselves. Nor did it necessarily mean the preservation or restoration of papal lands in central Italy. Otto III at least, perhaps also Henry III, took what from a papal and from a Roman point of view might seem an unhealthily close interest in Rome itself. At least at times popes and Roman clergy would find this too much. Up to the end of the tenth century there was a temptation to flirt with the Byzantine emperors; the last such flirtation in our period of any consequence led to the setting up of Otto III's tutor John Philagathos as anti-pope to Gregory V with covert Byzantine support. After John XII's time there were no contacts with more local opposition in the kingdom of Italy; neither Arduin nor Aribert of Milan found any support in Rome. On the other hand, popes did actually need protecting. The Roman aristocracy has had a bad press ever since the time of

Liutprand of Cremona – who, like many medieval authors before and since who wrote on Roman affairs, was writing for a north European audience evidently prepared to believe Romans capable of almost anything. Yet they were indeed capable of much, though here they were not noticeably different in their behaviour from aristocratic cliques in other Italian towns who tried to control their town and its surroundings by controlling the election to its bishopric. The fact that the bishop concerned was also the pope meant that the feuds, coups and usurpations of rights which took place were often conducted in the full glare of European publicity rather than in decent provincial obscurity, but the real difference lay in the prize: what the popes actually possessed represented considerable wealth, and this was only a fraction of what they had good claim to.

The Carolingians had enforced a settlement on Italy in the mid eighth century which left the papacy with a substantial territory shaped like an egg-timer which lay across the peninsula from south-west to north-east between the duchy of Spoleto and the Carolingian margravate of Tuscany. "Territory" is not here to be understood as evenly spread rule over an area but, as with any other early medieval principality, a collection of property, rights and claims. It embraced the popes' private landed wealth and their patrimony, as well as things like a claim to rule over Ravenna and its surroundings (in effect as successors to the Byzantine exarchs, who had ceased to be appointed after 751). After the disappearance of the Carolingians from Italy in 896 this territory, or at least the south-western part of it, had become in effect a secular principality under Theophylact, followed by his widow Marozia, her son Alberic, and his son Octavian, who became pope in 955 as John XII. Otto I did not destroy the basis of a secular principality over the papal patrimonium with the pope as house-bishop: it was to be revived by the Crescentii at the end of the tenth century and from 1012 by the counts of Tusculum, who were collateral descendants of Theophylact's family. What showed great continuity was the tradition among popes and Roman nobles of appealing to the German ruler as a move in their disputes: Otto II's expedition in 980, Otto III's in 996, Henry II's in 1014 and Henry III's in 1046 were all preceded by appeals from either a pope or a Roman aristocratic grouping or both. But it was not only here that traditions were preserved. Roman aristocrats and popes should not be seen as inherently antithetical, however acute the conflicts might sometimes become. The Roman church and the Roman nobility also regarded themselves as custodians of the traditions of Rome as a city. Throughout the ninth, tenth and eleventh centuries there were clerics and laymen in Rome who looked to the Rome of antiquity as a source of legitimation and as something in need of renewal and of rebirth. Once the Ottonians' initial suspicions had been overcome, these "Romanist" circles were seldom far or estranged from the circles around the emperor of the time.

The third player in the game was the Byzantine emperor. The Byzantines would have taken an interest in the German rulers in any case, and indeed did so, as can be seen from the pages devoted to them in Constantine Porphyrogenitos's *De administrando imperii*, compiled long before Otto I's imperial coronation. But they were brought more closely into contact and conflict with the Ottonians and Salians through the imperial title which the latter assumed than they might have been with rulers who, however powerful, continued to style themselves kings. The Ottonian imperial title affected Byzantine self-awareness and self-respect almost as deeply as the Carolingian title had done. The German rulers, on the other hand, generally sought Byzantine approval and friendship, particularly as expressed in Byzantine brides. Otto II was the only one of these rulers actually to marry a Byzantine princess, but a marriage had been arranged for Otto III – at the time of his death the princess had actually landed in Italy – and one was sought for Henry III, though without success. From the re-establishing of regular contacts in the 950s and 960s onwards there was a steady exchange of embassies between the two empires. There were elements of conflict as well, but these were played down most of the time. This was all the easier as the two empires barely touched. The main potential area of friction, the southern Italian principalities, was not of central importance to either side, while both sides valued the position of Venice in between the two empires sufficiently not to interfere with it too drastically. The roots of conflict lay much more in the two sides' views of themselves and – to an extent which can easily be exaggerated – in rivalry for spiritual hegemony in eastern Europe. This expressed itself primarily, as it had already done in the ninth century, in missionary disputes; but it is surprising how little the lines of demarcation were shifted. Bohemia was in the end converted by missionaries from Bavaria and Moravia, Poland by missionaries from Saxony and Bohemia, and Hungary by missionaries from Bavaria, while on the other hand Russia and Bulgaria were converted by Byzantine missionaries. We can see occasions when the lines were crossed. As early as 961 Adalbert, the later archbishop of Magdeburg, was ordained by the archbishop of Hamburg as missionary bishop for Russia, though he returned the next year without having accomplished anything. The famous story in the *Russian Primary Chronicle* about the conversion of the Russians (after looking at the practices of the Latin Christian Germans, of the Jewish Khazars and of the Muslim Bulgarians, the Russians chose Byzantine Christianity because the Greeks put on the best show)[9] also implies that German missionaries were active in Russia, and indeed Brun of Querfurt went there for a time at the end of Otto III's reign, as Adalbert had done two generations earlier. Yet although there continued to be occasional contacts between Germany and Kiev in the eleventh century – Kiev was a source of brides of acceptable rank, and occasionally, as in 1043, sent embassies to the imperial court – Russia belonged quite clearly to the Byzantine commonwealth. Contacts between Saxons and Bulgarians also did not amount to much, even if a Bulgarian embassy did appear at Quedlinburg in 973. In the other direction, Byzantine contacts with Poland and Hungary were equally limited in their scope and their effectiveness, especially in Poland. It is in any case doubtful whether such attempts to fish in each other's pond led to tensions between the two empires or were simply the expression of already existing tensions.

Against this complex background we may now look at the interactions between German rulers and popes. It was in the sixty years between Otto III's imperial coronation in 996 and Henry III's death in 1056 that the duality of empire and papacy at the head of Latin Christendom, familiar from the twelfth and thirteenth centuries, was to be established. The six years of Otto III's majority were to be of unusual importance for the development of the imperial idea. Even his first expedition to Rome for the imperial coronation brought significant changes. For the first time since the Greek emperors of the seventh century had appointed Greek popes, Otto appointed a non-Roman as pope on the death of John XV – his cousin Brun, who took the name of Gregory V. Nor did Otto follow his grandfather's example and confirm the papal patrimonies in a privilege. His chancery settled on the title of *imperator Romanorum* for use in his diplomata, but already there were signs of an increasing emphasis on Rome. Two diplomata referred to the "consent and advice of the bishops and laymen present, of Pope Gregory himself, the Romans, Franks, Bavarians, Saxons, Alsatians,

---

9. *The Russian Primary Chronicle. Laurentian Text* s.a. 986, 987, ed. and tr. S. H. Cross and O. P. Sherbowitz-Wetzor, Cambridge (Mass.) 1953, 96–8, 110–111.

Suabians and Lotharingians";[10] the man who composed the diplomata was probably a Bavarian cleric, not a member of the chancery, but the lists still show ideas current in Otto's entourage. Here we have Otto ruling over a polyethnic empire, with the Romans, not Saxons or Franks, listed in first place, and with the pope in a subordinate position as adviser. At first Otto showed interest in setting up Aachen as the New Rome (as his greatly admired predecessor Charles the Great had done, or as Otto I had done with Magdeburg), but though the cult of Charles the Great continued, culminating in Otto's famous visit to Aachen in 1000 and the opening of Charles's tomb, it was increasingly Rome itself which was to become the centre of Otto's interests. From the time of his return to Italy in 998 until the Roman uprising in early 1001, Otto resided almost continuously in Rome, apart from his pilgrimages to southern Italy in 999 and to Gnesen and Aachen in 1000. He had a new imperial palace built there, and ruled over the city in a way no emperor since Charles the Great had previously attempted. He set up a hierarchy of court officials very different from that known at Frankish or Saxon courts, with new, mostly Greek titles. These titles were applied not just to duties in his immediate surroundings, but within the empire as a whole: both his aunt Abbess Mathilda of Quedlinburg, who had de facto the functions of a regent in Saxony in his absence, as well as a Saxon count Ziazo, were given the title of *patricius*. Otto not only ruled Rome directly but also shared in the government of the church; his subscription appears occasionally in papal documents and he was not as scrupulous as his predecessors had generally been about participating in church councils. Otto had been given a very thorough education which included a knowledge of Greek, and soon gathered around him an eclectic circle of advisers and admirers. This included intellectuals like Gerbert of Rheims, whose career had been linked with the Ottonian court since the early 980s and Bishop Leo of Vercelli, a distinguished rhetorician and enthusiast for Roman antiquity. A different side of his personality was catered for by ascetics and missionaries like Adalbert of Prague, Romuald of Camaldoli, Nilus of Rossano and Brun of Querfurt.

The final phase of Otto's rule was initiated by Gerbert's election as Pope Silvester II in 999 in succession to Gregory V. The name was programmatic: Silvester I was the pope who in legend had cured the Emperor Constantine and accepted the Donation from him. The

---

10. D O III 197 for Freising and 208 for Salzburg.

titles Otto's chancery used for him stressed both the Christian and the Roman elements in his rule: Otto was *servus Iesu Christi et Romanorum imperator augustus secundum voluntatem Dei Salvatoris nostrique Liberatoris* (servant of Jesus Christ and august emperor of the Romans according to the will of God our saviour and liberator)[11] during the Gnesen pilgrimage. After his return to Italy in the summer of 1000 there was a series of titles, many including the element *servus apostolorum* (servant of the apostles). [12] The variety itself shows that the nature of Otto's rule was a matter of intense discussion at this period; normally titles and chancery clerks were conservative, and changed only gradually in response to new circumstances. The setting up of the kingdom of Hungary together with a Hungarian church on the one hand, and the new if undefined status for Boleslav of Poland together with a Polish church on the other, may hint at a new conception of empire, though as we have seen this was not made explicit. Instead of Franco-Saxon hegemony there was perhaps to be an *imperium Romanum* with which the new kings were to be associated. Ideas of a "family of kings", familiar in the Byzantine empire, may have played a role. The final years were also marked by very close cooperation between emperor and pope. Otto did not confirm the privileges of the Roman church issued by the Carolingian rulers and by his grandfather, but he did issue a diploma for Silvester II which both granted eight counties to the Roman church and at the same time rejected wider papal claims to territorial rule, especially those based on the Donation of Constantine. Its arenga began: "We hold Rome to be the head of the world, and acknowledge the Roman church as the mother of all churches, though by the carelessness and ignorance of its bishops the clarity of its claims has long been obscured."[13] This was not intended to cut the papacy down to size, but rather to include it in the renewal at which Otto aimed for the Roman empire.

Otto's rule ended darkly. In early 1001 there was an uprising of the Romans, who, whatever their feelings about *renovatio Romani imperii*, probably found having an emperor permanently on their doorstep too much to cope with. The eye-witness report by Thangmar, a Hildesheim cleric, of Otto's speech to the insurgent Romans has often been quoted: "Are you not my Romans? For your

---

11. First used in D O III 344, dated January 17 1000, and regularly though not exclusively in the following six months.
12. Wolfram 1973: 158 gives the details.
13. D O III 389.

sake I have deserted my fatherland and my kinsmen. For love of you I have cast out Saxons and all the Germans, and I have taken you into the furthest parts of our empire [a reference to the pilgrimage to Gnesen], where your fathers, when they ruled the world, never set foot."[14] Yet it would be dangerous to deduce from this that Otto intended for all time to rule the empire from Rome, still less that he could actually have done so. Thangmar was expressing not just Otto's own ideas, but also in good measure Saxon criticism of Otto's actions – we know that there was unrest in Saxony as well in the last year of Otto's reign. The sentiments about casting out Saxons and others are more likely to have reflected what people in Hildesheim thought Otto was capable of thinking rather than what Otto himself thought. In the last resort it is difficult to make out the intentions of Otto and his circle through the glare of rhetoric and contradiction. There was undoubtedly a different quality about these years. This was perceived by contemporaries; it is in fact one of the main differences between Otto III and his predecessors and successors that we have a good deal of direct evidence about what he and others in his circle thought they were doing – more than for the debates of the 960s or for the imperial idea in the first half of the eleventh century. But it is not always possible to tell what was experiment and what was design, and what would have lasted had Otto lived longer. What his brief rule as emperor did, for all its elements both of tradition and of rhetorical decoration, was to shift the meaning of the imperial title permanently: it was now firmly linked with both Christian and antique Rome. The troubles following his death prevented any immediate continuity, but it will become clear that his successors did not break radically with much of his imperial practice and aspirations.

Henry II appears on the face of it to have abandoned the ideas of his predecessor: the device *renovatio regni Francorum*, found on his bulls (metal seals) from 1003 onwards, and the campaigns against Boleslav of Poland seem a very conscious break with Otto's *Renovatio imperii Romanorum* and his alliance with Boleslav. Yet though there was evidently a change at the level of practice, this was determined by reality rather than ideology. Henry II was not in a position to rule from Rome in 1002, even had he wished to. The conceptual breach with Otto III was by no means total. The war with Boleslav was hardly about the nature of the *imperium*

---

14. Thangmar, *Vita Bernwardi episcopi Hildesheimensis* c. 25, MGH SS 4, 770.

Christianum, but had much more secular origins. *Renovatio regni Francorum* reflected not only reality (Henry II was not yet emperor and could not speak for or in 1002 convincingly claim to rule over the whole of the *imperium Romanum*) but, at the level of ideas, an indebtedness to the *Carolingian* tradition. Henry borrowed here from Louis the Pious, just as Otto III had been inspired by Louis's predecessor Charles the Great. Once Henry's rule had consolidated itself sufficiently for him to go to Rome and receive imperial coronation, we find notable continuities with the ideas of Otto III and his circle. Henry II, like Otto, did not confirm the Ottonianum immediately after his coronation; he left this until his second Italian expedition in 1020–2, though he promised to act as *defensor ecclesiae* (protector of the church). It is at his coronation that the use of the orb, a symbol of universal rule, is first recorded, and we are told that this was at the initiative of the pope, a good example of the papacy's fostering ideas of Roman rule over the world. For the end of Henry's reign we have a report that he planned a universal council to consider matters of peace and church reform, and he did indeed, as Otto III and Otto I had done before him, hold a synod jointly with the pope, at Pavia in 1022. In the acts of the synod Benedict VIII is presented as describing the state of the church in gloomy terms before promulgating canons on clerical marriage and church property and asking Henry to confirm these by an "august edict"; Henry did so "together with the senators of the earth, the officers of the palace and the friends of the commonwealth".[15] This kind of royal confirmation of conciliar canons was a Carolingian practice, but the Romanizing rhetoric it was clothed in was new – though not that new, as the author of the acts was probably Bishop Leo of Vercelli, one of Otto III's advisers.

Conrad's reign was remarkable for the speed with which he sought imperial coronation; he left for Italy even before the initial period of unrest was over. It was also marked by a further revival of Romanism, the link in thought between rule over Rome and rule over the empire, if not the world. The verbal equivalent of Henry II's orb was the device used on Conrad's bulls: *Roma caput mundi tenet orbis frena rotundi* (Rome, head of the world, holds the reins of the round globe), echoing in its tag the opening of Otto III's diploma for the Roman church. Equally noteworthy was the portrayal of Henry III as co-ruler on these bulls and his Byzantinizing title of *spes imperii*,

---

15. MGH Constitutiones et acta publica 1, ed. L. Weiland (Hannover 1893) 76–7, no. 34.

especially as Henry, unlike Otto II, was not actually a co-emperor. Even before his coronation there was an imperial flavour about Henry's rule, in particular in the emphasis on Henry as a peacemaker (not entirely justified when one recalls the hard campaigning in the south-east in the first few years of his reign) in the rhetoric of writers like Wipo and Bern of the Reichenau. When in 1045–6 there was once more a disputed election to the papacy, Henry III went south in fulfilment of a traditional imperial role: the protection of the papacy both from itself and from its opponents in and outside Rome. The situation was a complex one; Benedict IX had resigned in 1045 in favour of one John Gratianus, who became pope with the name of Gregory VI, but faced a rival candidate, Silvester III. Gregory VI had a good reputation, and it appeared at first that Henry III would deal with his rivals and accept him as pope; but when it turned out that he had paid Benedict to renounce his claims this was interpreted as simony, and at a council held at Sutri to investigate the matter he was in effect deposed (conceivably he deposed himself in accordance with the maxim that the pope may be judged by no one). To make assurance doubly sure, Henry III had him sent north of the Alps, as Otto I had done with Benedict V, and revived Otto III's practice by appointing popes from outside Rome. Clement II, who crowned Henry III on Christmas Day 1046 (echoing Charles the Great's coronation in 800), and his three successors, Damasus II, Leo IX and Victor II, were all bishops from German bishoprics. They kept their bishoprics after becoming pope; almost certainly this was an insurance policy, as Henry could not stay permanently in Rome, and there was no guarantee that the new popes would be able to hold their own there. Popes and emperor were to cooperate, as was now established tradition, but with some new elements in the cooperation. Henry III assisted in the summoning of papal councils, notably that at Mainz in 1050. Leo IX and Victor II, on the other hand, were prepared to act as the spiritual arm of the emperor: Leo IX excommunicated the peace-breaker Godfrey the Bearded of Lotharingia in 1049, while Victor II was in effect designated as regent by Henry III at the end of his reign. Cooperation was not limitless, as could be seen in Henry's refusal to give Leo IX any assistance against the Normans in 1052–3, but it was very close. Besides this, it is evident that the popes Henry nominated brought in their own outsiders, and thus began an internationalization of the papal entourage. Leo IX and Victor II in particular attracted ecclesiastics from north of the Alps to Rome: Frederick, brother of Godfrey the Bearded; Humbert, abbot of Moyenmoutier; Hugo Candidus. This was not just internationalization; it was a marriage between two streams within the church, that of papal authority and that of "church reform", to use a rather overworked and hard-to-define phrase. The consequences were to become more important after Henry's death.

Henry III's reign is often depicted as the culmination of the empire established by the Ottonians and Salians, and his rule as "theocratic", that is, as God-given and God-inspired in its presentation and in its conception of itself, and with elements of priestliness in Henry's rulership. At the same time it is customary to see his intervention at Sutri as creating a *damnosa haereditas* for his successor: the marriage between papal authority and church renewal just mentioned was to bring together forces which the German rulers could no longer control. Recently Henry's reign has also been seen as a period of crisis in terms of secular politics, as a reign in which the signs of the troubles to come in the 1060s and 1070s were already visible. A brief examination of his style of rulership may help to see how far these judgements are valid, as well as showing how far the Reich had come by the mid eleventh century. The first point to be made is that there is a danger in reading history backwards. What Henry III did at Sutri, for example, was not an anticipation of the later attempts by Henry IV and Henry V, not to mention the Staufer, to set up pliable popes. It was the last successful occasion in a series when rulers from north of the Alps intervened to restore order in Rome, as they perceived it and as most right-thinking people perceived it as well; there was probably less contemporary criticism of what Henry III did in 1046 than there had been of Otto I's actions in 963–4. The subsequent cooperation between Henry and the popes also followed very much in the traditions of good relations between emperors and popes: between John XIII and Otto I, for example, or between Gregory V, Silvester II and Otto III (whom Henry III resembled in a number of ways), or between Benedict VIII and Henry II. It is probably misleading to see Sutri as the central event of Henry's reign, or even as particularly typical of it. It is true that he was more sensitive than his father to new currents of religiosity: the delicate questions raised by the papal schism of 1045–6 were handled with a fair degree of tact, and this also marked Henry's dealings with ecclesiastics not entirely happy with the secular aspects of their offices, Halinard of Dijon or Wazo of Liège for example. It is also true that there were penitential and religious elements in his rule, as seen in his prostration before the relics of the cross on the battlefield at Menfö or in his attempts to set an example of peacemaking by forgiveness at Constance and Trier in 1043 and after his imperial coronation in 1046. Here he revived something of Otto III's practice and attitudes, as also on his death-bed, when he returned lands he had unjustly taken and forgave his enemies.

But Henry was just as much a war-lord as a theocratic ruler, and in some ways more so. The first five years of his reign were marked by continuous campaigning on the south-eastern frontier, against Bohemia and Hungary; this was followed by armed expeditions to Burgundy and Italy, campaigns in Lotharingia, a renewal of warfare in Hungary, and a further armed expedition to Italy. Besides this there were campaigns on the Saxon frontier which Henry directed, though he did not take part in person. At least as characteristic of Henry's rule as his public religiosity was an incident in 1041, when the young Liutpold, son of the Austrian margrave Adalbert, carried out a particularly daring raid against the Bohemians and was rewarded by Henry III with the gift of a "magnificent horse, the gift of the duke of Bohemia . . . with a saddle of great weight and workmanship, all of gold and silver",[16] much as Merovingian and Carolingian war-lords had rewarded their followers. The reigns of Henry II and Conrad II had hardly been marked by long periods of tranquillity, but there was a new intensity and aggressiveness apparent in the 1040s, and though Henry had domestic opposition in Lotharingia to contend with, he could devote more of his military efforts than his predecessors had done to warfare beyond the borders of the Reich, and was less constrained by internal opposition. The Reich and its rulers had survived the difficult thirty to forty years following the end of Otto II's reign, and were still formidable. What had hardly been developed, however, was any kind of institutional or ideological substratum. Some of the opposition to Henry may have been against his attempts to do so, but if so it was hardly articulate, and nor was the new palace and fiscal complex around Goslar a substitute for more wide-ranging institutions. In spite of a certain continuity provided by the imperial title, Henry III was still the leader of a very large scale war-band. He might be an anointed leader, but so were his contemporaries in France and England, who were anointed, moreover, using much the same liturgical formulae; no great differences of principle existed. What the readoption of the Frankish ceremony of unction for king- and emperor-making had not really preserved was the Frankish notion of kingship as an office,

16. *Annales Altahenses maiores* s.a. 1041, ed. E.L.B. von Oefele (MGH SRG, Hannover 1891), 28.

as a *ministerium*. The idea that the kingdom existed independently of whomever held it could indeed be formulated. Wipo did so in a famous anecdote recording Conrad II's answer to the citizens of Pavia, who had burnt the royal palace there on hearing the news of Henry II's death, and defended their action by saying that there was no king at the time and hence no owner of the palace: "If the king die, the kingdom still exists, just as a ship whose steersman has died still remains."[17] But – quite apart from the question of the historicity of this anecdote, which is doubtful – the kingdom could be made to exist as an abstraction more easily at the level of rhetoric than at that of politics or institutions. This was no inherent drawback; the Ottonians and Salians and their followers had done well with such arrangements, which were flexible and carried few overheads. It would remain to be seen whether the flexibility would allow the German polity to survive the rule of a child on Henry's death in 1056, as it had done after 900 and again more successfully after 983.

17. Wipo, c. 7, p. 30.

Further reading and bibliography

The following suggestions for further reading and the bibliography are necessarily highly selective and are confined except for a handful of classics to works which have appeared since 1960; even here only a fraction of the literature is given, and in particular work with a regional emphasis is only occasionally cited. Fuller bibliographies, including details of the very extensive battery of bibliographical and other reference works available for German history, may be found in Prinz 1985, Keller 1986 and Hlawitschka 1986. Current bibliographical information may be obtained from a number of periodicals: *Historische Zeitschrift*, *Deutsches Archiv* and the *Blätter für deutsche Landesgeschichte*.

SOURCES AND HISTORIOGRAPHY

There is not a great deal on the historiography of the nineteenth and early twentieth centuries. Keller 1986: 13–55 is a superb survey; see also Böckenförde 1961 and Schorn-Schütte 1984 on aspects of the nineteenth century and the essays in P. Fried 1978 on *Landesgeschichte*. For the debate on *Kaiserpolitik* see Schneider 1941. Jordan 1980, Mayer 1958 and Schreiner 1989 are reflections by practitioners on the changes of their own lifetime. This is perhaps the most appropriate point to mention the general surveys of Frankish/German history in our period. The classic starting-points are still Giesebrecht 1881 and 1885 and Waitz 1880–96, which may be supplemented by Mühlbacher 1896 and Holtzmann 1955. The 1970s and 1980s have seen the appearance of several general textbooks, many of high quality. Besides the handbooks, Gebhardt 1970 and Schieffer 1976, we have Fleckenstein 1978 and Fuhrmann 1986 (mainly on the period following ours), Cuvillier 1979, Herrmann *et al.* 1982, Prinz 1985, Hlawitschka 1986, Keller 1986, Schulze 1987, as well as surveys of shorter periods in Beumann 1987a and Boshof 1987. J. Fried 1987 provides a critical review of several of these works. In English there is McKitterick 1983 and Halphen 1977 for the Carolingians; for German history Barraclough 1938a, 1938b and 1946 are still classic, but should be taken with the pungent corrective by Gillingham 1971. Kempf 1968 should also be used, as it covers much more than just church history, though for fullness of detail Hauck 1912 and 1913 must still be consulted. Tellenbach 1988, Pitz 1979, Ennen and Janssen 1979, Brunhölzl 1975 and Grodecki 1973 provide surveys of specific aspects of history relevant to more than one of the following sections.

The Frankish kingdom

On the Carolingian empire see, besides McKitterick 1983, Bullough 1965 and 1970, Halphen 1977, Fichtenau 1957b. Institutions are dealt with by Ganshof 1968; see also Fleckenstein 1959, Werner 1984: 108–56, Hannig 1983, Metz 1971 and 1978a. Structural aspects are considered by J. Fried 1982, Fleckenstein 1989: 315–32 and Reuter 1985. The nobility is an inexhaustible topic; see the articles and bibliography in Reuter 1978, plus Zotz 1977, Schulze 1978, Goetz 1983, Freed 1986. See also Brunner 1979 and Hannig 1982 on the political role of the nobility. On the free see Müller-Mertens 1963, Schulze 1974, Schmitt 1977 and Staab 1980. For the renewed Frankish church of the eighth century Wallace-Hadrill 1983 gives a fine if idiosyncratic survey; see also Büttner 1965 on mission, Hartmann 1989 on councils and Semmler 1961, 1980 on monasticism.

Gentes ultra Rhenum

The reign of Louis the Pious is now best approached through the essays in Godman and Collins 1990. Reuter 1990 offers an explanation of the end of expansion; see also Schieffer 1957 and several of the articles in Ganshof 1971. Ewig 1981 provides the most recent account of the various divisions of the 830s; on the geographical background see the essays in Ewig 1976 and 1979, and on the practice of division see Classen 1983: 205–30. On "Germany" and "German" see Weisgerber 1953, Eggers 1970, Strasser 1984 and Thomas 1988; and Geuenich 1983 should also be consulted. The question of when "Germany" first came into existence has been much discussed; the older discussion can be found largely in the articles in Kämpf 1956, while more recent discussions are Bartmuß 1966, Brühl 1972, Fleckenstein 1987 and Hlawitschka 1988. Geary 1988 is a good introduction to Frankish "Germany"; see also Wenskus 1986: 96–137. Wolfram 1987 provides a good approach to Bavaria, as does Dannheimer and Dopsch 1988; on Tassilo's end see Classen 1983: 231–48. Alemannia is less well served and more difficult; try Behr 1975 (with Keller 1976), and Borgolte 1984. Several of the essays in Wolfram and Schwarcz 1985 are valuable on both duchies, as is the collection Beumann and Schröder 1985. On central Germany see Schlesinger 1975 and Bosl 1969. Saxony may be approached via the work of Martin Lintzel, mostly reprinted in Lintzel 1961a, and via the articles in Lammers 1967 and 1970; see also Beumann 1987b: 289–323, Kahl 1982 and Schmidt 1977 on the conversion.

East Frankish kingdom

On relations between the Carolingians see Schlesinger 1987: 49–124. There is surprisingly little on Louis the German, but see Fried 1982 on Louis the Younger. On Frankish togetherness after 843 see Penndorf 1974 and Schneider 1964; Borgolte 1977 covers the east Frankish divisions. The southern half of the Slav frontier can be studied in Herrmann 1965, Sós 1973, Wolfram 1979. On the north there is less; see Ernst 1974, Dralle 1981 and Friedmann 1986. Mitterauer 1963 is important on the frontier commands in the south. In English see Dvornik 1970 and Vlasto 1970, who both concentrate on the missionary aspect, on which see also Dopsch 1986. On the institutions of the east Frankish kingdom, such as they were, see Brühl 1968a and 1968b on itineration, Flach 1976, Gockel 1970, Metz 1971, 1978a and Schalles-Fischer 1969 on fiscal organization, Weber 1962 on assemblies, Deutsche Königspfalzen 1963, 1965 and 1979, Schmitz 1974, Schmid 1976 and Zotz 1983ff. on palaces. Counties have been examined most recently by Borgolte 1984, Nonn 1983 and Schulze 1973 and 1985. On the east Frankish economy Dopsch 1921 and 1922 is still fundamental; for good recent regional studies see

Kuchenbuch 1978 and Staab 1975. On *Grundherrschaft* and the dependent population see Njeussychin 1961, Verhulst 1966, Epperlein 1969, Janssen and Lohrmann 1983, Müller-Mertens 1985, Rösener 1980, 1985, 1989 and Verhulst 1985; for village structure see also Heinzelmann 1977 and Schwind 1977. The non-rural economy can be studied via a number of articles on coinage and markets: Berghaus 1973, Hardt-Friederichs 1980, Heß 1962, Kaiser 1976. Hartmannn 1989 is now the standard work on church councils; for the ground-level work of the east Frankish church see Hammer 1980, Hartmann 1982, McKitterick 1977, Semmler 1982, 1983. Fleckenstein 1959 deals with the links between king and episcopate; see on this and on episcopal families Schmid 1983: 305–36, and Schieffer 1976 on the internal development of bishoprics. The cultural life of the east Frankish church may be approached through the works of Bischoff on manuscripts and their contents; on Hrabanus Maurus see Heyse 1969 and Kottje and Zimmermann 1982.

Kings, dukes and invaders 882–936

The events of 887 have been much discussed; Kämpf 1956 and Hlawitschka 1975 contain most of the significant essays, but see also Hlawitschka 1968 (valuable on the whole of Charles's and Arnulf's reigns) and Tellenbach 1979. On Arnulf see Appelt 1961 and Eibl 1984. There is little on Louis the Child apart from Beumann 1987b: 44–65, but much may be found in the two recent large-scale investigations of the emergent dukes of the early tenth century: Goetz 1977 and Stingl 1974; Maurer 1978, Reindel 1953 and Werner 1984: 278–328 are also indispensable here. On the Magyars see Büttner 1956b, Fasoli 1959, de Vajay 1968. Conrad's reign is better studied: see Goetz 1982, and for particular aspects Büttner and Dietrich 1952, Dietrich 1953, Fuhrmann 1987. Henry's accession has been studied recently by Althoff and Keller 1985, who offer an important and coherent account of his reign and that of Otto I. For Arnulf's accession and the question of the *regnum Teutonicum/Teutonicorum* see Beumann 1987b: 317–65 and Thomas 1976a, and on both accessions see the collections of articles in Erdmann 1968, Hlawitschka 1971, Kämpf 1956 and Lintzel 1961b. On Henry's military reforms, real and supposed, see Baaken 1961, Büttner 1956a, Leyser 1982: 11–42, Fleckenstein 1989: 315–32, Jäschke 1975. For Henry's relations with his magnates and the importance of *amicitia* see Althoff 1986, for his relations with Burgundy, Lotharingia and west Francia Büttner 1964, and for his eastern frontier Dralle 1980.

Schmid 1964 is still convincing on the designation of Otto I and its date, in spite of the objections in Hoffmann 1972.

Otto I and II

The most important work on the coronation of 936 is collected in Hlawitschka 1971 and Zimmermann 1976; the question of indivisibility has been recently discussed by Schmid 1985 and Hlawitschka 1988. On the uprisings of 937–41 see Leyser 1979, Althoff 1982 and Althoff and Keller 1985. These should also be consulted for the uprising of 953–4, on which see also Naumann 1964 and Erkens 1982. On Brun and Otto's use of the episcopate see Fleckenstein 1966, Hoffmann 1957, Lotter 1958, Prinz 1971, Reuter 1982. On the Lechfeld and the Magyars see de Vajay 1968 and Leyser 1982: 43–68. There is a large technical literature on the new episcopal foundations: see the articles in Beumann 1972 and 1987b, Büttner 1965b, 1967, 1968, as well as Claude 1972. On mission and conversion more generally see the difficult work by Petersohn 1979 and the articles in Beumann 1963. Relations with the Slavs can be studied from Herrmann 1972, Lübke 1982 and 1985; see also the classic articles in Ludat 1960 and Schlesinger 1961. Zimmermann 1962 and Dunbabin 1980 deal with the Ottonians and west Francia, and Dupré-Theseider 1962 with Otto and Italy (Wickham 1981 is an excellent general introduction to the Italian kingdom in the tenth century). The main essays on the imperial coronation of 962 are in Zimmermann 1976, but see also Stengel 1965. On the Carolingian prehistory of the Ottonianum see most recently Drabek 1976. There is no recent work on the Ottonians and southern Italy or on the uprisings of Henry the Quarrelsome in the 970s. For the Slav uprising of 983 and its background see Brüske 1955, Fritze 1958 and Fritze 1984.

The politics of the kingdom

The starting point is Mitteis 1944, and Böhme 1970 provides a useful collection of sources for the study of royal accessions; see also Haider 1968 and Reuling 1979. The year 1002 has been much studied recently, for example by Schlesinger 1987: 221–72 and Keller 1983. On the new king's perambulation of his kingdom see Schmidt 1961. On appointments and privileges see Kienast 1968 and Tellenbach in Reuter 1978: 203–42 for the duchies, Fleckenstein 1966 and 1985,

Reuter 1982 and Zielinski 1984 for the bishoprics, and on privileges and royal gifts see Krause 1965 and (from a quite different perspective) Leyser 1983. On rebellions there has been a good deal of recent work: see Leyser 1979, Althoff 1982, Erkens 1982, Keller 1986, Althoff 1989, Reuter 1991. See also specifically Giese 1979 on Saxony and Boshof 1978a on Lotharingia. The government of the Reich has been studied in a number of articles by Keller (1982, 1985a, 1989) and by Leyser 1982: 69–102; Weinfurter 1986 points to the importance of the changes of Henry II's reign. Müller-Mertens 1980 is fundamental on the principles and practice of itinerant rulership. Warfare has been studied by Werner 1968, Auer 1976b and Scherf 1985; the contribution of the clergy is measured in Auer 1971 and 1972. On peace-making see Minninger 1979, Kaiser 1983 and Reuter 1990b. Much of the literature cited above on the east Frankish kingdom in the ninth century is also relevant here, and Waitz 1880–96 is still indispensable. On the advocacy see most recently Boshof 1979b.

Being and consciousness

Leyser 1982: 161–90 is a brilliant social survey of the German nobility. On family structure see the articles in Reuter 1978 and Schmid 1983, and also Freed 1986. Althoff 1984 is a difficult but rewarding introduction to much recent work on family conscious-ness as reflected in *libri memoriales*. On Hermann and Thietmar see Borgolte 1979 and Lippelt 1973 respectively. On castles see Maurer 1969, Streich 1984, Ebner 1976 and Lewald 1976. Fichtenau 1984 is a remarkably wide-ranging and thoughtful study of tenth-century being and consciousness. The standard handbooks – Abel 1978, Luetge 1960, Ennen and Janssen 1979 – have little specific to say about rural economy and country life in the period 900–1050. Dollinger 1949/1982 is more rewarding. The classic study of *ministeriales* is still Bosl 1950 and 1951, though a new synthesis is needed; on *censuales* see Schulz 1982. Barley 1977 and Clarke and Simms 1985a and 1985b have a number of short contributions on German towns; in German there is much more, which may be approached through Diestelkamp 1982 and Schwineköper 1977, and Herzog 1964 on the topography (see also Maurer 1973). On coinage and trade with the north see Hatz 1974, Heß 1982.

Tellenbach 1988 is a deeply learned and thoughtful survey of all aspects of church life in this period. For the synodal activity of the church see most recently Wolter 1988. On relations with the papacy see Boshof 1972 and 1978b, Zotz 1982. For studies of individual bishoprics see for example Bannasch 1972, Große 1987, Kupper 1981, Maurer 1973, and on the episcopal ideal Engels 1989. On the relations between rulers and the church see in general Santifaller 1964, Köhler 1968, Reuter 1982, Zielinski 1984, Fleckenstein 1985, Schieffer 1989. For the question of differences between rulers in this respect see Benz 1977 and 1979, Schieffer 1951. Blumenthal 1988 is good on monastic reform; the starting point is still the classic study by Hallinger 1950, 1951, but see further Bulst 1973, Richter 1975, Wollasch 1973, 1977 and the essays in Kottje and Maurer 1989; on individual monasteries see the studies by Kaminsky 1972, Wehlt 1970, Wisplinghoff 1970, all of which deal essentially with relations with rulers, as does Willmes 1976. On schools, intellectual and court life see in general Riché 1989 and Fleckenstein 1989: 168–92; for individual rulers see Schramm 1957 (on Otto III), Schmidt 1983 (on Henry III). On canon law see Fuhrmann 1972–4 and most recently Müller 1989; forthcoming studies by Hoffmann and Pokorny on Burchard and the history of medieval canon law to be edited by Hartmann and Pennington will be relevant here. On historiography and historians see Lippelt 1973, Buchner 1970, Karpf 1985; see also Butzer 1976, Lindgren 1976, Blank 1968 and above all Borst 1988 for the links between historical studies and the quadrivium. Grodecki 1973 is a fine survey of Ottonian art; on the manuscripts dedicated to rulers and their illuminations see Deshman 1976, Keller 1985b, Hoffmann 1986 and above all the collections by Schramm and Mütherich 1981 and 1983. The building activities of prelates are studied by Giese 1982. Sacred art is best approached through recent exhibition catalogues, for example Ornamenta 1985 and Rhein und Maas 1972.

Hegemony and empire

On Poland and Bohemia see Graus 1980; on Hungary see Bogyay 1967 and Boshof 1986; on Denmark see Hoffmann 1984; and on the Abodrites and Elbe Slavs see Lübke 1982–7, Dralle 1981, Friedmann 1986. Ludat 1971 is important on the links between Saxon and Slav nobilities. Fried 1989 is the most recent attempt to make sense of the complex events of 1000; on missionary politics, aims and methods see also Wenskus 1956, Dvornik 1974 and Angenendt 1984. On France and Burgundy see Schneidmüller 1979, Kienast 1974 and Kahl 1969. Ottonian and Salian policies towards Italy are studied in Anton 1972, Pauler 1982; see Hoffmann 1969 and 1978 on southern Italy.

Germany in the early middle ages

On the "papal state" see Noble 1984 and Partner 1973. On the developments in the imperial idea, as well as on relations between the Ottonians, Rome and Byzantium, Schramm 1957 is still fundamental, and can be supplemented by Wolfram 1973 and 1988 as well as by the articles in Schramm's own collected essays (1968–71). For Byzantium see also (with caution) Ohnsorge 1958 and 1966, and the illuminating survey by Leyser 1982: 103–37. Struve 1988 is helpful on the Salian imperial idea; the account of imperial and papal ideology in Ullmann 1970 is interesting but should be treated with caution. The representation of rulers in art and in the liturgy, hardly touched on here, must be approached through the numerous works by Schramm. On Henry III's relations with the papacy see most recently Schmale 1979 and Vollrath 1974; Tellenbach 1988 and Blumenthal 1988 provide a more general context to the church history, while Boshof 1979a and Prinz 1988 are recent discussions of the reign of Henry III as a turning-point.

The alphabetical bibliography which follows is intended to support the suggestions for further reading above and at the same time indicate my principal debts. Only the bibliographical minimum has been given: series titles and lengthy subtitles have normally been excluded. For simplicity, the *Vorträge und Forschungen* of the Konstanzer Arbeitskreis and the *Settimane di studi* of Spoleto have been cited as if they were periodicals, by short title and volume number only. Where authors have published their essays in collections, reference has generally been made to these rather than to the original place of publication; this means that the dates given are not necessarily those of first publication.

The German diacritics Ä/ä, Ö/ö and Ü/ü and the "sharp s" ß are treated alphabetically as if they were ae, oe, ue and ss, respectively.

Abel, W. (1978), *Geschichte der deutschen Landwirtschaft vom frühen Mittelalter bis zum 19 Jahrhundert*, 3rd edn, Stuttgart.
Althoff, G. (1982), "Zur Frage nach der Organisation sächsischer coniurationes in der Ottonenzeit", *FmaSt* 16, 129–142.
Althoff, G. (1984), *Adels- und Königsfamilien im Spiegel ihrer Memorialüberlieferung*. Munich.
Althoff, G. (1986), "Unerforschte Quellen aus quellenarmer Zeit IV: Zur Verflechtung der Führungsschichten in den Gedenkquellen des frühen zehnten Jahrhunderts", in *Medieval lives and the historian*, ed. N. Bulst and J.-P. Genet, Kalamazoo, 37-71

Althoff, G. (1989), "Königsherrschaft und Konfliktbewältigung im 10 und 11 Jahrhundert", *FmaSt* 23, 265–90

Althoff, G. and Keller, H. (1985), *Heinrich I und Otto der Große. Neubeginn auf karolingischem Erbe*, Göttingen.

Angenendt, A. (1984), *Kaiserherrschaft und Königstaufe*, Berlin.

Angerer, J. F. and Lenzenweger, J., eds (1982), *Consuetudines monasticae. Eine Festgabe für Kassius Hallinger aus Anlaß seines 70, Geburtstages*, Rome.

Anton, H. H. (1972), "Bonifaz von Canossa, Markgraf von Tuszien, und die Italienpolitik der frühen Salier", *HZ* 214, 529–56

Appelt, H. (1961), "Arnulf von Kärnten und das Karolingerreich", in *Kärnten in europäischer Schau*, Graz, 1–15.

Auer, L. (1971, 1972), "Der Kriegsdienst des Klerus unter den sächsischen Kaisern", *MIÖG* 79, 316–407 and 80, 48–70.

Bannasch, H. (1972), *Das Bistum Paderborn unter den Bischöfen Rethar und Meinwerk (983–1036)*, Paderborn.

Barley, M. W., ed. (1977), *European towns: their archaeology and early history*, London.

Barraclough, G. (1938a and b), *Medieval Germany*, 2 vols, Oxford.

Barraclough, G. (1946) *The origins of modern Germany*, Oxford.

Bartmuß, H-J. (1966), *Die Geburt des ersten deutschen Staates*, Berlin [E.].

Beck, H., Denecke, D. and Jankuhn, H., eds (1979, 1980), *Untersuchungen zur eisenzeitlichen und frühmittelalterlichen Flur in Mitteleuropa und ihrer Nutzung*, Göttingen.

Behr, B. (1975), *Das alemannische Herzogtum bis 750*, Bern.

Benz, K. J. (1977), "Kaiser Konrad II und die Kirche", *ZKG* 88, 190–217.

Berghaus, P. (1973), "Karolingische Münzen in Westfalen", *Westfalen*, 51, 22–32.

Beumann, H. (1950), *Widukind von Korvei*, Weimar.

Beumann, H., ed. (1963), *Heidenmission und Kreuzzugsgedanke in der deutschen Ostpolitik des Mittelalters*, Darmstadt.

Beumann, H., ed. (1965), *Karl der Große. Persönlichkeit und Geschichte*, Düsseldorf.

Beumann, H. (1972), *Wissenschaft vom Mittelalter. Ausgewählte Aufsätze*, Cologne.

Beumann, H. and Schröder, W., eds (1978), *Aspekte der Nationenbildung im Mittelalter*, Sigmaringen.

Beumann, H. (1981), *Der deutsche König als "Romanorum rex"*. Wiesbaden.

Beumann, H. and Schröder, W., eds (1985) *Frühmittelalterliche Ethnogenese im Alpenraum*, Sigmaringen.

Germany in the early middle ages

Beumann, H. (1987a), *Die Ottonen*, Stuttgart.

Beumann, H. (1987b), *Ausgewählte Aufsätze aus den Jahren 1966–1986*, eds J. Petersohn and R. Schmidt, Sigmaringen.

Bischoff, B. (1960, 1980), *Die südostdeutschen Schreibschulen und Bibliotheken in der Karolingerzeit*, 2 vols, vol. 1 2nd edn, Wiesbaden.

Bischoff, B. (1966, 1967, 1981), *Mittelalterliche Studien. Ausgewählte Aufsätze zur Schriftkunde und Literaturgeschichte*, 3 Bde, Stuttgart.

Blank, R. (1968) *Weltdarstellung und Weltbild in Würzburg und Bamberg vom 8 bis zum Ende des 12 Jahrhunderts*, Bamberg.

Blumenthal, U.-R. (1988), *The investiture controversy*, Philadelphia.

Boba, I. (1971), *Moravia's history reconsidered. A reinterpretation of medieval sources*, The Hague.

Böckenförde, E. W. (1961) *Die deutsche verfassungsgeschichtliche Forschung des 19 Jahrhunderts*, Berlin.

Böhme, W. (1970), *Die deutsche Königserhebung im 10–12 Jahrhundert, 1: Die Erhebungen von 911 bis 1105*, Göttingen.

Bogyay, T. v. (1967), *Grundzüge der Geschichte Ungarns*, Darmstadt.

Borgolte, M. (1977), "Karl III und Neuendingen", *ZGO* 125, 21–56.

Borgolte, M. (1979), "Über die persönlichen und familiengeschichtlichen Aufzeichnungen Hermanns des Lahmen", *ZGO* 127, 1–15.

Borgolte, M. (1984), *Geschichte der Grafschaften Alemanniens in fränkischer Zeit*, Sigmaringen.

Borst, A. (1988), "Computus – Zeit und Zahl im Mittelalter, *DA* 44, 1–82.

Boshof, E. (1972), *Das Erzstift Trier und seine Stellung zu Königtum und Papsttum im ausgehenden 10, Jahrhundert*, Cologne.

Boshof, E. (1978a), "Lothringen, Frankreich und das Reich in der Regierungszeit Heinrichs III", *RhVjBll* 42, 63–127.

Boshof, E. (1978b), "Köln, Mainz, Trier – Die Auseinandersetzung um die Spitzenstellung im deutschen Episkopat in ottonisch-salischer Zeit", *Jahrbuch des Kölner Geschichtsvereins* 49, 19–48.

Boshof, E. (1979a), "Das Reich in der Krise. Überlegungen zum Regierungsausgang Heinrichs III", *HZ* 228, 265–87.

Boshof, E. (1979b), "Untersuchungen zur Kirchenvogtei in Lothringen im 10 und 11 Jahrhundert", *ZRGKA* 65, 55–119.

Boshof, E. (1986), "Das Reich und Ungarn in der Zeit der Salier", *Ostbairische Grenzmarken* 28, 178–94.

Boshof, E. (1987), *Die Salier*, Stuttgart.

Bosl, K. (1950, 1951), *Die Reichsministerialität der Salier und Staufer*, Stuttgart.

Bosl, K. (1969), *Franken um 800. Strukturanalyse einer fränkischen Königsprovinz*, 2nd edn, Munich.

Bowlus, C.R. (1987), "Imre Boba's reconsiderations of Moravia's early history and Arnulf of Carinthia's *Ostpolitik* (887–892)", *Speculum* 62, 552–74.

Breßlau, H. (1912, 1931), *Handbuch der Urkundenlehre*, 2 vols, 2nd, edn by H.-W. Klewitz, Berlin.

Brück, A. P., ed. (1975), *Willigis und sein Dom*, Mainz.

Brühl, C. (1968), *Fodrum, Gistum, Servitium Regis*, 2 vols, Cologne.

Brühl, C. (1972), *Die Anfänge der deutschen Geschichte*, Wiesbaden.

Brüske, W. (1955), *Untersuchungen zur Geschichte des Liutizenbundes*, Münster.

Brunhölzl, F. (1975), *Geschichte der lateinischen Literatur des Mittelalters 1: Von Cassiodor bis zum Ausklang der karolingischen Erneuerung*, Munich.

Brunner, K. (1979), *Oppositionelle Gruppen im Karolingerreich*, Vienna.

Buchner, R. (1970), "Die frühsalische Geschichtsschreibung in Deutschland", *Settimane* 17, 895–944.

Büttner, H. and Dietrich, I. (1952), "Weserland und Hessen im Kräftespiel der karolingischen und frühen ottonischen Politik", *Westfalen* 30, 133–149.

Büttner, H. (1956a), "Zur Burgenbauordnung Heinrichs I", *BDLG* 92, 1–17.

Büttner, H. (1956b), "Die Ungarn, das Reich und Europa bis zur Lechfeldschlacht des Jahres 955", *ZBLG* 19, 433–458.

Büttner, H. (1957), "Verfassungsgeschichte und lothringische Klosterreform", in Engel and Klinkenberg 1957, 17–27.

Büttner, H. (1964), *Heinrichs I. Südwest- und Westpolitik*, Sigmaringen.

Büttner, H. (1965), "Mission und Kirchenorganisation des Frankenreiches bis zum Tode Karls des Großen", in Beumann 1965, 454–487.

Büttner, H. (1975), *Zur frühmittelalterlichen Reichsgeschichte an Rhein, Main und Neckar*, ed. A. Gerlich, Darmstadt.

Bullough, D. (1970), "Europae Pater: Charlemagne and his achievement in the light of recent scholarship", *EHR* 85, 59–105.

Bullough, D.A. (1965), *The age of Charlemagne*, London.

Bulst, N. (1973), *Untersuchungen zu der Klosterreform Wilhelms von Dijon (962–1031)*, Bonn.

Butzer, P. L. (1976), "Die Mathematiker des Aachen-Lütticher

Raumes von der karolingischen bis zur spätottonischen Epoche", *AHVNRh* 178, 7–30.

Clarke, H. B. and Simms, A., eds (1985a, 1985b), *The comparative history of urban origins in non-Roman Europe: Ireland, Wales, Denmark, Germany, Poland and Russia from the ninth to the thirteenth century*, Oxford.

Classen, P. (1983), *Ausgewählte Aufsätze*, ed. J. Fleckenstein, Sigmaringen.

Classen, P. (1985), *Karl der Große, das Papsttum und Byzanz. Die Begründung des karolingischen Kaisertums*, 3rd edn, Sigmaringen.

Claude, D. (1972), *Geschichte des Erzbistums Magdeburg bis in das 12 Jahrhundert 1: Die Geschichte der Erzbischöfe bis auf Ruotger (1124)*, Cologne.

Corbett, P. (1986), *Les saints ottoniens*, Sigmaringen.

Cuvillier, J.P. (1979), *L'Allemagne médiévale. Naissance d'un état (VIIIe-XIIIe siècles)*, Paris.

Dannheimer, H. and Dopsch, H. (1988), *Die Bajuwaren. Von Severin bis Tassilo 488–788*, Salzburg.

Deshman, R. (1976), "Christus rex et magi reges: Kingship and Christology in Ottonian and Anglo-Saxon art", *FmaSt* 10, 367–405.

Deutsche Königspfalzen (1963, 1965, 1979), *Deutsche Königspfalzen*, 3 vols, Göttingen.

Diestelkamp, B., ed. (1982), *Beiträge zum hochmittelalterlichen Städtewesen*, Cologne.

Dietrich, I. (1953), "Die Konradiner im fränkisch-sächsischen Grenzraum von Thüringen und Hessen", *HJLG* 3, 57–95.

Dölger, F. (1953), *Byzanz und die europäische Staatenwelt*, Ettal.

Dollinger, P. (1982), *Der bayerische Bauernstand vom 9. bis zum 13. Jarhundert*, ed. F. Irsigler, Munich [lightly revised German translation of the French original, Paris 1949].

Dopsch, A.(1921, 1922), *Die Wirtschaftsentwicklung der Karolingerzeit vornehmlich in Deutschland*, 2 vols, 2nd edn, Weimar.

Dopsch, H., ed. (1986), *Salzburg und die Slawenmission. Zum 1100. Todestag des hl. Methodius*, Salzburg.

Drabek, A. M. (1976), *Die Verträge der fränkischen und deutschen Herrscher und das Papsttum von 754 bis 1020,* Vienna.

Dralle, L. (1980), "Zu Vorgeschichte und Hintergründen der Ostpolitik Heinrichs I", in Grothusen and Zernack 1980, 99–126

Dralle, L. (1981), *Slaven an Havel und Spree. Studien zur Geschichte des hevellisch-wilzischen Fürstentums (6 bis 10 Jh.)*, Berlin.

Dupré-Theseider, E. (1964), "La grande rapina dei corpi Santi dell'Italia al tempo di Ottone I", in *Festschrift Percy Ernst Schramm* 1, Wiesbaden, 420–32.

Dupré-Theseider, E. (1962), "Otto I und Italien", *MIÖG EB* 20/1, 53–69.

Dvornik, F. (1970), *Byzantine Missions among the Slavs. SS. Constantine-Cyril and Methodius*, New Brunswick, NJ.

Dvornik, F. (1974), *The making of central and eastern Europe*, 2nd edn, Gulf Breeze, Florida.

Ebner, H. (1976), "Die Burg als Forschungsproblem mittelalterlicher Verfassungsgeschichte", *VuF* 19, 11–82.

Eggers, H., ed. (1970), *Der Volksname Deutsch*, Darmstadt.

Eggert, W. (1973), *Das ostfränkisch-deutsche Reich in der Auffassung seiner Zeitgenossen*, Berlin [E.].

Eggert, W. (1975), "Rebelliones servorum", *ZfG* 23, 1147–64.

Eggert, W. and Pätzold, B. (1984), *Wir-Gefühl und regnum Saxonum bei frühmittelalterlichen Geschichtsschreibern*, Berlin [E.].

Ehlers, J. (1989), "Schriftkultur, Ethnogenese und Nationsbildung in ottonischer Zeit", *FmaSt* 23, 302–17.

Eibl, E.-M. (1984), "Zur Stellung Bayerns und Rheinfrankens im Reiche Arnulfs von Kärnten", *JGF* 8, 73–113.

Ennen, E. and Janssen, W. (1979), *Deutsche Agrargeschichte. Vom Neolithikum bis zur Schwelle des Industriezeitalters*, Wiesbaden.

Engel, J. and Klinkenberg, H., eds (1957), *Aus Mittelalter und Neuzeit: Gerhard Kallen zum 70 Geburtstag*, Bonn.

Engels, O. (1989), "Der Reichsbischof in ottonischer und frühsalischer Zeit", in *Beiträge zu Geschichte und Struktur der mittelalterlichen Germania Sacra*, ed. I. Crusius, Göttingen.

Epperlein, S. (1969), *Herrschaft und Volk im karolingischen Imperium*, Berlin [E.].

Erbe, M. (1960), *Studien zur Entwicklung des Niederkirchenwesens in Ostsachsen vom 8 bis zum 12 Jahrhundert*, Göttingen.

Erdmann, C. (1951), *Forschungen zur politischen Ideenwelt des Frühmittelalters*, ed. F. Baethgen, Berlin.

Erdmann, C. (1968), *Ottonische Studien*, ed. H. Beumann, Darmstadt.

Erkens, F.-R. (1982), "Fürstliche Opposition in ottonisch-salischer Zeit", *Archiv für Kulturgeschichte* 64, 307–70.

Ernst, R. (1974), *Die Nordwestslaven und das fränkische Reich*, Berlin.

Ewig, E. (1976, 1979), *Spätantikes und fränkisches Gallien. Gesammelte Schriften (1952–1973)*, 2 vols, ed. H. Atsma, Sigmaringen.

Ewig, E. (1981), "Überlegungen zu den merowingischen und karolingischen Teilungen", *Settimane* 27, 225–53.

Fasoli, G. (1959), "Points de vue sur les incursions hongroises en Europe au Xe siècle", *CCM* 2, 17–36.

Fenske, L., Rösener, W. and Zotz, T., eds (1984), *Institutionen, Kultur und Gesellschaft im Mittelalter. Festschrift für Josef Fleckenstein zu seinem 65 Geburtstag*, Sigmaringen,

Fichtenau, H. (1957a), *Arenga*, Vienna.

Fichtenau, H. (1957b), *The Carolingian Empire*, Oxford.

Fichtenau, H. (1984), *Lebensordnungen des 10 Jahrhunderts*, 2 vols, Stuttgart; an English translation by P. Geary is forthcoming.

Flach, D. (1976), *Untersuchungen zur Verfassung und Verwaltung des Aachener Reichsgutes von der Karlingerzeit bis zur Mitte des 14 Jahrhunderts*, Göttingen.

Fleckenstein, J. (1959), *Die Hofkapelle der deutschen Könige, 1. Teil: Grundlegung. Die karolingische Hofkapelle*, Stuttgart.

Fleckenstein, J. (1966), *Die Hofkapelle der deutschen Könige, 2. Teil: Die Hofkapelle im Rahmen der ottonisch-salischen Reichskirche*, Stuttgart.

Fleckenstein, J. and Schmid, K, eds (1968), *Adel und Kirche. Festschrift Gerd Tellenbach zum 65 Geburtstag*, Freiburg.

Fleckenstein, J. (1978), *Early medieval Germany*, translated by B. S. Smith, Amsterdam.

Fleckenstein, J. (1987), *Über die Anfänge der deutschen Geschichte*, Opladen.

Fleckenstein, J. (1989), *Ordnungen und formende Kräfte des Mittelalters*, Göttingen.

Freed, J. B. (1976), "The origins of the European nobility: the problem of the ministerials", *Viator* 7, 211–41.

Freed, J. B. (1978), "The formation of the Salzburg ministerialage in the tenth and eleventh centuries: an example of upward social mobility in the early middle ages", *Viator* 9, 67–102.

Freed, J. B. (1986), "Reflections on the medieval German nobility", *American Historical Review* 91, 553–75.

Fried, J. (1982), "Der karolingische Herrschaftsverband im 9 Jh. zwischen 'Kirche' und 'Königshaus'", *HZ* 235, 1–43.

Fried, J. (1984), *König Ludwig der Jüngere in seiner Zeit. Zum 1100 Todestag des Königs*, Lorsch.

Fried, J. (1987), "Deutsche Geschichte im früheren und hohen Mittelalter: Bemerkungen zu einigen neuen Gesamtdarstellungen", *HZ* 245, 625–59.

Fried, J. (1989), *Otto III und Boleslaw Chrobry*, Stuttgart.

Fried, P., ed. (1978), *Probleme und Methoden der Landesgeschichte*, Darmstadt.

Friedmann, B. (1986), *Untersuchungen zur Geschichte des abodritischen Fürstentums bis zum Ende des 10 Jahrhundert*, Berlin.

Fritze, W. H. (1958), "Beobachtungen zu Entstehung und Wesen des Liutizenbundes", *JGMOD* 7, 1–38.

Fritze, W. H. (1984), "Der slawische Aufstand von 983: Eine Schiksalswende in der Geschichte Mitteleuropas", in *Festschrift der Landesgeschichtlichen Vereinigung für die Mark Brandenburg zu ihrem hundertjährigen Bestehen 1884–1984*, Berlin.

Fuhrmann, H. (1972–4), *Einfluß und Verbreitung der pseudoisidorischen Fälschungen*. 3 vols, Stuttgart.

Fuhrmann, H. (1986), *Germany in the high middle ages, c. 1050–1200*, translated by T. Reuter, Cambridge.

Fuhrmann, H. (1987), "Die Synode von Hohenaltheim (916) – quellenkundlich betrachtet", *DA* 43, 440–68.

Ganshof, F. L. (1968), *Frankish institutions under Charlemagne*, Providence, RI.

Ganshof, F.L. (1971), *The Carolingians and the Frankish Monarchy. Studies in Carolingian History*, translated by Janet Sondheimer, London.

Geary, P.J. (1985), *Aristocracy in Provence. The Rhône basin at the dawn of the Carolingian age*, Stuttgart.

Geary, P. (1988), *Before France and Germany*, Oxford.

Gebhardt, B., ed. (1970), *Handbuch der deutschen Geschichte*, 1, 9th edn by H. Grundmann, Stuttgart.

Geuenich, D. (1983), "Die volkssprachige Überlieferung der Karolingerzeit aus der Sicht des Historikers", *DA* 39, 104–30.

Giesebrecht, W. v. (1881, 1885), *Geschichte der deutschen Kaiserzeit, 1: Gründung des Kaiserthums; 2: Blüthe des Kaiserthums*, 5th edn, Leipzig.

Giese, W. (1979), *Der Stamm der Sachsen und das Reich in ottonischer und salischer Zeit*, Wiesbaden.

Giese, W. (1982), "Zur Bautätigkeit von Bischöfen und Äbten des 10 bis 12 Jahrhunderts", *DA* 38, 388–438.

Gillingham, J. B. (1971), *The kingdom of Germany in the high middle ages*, London.

Glauche, G. (1970), *Schullektüre im Mittelalter*, Munich.

Gockel, M. (1970), *Karolingische Königshöfe am Mittelrhein*, Göttingen.

Gockel, M. (1976), "Die Träger von Rodung und Siedlung im Hünfelder Raum in karolingischer Zeit", *HJLG* 26, 1–24.

Godman, P. and Collins, R., eds (1990), *Charlemagne's Heir. New perspectives on the reign of Louis the Pious*, Oxford.

Goetz, H.-W. (1977), *"Dux" und "ducatus"*, Bochum.

Goetz, H.-W. (1982), "Der letzte 'Karolinger'? Die Regierung Konrads I im Spiegel seiner Urkunden", *AfD* 26, 56–125.

Goetz, H.-W. (1983), "Nobilis. Der Adel im Selbstverständnis der Karolingerzeit", *VSWG* 70, 153–91.

Graus, F. (1980), *Die Nationenbildung der Westslawen im Mittelalter*, Sigmaringen.

Grodecki, L. et al, (1973), *Die Zeit der Ottonen und Salier*, Munich.

Gross, R. (1987), *Das Bistum Utrecht und seine Bischöfe im 10 und frühen 11 Jahrhundert*, Cologne.

Grothusen, K.-D. and Zernack, K., eds (1980), *Europa Slavica – Europa Orientalis. Festschrift für Herbert Ludat zum 70 Geburtstag*, Berlin.

Hauck, K. and Mordek H., eds (1978), *Geschichtsschreibung und geistiges Leben im Mittelalter. Festschrift für Heinz Löwe zum 65 Geburtstag*, Sigmaringen.

Hallinger, K. (1950, 1951), *Gorze-Kluny. Studien zu den monastischen Lebensformen und Gegensätzen im Hochmittelalter*, Rome.

Halphen, L. (1977), *Charlemagne and the Carolingian empire*, Amsterdam.

Hammer, C. J. (1980), "Country churches, clerical inventories and the Carolingian renaissance in Bavaria", *Church History* 49, 5–17.

Hannig, J. (1982), *Consensus fidelium*, Stuttgart.

Hannig, J. (1983), "Pauperiores vassi de infra palatio? Zur Entstehung der karolingischen Königsbotenorganisation", *MIÖG* 91, 309–74.

Hardt-Friederichs, F. (1980), "Markt, Münze und Zoll im ostfränkischen Reich bis zum Ende der Ottonen", *BDLG* 116, 1–31.

Hartmann, W. (1982), "Der rechtliche Zustand der Kirchen auf dem Lande: Die Eigenkirche in der fränkischen Gesetzgebung des 7–9 Jahrhunderts", *Settimane* 28, 397–441.

Hartmann, W. (1989), *Die Synoden der Karolingerzeit im Frankenreich und in Italien*, Paderborn.

Hatz, G. (1974), *Handel und Verkehr zwischen dem Deutschen Reich und Schweden in der späten Wikingerzeit. Die deutschen Münzen des 10 und 11 Jh. in Schweden*, Stockholm.

Hauck, A. (1912), *Kirchengeschichte Deutschlands 2: Die Karolingerzeit*, 3rd edn, Leipzig.

Hauck, A. (1913), *Kirchengeschichte Deutschlands 3: Die Zeit der sächsischen und fränkischen Kaiser*, 3rd edn, Leipzig.

Heidrich, I. (1971), "Die Absetzung Herzog Adalberos von Kärnten durch Kaiser Konrad II 1035", *HJb* 91, 70–94.

Heinzelmann, M. (1977), "Beobachtungen zur Bevölkerungsstruktur einiger grundherrschaftlicher Siedlungen im karolingischen Bayern", *FmaSt* 11, 202–17.

Herrmann, J. *et al.* (1982), *Deutsche Geschichte von den Anfängen bis zur Ausbildung des Feudalismus Mitte des 11 Jahrhunderts.* Cologne.

Herrmann, J., ed. (1972), *Die Slawen in Deutschland*, 2nd edn, Berlin [E.].

Herrmann, K.-J. (1973), *Das Tuskulanerpapsttum. 1012–1046 Benedikt VIII, Johannes XIX, Benedikt IX,* Stuttgart.

Herzog, E. (1964), *Die ottonische Stadt,* Berlin.

Heß, W. (1962), "Geldwirtschaft am Mittelrhein in karolingischer Zeit", *BDLG* 98, 26–63.

Heß, W. (1982), "Münzstätten, Geldverkehr und Märkte am Rhein in ottonischer und salischer Zeit", in Diestelkamp 1982, 111–133.

Heyse, E. (1969), *Hrabanus Maurus' Enzyklopädie "De rerum naturis". Untersuchungen zu den Quellen und zur Methode der Kompilation* Munich.

Hiestand, R. (1964), *Byzanz und das Regnum Italicum im 10 Jahrhundert,* Zurich.

Hlawitschka, E. (1960), *Franken, Alemannen, Bayern und Burgunder in Oberitalien (774–962),* Freiburg.

Hlawitschka, E. (1968), *Lothringen und das Reich an der Schwelle der deutschen Geschichte,* Stuttgart.

Hlawitschka, E., ed. (1971), *Königswahl und Thronfolge in ottonischfrühdeutscher Zeit.* Darmstadt.

Hlawitschka, E., ed. (1975), *Königswahl und Thronfolge in fränkischkarolingischer Zeit,* Darmstadt.

Hlawitschka, E. (1986), *Vom Frankenreich zur Formierung der europäischen Staaten- und Völkergemeinschaft 840–1046,* Darmstadt.

Hlawitschka, E. (1988), *Von der großfränkischen zur deutschen Geschichte,* Munich.

Hlawitschka, E. (1989), *Stirps regia. Forschungen zum Königtum und Führungsschichten im früheren Mittelalter,* ed. G. Thoma and W. Giese, Frankfurt.

Hoffmann, E. (1984), "Beiträge zur Geschichte der Beziehungen zwischen dem deutschen und dem dänischen Reich für die Zeit von 934 bis 1035", in *850 Jahre St-Petri-Dom zu Schleswig, 1134–1984,* ed. C. Radtke and W. Körber, Schleswig, 97–132.

Hoffmann, H. (1957), "Politik und Kultur im ottonischen Reichskirchensystem", *RhVjBll* 22, 31–55.

Hoffmann, H. (1964), *Gottesfriede und Treuga Dei*, Stuttgart.

Hoffmann, H. (1969), "Die Anfänge der Normannen in Süditalien", *QFIAB* 49, 95–144.

Hoffmann, H. (1969), "Böhmen und das deutsche Reich im hohen Mittelalter", *JGMOD* 18, 1–62.

Hoffmann, H. (1978), "Langobarden, Normannen, Päpste", *QFIAB* 58, 137–80.

Hoffmann, H. (1986), *Buchkunst und Königtum im ottonischen und frühsalischen Reich*, Stuttgart.

Holtzmann, R. (1955), *Geschichte der sächsischen Kaiserzeit* (900–1024), 3rd edn, Darmstadt.

Irsigler, F. (1976–77), "Bischof Meinwerk, Graf Dodiko und Warburg", *Westfälische Zeitschrift* 126/127, 181–200.

Jäschke, K.-U. (1975), *Burgenbau und Landesverteidigung um 900*. Sigmaringen.

Jäschke, K.-U. and Wenskus, R., eds (1977), *Festschrift für Helmut Beumann zum 65 Geburtstag*, Sigmaringen.

Jankuhn, H., Schlesinger, W. and Steuer, H., eds (1973), *Vor- und Frühformen der europäischen Stadt im Mittelalter, 1*, Göttingen.

Jankuhn, H., Schützeichel, R. and Schwind, F., eds (1977), *Das Dorf der Eisenzeit und des frühen Mittelalters*, Göttingen.

Jankuhn, H., Schmidt-Wiegand, R. and Tiefenbach, H., eds (1981, 1983), *Das Handwerk in vor- und frühgeschichtlicher Zeit*, Göttingen.

Janssen, W. (1968), "Mittelalterliche Dorfsiedlung als archäologisches Problem", *FmaSt* 2, 305–67.

Janssen, W. (1977), "Dorf und Dorfformen des 7 bis 12 Jahrhunderts im Lichte neuer Ausgrabungen in Mittel- und Nordeuropa", in Jankuhn, Schützeichel and Schwind 1977, 285–356.

Janssen, W. and Lohrmann, D., eds (1983), *Villa – curtis – grangia*, Sigmaringen.

Johanek, P. (1977), "Zur rechtlichen Funktion von Traditionsnotiz, Traditionsbuch und früher Siegelurkunde", *VuF* 23, 131–62.

Johanek, P. (1982), "Die Raffelstetter Zollordnung und das Urkundenwesen der Karolingerzeit", in Maurer and Patze 1982, 87–103.

Jordan, K. (1980), "Aspekte der Mittelalterforschung in Deutschland in den letzten fünfzig Jahren", in: *Ausgewählte Aufsätze zur Geschichte des Mittelalters*. Stuttgart, 329–44.

Kahl, H.-D. (1982), "Karl der Große und die Sachsen. Stufen und Motive einer historischen 'Eskalation'", in: Ludat and Schwinges 1982, 49–130.

Kaiser, R. (1976), "Münzprivilegien und bischöfliche Münzprägung in Frankreich, Deutschland und Burgund im 9–12 Jahrhundert", *VSWG* 63, 289–338.

Kaiser, R. (1983), "Selbsthilfe und Gewaltmonopol. Königliche friedenswahrung in Deutschland und Frankreich im Mittelalter", *FmaSt* 17, 55–72.

Kaminsky, H. H. (1972), *Studien zur Reichsabtei Corvey in der Salierzeit*, Cologne.

Kamp, N. and Wollasch, J., eds (1982), *Tradition als historische Kraft*, Berlin.

Karpf, E. (1984), "Königserhebung ohne Salbung. Zur politischen Bedeutung von Heinrichs I. ungewöhnlichem Verzicht in Fritzlar (919)", *HJLG* 34, 1–24.

Karpf, E. (1985), *Herrscherlegitimation und Reichsbegriff in der ottonischen Geschichtsschreibung des 10 Jahrhunderts*, Stuttgart.

Keller, H. (1976), "Fränkische Herrschaft und alemannisches Herzogtum im 6 und 7 Jahrhundert", *ZGO* 124, 1–30.

Keller, H. (1982), "Reichsstruktur und Herrschaftsauffassung in ottonisch-frühsalischer Zeit", *FmaSt* 16, 74–128.

Keller, H. (1983), "Schwäbische Herzöge als Thronbewerber: Hermann II (1002), Rudolf von Rheinfelden (1077), Friedrich von Staufen (1125)", *ZGO* 131, 123–62.

Keller, H. (1985a), "Grundlagen ottonischer Königsherrschaft", in Schmid 1985a, 17–34.

Keller, H. (1985b), "Herrscherbild und Herrschaftslegitimation. Zur Deutung der ottonischen Denkmäler", *FmaSt* 19, 290–311.

Keller, H. (1986), *Zwischen regionaler Begrenzung und universalem Horizont. Deutschland im Imperium der Salier und Staufer 1024–1250*, Berlin.

Keller, H. (1989), "Zum Charakter der 'Staatlichkeit' zwischen karolingischem Reichsreform und hochmittelalterlichem Herrschaftsausbau", *FmaSt* 23, 248–64.

Kempf, F., ed. (1968), *The church in the age of feudalism*, translated by A. Biggs, London.

Kern, F. (1954), *Gottesgnadentum und Widerstandsrecht im frühen Mittelalter*, 2nd edn by R. Buchner, Darmstadt; English translation of the 1st edn by S. B. Chrimes as *Kingship and law in the middle ages*, Oxford 1939.

Kienast, W. (1968), *Der Herzogstitel in Frankreich und Deutschland (9 bis 12 Jh.)*, Munich.

Kienast, W. (1974a, 1974b, 1975), *Deutschland und Frankreich in der Kaiserzeit (900–1270). Weltkaiser und Einzelkönige*, 3 vols, Stuttgart.

Germany in the early middle ages

Kloster und Stift (1980), *Untersuchungen zu Kloster und Stift*, Göttingen.

Köhler, O. (1968), "Die ottonische Reichskirche. Ein Forschungsbericht", in Fleckenstein and Schmid 1968, 141–205.

Konecny, S. (1976), *Die Frauen des karolingischen Königshauses*, Vienna.

Kottje, R., and Maurer, H. (1989), *Monastische Reformen im 9 und 10 Jahrhundert*, Sigmaringen.

Kottje, R. and Zimmermann, H., eds (1982), *Hrabanus Maurus. Lehrer, Abt und Bischof*, Wiesbaden.

Krause, H. (1965), "Königtum und Rechtsordnung in der Zeit der sächsischen und salischen Herrscher", *ZRGGA* 82, 1–98.

Kuchenbuch, L. (1978), *Bäuerliche Gesellschaft und Klosterherrschaft im 9. Jahrhundert*, Wiesbaden.

Kugler, G. J. (1986), *Die Reichskrone*, 2nd edn Vienna.

Kupper, J.-L. (1981), *Liège et l'église impériale, XIe–XIIe siècles*, Paris.

Lammers, W., ed. (1967), *Entstehung und Verfassung des Sachsenstammes*, Darmstadt.

Lammers, W., ed. (1970), *Die Eingliederung der Sachsen in das Frankenreich*, Darmstadt.

Lang, H. J. (1974), "The fall of the monarchy of Mieszko II Lambert," *Speculum* 49, 623–39.

Lewald, U. (1976), "Burg, Kloster, Stift", *VuF* 19/1, 155–180.

Leyser, K. (1979), *Rule and conflict in an early medieval society*, London.

Leyser, K. (1982), *Medieval Germany and its neighbours, 900–1250*, London.

Leyser, K. (1983), "The crisis of medieval Germany", *Proceedings of the British Academy* 69, 409–43.

Lindgren, U. (1976), *Gerbert von Aurillac und das Quadrivium*, Wiesbaden.

Lintzel, M. (1961a, 1961b), *Ausgewählte Schriften*, 2 vols, Berlin [E.].

Lippelt, H. (1973), *Thietmar von Merseburg. Reichsbischof und Chronist*, Cologne.

Lotter, F. (1958), *Die "Vita Brunonis" des Ruotger*, Bonn.

Ludat, H., ed. (1960), *Siedlung und Verfassung der Slawen zwischen Elbe, Saale und Oder*, Giessen.

Ludat, H. (1971), *An Elbe und Oder um das Jahr 1000*, Cologne.

Ludat, H. and Schwinges, R. C., eds (1982), *Politik, Gesellschaft, Geschichtsschreibung. Giessener Festgabe für Frantiek Graus zum 60 Geburtstag*, Cologne.

Lübke, C. (1982, 1985, 1986, 1987), *Regesten zur Geschichte der Slaven an Elbe und Oder (vom Jahr 900 an)*, 4 vols, Berlin [W.].

Lütge, F. (1966), *Deutsche Sozial- und Wirtschaftsgeschichte. Ein Überblick*. 3rd edn, Berlin.

Maurer, H. (1969), "Die Entstehung der hochmittelalterlichen Adelsburg in Südwestdeutschland", *ZGO* 117, 295–332.

Maurer, H. (1973), *Konstanz als ottonischer Bischofssitz*, Göttingen.

Maurer, H. (1978), *Der Herzog von Schwaben*, Sigmaringen.

Maurer, H. and Patze, H., eds (1982), *Festschrift für Berent Schwineköper zu seinem siebzigsten Geburtstag*, Sigmaringen.

Mayer, T. (1950), *Fürsten und Staat*, Weimar.

Mayer, T. (1958), *Mittelalterliche Studien*, Lindau.

McKitterick, R. (1977), *The Frankish church and the Carolingian reforms, 789–895*, London.

McKitterick, R. (1983), *The Frankish kingdoms under the Carolingians, 751–987*, London.

Metz, W. (1971), *Zur Erforschung des karolingischen Reichsgutes*, Darmstadt.

Metz, W. (1972), "Marktrechtfamilie und Kaufmannsfriede in ottonisch-salischer Zeit", *BDLG* 108, 28–55.

Metz, W. (1978a), *Das Servitium regis*, Darmstadt.

Metz, W. (1978b, 1981b), "Quellenstudien zum Servitium regis (900–1250)", *AfD* 22, 187–271; 24, 203–91.

Metz, W. (1981a), "Zu Wesen und Struktur der geistlichen Grundherrschaft", *Settimane* 27, 147–69.

Minninger, M. (1979), Heinrichs III interne Friedensmaßnahmen und ihre etwaigen Gegner in Lothringen", *JwLG* 5, 33–52.

Mitteis, H. (1944), *Die Deutsche Königswahl. Ihre Rechtsgrundlagen bis zur Goldenen Bulle*, 2nd edn, Vienna.

Mitteis, H. (1975), *The state in the high middle ages*, translated by H. F. Orton, Amsterdam.

Mitterauer, M. (1963), *Karolingische Markgrafen im Südosten*, Vienna.

Moehs, T.E. (1972), *Gregorius V, 996–999*, Stuttgart.

Mordek, H., ed. (1983), *Aus Kirche und Reich. Festschrift für Friedrich Kempf zu seinem fünfundsiebzigsten Geburtstag und fünfzigjährigen Doktorjubiläum*, Sigmaringen.

Mühlbacher, E. (1896), *Deutsche Geschichte unter den Karolingern*, Stuttgart.

Müller, J. (1989), *Untersuchungen zur Collectio duodecim partium*, Ebelsbach.

Müller-Mertens, E. (1963), *Karl der Große, Ludwig der Fromme und die Freien*, Berlin [E.].

Müller-Mertens, E. (1970), *Regnum Teutonicum*, Berlin [E.].

Müller-Mertens, E. (1980), *Die Reichsstruktur im Spiegel der Herrschaftspraxis Ottos des Großen*, Berlin [E.].

Müller-Mertens, E., ed. (1985), *Feudalismus. Entstehung und Wesen*, Berlin [E.].

Naumann, H. (1964), "Rätsel des letzten Aufstandes gegen Otto I (953–954)", in Zimmermann 1976, 70–136.

Nelson, J. L. (1986), *Politics and ritual in the early middle ages*, London.

Njeussychin, A. J. (1961), *Die Entstehung der abhängigen Bauernschaft als Klasse der frühfeudalen Gesellschaft in Westeuropa vom 6–8 Jahrhundert*, Berlin [E.].

Noble, T. F. X. (1984), *The Republic of St Peter. The Birth of the Papal State, 680–825*, Philadelphia.

Nonn, U. (1983), *Pagus und Comitatus in Niederlothringen*, Bonn.

Ohnsorge, W. (1958), *Abendland und Byzanz*, Darmstadt.

Ohnsorge, W. (1966), *Konstantinopel und der Okzident*, Darmstadt.

Ornamenta (1985a, b and c), *Ornamenta Ecclesiae*, 3 vols, Cologne.

Parisse, M. (1976), *La noblesse lorraine. XIe–XIIIe siècles*, 2 vols, Paris.

Parisse, M. (1978), "Les chanoinesses dans l'Empire germanique (IXe–XIe siècles)", *Francia* 6, 107–26.

Parisse, M. (1984), "L'évêque impérial dans son diocèse. L'exemple Lorrain aux Xe et XIe siècles", in Fenske, Rösener and Zotz 1984, 179–93.

Partner, P. (1973), *The lands of St Peter*, London.

Pauler, R. (1982), *Das Regnum Italiae in ottonischer Zeit. Markgrafen, Grafen und Bischöfe als politische Kräfte*, Tübingen.

Penndorf, U. (1974), *Das Problem der "Reichseinheitsidee" nach der Teilung von Verdun (843)*, Munich.

Petersohn, J. (1979), *Der südliche Ostseeraum im kirchlich-politischen Kräftespiel des Reichs, Polens und Dänemarks vom 10 bis 13 Jahrhundert*, Cologne.

Pitz, E. (1979), *Wirtschafts- und Sozialgeschichte Deutschlands im Mittelalter*, Wiesbaden.

Prinz, F. (1970), *Klerus und Krieg im frühen Mittelalter*, Stuttgart.

Prinz, F, ed. (1976), *Mönchtum und Gesellschaft im Frühmittelalter*, Darmstadt.

Prinz, F. (1985), *Grundlagen und Anfänge. Deutschland bis 1056*, Munich.

Prinz, F. (1988), "Kaiser Heinrich III. Seine widersprüchliche Beurteilung und deren Gründe", *HZ* 246, 529–48.

Reindel, K. (1953), *Die bayerischen Liutpoldinger 893–989*, Munich.

Reindel, K. (1954), "Herzog Arnulf und das Regnum Bavariae", *ZBLG* 17, 187–252.

Reindel, K. (1981), "Die Bajuwaren. Quellen, Hypothesen, Tatsachen", *DA* 37, 451–73.

Reuling, U. (1979), *Die Kur in Deutschland und Frankreich*, Göttingen.

Reuter, T., ed. (1978), *The medieval nobility*, Amsterdam.

Reuter, T. (1981), "A new history of medieval Germany", *History* 61, 440–4.

Reuter, T. (1982), "The 'imperial church system' of the Ottonian and Salian rulers: a reconsideration", *JEcclH* 32, 347–74.

Reuter, T. (1985), "Plunder and tribute in the Carolingian Empire", *TRHS* 5th series 35, 75–94.

Reuter, T. (1990), "The end of Carolingian military expansion", in Godman and Collins 1990, 391–405.

Reuter, T. (1991), "Unruhestiftung, Fehde, Rebellion, Widerstand: Gewalt und Frieden in der Politik der Salierzeit", in Weinfurter 1991c.

Rexroth, K. H. (1978), "Volkssprache und werdendes Volksbewußtsein im ostfränkischen Reich", in Beumann and Schröder 1978, 275–315.

Reynolds, S. (1984), *Kingdoms and communities in Western Europe, 900–1300*, London.

Rhein und Maas (1972a and b), *Rhein und Maas. Kunst und Kultur 800–1400*. 2 vols, Cologne.

Riché, P. (1989), *Les écoles et l'enseignement dans le haut moyen âge*, Paris.

Richter, H., ed. (1975), *Cluny. Beiträge zu Gestalt und Wirkung der cluniazensischen Reform*, Darmstadt.

Rösener, W. (1980), "Strukturformen der älteren Agrarverfassung im sächsischen Raum", *NJLG* 52, 107–43.

Rösener, W. (1985), *Bauern im Mittelalter*, Munich.

Rösener, W. ed. (1989), *Strukturen der Grundherrschaft im frühen Mittelalter*, Göttingen.

Santifaller, L. (1964), *Zur Geschichte des ottonisch-salischen Reichskirchensystems*, 2nd edn, Vienna.

Schalles-Fischer, M. (1969), *Pfalz und Fiskus Frankfurt*, Göttingen.

Scherff, B. (1985), *Studien zum Heer der Ottonen und der ersten Salier 919–1056)*, Ph.D. thesis, Bonn.

Schieffer, R. (1976), *Die Entstehung von Domkapiteln in Deutschland*, Bonn.

Schieffer, R. (1989), "Der ottonische Reichsepiskopat zwischen Königtum und Adel", *FmaSt* 23, 291–300.

Schieffer, T. (1951), "Heinrich II und Konrad II. Die Umprägung des Geschichtsbildes durch die Kirchenreform des 11 Jh.", *DA* 8, 384–437.

Schieffer, T. (1957), "Die Krise des karolingischen Imperiums", in Engel and Klinkenberg 1957, 1–15.

Schieffer, T., ed. (1976), *Handbuch der europäischen Geschichte, 1,* Stuttgart.

Schlesinger, W. (1961), *Mitteldeutsche Beiträge zur deutschen Verfassungsgeschichte des Mittelalters,* Göttingen.

Schlesinger, W. (1962), *Kirchengeschichte Sachsens im Mittelalter 1,* Cologne.

Schlesinger, W. (1963a and b), *Beiträge zur deutschen Verfassungsgeschichte des Mittelalters,* 2 vols, Göttingen.

Schlesinger, W., ed. (1975), *Althessen im Frankenreich,* Sigmaringen.

Schlesinger, W. (1987), *Ausgewählte Aufsätze von Walter Schlesinger 1965–1979,* ed. H. Patze and F. Schwind, *VuF* 34, Sigmaringen.

Schmale, F.-J. (1979), "Die Absetzung Gregors VI in Sutri und die synodale Tradition", *AHC* 11, 55–103.

Schmid, K. (1964), "Die Thronfolge Ottos des Großen", *ZRGGA* 81, 80–163.

Schmid, K. (1983), *Gebetsgedanken und adliges Selbstverständnis im Mittelalter,* Sigmaringen.

Schmid, K., ed. (1985a), *Reich und Kirche vor dem Investiturstreit. Gerd Tellenbach zum achtzigsten Geburtstag,* Sigmaringen.

Schmid, K. (1985b), "Das Problem der 'Unteilbarkeit des Reiches'", in Schmid 1985a, 1–15.

Schmid, P. (1976), *Regensburg, Stadt der Könige und Herzöge im Mittelalter,* Kallmünz.

Schmidt, H. (1977), "Über Christianisierung und gesellschaftliches Verhalten in Sachsen und Friesland", *NJLG* 49, 1–44.

Schmidt, P.G. (1983), "Heinrich III – Das Bild des Herrschers in der Literatur seiner Zeit", *DA* 39, 582–590.

Schmidt, R. (1961), "Königsumritt und Huldigung in ottonisch-salischer Zeit", *VuF* 6, 97–233.

Schmitt, J. (1977), *Untersuchungen zu den liberi homines der Karolingerzeit,* Frankfurt.

Schmitt, U. (1974), *Villa Regalis Ulm und Kloster Reichenau,* Göttingen.

Schmitz, H. (1974), *Pfalz und Fiskus Ingelheim,* Marburg.

Schneider, F., ed. (1941), *Universalstaat oder Nationalstaat,* Innsbruck.

Schneider, R. (1964), *Brüdergemeine und Schwurfreundschaft,* Lübeck.

Schneidmüller, B. (1979), "Französische Lothringenpolitik im 10 Jahrhundert", *JwLG* 5, 1–31.

Schnith, K. (1962), "Recht und Friede. Zum Königsgedanken im Umkreis Heinrichs III", *HJb* 81, 22–57.

Schorn-Schütte, L. (1984), *Karl Lamprecht*. Göttingen.

Schramm, P. E. (1954, 1955, 1956), *Herrschaftszeichen und Staatssymbolik*, Stuttgart.

Schramm, P. E. (1957, 1929), *Kaiser, Rom und Renovatio*, 2 vols, vol. 1 2nd edn, London.

Schramm, P. E. (1968a, 1968b, 1969, 1970, 1971), *Kaiser, Könige und Päpste*, 4 vols in 5, Stuttgart.

Schramm, P.E. and Mütherich, F. (1981), *Denkmale der deutschen Könige und Kaiser, 1*, Munich.

Schramm, P. E. (1983), *Die deutschen Kaiser und Könige in Bildern ihrer Zeit: 751–1190*, revised edition by F. Mütherich *et al.*, Munich.

Schreiner, K. (1989), "Wissenschaft von der Geschichte des Mittelalters im geteilten Deutschland", in *Deutsche Geschichtswissenschaft nach dem Zweiten Weltkrieg (1945–1965)*, ed. E. Schulin, Munich.

Schröder, W. (1978), "Zum Verhältnis von Lateinisch und Deutsch um das Jahr 1000", in Beumann and Schröder 1978, 425–38

Schulz, K. (1982), "Zensualität und Stadtentwicklung im 11/12 Jahrhundert", in Diestelkamp 1982, 73–93.

Schulze, H. K. (1973), *Die Grafschaftsverfassung der Karolingerzeit in den Gebieten östlich des Rheins*, Berlin.

Schulze, H.K. (1974), "Rodungsfreiheit und Königsfreiheit", *HZ* 219, 529–50.

Schulze, H.K. (1978), "Reichsaristokratie, Stammesadel und fränkische Freiheit", *HZ* 227, 353–73.

Schulze, H. K. (1985), "Grundprobleme der Grafschaftsverfassung", *ZWLG* 44, 265–82.

Schulze, H. K. (1987), *Vom Reich der Franken zum Land der Deutschen*, Berlin.

Schwind, F. (1977), "Beobachtungen zur inneren Struktur des Dorfes in karolingischer Zeit", in: Jankuhn, Schützeichel and Schwind 1977, 444–93.

Schwineköper, B. (1977), *Königtum und Städte bis zum Ende des Investiturstreits*, Sigmaringen.

Semmler, J. (1970), "Corvey und Herford in der benediktinischen Reformbewegung des 9 Jahrhunderts", *FmaSt* 4, 289–319).

Semmler, J. (1980), "Mönche und Kanoniker im Frankenreich Pippins III und Karls des Großen", in Kloster und Stift 1980, 78–111.

Germany

Semmler, J. (1982), "Mission und Pfarrorganisation in den rheinischen, mosel- und maasländischen Bistümern 5–10 Jahrhundert", *Settimane* 28, 813–88.

Semmler, J. (1983), "Zehntgebot und Pfarrtermination in karolingischer Zeit", in Mordek 1983, 33–44.

Sonderegger, S. (1978), "Tendenzen zu einen überregional geschriebenen Althochdeutsch", in Beumann and Schröder 1978, 229–73.

Sós, A. C. (1974) *Die slawische Bevölkerung Westungarns im 9 Jahrhundert*, Munich.

Sprandel, R. (1978), "Gerichtsorganisation und Sozialstruktur Mainfrankens im früheren Mittelalter", *JFLF* 38, 7–38.

Staab, F. (1975), *Untersuchungen zur Gesellschaft am Mittelrhein in der Karolingerzeit*, Wiesbaden.

Staab, F. (1980), "A reconsideration of the ancestry of modern political liberty: the problem of the so-called 'King's Freemen' (Königsfreie)", *Viator* 11, 51–69.

Staats, R. (1976), *Theologie der Reichskrone. Ottonische "Renovatio Imperii" im Spiegel einer Insignie*, Vienna.

Stengel, E. E. (1965), *Abhandlungen und Untersuchungen zur Geschichte des Kaisergedankens im Mittelalter*, Cologne.

Stingl, H. (1974), *Die Entstehung der deutschen Stammesherzogtümer am Anfang des 10 Jahrhunderts*, Aalen.

Störmer, W. (1973), *Früher Adel*, 2 vols, Stuttgart.

Strasser, I. (1984), *Diutisk – deutsch. Neue Überlegungen zur Entstehung der Sprachbezeichnung*, Vienna.

Streich, G. (1984), *Burg und Kirche während des deutschen Mittelalters*, Sigmaringen.

Struve, T. (1988), "Kaisertum und Romgedanke in salischer Zeit", *DA* 44 424–54.

Tellenbach, G. (1939), *Königtum und Stämme in der Werdezeit des Deutschen Reiches*, Weimar.

Tellenbach, G. (1979), "Die geistigen und politischen Grundlagen der karolingischen Thronfolge", *FmaSt* 13, 184–302.

Tellenbach, G. (1988), *Die westliche Kirche vom 10. bis zum frühen 12. Jahrhundert*, Göttingen; English translation by T. Reuter to appear Cambridge 1991.

Thomas, H. (1976), "Regnum Teutonicorum = Diutiskono Richi? Bemerkungen zur Doppelwahl des Jahres 919", *RhVjbll* 40, 17–45.

Thomas, H. (1988), "Der Ursprung des Wortes theodiscus", *HZ* 247, 295–331.

Ullmann, W. (1970) *The growth of papal government in the middle ages.* 3rd edn, London.

Vajay, S. de (1968), *Der Eintritt des ungarischen Stämmebundes in die europäische Geschichte (862–933)*, Mainz.

Verhulst, A. (1966), "La genèse du régime domainal classique en France au haut moyen âge", *Settimane* 13, 134–60.

Verhulst, A., ed. (1985), *Le grand domain aux époques mérovingiennes et carolingiennes*, Ghent.

Vlasto, A. (1970), *The entry of the Slavs into Christendom*, Cambridge.

Vollrath, H. (1974), "Kaisertum und Patriziat in den Anfängen des Investiturstreits", *ZKG* 85, 11–44.

Waitz, G. (1880, 1882, 1883, 1885, 1893, 1896, 1876, 1878) *Deutsche Verfassungsgeschichte*, 8 vols, vols 1–3 3rd edn, vols 4–6 2nd edn, Berlin.

Wallace-Hadrill, J. M. (1970), *Early Germanic Kingship in England and on the Continent*, Oxford.

Wallace-Hadrill, J. M. (1975), *Early medieval history*, Oxford.

Wallace-Hadrill, J. M. (1983), *The Frankish Church*, Oxford.

Warnke, C. (1980), "Ursachen und Voraussetzungen der Schenkung Polens an den Heiligen Petrus", in Grothusen and Zernack 1980, 127–77.

Wattenbach, W., Holtzmann, R. and Schmale, F.-J. (1967a, 1967b, 1971), *Deutsche Geschichtsquellen im Mittelalter. Die Zeit der Sachsen und Salier*, Darmstadt.

Wattenbach, W., Levison, W. and Löwe, H. (1952–90), *Deutsche Geschichtsquellen im Mittelalter. Vorzeit und Karolinger*, Weimar.

Weber, H. (1962), *Die Reichsversammlungen im ostfränkischen Reich, 840–918*, Diss, Würzburg.

Wehlt, H. P. (1970), *Reichsabtei und König, dargestellt am Beispiel der Abtei Lorsch mit Ausblicken auf Hersfeld, Stablo und Fulda*, Göttingen.

Weinfurter, S. (1986), "Die Zentralisierung der Herrschaftsgewalt im Reich durch Kaiser Heinrich II", *HJb* 106, 241–97.

Weinfurter, S., ed. (1991a, 1991b, 1991c), *Die Salier und das Reich*, 3 vols, Sigmaringen.

Wenskus, R. (1956), *Studien zum historisch-politischen Gedankenwelt Bruns von Querfurt*, Münster.

Wenskus, R. (1986), *Ausgewählte Aufsätze zum frühen und preußischem Mittelalter*, ed. H. Patze, Sigmaringen.

Wenskus, R., Jankuhn, H. and Grinda, K., eds (1975), *Wort und Begriff Bauer*, Göttingen.

Germany in the early middle ages

Werner, K. F. (1967), *Das NS-Geschichtsbild und die deutsche Geschichtswissenschaft*, Stuttgart.

Werner, K. F. (1968), "Heeresorganisation und Kriegsführung im deutschen Königreich des 10 und 11 Jh.", *Settimane* 15, 799–884.

Werner, K. F. (1984), *Vom Frankenreich zur Entfaltung Deutschlands und Frankreichs*, Sigmaringen.

Wickham, C. (1981), *Early medieval Italy 400–1000*, London.

Wilke, S. (1970), *Das Goslarer Reichsgebiet und seine Beziehungen zu den territorialen Nachbargewalten*, Göttingen.

Willmes, P. (1976), *Der Herrscher-"Adventus" im Kloster des Frühmittelalters*, Munich.

Wolfram, H., ed. (1967, 1973, 1988), *Intitulatio*. 3 vols, Vienna.

Wolfram, H. (1987), *Die Geburt Mitteleuropas. Geschichte Österreichs vor seiner Entstehung 378–907*, Vienna.

Wolfram, H. and Schwarcz, A., eds (1985), *Die Bayern und ihre Nachbarn*, Vienna.

Wolfram, H., ed. (1979), *Conversio Bagoariorum et Carntanorum*, Vienna.

Wollasch, J. (1973), *Mönchtum des Mittelalters zwischen Kirche und Welt*, Munich.

Wollasch, J. (1977), "Neue Methoden zur Erforschung des Mönchtums im Mittelalter", *HZ* 225, 529–71.

Wolter, H. (1988), *Die Synoden im Reichsgebiet und im Reichsitalien von 916 bis 1056*, Paderborn.

Zielinski, H. (1984), *Der Reichsepiskopat in spätottonischer und salischer Zeit (1002–1125)*, 1, Stuttgart.

Zimmermann, H. (1968), *Papstabsetzungen des Mittelalters*, Graz.

Zimmermann, H., ed. (1976), *Otto der Große*, Darmstadt.

Zimmermann, H. (1986), *Im Bann des Mittelalters*, Sigmaringen.

Zotz, T. (1974), *Der Breisgau und das alemannische Herzogtum*, Sigmaringen.

Zotz, T. (1977), "Adel, Oberschicht, Freie", *ZGO* 125, 3–20.

Zotz, T. (1982), "Pallium et alia quaedam archiepiscopatus insignia", in Maurer and Patze 1982, 155–75.

Zotz, T., ed. (1983ff.), *Die deutschen Königspfalzen. Repertorium der Pfalzen, Königshöfe und üblichen Aufenthaltsorte der Könige im deutschen Reich des Mittelalters*, Göttingen.

Chronological table

714		Charles Martel ruler of Francia.
716		Plan for erection of bishoprics in Bavaria.
722		Boniface ordained bishop by Pope Gregory II.
735		Frankish conquest of Frisia.
739		Boniface establishes bishoprics in Bavaria.
741		Charles Martel d.; succeeded by Pippin and Carloman.
(or 742)		Bishoprics established in Erfurt, Büraburg, Würzburg.
742 (or 743)		Council of east Frankish bishops.
743		Frankish campaign against Bavaria.
746		Alemans defeated at Cannstatt; Frankish conquest of Alemannia.
749		Pope Zachary sanctions Frankish change of dynasty.
751	autumn	Pippin III elected and anointed king of Franks.
754	January	Pope Stephen II comes to Francia.
	June	Boniface martyred in Frisia.
755 (or 754?)		Franks invade Italy.
756		Franks again invade Italy.
757		Tassilo of Bavaria swears fidelity to Pippin at Compiègne.
768		Pippin III d.; Charles and Carloman succeed him.
771		Carloman d.; Charles sole ruler in Francia.

772		First campaign of Charles against Saxons.
774		Charles becomes king of Lombardy.
776–785		Conquest of Saxony.
788		Tassilo of Bavaria deposed; Charles takes over in Bavaria.
789		Campaign against Slavs of north-east.
791		Campaign against Avars.
794		Synod of Frankfurt.
795		Destruction of Avar kingdom, capture of their treasure.
800	Dec. 25	Charles crowned emperor by Leo III.
803 (?)		Final peace with Saxons.
806		Charles divides kingdom among sons.
814	Jan. 28	Death of Charles; Louis the Pious succeeds. Lothar sub-king in Bavaria.
817		Ordinatio Imperii. Louis the German nominally sub-king in Bavaria.
819–23		Uprising of Liudewit on Carinthian border.
826		Louis begins rule in Bavaria.
827		Bulgars raid south-east.
828		Northern part of Friuli comes to Bavaria.
829		New division of Frankish empire.
833	October	Deposition of Louis the Pious.
834–5		Restoration of Louis the Pious.
838		Louis the Pious divides empire between Lothar and Charles, leaving Louis the German with Bavaria only
840	June 20	Louis the Pious d.
842	April	Louis and Charles divide up Frankish empire north of Alps.
843	August	Treaty of Verdun; equal division of Frankish empire between three sons of Louis the Pious.
844		Kings meet at Thionville.
845		Vikings sack Hamburg.
847		Kings meet at Meerssen.
	October	Council at Mainz.
848		Council at Mainz.
851		Kings meet at Meerssen.
852		Council at Mainz.

855	Sep. 29	Lothar I d.; kingdom divided between three sons.
856		Carloman becomes margrave of eastern March.
858	August	Louis invades west Francia.
859	January	Charles recovers rule in west Francia.
860	June	Kings meet at Coblenz.
861		Purge of east Frankish aristocracy.
862		Revolt of Carloman against Louis the German.
866		Revolt of Louis the Younger against Louis the German.
867		Mission of Ermanrich of Ellwangen to Bulgarians.
868	May	Council at Worms.
869	Aug. 8	Lothar II d.
	autumn	Charles the Bald claims Lotharingia, crowned at Metz.
870	August	Treaty of Meerssen divides Lotharingia between Charles the Bald and Louis the German
	autumn	Synod of Regensburg condemns Methodius. Rastiz deposed as ruler of Moravia; succeeded by Zwentibald.
872		Peace treaty with Danes.
873		Division of east Frankish kingdom confirmed.
874		Peace treaty with Moravians.
875	Aug. 12	Louis II of Italy d.; succeeded by Charles the Bald.
876	Aug. 28	Louis the German d.
	Oct. 8	Charles the Bald defeated at Andernach by Louis the Younger.
		Eastern Lotharingia divided between Louis and Charles III.
877	Oct. 6	Charles the Bald d.
879		Charles III king in Italy.
		Boso becomes king in Provence.
880		Carloman d., succeeded by Louis the Younger.
		Louis the Younger invades west Francia; treaty of Ribemont concedes him

		western Lotharingia.
881		Viking Great Army established at Asselt.
882	Jan. 20	Louis the Younger d.
	April	Charles III king in east Francia
	summer	Unsuccessful siege of Vikings at Asselt.
884		Dispute over Pannonian margravate.
	October	Charles III king in west Francia.
886	summer	Siege of Paris.
887	May	Liutward of Vercelli deposed at Kirchheim.
	summer	Charles III adopts Louis of Provence, Boso's son.
	November	Charles III deserted by followers; Arnulf becomes king in east Francia.
888	Jan. 13	Charles III d.
	summer	Council of Mainz.
		Arnulf recognizes Odo, Rudolf, Berengar as kings.
890		Aleman revolt crushed.
		Louis of Provence crowned with Arnulf's approval.
891	November	Vikings defeated at battle of River Dyle.
894		Arnulf's first Italian expedition.
895	May	Council of Tribur.
		Zwentibald becomes king in Lotharingia.
896		Arnulf's second Italian expedition.
	February	Arnulf crowned emperor.
898		Odo d.; Charles the Simple king in west Francia.
899	Dec. 8	Arnulf d.; Louis the Child succeeds.
900	Aug. 16	Zwentibald d.
906		Feud between Babenberger and Conradines; Adalbert executed.
907		Bavarians defeated by Magyars at Preßburg; Arnulf succeeds Liutpold.
908		Franks and Thuringians defeated by Magyars.
910		Defeat of east Frankish forces by Magyars.
911	November	Conrad of Franconia elected king in east Francia.

		Lotharingians recognize Charles the Simple.
913		Magyars defeated by Suabians and Bavarians.
915		Battle of Wahlwies; Erchanger elected *dux* by Suabians.
		Henry of Saxony defeats Eberhard of Franconia.
916	September	Synod of Hohenaltheim.
917	January	Execution of Suabian magnates Berthold and Erchanger;
		Burchard becomes *dux* in Suabia.
918	Dec. 23	Conrad I d.
919		Henry of Saxony elected king at Fritzlar.
		Arnulf of Bavaria elected king.
		Burchard of Suabia submits to Henry.
920		Gilbert becomes king (?) of Lotharingia.
921		Arnulf of Bavaria submits to Henry.
		Meeting of Henry and Charles the Simple at Bonn.
922		Council at Coblenz.
923		Meeting of Henry and Rudolf of west Francia at Coblenz.
		Henry visits Lotharingia.
924		Magyars invade Saxony.
925		Henry acknowledged in Lotharingia.
926		Magyars attack; nine years' truce.
	November	Rudolf II acknowledges Henry's overlordship.
		Henry appoints Hermann duke of Suabia.
928–9		Campaigns against Hevelli, Daleminzi, Bohemians.
930		Henry I visits Franconia, Suabia, Bavaria.
		Otto I m. Edith, sister of Æthelstan of Wessex.
		Designation of Otto I as successor.
933	March 14	Henry I defeats Magyars at Riade.
935		Meeting of Henry, Rudolf of west Francia, Rudolf of Burgundy.
		Eberhard acknowledged Arnulf's successor by Bavarians.
936		Otto acknowledged successor at Erfurt.
	July 7	Henry I d.

	Aug. 8	Otto I crowned at Aachen.
		Bohemians rebel.
937	July 14	Arnulf of Bavaria d.
		Saxon marches reorganized; unrest in Saxony.
		Foundation of St Maurice, Magdeburg.
938		Bavarian revolt suppressed.
		Magyar invasion.
		Revolt of Eberhard and Thankmar.
939		Revolt of Eberhard, Gilbert and Henry.
		Otto and supporters win battles at Birten, Andernach.
		Abodrites rebel.
941		Final revolt of Henry and east Saxons.
944		Conrad duke of Lotharingia.
947	November	Berthold of Bavaria d.; Otto's brother Henry succeeds him.
948	June	Council at Ingelheim; Danish and Slav bishoprics founded.
949	December	Hermann of Suabia d.; Otto's son Liudolf succeeds him.
950		Bohemians restored to tributary status.
951	October	Otto I crowned king of Italy.
952	August	Berengar II under-king in Italy.
953	Easter	Beginning of rebellion of Liudolf and Conrad.
	August	Brun becomes archbishop of Cologne.
954	February	Magyar invasion.
		Otto besieges Regensburg.
	June	Conrad and Frederick of Mainz submit at Langenzenn.
	autumn	Liudolf submits.
955	Aug. 10	Otto I defeats Magyars at Lechfeld (Augsburg).
	Oct. 16	Otto I defeats Slavs at Recknitz.
		First proposals to Pope Agapetus II for an archbishopric at Magdeburg.
957		Campaign against Elbe Slavs.
959		Campaign against Elbe Slavs.
961	August	Otto II elected king.
	autumn	Otto I's second Italian expedition.

962	Feb. 2	Otto I crowned emperor by Pope John XII.
	Feb. 12	John XII gives approval to Magdeburg archbishopric.
	Feb. 13	Otto I confirms privileges of Roman church.
963	November	Otto I deposes John XII, has Leo VIII elected.
964	spring	Romans attempt to elect Benedict V on John's death.
965	January	Otto returns to Germany.
	Oct. 11	Brun d.
966	autumn	Otto I's third Italian expedition.
967	December	Otto II crowned emperor.
	April	Synod of Ravenna under Pope John XIII confirms foundation of Magdeburg.
968	spring	Expedition to southern Italy.
972	April	Otto II m. Theophanu.
	August	Otto I and Otto II return to Germany.
973	March	Assembly at Quedlinburg.
	May 7	Otto I d.
974		First revolt of Henry of Bavaria.
976		Duchy of Carinthia and march of Austria established.
977		Second revolt of Henry of Bavaria.
978		War between Otto II and Lothar.
980		Meeting of Otto II and Lothar at Margut. Otto II's first Italian expedition.
981		Bishopric of Merseburg merged with Magdeburg. Otto campaigns in southern Italy.
982	July 13	Otto II's army defeated by Muslims at Cap Colonne.
983	May	Assembly at Verona elects Otto III king.
	June	Uprising of Liutizi, Abodrites, Danes against Saxons.
	Dec 7	Otto II d.
	Dec 24	Otto III crowned king at Aachen.
984	Easter	Henry of Bavaria claims kingship.
	June	Henry forced to hand over Otto III to Theophanu and Adelheid.
986	Easter	General recognition of Otto III at Quedlinburg.
987	May	Louis V of west Francia d.; Hugo

		Capet succeeds.
990		Campaign against Bohemia.
991	June 15	Theophanu d.; Adelheid regent.
992		Brandenburg recaptured.
994	Sep.	Otto III comes of age.
996		Otto III's first Italian expedition.
	May	Otto III's cousin Brun elected pope as Gregory V.
	May 21	Otto III crowned emperor.
	autumn	Return to Germany.
997		Adalbert of Prague martyred by Prussians.
	Christmas	Otto III's second Italian expedition.
999	April 9	Gerbert becomes pope as Silvester II.
1000	February	Otto III's pilgrimage to Gnesen; Polish church province established.
	June	Otto III returns to Italy.
1001		Uprisings in Rome and northern Italy; unrest in Saxony.
	August	Stephen I of Hungary crowned king; Hungarian church province established.
1002	Jan. 24	Otto III d.
	June 7	Henry II crowned at Mainz.
1003		Boleslav Chrobry occupies Bohemia; Henry II allies with Liutizi against Boleslav.
1004		Bishopric of Merseburg restored.
	April	Henry II's first Italian expedition.
	May 14	Henry II crowned king of Italy.
1005	July	Council at Dortmund.
		Campaign against Boleslav Chrobry.
1006		Henry II visits Burgundy; Basle restored to Reich.
1007		Campaigns against Boleslav Chrobry, Baldwin of Flanders.
	November	Council at Frankfurt; bishopric of Bamberg established.
1008		Rebellion in Lotharingia.
1009		Brun of Querfurt martyred by Prussians. Henry of Bavaria deposed.
1010		Campaign against Boleslav Chrobry.
1011		Campaign in Lotharingia.
1012		Campaign against Boleslav Chrobry.

1013	May	Peace of Merseburg with Boleslav Chrobry.
	autumn	Henry II's second Italian expedition.
1014	Feb. 14	Henry II crowned emperor.
1015		End of Lotharingian rebellion.
		Campaign against Boleslav.
1016		Campaign against Otto-William of Burgundy.
		Rudolf III acknowledges Henry II as successor.
1017		Campaign against Boleslav.
1018		Peace of Bautzen with Boleslav Chrobry.
		Rudolf III again acknowledges Henry II's succession.
1020		Benedict VIII visits Germany.
		Saxon uprising.
1021	November	Henry II's third Italian expedition.
1022	March–July	Campaign in southern Italy.
	Aug. 1	Council at Pavia.
1023	August	Council at Seligenstadt.
1024	July 13	Henry II d.
	September	Conrad II elected and crowned.
1025		Lotharingians submit to Conrad.
1026		Conrad's first Italian expedition.
1027	March 26	Conrad II crowned emperor.
	September	Council at Frankfurt.
1028	April	Henry III crowned king at Aachen.
1030		Campaign against Hungary.
		Ernest II d.
1031		Peace with Hungary.
1032		Campaigns against Bohemia and Poland.
		Miesco II forced to resign kingship.
1033	January	Rudolf III of Burgundy d.; Conrad becomes king of Burgundy.
		Campaign against Odo of Champagne.
1034		Miesco II of Poland d.
1035		Campaign against Liutizi.
1036		Campaign against Liutizi.
	May	Council at Tribur.
1037	January	Conrad's second Italian expedition.
		Odo of Champagne d.
1038		Henry III elected king of Burgundy.
1039	June 4	Conrad II d.

1040		Campaign against Bohemia.
1041		Campaign against Bohemia.
1042		Henry III visits Burgundy.
		Campaign against Hungary
1043		Campaign against Hungary.
1044		Hungarians defeated at Menfö.
		Revolt of Godfrey of Lotharingia.
1045	January	Henry III visits Burgundy.
		Campaign against Liutizi.
1046	autumn	Henry III's first Italian expedition.
	Dec. 20	Synod of Sutri: Pope Gregory VI deposed.
	Dec. 25	Henry III crowned emperor.
1049		Leo IX elected pope.
		Synod of Rheims under Leo IX.
1050		Synod of Mainz under Leo IX.
1052		Henry III visits Burgundy.
1053		Henry IV elected king.
		Papal army defeated at Civitate by Normans.
1054		Victor II elected pope.
1055		Henry III's second Italian expedition.
		Revolt of Bavarian magnates.
1056		Liutizi defeat Saxon army.
	Oct. 5	Henry III d.

Maps and genealogical tables

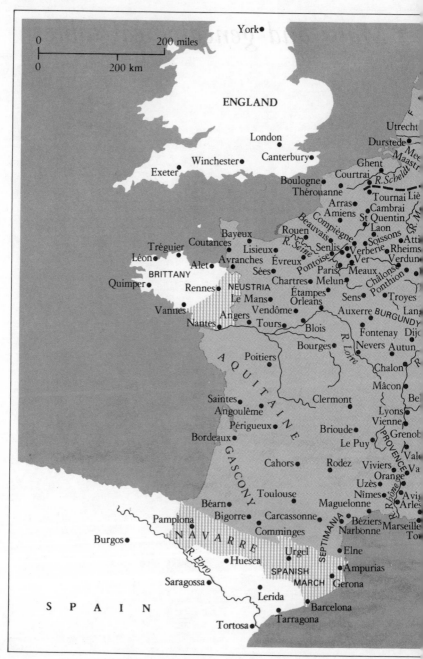

Map 1.   The Frankish Empire, 768–840

	The core-lands of Francia in 768
	The accquisitions of Charles the Great
	The marches
– – –	The 'linguistic frontier' between Romance and Germanic

Hamburg

Bremen
Verden
SAXONY
Osnabrück
WESTFALIA
Hildesheim
OSTFALIA
Magdeburg
egen Münster
Paderborn Corvey Halberstadt
R. Elbe
THURINGIA
Fritzlar
Cologne Erfurt
en Andernach
Frankfurt
F R A N C O N I A
R. Main
Mainz
rier
tz Worms Würzburg
Speyer Eichstätt Regensburg
ALSACE
Strasbourg Ingolstadt Passau
Freising
R. Rhine
Augsburg R. Danube
ALEMANNIA
Reichenau Salzburg
Basle Kempten EASTERN MARCH OF BAVARIA
ançon Constance B A V A R I A
Zurich CARINTHIA
ausanne RAETIA Chur PANNONIA

MORAVIA

eva
L O M B A R D Y Friuli
Novara Ivrea Milan Verona Padua
ntaise Cremona Venice
Turin Vercelli Mantua
Pavia R. Po
Bobbio
Genoa Bologna Ravenna

gne
PATRIMONY
Pisa R. Arno OF
Nice Perugia DUCHY OF SPOLETO
Fréjus Chiusi
ST PETER Spoleto

CORSICA DUCHY
OF
Ajaccio Rome BENEVENTO
Monte Cassino
Teano Benevento
Capua
Naples Salerno

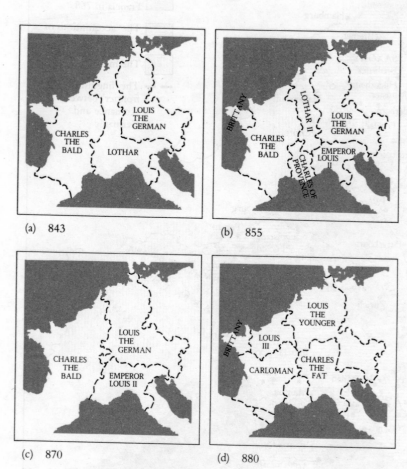

(a) 843

(b) 855

(c) 870

(d) 880

Map 2. The Frankish kingdoms, 843–80

Map 3. The east Frankish kingdom and its neighbours in the early tenth century

Map 4. The east Frankish/German kingdom: territorial divisions

Map 5. Ottonian palaces

Map 6.   The German church

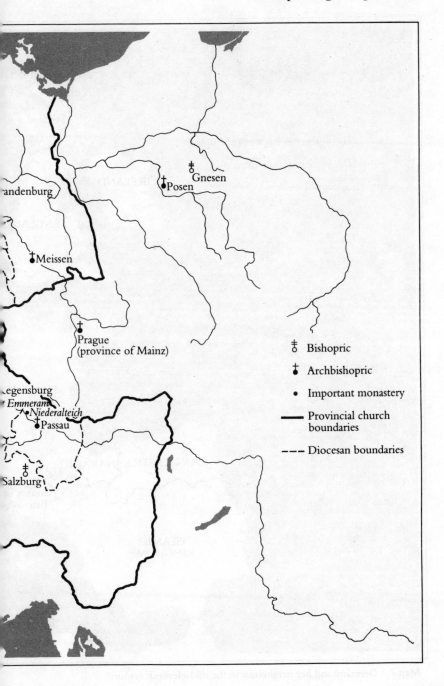

andenburg

†Meissen

†Prague
(province of Mainz)

egensburg
Emmeram
Niederalteich
†Passau

Salzburg

Gnesen

†Posen

Bishopric

Archbishopric

• Important monastery

Provincial church
boundaries

Diocesan boundaries

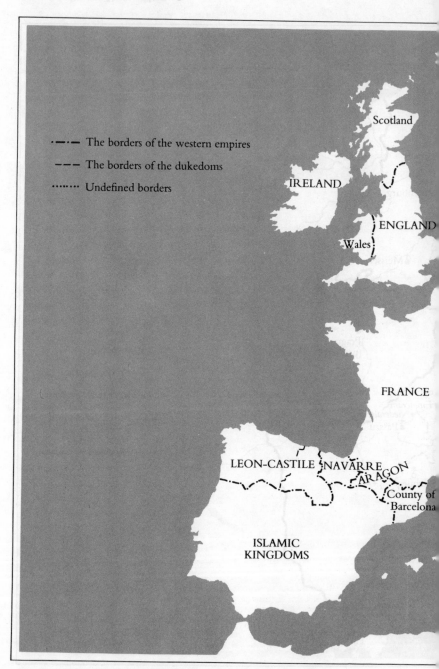

Map 7.   Germany and her neighbours in the mid–eleventh century

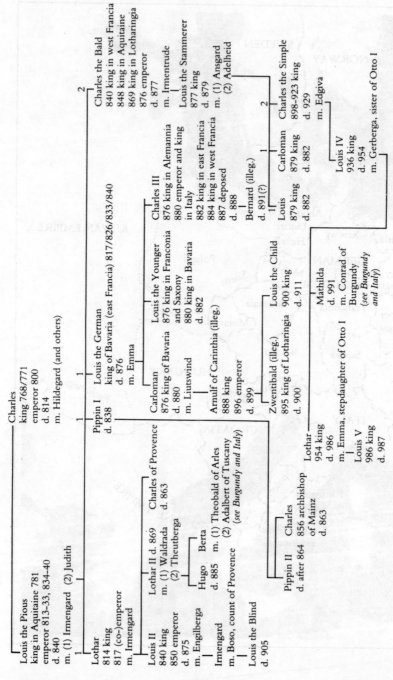

Table 1. The Carolingians (in this and the other tables only essential names are given)

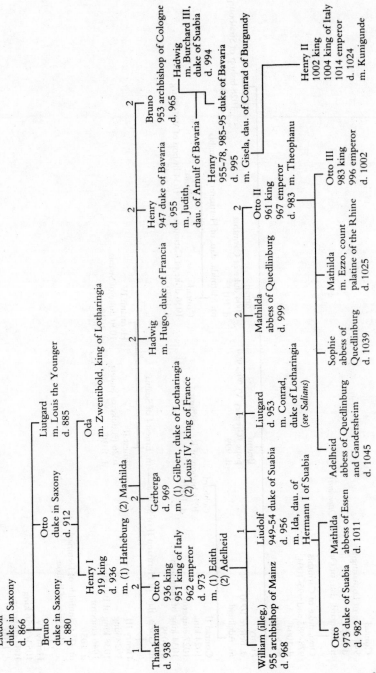

Table 2. The Ottonians

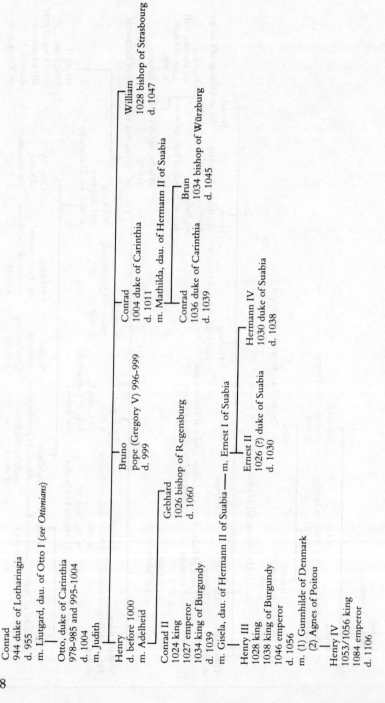

Table 3. The Salians

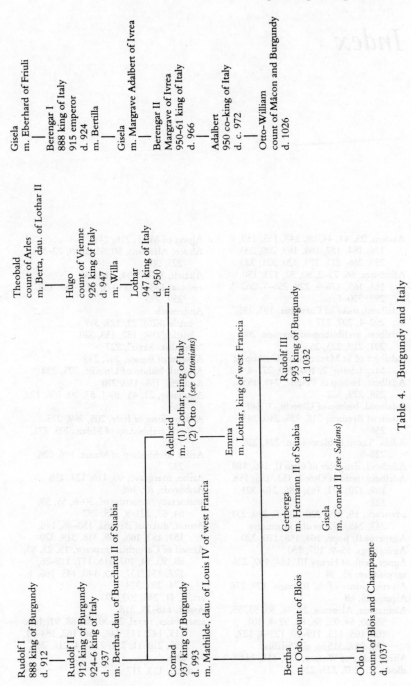

Table 4. Burgundy and Italy

Index

340

Index

192–4, 197, 226, 229, 251
Gisilher, archbishop of Magdeburg, 179, 189, 195, 241
Gnesen, 238, 258, 260, 264, 279–80, 293, 322
Godfrey the Bearded, duke of Lotharingia, 192, 195, 201, 202, 206, 217, 283, 324
Gorze, 243–4
Goseck, 223, 246
Goslar, 8, 209, 252, 285
Gozelo I, duke of Lotharingia, 190, 201
Gozelo II, duke of lower Lotharingia, 192, 201
Gregory II, pope, 52, 315
Gregory V, pope, 197, 275, 278, 284, 322
Gregory VI, pope, 283, 324
Gundechar, bishop of Eichstätt, 252, 270
Gunzelin, margrave of Meißen, 194, 204, 207, 227, 260

Hadrian I, pope, 40, 170
Hadwig, daughter of Henry I, 167–8
Hainault, counts of, 201–2
Haithabu, 233, 263
Halberstadt, 68, 107, 163–4, 187, 239
Hamburg, 91, 98, 105, 163–4, 171, 179, 233, 239, 252, 277, 316 see also Bremen
Harald Bluetooth, 165, 255
Harzburg, 226
Hatto I, archbishop of Mainz, 127, 135, 137
Hatto II, archbishop of Mainz, 164, 239
Havelberg, 162–5, 179, 241, 263
hegemony, 84, 94, 123, 140, 147, 149–50, 161–2, 166–75, 179–80, 258, 261, 264, 273, 280
Henry I, duke of Saxony, king, 11, 130, 133, 136–47, 148, 166, 168, 169, 178, 179, 192, 212, 222, 267, 290, 319
Henry II, emperor, 3, 179, 183, 186–7, 190–217 passim, 224–5, 232, 236, 240, 244, 252, 254, 260, 264–5, 267, 269–70, 273–4, 276, 281, 284, 292, 322–3
Henry III, 3, 4, 8, 183, 184, 190–217 passim, 226, 228, 232, 234, 242, 247, 251, 254–5, 262, 265–78 passim, 282–6, 294, 323–4
Henry IV, 8, 127, 183–4, 201, 232, 234, 255, 286, 324
Henry V, 232, 234
Henry I, king of France, 202, 265–6

Henry, Babenberger, 85, 93, 116, 118, 131
Henry, bishop of Augsburg, 158, 176–7
Henry, duke of Carinthia and Bavaria, 176, 185
Henry I, bishop of Würzburg, 198, 242
Henry I, duke of Bavaria, 149, 151, 152, 153, 154, 155, 157, 158, 159, 167, 169, 183, 184, 199, 206, 207, 320
Henry II the Quarrelsome, duke of Bavaria, 150, 159, 162, 175–6, 184–5, 199, 202, 203, 205, 217, 258, 321
Henry IV, duke of Bavaria, see Henry II, emperor
Henry of Luxemburg, duke of Bavaria, 192–3, 195, 202, 217
Henry of Schweinfurt, 193, 202–3, 206–7, 226–7, 240
Herford, 68, 86, 107, 244
Heribert, archbishop of Cologne, 186, 198
Heriger, archbishop of Mainz, 137, 139–40
Hermann Billung, 15, 152, 155–6, 160, 165–6
Hermann I, duke of Suabia, 142, 148, 153–4, 319, 320
Hermann II, duke of Suabia, 186–7, 189, 192, 203–4, 218
Hermann IV, duke of Suabia, 192, 271
Hermann, margrave of Meißen, 194, 204, 227
Hermann of the Reichenau, 3, 228–9, 249
hermits, 242–3, 279
Herold, archbishop of Salzburg, 151, 156
Hersfeld, 3, 104–5, 109, 133, 244, 249
Hessen, 53, 61–2, 208
Hevelli, 144, 165, 319
Hildesheim, 68, 97, 106, 197, 237, 239, 242, 247, 272, 281
Hildiward, bishop of Halberstadt, 164, 197
historiography, 14, 249–50, 287, 293
Hodo, margrave, 257, 264
Hohenaltheim, council (916), 102–3, 131, 133, 136, 145, 319
Holy Lance, 145, 165, 186–9, 254, 259
hospitality, 44
Hrabanus Maurus, 75, 85, 109–10
Hrotswitha of Gandersheim, 249, 251
Hugo Capet, king of France, 168, 265, 266, 321
Hugo, king of Italy, 147, 166, 168–70
Hugo, son of Lothar II, 15, 117
Hugo, duke of Francia, 152, 167–8

Index

Lothar II, king of Lotharingia, 71–5, 77, 86, 103, 117–18, 125, 317
Lothar, king of West Francia, 168, 176, 185, 212, 265, 321
Lotharingia, Lotharingians, 53, 71–3, 85, 93, 110, 115, 117–18, 121–3, 125–6, 129, 131–2, 135, 140–1, 145–6, 148, 151, 153–60, 167, 176, 187–8, 191–3, 196, 201, 208–9, 222, 225, 232, 234, 242, 265–8, 286, 317, 319, 322–3
Louis the German, 4, 45, 50, 51, 58, 64, 70–98 *passim*, 107, 109, 116, 120, 126, 134, 137, 174, 211, 247, 289, 316–17
Louis the Pious, 22–50 *passim*, 68, 72, 79, 89, 92, 103, 105, 107–8, 110, 119–20, 247, 282, 288, 316
Louis II, king of Italy, 71–5, 84, 116, 173–4, 273, 317
Louis III, king of west Francia, 74, 111, 118
Louis IV, king of west Francia, 148, 152, 167–8
Louis, king of Provence, 119–22, 135, 169, 318
Louis the Child, king, 92, 125–9, 134–5, 139–40, 186, 290, 318
Louis the Stammerer, king of west Francia, 74, 77, 115, 117
Louis the Younger, king, 71–7, 86, 92, 115, 117–18, 120, 131, 132, 289, 317–18
Louis V, king of west Francia, 265, 321
Lüneburg, 226, 233, 241
Luxemburger, 192–3, 196, 201–3

Magdeburg, 98, 163–5, 172, 174, 185, 195, 204, 207, 209, 215, 234–5, 237–41, 244, 247–8, 253, 259, 261, 271, 279, 320–1
Magyars *see* Hungary
Mainz, 3, 25, 38, 48, 51, 53, 60–1, 63–4, 68–9, 73, 76, 86–90, 95–6, 98, 102–6, 109, 140, 144, 148, 155, 163–4, 187–9, 197, 232, 234–5, 237, 239, 241, 244, 253, 262, 322
  council (852), 85, 89, 104, 316
  council (888), 104, 124, 318
  council (1050), 238, 283, 324
manuscripts, 39–41, 95, 104, 108–9, 245–6, 251–2
marches, margraves, 24, 77, 78–80, 92, 129, 132, 134, 137, 165–7, 176–7, 194, 204, 209, 217–18, 224, 257
Margut, 176, 321
markets, 97, 198, 230, 233–5

Marklohe, 66–7
marriage, 32, 38, 101, 192, 225, 228
Marx, Karl, 10, 16
Matfridings, 125, 127, 159
Mathilda, abbess of Quedlinburg, 197, 279
Mathilda, sister of Otto III, 192, 226
Mathilda, wife of Henry I, 138, 145, 153, 159
Mauritius, 163, 165
mausolea, 43, 226–7, 240
Mecklenburg, 241, 263
Meerssen, 70, 72, 103, 316
Meinwerk, bishop of Paderborn, 225, 243, 248
Meißen, 143, 164–5, 224, 230, 253, 258
Menfö, 214, 255, 284, 324
merchants, 91, 232–5
Merovingians, 21–36 *passim*, 55–61
Merseburg, 138, 143, 152, 164–5, 230, 235, 241, 253, 260, 321–3
Methodius, 82–4, 104, 317
Metz, 25, 96, 196, 317
Miesco I, ruler of Poland, 160–1, 164–5, 175–8, 185, 257–8, 264
Miesco II, king of Poland, 261, 323
military service, 31, 34, 99, 143, 151, 213, 214
Minden, 68, 85, 87, 88, 188, 241, 252
ministeriales, 219, 231, 232, 292
minority, royal, 126–7, 185–6, 279, 286
missi dominici, 28–9, 48, 67, 92, 94, 211
mission, Christianization, 22, 37, 41, 43, 47, 56, 62–3, 67–9, 77, 80–4, 102, 105, 110, 144, 163–5, 172, 174, 239–40, 251, 253, 256, 263–4, 277, 289, 291, 293
Mistui, Abodrite ruler, 179, 185, 264
monasteries, 37, 42–4, 95, 105–8, 224–6, 229, 241–7, 293
Mondsee, 90, 110
Monte Cassino, 244, 270
Moravia, Moravians, 81–4, 91, 107, 116, 128–9, 161, 263, 277
Münster, 68, 101, 107
Muslims, 37, 47, 70, 75, 173–5, 273

Naumburg, 234, 241
Neckar, 59, 61
Neutra, 82, 83
Nicholas I, pope, 103, 110
Niederaltaich *see* Altaich
Nimwegen, 69, 206, 208, 238
Nordgau, 54, 202
Noricum, 54, 56
Normans, 273, 283, 324

Index

Riade, battle, 142–4, 319
Ribemont, treaty (880), 74, 317
Robert, king of west Francia, 140, 167
Robert II, king of France, 202, 265–6,
   269
Robertines, 64, 167
Rome, Romans, 21, 41, 142, 146–7,
   168–74, 177, 200, 252, 258, 269,
   274–82, 294, 322
Royal Frankish Annals, 2, 30
Rudolf I, king of Burgundy, 121–3, 125,
   318
Rudolf II, king of Burgundy, 140, 142,
   144–5, 147, 166, 169, 267, 319
Rudolf III, king of Burgundy, 255, 267,
   271, 323
Rudolf, king of west Francia, 144, 147,
   319
rule of St Benedict, 39, 43–4, 241–3
Ruodlieb, 221–9
Ruotger, 157, 171, 249
Russia *see* Kiev

Saint-Denis, 42–3, 145
Salerno, 174, 273
Salians, 13, 183–4, 188, 190, 201, 209,
   226, 234, 256, 268
Salzburg, 55–6, 60, 79, 82, 84, 90, 101,
   103–5, 128, 196, 237, 241
   annals of, 116, 138
Saucourt, battle, 111, 118
Saxony, Saxons, 21, 42, 46, 50, 53, 60,
   63–5, 68–9, 79, 80, 85–8, 92–3, 101,
   103, 105, 120, 123, 127, 132, 134–5,
   140, 148, 150–3, 155, 159, 161,
   163–5, 170–1, 177, 185, 187–8, 191,
   196, 199–200, 209, 221, 225, 228–9,
   253–4, 277, 281, 289, 316, 319, 322,
   324
   bishoprics, 63, 95–6, 105, 107, 109,
      133, 164, 238, 241
   revolt of 1073, 226, 252
Scandinavia, 21, 98, 105, 163, 236
schools, 39, 109, 241, 248, 293
seigneurie banale, 230–1
Seligenstadt, council (1023), 237–8, 323
serfdom, 99, 101, 231–2
Sicily, 174, 177, 273
silver, 179, 236
Silvester II, pope, 254, 279–80, 284, 322
slaves, 34, 67, 97–101, 231
Slavs, *see* Abodrites, Bohemians,
   frontier, Liutizi, Poland
   uprising of, 983, 162, 166, 178–9,
      252, 257, 262–3, 291
Soest, 65, 233

Solomon III, bishop of Constance, 107,
   137
Solothurn, 215, 267
Sophie, sister of Otto III, 186, 188, 197
Sorbs, 80–2, 91, 106, 129, 165, 178, 179,
   230
sources, historical, 2–7
southern Italy, 75, 160, 162–3, 173–5,
   177–9, 269, 273–4, 278–9, 291, 293,
   321, 323
Spain, 21, 173, 231
Speyer, 51, 61, 63–4, 73, 90, 96, 209,
   226, 232, 239
St Emmeram, 89, 97, 108, 215, 233, 246
St Gallen, 60, 89–90, 104, 106, 107, 109,
   133, 245, 247–8, 251
   annals of, 187
St Maximin, 163, 245
Stade, counts of, 138, 255
state, nature of, 16, 27, 45–7, 89–94,
   208–20, 285–6
Stavelot, 244, 245
Stellinga uprising, 67, 102, 178
stem-duchies, 127, 130–4
Stephen I, king of Hungary, 254–5, 259,
   322
Stephen II, 40, 170, 315
Strasbourg, 60, 63, 197, 204
Strasbourg oaths, 70, 111
Suabia, Suabians, 131–4, 137, 139–42,
   145–6, 153–5, 160–1, 168–9, 175,
   185, 187, 194, 196, 202, 208–9,
   221–2, 225, 242, 257, 319 *see also*
   Alemannia
sub-kingdoms, sub-kings, 23, 45, 73, 77,
   86, 92, 134, 149, 154, 175, 270
Sutri, council (1046), 283, 284, 324
Svein Forkbeard, king of Denmark, 236,
   255, 256
symbolism of state, 12, 15, 89, 120, 145,
   185, 212, 214, 282, 285 *see also*
   insignia, Holy Lance, unction

Tagino, archbishop of Magdeburg, 195,
   197, 206
Tassilo, duke of Bavaria, 36, 40, 57, 59,
   64, 108, 315, 316
Tegernsee, 5, 133, 221, 244, 248
Tellenbach, Gerd, 14, 75
territorialization, 179, 230
Thangmar, episcopal biographer, 249,
   280
Thankmar, son of Henry I, 149–52, 320
Theodulf, bishop of Orleans, 25, 104
Theophanu, wife of Otto II, 154, 174,
   185–6, 192, 258, 321–2